Classical Islam

This definitive sourcebook presents more than fifty authoritative new translations of key Islamic texts. Edited and translated by three leading specialists and clearly contextualised for introductory-level students, it illustrates the growth of Islamic thought from its seventh-century origins through to the end of the medieval period. Eight thematically-organized sections cover the Qur'ān and its interpretation, the life of Muḥammad, *ḥadīth*, law, ritual, mysticism and Islamic history. Among the selections are Ibn 'Abbās's account of the heavenly journey; al-Taftāzānī on the uncreatedness of the Qur'ān as God's speech; al-Fārābī on the faculties of the soul; and extracts from Rūmī's *Mathnawī*.

Classical Islam includes a glossary, extensive bibliography and explanatory prefaces for each text. It pays special attention to the literary genres of medieval Muslim scholarship, within whose creative variations Islamic doctrine took form and matured. With many extracts translated here for the first time into English, fresh from Arabic and Persian sources, ***Classical Islam*** is an essential resource for the study of early and medieval Islam and its legacy.

Norman Calder, who died in 1998, was Senior Lecturer in Arabic at the University of Manchester. His *Studies in Early Muslim Jurisprudence* (Oxford 1993) and numerous articles have had a lasting impact on the study of Islamic law. **Jawid Mojaddedi**, Associate Research Scholar in Iranian Studies at Columbia University, is the author of *The Biographical Tradition in Sufism* (Curzon 2001) and an editor of *Encylopaedia Iranica*. **Andrew Rippin**, Professor of Islamic History and Dean of the Faculty of Humanities at the University of Victoria, Canada, is the author of *Muslims: Their Religious Beliefs and Practices* (2nd edition, Routledge 2001).

Classical Islam

A sourcebook of religious literature

Edited and translated by

Norman Calder, Jawid Mojaddedi and Andrew Rippin

Routledge
Taylor & Francis Group
LONDON AND NEW YORK

First published 2003 by Routledge
11 New Fetter Lane, London EC4P 4EE

Simultaneously published in the USA and Canada
by Routledge
29 West 35th Street, New York, NY 10001

Routledge is an imprint of the Taylor & Francis Group

Typeset in Times and Helvetica by
Florence Production Ltd, Stoodleigh, Devon
Printed and bound in Great Britain by
TJ International, Padstow, Cornwall

British Library Cataloguing in Publication Data
A catalogue record for this book is available from the British Library

Library of Congress Cataloging in Publication Data
Classical Islam: a sourcebook of religious literature/edited and translated by Norman Calder, Jawid Mojaddedi and Andrew Rippin.
p. cm.
Includes index
1. Islamic literature–Sources 2. Islamic literature–History and criticism. I. Calder, Norman. II. Mojaddedi, J.A. (Jawid Ahmad) III. Rippin, Andrew, 1950–

BP89.C56 2003
297–dc21 2003043132

ISBN 0–415–24032–8 (hbk)
ISBN 0–415–24033–6 (pbk)

Contents

Preface

The genesis of this book lies with Norman Calder, from shortly before he died in 1998. In 1997 Norman had been approached by a publisher to put together a book of readings on Islam. While neither a full prospectus nor a contract for the work had been finalized by the time of Norman's death, a collation of some texts upon which he had been working and which he was planning to put into this book was among his papers. Many of these texts will be familiar to those who have studied Norman's articles; he had reworked most of them with an eye to their publication in this setting and we have, on occasion, taken the liberty of making further alterations to make them fit within the overall context of this book. Other texts will be familiar to Norman's students from their use in the classroom setting.

Upon Norman's death, Jawid Mojaddedi, Norman's last PhD student, with whom he had discussed publishing his translations as part of a collaborative project, contacted Andrew Rippin, a friend of Norman's since they were completing their own dissertations, with the idea of finishing off the textbook which Norman had started (Norman had completed about one-third of the overall book). The goal was to put the material to good use and to honour Norman's legacy at the same time. We were fortunate in obtaining the agreement of Norman's sister and executor of his estate, Anne Hall, to this plan; we are most grateful to her for entrusting this material to us and allowing us to publish this book under all three of our names.

In bringing this book to its completion, we have tried to follow what we understood Norman would have wanted to do in terms of the overall aim. This work has been conceived as a compilation of translated sources illustrating the development of Muslim scholarship through the form and content of its most celebrated examples. It is designed as a textbook for undergraduate classes on Islam within the context of Middle Eastern and religious studies. Although we have certainly not created the same work as Norman would have in terms of its eloquence, incisive analyses and wit – characteristics of all of Norman's best work – the attention to the structure of each text has been the driving force behind the presentation. While not attempting to provide a comprehensive overview of Islam in terms of doctrine, we have tried to illustrate most of the genres of literature in which the development of the doctrines of Islam is expressed and the creative variations within those genres.

In the selection of texts we have taken into account the range of material readily available to students in translation either as entire works or as extracts in other readers. Some guidance has also been taken from Andrew Rippin, *Muslims: their religious beliefs and practices* (London 1990, second edition 2001), in that we have identified texts which complement the content of that work; by no means, however, are the two works directly connected or dependent upon one another.

Dates are AH/CE except where only CE is indicated, as appropriate. Qur'ān citations are in italics where they appear within other texts. In virtually every case, the numbering of the paragraphs in translated texts is our own; such numbering not only makes reference easier but also provides the editors with the ability to offer interpretive guidelines to the reader.

Two major reference works are frequently cited in the 'Further reading' list which is appended to each section. Both sources are available in print and electronically, so we have not provided volume and page references for these alphabetically organized works. The full bibliographical citations for those works are:

H. A. R. Gibb et al. (eds), *Encyclopaedia of Islam*, new edition, Leiden 1960–2003.
Ehsan Yarshater (ed.), *Encyclopaedia Iranica*, New York 1985 – in progress.

Acknowledgements

We would like to extend our thanks to the following:

Crystal Procyshen, a student of Andrew Rippin in Calgary, now at McGill University, for her initial work on a number of the translations which helped move this work along;

Oxford University Press, for allowing Jawid Mojaddedi to publish selections from his forthcoming translation, Rumi, *The Masnavi* (Oxford World's Classics series).

PART ONE

Formation and salvation history

Chapter 1

The Qur'ān

THE QUR'ĀN IS UNDERSTOOD within the Islamic faith to be the revelatory word of God, dictated in segments by the angel Gabriel to the prophet Muḥammad between the years 610 and 632 CE. The revelations were memorized and recorded word for word, and are today found in the Arabic text of the Qur'ān in precisely the manner God intended.

The Qur'ān is arranged approximately according to the length of its 114 *sūra*s, or chapters, from the longest to the shortest. Each chapter is divided into verses which are generally dictated by consideration of the rhyme structure of the chapter. This is illustrated by the transliteration provided for *sūra*s 104 and 98 (sections 1.1 and 1.2 respectively), both of which use the rhyme of an 'a' sound to punctuate the chapter. Prefacing each chapter (with the exception of *sūra* 9, the beginning of which is in section 1.5) is the *basmala,* the statement, *In the name of God, the All-merciful, the All-compassionate.* This phrase acts as an opening to all Muslim religious statements. Muslims understand that God speaks throughout the text of the Qur'ān even though He refers to Himself in both the singular and plural first-person forms, as well as in the third person. Statements which might be understood to be Muḥammad's speech are usually, but not always (see Q 3/8–9 in section 1.4 for an ambiguous example), preceded by the word 'Say', understood to be a command from God to allow for Muḥammad's voice in the text. Illustrations of these narrative points of view are found in the passages which follow.

Apart from the arrangement of the Qur'ān by length of chapter, the organizational principle behind the text has never been convincingly explained. Historical, biographical, thematic, aesthetic and poetic criteria by which one could understand the overall structure of the work do not seem to apply. Muḥammad himself is excluded from any role in the collection and organization of the text according to Muslim accounts. The community, working on the basis of pieces of text written 'on palm leaves or flat stones or in the hearts of men', compiled the text some thirty years after the death of Muḥammad; theologically, it is held that the form which the text was in at this point was an image of the 'heavenly tablet', suggesting that its structure and content were precisely that which God desired for it. The emergence of the written text is moot for Muslims; it is held that an oral tradition preserved the full text from the time of its revelation, the written form serving only as a mnemonic device for memorization of the text. The poetic form of the text is held to have helped in this memorization process. Some of the *sūra*s are in a short, well-defined rhythmic form as in *sūra* 104 (section 1.1); others are well marked and fairly regular in structure as in *sūra* 79 (section 1.3); others are more narrative or didactic pieces and their poetic form only comes through in the verse-ending rhyme words, as in *sūra*s 3, 9 and 19 (sections 1.4, 1.5 and 1.6 respectively).

The Qur'ān has a thematic preoccupation with three major topics: law, the previous prophets and the final judgement. Ruling over all of the Qur'ān, and the reference point for the development of its major themes, is the figure of God, Allāh in Arabic. In all the *sūra*s provided here as illustration, God is present, whether in the foreground or as an actor in the background. The all-mighty, all-powerful and all-merciful God created the world for the benefit of His creatures. He has sent messengers to them in the past to guide them in the way of living most befitting to them and to Him; this is illustrated by the stories of the prophets of the past, in the case of Moses being referred to in *sūra* 79 (section 1.3). He has given them the law by which they should live, a law which has reached its perfection and completion in Islam; *sūra* 3 (section 1.4) exemplifies this. He will bring about the end of the world at a time known only to Him, when all people will be judged strictly according to their deeds; a vivid picture of this is painted in *sūra*s 104 and 79 (sections 1.1 and 1.3 respectively). The message is the one familiar from the Judaeo-Christian tradition, in keeping with the claims of the Qur'ān that Muḥammad stands at the end of the line of the biblical prophets. This aspect is emphasized by the familiarity of certain passages to those who know the Bible; the story of Mary, mother of Jesus, recounted in *sūra* 19 (section 1.6) is a good example. But there are other elements as well which speak of a local context, including references to places (as in the mention of Ḥunayn in Q 9/25) and to polemical issues unfamiliar to contemporary Judaism and Christianity (as in Q 9/30).

The Qur'ān is, and has been from the beginning of the emergence of the religion, the primary reference point for Islam and the defining symbol of Islamic identity. The Qur'ān, knowledge of which is traditionally instilled in most children through memorization, is spoken of as an unrivalled literary production in Arabic. It has been, and continues to be, the focal point of all Islamic devotion, manifesting itself especially in calligraphic art and epigraphy. The recitation of the text is a highly prized art and listening to such a recitation in conjunction with the transliterated texts provided of *sūra*s 104 and 98 (sections 1.1 and 1.2) will illustrate this fact. (The transliteration in those chapters reflects the practice of Arabic pronunciation when reciting the Qur'ān and not a technical transliteration as normally found in scholarly works.)

The following passages have been selected as representative examples of the various styles and the content of the Qur'ān; consulting a full translation is the only way to gain a good sense of the entire work.

Further reading

Michael Cook, *The Koran: a very short introduction*, Oxford 2000.
Jane Dammen McAuliffe (ed.), *Encyclopaedia of the Qur'ān*, Leiden 2001 – ongoing.
Neal Robinson, *Discovering the Qur'an: a contemporary approach to a veiled text*, London 1996.

Source text

The standard edition of the Qur'ān is referred to as the Cairo Royal text, published in 1924. The verse numbering of that edition is followed here. The translations have been made with constant reference to earlier versions, especially those of A. J. Arberry, *The Koran interpreted*, London 1955, and Richard Bell, *The Qur'ān, translated with a critical re-arrangement of the surahs*, Edinburgh 1935. Both of those translations follow the earlier, European (Flügel) verse numbering scheme.

1.1 Warning: *sūrat al-humaza* (104), 'The backbiter'

In the name of God, the All-merciful, the All-compassionate.
bismi'llāhi 'r-raḥmān ir-raḥīm

1. Woe unto every backbiting slanderer
waylul li kulli humazati lumaza

2. who has gathered riches and counted them.
alladhī jamaʿa mālan wa ʿaddadah

3. He thinks his riches will make him immortal!
yaḥsabu anna mālahu akhladah

4. No indeed; he shall certainly be thrown into the crushing fire.
kallā la-yunbadhanna fi 'l-ḥuṭama

5. What shall teach you what the crushing fire is?
wa mā adrāka mā 'l-ḥuṭama

6. It is the fire of God kindled,
nāru'llāhi 'l-mūqada

7. rising over the hearts,
allatī taṭṭaliʿu ʿalā 'l-af'ida

8. vaulted over them,
innahā ʿalayhim mu'ṣada

9. in outstretched columns.
fī ʿamadim mumaddada

1.2 Faith: *sūrat al-bayyina* (98), 'The clear sign' (also known as *sūrat lam yakun*, 'It would not be')

In the name of God, the All-merciful, the All-compassionate.
bismi'llāhi 'r-raḥmān ir-raḥīm

1. The unbelievers of the people of the book and the idolaters would not leave off until the clear sign comes to them,
lam yakuni 'lladhīna kafarū min ahli 'l-kitābi wa'l-mushrikīna munfakkīna ḥattā ta'tiyahumu 'l-bayyina

2. a messenger from God, reading aloud pages purified,
rasūlum mina 'llāhi yatlū ṣuḥufam muṭahhara

3. therein true books.
fīhā kutubun qayyima

4. And those who were given the book did not separate except after the clear sign came to them.
wa mā tafarraqa 'lladhīna ūtū 'l-kitāba illā min ba'di mā jā'athumu 'l-bayyina

5. They were commanded only to serve God, making the religion His, sincerely as men of true faith, and to establish prayer and pay the alms; and that is the religion of the true.
wa mā umirū illā li-ya'budū 'llāha mukhliṣīna lahu 'd-dīna ḥunafā'a wa-yuqīmū 'ṣ-ṣalāta wa yutū 'z-zakā wa dhālika dīnu 'l-qayyima

6. The unbelievers of the people of the book and the idolaters will be in the fire of Gehenna, therein dwelling forever. Those are the worst of creatures.
inna 'lladhīna kafarū min ahli 'l-kitābi wa 'l-mushrikīna fī nāri jahannama khālidīna fīhā ulā'ika hum sharru 'l-bariyya

7. But those who believe and do righteous deeds, those are the best of creatures,
inna 'lladhīna āmanū wa 'amilū 'ṣ-ṣāliḥāti ulā'ika hum khayru 'l-bariyya

8. their recompense is with their Lord; gardens of Eden, underneath which rivers flow, therein dwelling forever and ever; God is well pleased with them and they are well pleased with Him; that is for him who fears his Lord.
jazā'uhum 'inda rabbihim jannātu 'adnin tajrī min taḥtihā 'l-anhāru khālidīna fīhā abadar raḍiya 'llāhu 'anhum wa raḍū 'anh dhālika li-man khashiya rabbah

1.3 The hereafter: *sūrat al-nāziʿāt* (79), 'The pullers'

In the name of God, the All-merciful, the All-compassionate.

1. By those who pull violently
2. and those who take out gently;
3. by those who swim serenely
4. and those who race ahead;
5. by those who manage an affair!
6. Upon the day when the first blast quakes
7. and the second blast follows it,
8. hearts upon that day shall be throbbing,
9. their eyes downcast.
10. They will say, 'Are we being returned to what we were before?
11. After we are crumbled bones?'
12. They shall say, 'That then is a return with a loss!'
13. But it shall be only a single cry,
14. and behold, they are wide awake.
15. Have you heard the story of Moses?
16. When his Lord called out to him in the sacred valley, Ṭūwā:
17. 'Go to Pharaoh; he has transgressed.
18. And say, "Do you have the desire to purify yourself,
19. and to have me guide you to your Lord, as you fear?"'
20. So he showed him the great sign,
21. but he cried lies, and resisted.
22. Then he turned away purposefully,
23. and he mustered and proclaimed,
24. saying, 'I am your lord, most high!'
25. So God seized him with the chastisement of the last and the first.
26. In that is a lesson for those who fear!
27. Are you more difficult to create or is it the heaven? He built it.
28. He raised its roof, and set it in order,
29. and darkened its night, and brought forth its forenoon;
30. and the earth – after that He spread it out,
31. from there brought forth its waters and its pastures,
32. and the mountains He fixed firmly,
33. a provision for you and your flocks.
34. Then, when the greatest catastrophe comes,
35. upon the day when people shall remember what they have striven for,
36. and hell is set forth for everyone to see,
37. then as for him who has transgressed
38. and preferred the present life,
39. surely hell will be the place.
40. But as for him who feared standing before his Lord and forbade the soul its desire,
41. surely paradise will be the place.
42. They will ask you about the hour, when will it arrive?
43. What are you to say about it?

44. To your Lord is its final end.
45. You are only the warner to those who fear it.
46. On the day they see it, it will be as if they had waited for only an evening or its forenoon.

1.4 The religion of Islam: a selection from *sūrat āl ʿImrān* (3), 'The people of ʿImrān'

In the name of God, the All-merciful, the All-compassionate.

1. *Alif, lām, mīm.*
2. God, there is no god but He, the Living, the Eternal.
3. He has sent down to you the book with the truth, confirming what was before it, and He sent down the Torah and the Gospel
4. before, as a guidance for the people, and He sent down the *furqān*. For those who disbelieve in the signs of God, a terrible chastisement awaits them; God is All-mighty, the Possessor of vengeance.
5. From God nothing is hidden in heaven nor in the earth.
6. It is He who forms you in the womb as He wills. There is no god but He, the All-mighty, the All-wise.
7. It is He who has sent down to you the book; in it are clear verses that are the mother of the book, and others ambiguous. As for those in whose hearts is deviation, they follow the ambiguous part, out of desire for dissension, and out of desire for its interpretation; and no one knows its interpretation, save only God. And those firmly grounded in knowledge say, 'We believe in it; all of it is from our Lord'; but no one remembers other than those with understanding.
8. Our Lord, do not let our hearts deviate after You have guided us; and give us mercy from yourself; You are the Giver.
9. Our Lord, it is You who will gather the people for a day of which there is no doubt; indeed God will not miss the appointment.
10. As for those who disbelieve, their riches will not help them, nor their children, at all against God; those ones – they are the fuel of the fire
11. like Pharaoh's folk, and the people before them, who declared our signs false; God seized them because of their sins; God is severe in punishment.
12. Say to those who disbelieve, 'You will be overthrown, and gathered together into hell – a bad place of rest!'
13. There has already been a sign for you in the two companies that met, one fighting in the way of God and the other unbelieving; they saw twice the number of them as there were, but God supports with His help whom He will. Surely in that is a lesson for those who see.
14. Made attractive to the people is the love of desires, women, children, private hoards of gold and silver, distinguished horses, cattle and land. Those are the goods of the present life; but with God is the best resort.
15. Say, 'Shall I tell you of something better than that?' For those who are godfearing, with their Lord, are gardens underneath which rivers flow, in which to dwell forever, and pure spouses, and God being pleased. God sees His servants
16. who say, 'Our Lord, we believe; forgive us our sins, and protect us from the punishment of the fire.'
17. They are the patient, the truthful, the obedient, the contributors, and the askers of forgiveness in the morning.
18. God testifies that there is no god but He, and the angels and those possessing knowledge who uphold justice; there is no god but He, the All-mighty, the All-wise.

19. The religion with God is Islam. Those to whom the book had been given only differed after they received knowledge, because of jealousy among themselves. Whoever disbelieves in the signs of God, God will quickly call to account.

1.5 Legal requirements: a selection from *sūrat al-barā'a* (9), 'The acquittal' (also known as *sūrat al-tawba*, 'Repentance')

1. An acquittal, from God and His messenger, to the idolaters with whom you have covenanted:
2. Go about in the land for four months; and know that you cannot frustrate God, and that God humiliates the unbelievers.
3. A proclamation, from God and His messenger, to humanity on the day of the greatest pilgrimage: God and His messenger renounce the idolaters. So if you repent, that will be better for you; but if you turn your backs, know that you cannot frustrate God. And announce to the unbelievers a painful chastisement,
4. except those of the idolaters with whom you have covenanted, who then did not fail you or lend support to anyone against you. Fulfil your covenant with them through its term. Surely God loves the godfearing.
5. Then, when the sacred months are passed, slay the idolaters wherever you find them, and seize them, and confine them, and lie in ambush for them everywhere. If they repent, perform the prayer and pay the alms, then let them go free; God is All-forgiving, All-compassionate.
6. And if any of the idolaters seeks your protection, grant him protection till he hears the words of God; then take him to his place of security – that is because they are a people who do not know.
7. How can there be a covenant between God and His messenger and the idolaters, other than with those with whom you covenanted at the holy mosque; as they are true with you, stand true with them; surely God loves the godfearing.
8. How? If they overpower you, they will not observe any kinship or treaty with you but will give you satisfaction with their mouths while in their hearts they will refuse; most of them are ungodly.
9. They have sold the signs of God for a small price, and have hindered from His way; truly evil is what they have been doing,
10. observing neither kinship nor treaty with a believer; they are the transgressors.
11. If they repent, perform the prayer and pay the alms, then they are your brothers in religion; and We explain the signs for a people who know.
12. But if they break their oaths after their covenant and attack your religion, then fight the leaders of unbelief. Their oaths mean nothing; perhaps they will reach an end.
13. Will you not fight a people who have broken their oaths and intended to expel the messenger, who began against you the first time? Do you fear them? God is the best one to fear, if you are believers.
14. Fight them, and God will punish them at your hands and degrade them. He will help you against them, and bring health to the breasts of a people who believe,
15. and He will remove the anger within their hearts. God accepts the repentance of whoever He wills; God is All-knowing, All-wise.
16. Did you think that you would be left when God does not yet know those of you who have struggled, and become attached to anything other than God and His messenger and the believers – any intimate? God is aware of what you do.

17. It is not for the idolaters to inhabit God's places of worship while witnessing against themselves unbelief; those are the ones whose works have failed them, and they will reside forever in the fire.
18. Only he shall inhabit God's places of worship who believes in God and the last day, and performs the prayer, pays the alms, and fears only God; it may be that they will be among the guided.
19. Do you consider the giving of water to pilgrims and the inhabiting of the holy mosque equal to one who believes in God and the last day and who struggles in the way of God? They are not equal to God; God does not guide the people of the evildoers.
20. Those who believe, have emigrated, and have struggled in the way of God with their possessions and their lives are greater in rank with God; they are the triumphant;
21. their Lord gives them good tidings of mercy from Him and pleasure; they will have gardens wherein is lasting bliss,
22. therein to dwell forever; surely with God is a mighty reward.
23. O believers, take not your fathers and your brothers to be your friends, if they prefer unbelief over belief; whoever of you takes them for friends, they are the evildoers.
24. Say, 'If your fathers, your sons, your brothers, your wives, your clan, your possessions that you have gained, any commerce you fear may decline, any dwellings you love – if these are dearer to you than God, His messenger and struggling in His way, then wait until God brings His command! God does not guide the people of the ungodly.'
25. God has already helped you on many battlefields, and on the day of Ḥunayn, when you were happy in your great number, but it did not benefit you and the land, for all its breadth, was too narrow for you, and you turned around in retreat.
26. Then God sent down His *sakīna* [Shechina] upon His messenger and the believers, and He sent down hosts which you did not see, and He punished those who disbelieved. That is the recompense of the unbelievers.
27. Thereafter God will accept the repentance of whom He will; God is All-forgiving, All-compassionate.
28. O believers, the idolaters are unclean; they should not approach the holy mosque after this year of theirs. If you fear poverty, God will surely enrich you from His bounty, if He wills; God is All-knowing, All-wise.
29. Fight those who do not believe in God and the last day, who do not forbid what God and His messenger have forbidden, and who do not practise the religion of truth among those who have been given the book, until they pay the tribute tax out of hand and have been subdued.
30. The Jews say that Ezra is the son of God; the Christians say that the Messiah is the son of God. That is what they say with their mouths, following the unbelievers before them. God fight them! How they are perverted!
31. They have taken their rabbis and their monks as lords apart from God, as well as the Messiah, Mary's son, even though they were commanded to serve but one God besides whom there is no god but Him. Glory be to Him, above what they associate,
32. desiring to extinguish the light of God with their mouths. But God refuses to do other than perfect His light, even though the unbelievers detest it.

33. He is the one who has sent His messenger with the guidance and the religion of truth in order to set it above every religion, though the idolaters detest it.
34. O believers, many of the rabbis and monks consume the goods of the people in vanity and turn others from the way of God. Those who store gold and silver and do not expend them in the way of God – give them the good tidings of a painful chastisement
35. on the day they shall be burned in the fire of Gehenna and their foreheads and their sides and their backs shall be branded. This is what you have stored for yourselves; therefore taste you now what you were storing!
36. The number of the months with God is twelve. In the book of God on the day that He created the heavens and the earth, there are four of them that are sacred. That is the right religion. So do not wrong yourselves during them. Fight the idolaters continuously as they fight you continuously; and know that God is with those who fear God.
37. The postponement (of a month) is an increase of unbelief in which the unbelievers go astray; they make it profane one year, and then make it sacred another, in order to agree with the number that God has made sacred. In this way they make profane what God has made sacred. Their evil deeds seem good to them, but God does not guide the people of the unbelievers.

1.6 The birth of Jesus: a selection from *sūrat Maryam* (19), 'Mary'

16. Mention in the book of Mary, when she withdrew from her people to a place facing east,
17. and she took a veil apart from them; so We sent to her Our spirit who presented himself to her as a man without faults.
18. She said, 'I take refuge in the All-merciful from you! If you fear God. . . .'
19. He said, 'I am a messenger from your Lord, to give you a boy, pure.'
20. She said, 'How shall I have a boy when no mortal has touched me, nor have I been unchaste?'
21. He said, 'It shall be so! Your Lord has said: "It is easy for Me; We have appointed him as a sign to the people and a mercy from Us; it is a thing decreed."'
22. So she conceived him, and withdrew with him to a far-away place.
23. And the pains of birth drove her to the trunk of the palm-tree. She said, 'I wish I had died before this happened, and had become a thing forgotten!'
24. But he who was below her called to her, 'No, do not sorrow; see, your Lord has set below you a stream.
25. Shake the palm-trunk towards you, and fresh, ripe fruit will tumble down on you.
26. So eat thereof and drink, and be comforted; and if you should see any human being, say, "I have vowed a fast to the All-merciful, and today I will not speak to any human being."'
27. Then she brought him to her folk, carrying him. They said, 'Mary, you have surely committed an improper thing!
28. Sister of Aaron, your father was not an impure man, nor was your mother an unchaste woman.'
29. Then she pointed to him but they said, 'How can we speak to one who is still in the cradle, a child?'
30. He said, 'Lo, I am God's servant; God has given me the book, and has made me a prophet.
31. He has made me blessed, wherever I may be; He has enjoined me to pray, and to give the alms, so long as I live,
32. and likewise to cherish my mother; He has not made me a tyrant, unprosperous.
33. Peace be upon me, the day I was born, and the day I die, and the day I am raised up alive!'
34. That is Jesus, son of Mary, a statement of the truth concerning which they are in doubt.
35. It is not for God to take a child unto Him. Glory be to Him! When He decrees something, He simply says to it 'Be,' and it is.
36. Surely God is my Lord, and your Lord; so serve Him. This is a straight path.

Chapter 2

The life of Muḥammad

2.1 Muḥammad in the Qur'ān

The Qur'ān is conceived by Muslims to be the word of God spoken to Muḥammad and then passed on to humanity in exactly the same form as it was received. On one level, the entire text is seen as having Muḥammad thoroughly imbued in it. When the text says 'Say!', this is interpreted as God addressing Muḥammad and ordering him to repeat what is being dictated. In that sense, the first-person speaking voice of some of the text is Muḥammad, but that is deflected in the narrative through the command 'Say!' to become the word of God. Clear examples of this are present in some of the passages of the Qur'ān provided above (e.g., section 1.4, *sūrat āl 'Imrān* [3], verse 15; section 1.5, *sūrat al-barā'a* [9], verse 24). The life story of Muḥammad is also held to be the basis of what builds the narrative of some sections of the text. One of the most famous of such sections is *sūrat al-ḍuḥā,* 'The morning' (93), in section 2.1.5 below, which is generally understood as a reference to Muḥammad's own childhood. Given that there is no independent source material on the early life of Muḥammad, this reading of the text of the Qur'ān remains highly speculative, but it is compelling in light of the weight of Muslim tradition behind it. Still, the life story of Muḥammad is certainly present in the Qur'ān. While some of the references are just in passing, others seem to refer to disputes in the community. The actual name 'Muḥammad' is used four times in the Qur'ān, as found in sections 2.1.1 to 2.1.4 below.

Further reading

Harris Birkeland, *The Lord guideth: studies on primitive Islam*, Oslo 1956.

Andrew Rippin, 'Muḥammad in the Qur'ān: reading scripture in the 21st century,' in Harald Motzki (ed.), *The biography of Muḥammad: the issue of the sources*, Leiden 2000, pp. 298–309.

Alford T. Welch, 'Muhammad's understanding of himself: the Koranic data,' in R. G. Hovannisian, S. Vryonis, Jr. (eds), *Islam's understanding of itself*, Malibu CA 1983, pp. 15–52.

Source text

The standard edition of the Qur'ān is referred to as the Cairo Royal text, published in 1924. The verse numbering of that edition is followed here. The translations have been made with constant reference to earlier versions, especially those of A. J. Arberry, *The Koran interpreted*, London 1955, and Richard Bell, *The Qur'ān, translated with a critical re-arrangement of the surahs*, Edinburgh 1935. Both of those translations follow the earlier, European (Flügel) verse numbering scheme.

2.1.1 Selection from sūrat āl ʿImrān, *'The people of ʿImrān' (3)*

144. Muḥammad is only a messenger; messengers have passed away before him. If he should die or be killed, will you turn around on your heels? Whoever turns around on his heels does not harm God at all. God will reward the thankful!

145. It is not for any soul to die except by the leave of God at an appointed time. Whoever desires the reward of this world, We will give it to him. Whoever desires the reward of the hereafter, We shall give it to him. We will reward the thankful!

2.1.2 Selection from sūrat al-akhzāb, *'The confederates' (33)*

37. When you said to him whom God favoured and whom you had favoured, 'Keep your wife for yourself and fear God,' you concealed inside yourself what God would make manifest. You were fearing the people, while by right it was God that you should have been fearing. So, when Zayd had finished with her, We married her to you so that there would be no blame on the believers regarding the wives of their adopted sons when they have finished with them. The command of God is to be performed.

38. There is no blame on the prophet concerning that which God has made a duty for him. This was the custom of God with those who passed away before – the command of God is a determined decree –

39. who delivered the messages of God and fear Him and do not fear anyone other than God. God suffices as a keeper of accounts.

40. Muḥammad is not the father of any one of your men, but the messenger of God, and the seal of the prophets; God has knowledge of everything.

2.1.3 Selection from **sūrat Muḥammad,** *'Muḥammad' (47)*

2. Those who believe and do righteous deeds and believe in what is sent down to Muḥammad, which is the truth from their Lord – He will absolve them of their evil deeds and make right their state.

2.1.4 Selection from **sūrat al-fatḥ,** *'Victory' (48)*

28. He it is who has sent His messenger with guidance and the religion of truth so that He may raise it above all other religions; God suffices as a witness.

29. Muḥammad is the messenger of God and those who are with him are severe against the unbelievers, merciful to each another. You see them bowing, prostrating, seeking bounty and acceptance from God. They bear the mark on their faces, their trace of prostration.

2.1.5 **Sūrat al-ḍuḥā,** *'The morning' (93)*

1. By the morning!
2. By the night when it is still!
3. Your Lord has not forsaken you, nor does he hate you.
4. The last will be better for you than the first.
5. Your Lord will give to you so that you will be pleased.
6. Did He not find you as an orphan and then give you shelter?
7. Did He not find you erring and then guide you?
8. Did He not find you poor and then enrich you?
9. So, as for the orphan, do not oppress him,
10. and, as for the beggar, do not scold him,
11. and, as for the favour of your Lord, spread it widely!

2.2 Ibn ʿAbbās on the heavenly ascension

ʿAbd Allāh Ibn ʿAbbās is one of the most famous transmitters of traditions in early Islam, especially those related to the interpretation of the Qurʾān. A cousin of Muḥammad, Ibn ʿAbbās is said to have been born in 619 CE, three years before the *hijra* of Muḥammad, and he died in 68/687. He was the grandfather of those who are later called the dynasty of the ʿAbbāsid caliphs, and so he became a very important figure for later tradition because of the political significance which his authority conveyed in affirming the solid Muslim foundation of the ruling family.

A number of books are ascribed to Ibn ʿAbbās, but it is doubtful that any of them was actually written by him. Rather, his name has become attached to a series of texts which establish basic methods of approach to crucial Islamic religious topics. The *Kitāb al-isrāʾ waʾl-miʿrāj* is an example of precisely that. The work is probably the most widely circulated of all the texts dealing with the subject of Muḥammad's night journey and heavenly ascension. It has been characterized as a work which provides a firm foundation for Islamic doctrine and law, while at the same time allowing the Muslim imagination to flourish. As such, it is likely to be a reflection of ideas current in mature Muslim religious perception, rather than from the formative period.

In terms of the development of the story, this version can be profitably compared with those found in Ibn Isḥāq [Ibn Hishām], *Al-Sīra al-nabawiyya*, Cairo 1955, vol. 1, pp. 396–408, A. Guillaume (trans.), *The life of Muḥammad: a translation of [Ibn] Isḥāq's* Sīrat rasūl Allāh, Oxford 1955, pp. 181–7, al-Ṭabarī, *Taʾrīkh al-rusul waʾl-mulūk*, ed. M. J. de Goeje, Leiden 1879–1901, vol. 1, pp. 1157–9, and W. M. Watt, M. V. McDonald (trans.), *The history of al-Ṭabarī, volume VI: Muḥammad at Mecca*, Albany NY 1988, pp. 78–80. Ibn Isḥāq's version may be characterized as a composite of the earliest stories in which the emphasis falls on Muḥammad's interaction with the Meccans. In Ibn ʿAbbās's work, on the other hand, three accounts are combined, as they frequently are in other later works dealing with the heavenly ascension. The first deals with the miraculous initiation of Muḥammad, here treated fairly simply via the appearance of Gabriel and Burāq. Then follows the night journey to Jerusalem on Burāq and the test of the three drinks. Finally comes the ascension to the seven heavens themselves, with a glimpse of heaven and hell and a discussion with God. This is concluded by a return to the world. This latter section has much in common with literature dealing specifically with the events related to the resurrection, judgement day and the afterlife, the *aḥwāl al-qiyāma* ('the stages of the resurrection day'). Overall, one can see the role of the popular preacher in the development of such accounts; the details are filled in with much embellishment, while the main aims of the story are to provide vivid accounts of the wonders of the divine realm, to assert the special qualities of Muḥammad through his experiences, and to provide an appropriate vehicle for the adoration of God and Muḥammad.

Ibn ʿAbbās's work is short, being only forty-six pages of a dense but small format booklet published in Beirut in recent years; it is available in many prints but none of them is a critical edition. Such booklets reflect the popular nature of the work among Muslims in general. The repetitive nature of the story, with identical pieces of text structuring the visit to the seven heavens, for example, marks this as a popular folktale.

Further reading

Mohammad Ali Amir-Moezzi (ed.), *Le voyage initiatique en terre d'Islam. Ascensions célestes et itinéraires spirituels*, Louvain-Paris 1996.
Jamel Eddine Bencheikh, *Le voyage nocturne de Mahomet*, Paris 1988.
Heribert Busse, 'Jerusalem in the story of Muḥammad's night journey and ascension,' *Jerusalem studies in Arabic and Islam*, 14 (1991), pp. 1–40; reprinted in Uri Rubin (ed.), *The life of Muḥammad*, Aldershot 1998, pp. 279–318.
B. Schrieke, J. Horovitz, J. E. Bencheikh, '*Miʿrādj*,' in *Encyclopaedia of Islam*, new edition.
Jane Idleman Smith, Yvonne Yazbeck Haddad, *The Islamic understanding of death and resurrection*, Albany NY 1981.
For some background on the image of the 'seven heavens', see Adela Y. Collins, 'The seven heavens in Jewish and Christian apocalypses,' in John J. Collins, Michael Fishbane (eds), *Death, ecstasy, and other worldly journeys*, Albany NY 1995, pp. 59–93; other chapters of this book are also helpful in coming to an understanding of this text.

Source text

Ibn ʿAbbās, *Kitāb al-isrāʾ waʾl-miʿrāj*, Beirut n.d. The extracts translated here are taken from pp. 2–5 (part I), 6 (part II), 7–8 (part III), 9–12 (part IV), 23–4 (part V), 24–5 (part VI), 38–40 (part VII), 42–4 (part VIII) and 44–6 (part IX).

I Gabriel and Burāq

God, Most High, said, *Glory be to He who sent His servant on a journey by night from the holy mosque to the furthest mosque, which We have blessed, in order that We might show him some of Our signs. He is All-hearing, All-seeing* (Q 17/1).

It is reported on the authority of Ibn ʿAbbās who reported on the authority of the prophet that he said that he was in the house of Umm Hāniʾ, daughter of Abū Ṭālib, who was called Fākhita, on Monday, the twenty-seventh of Rajab, eight years after the beginning of the prophetic mission. Fāṭima al-Zahrāʾ was also there; she was nine years old and she had not yet married ʿAlī (having been married later in Medina).

That night a visitor knocked on the door and Fāṭima went to see who was there. She saw an individual upon whom were jewels and vestments; he had green wings which covered the east and the west. Upon his head was a crown inlaid with pearls and jewels. Written on the front of it was, 'There is no god but God and Muḥammad is the messenger of God.'

Fāṭima asked, 'What do you want?' He replied, 'I want Muḥammad.' So she turned back and called the messenger of God and said, 'Father, there is someone at the door. He made me afraid, as I have never seen anything like him! He said to me, "I want Muḥammad."' I [i.e., Muḥammad] then went to the door and, when I saw him, I realized that it was Gabriel. Gabriel greeted me saying, 'Blessings and peace be upon you, lover of the truth and master of the creatures.' So I said, 'My brother Gabriel, is this a revelation sent down, a promise made manifest, or a decree come to pass?' He said, 'My love, stand and don your cloak and quieten your heart, for in this night you will approach your Lord, whom age and sleep do not affect.' When I heard the words of my brother Gabriel, I rose up excitedly, drew my clothing around me, and went out into the desert. There stood Burāq with Gabriel leading it.

It was a beast unlike any other, something between a donkey and a mule. It had a face like that of a human and its body was that of a horse. It was a finer beast than any other on earth. Its mane was made of the finest pearls woven with precious stones sparkling in the light. Its ears were of green emerald and its eyes were like circular stars. Its eyes shone like rays of the sun. It was grey and black with three white feet and was decorated with pearls and jewels. A full description of it is impossible unless God Himself composes it, since the essence of the beast is like that of a human.

When I saw Burāq I was amazed by it. Gabriel said, 'Stand up, lover of God, and mount it.' I rose up to mount it but Burāq was shaking like a fish in the net. Gabriel admonished it, saying, 'Burāq, be settled! Are you not ashamed to turn away from the master of the creatures and the lover of the truth? By He who created me and created you, no one has mounted you who is more esteemed before God than Muḥammad.' Burāq said, 'Adam, the chosen of God, rode me, as did Abraham, the friend of God.' Gabriel said, 'Burāq, this is the lover of God and the messenger of the Lord of the worlds. He is the most favoured of the people of heaven and earth. His *qibla* is the Kaʿba and his religion is Islam. All creatures hope for his intercession on the day of resurrection. With paradise on his right and the fire on his left, those who believe in him will enter paradise, while those who deny him will enter the fire.'

II The three vessels

Then Gabriel went ahead to the holy house (in Jerusalem) and I followed him. When I approached, he had three vessels. In the first was milk, in the second, wine, and in the third, water. Gabriel said to me, 'Drink whichever you desire.' So I took the milk and drank virtually all of it. Gabriel said to me, 'You took all of the natural disposition which is Islam. If you had taken the wine, your community would have gone astray. If you had taken the water, your community would have drowned. Since you drank all of the milk, no one from your community will enter the fire.'

III The first heaven

Gabriel said, 'Rise, Muḥammad.' So I rose up alongside Gabriel. He allowed me to view the many places of worship. Angels, the number of which can only be calculated by God, were unceasingly worshipping and glorifying God. I saw stars attached like suspended candelabras in the mosque. The smallest one was larger than the biggest mountain. I then ascended to the sky of the world during this night journey in the twinkling of an eye. Between the lowest heaven and the earth is a distance of five hundred years and its breadth is the same.

Gabriel then knocked on the door. They said, ' Who's there?' He replied, 'Gabriel.' They said, 'Who is with you?' He said, 'Muḥammad.' They said, 'Has he been sent for?' He said, 'Yes.' They said, 'Welcome to you and to him who is with you. Your arrival is wonderful!'

Then they opened the door for us and we entered. It was a heaven of mist, known as al-Rafīʿa ['the highest']. There was no open spot because everywhere was occupied by angels kneeling or prostrating in prayer. I saw two great flowing rivers and I asked, 'Which rivers are these, Gabriel?' He said, 'Those are the Nile and the Euphrates. Their source is in paradise.' There was another river and beside it was a palace of pearls and green jewels like chrysolites; I put my hand on the riverbank and it smelled of fragrant musk. Then I asked, 'Which river is this?' Gabriel said, 'This is al-Kawthar which God has guarded for you.'

I glanced over and there was an angel with a regal demeanour. He was riding on a horse of light and he was wearing a vestment of light. He was the leader of seventy thousand angels wearing different jewels and clothes. Every one of them held a lance of light. They were the army of God. If one person on earth, just one person, rebels against God, they proclaim that God is angry with so-and-so and they also become angry with him. If the worshippers seek forgiveness and repent, they will proclaim that God is pleased with so-and-so and they also are pleased with him.

I asked, 'My brother Gabriel, who is this great angel?' He said, 'This is Ishmael, treasure-keeper of the heaven of the world. Draw near to him and greet him.' So I approached him and greeted him. He greeted me in return and congratulated me on the favour which my Lord had bestowed on me. He said, 'Spread the good news, Muḥammad! The best of all creation are you and your community until the day of resurrection.' I said, 'To my Lord, I give praise and thanks.'

IV The second, third and fourth heavens

Then we were elevated to the second heaven during this night journey in a twinkling of an eye. Between it and the sky of the world is five hundred years and its breadth is the same. Gabriel then knocked on the door. They said, 'Who's there?' He said, 'Gabriel.' They said, 'Who is with you?' He said, 'Muḥammad.' They said, 'Has he been sent for?' He said, 'Yes.' They said, 'Welcome to you and to him who is with you.' They opened the door for us and we entered. It was the heaven of iron (like a flat sheet, not joined or separated), which is called al-Māʿūn ['the vessels']. There I saw angels mounted for us on their horses holding variously decorated swords in their hands for battle. I asked, 'Who are those beings, Gabriel?' He said, 'They are the army from the angels whom God created to be the aides of Islam until the day of resurrection.'

I saw two young men who looked alike and I asked Gabriel who they were. He said, 'One of them is John, the son of Zachariah, and the other is Jesus, the son of Mary, on them may there be peace. Draw near to them and greet them.' So I approached them and greeted them. They greeted me in return.

Jesus had beautiful medium-length hair and a white-coloured face mixed with a reddish hue. As for John, his face displayed traces of humility. They greeted me in turn and congratulated me on the favour which my Lord had bestowed on me. They said, 'Spread the good news, Muḥammad! The best of all creation are you and your community until the day of resurrection.' I said, 'To my Lord, I give praise and thanks.' Then Gabriel introduced me and I prayed two *rakʿa*s for the community of Abraham, the friend of God.

We then went up to the third heaven in this night journey in the twinkling of an eye. Between it and the second heaven are five hundred years and its breadth is the same. Gabriel knocked on the door and they said, 'Who's there?' He said, 'Gabriel.'

They said, 'Who is with you?' He said, 'Muḥammad.' They said, 'Welcome to you and to he who is with you.' They opened the door and we entered. This was the heaven of copper which is called al-Muzayyana ['the decorated']. In it I saw angels and with them was a green brigade. I said, 'Who are they, Gabriel?' He said, 'They are the angels of the night of power (of the revelation of the Qurʾān) in the month of Ramaḍān. They are searching for religious gatherings and gatherings of martyrs and those of the religious community to protect the people of prayer at night.' In the group I saw an old man and a young one and I said, 'Who are they, Gabriel?' He said, 'David and Solomon; draw near to them and greet them.' So I approached them and greeted them and they returned the greeting. They congratulated me on the favour which my Lord had bestowed on me and said, 'Spread the good news, Muḥammad! The best of all creation are you and your community until the day of resurrection.' I said, 'To my Lord, I give praise and thanks.'

I saw that between them was a young man, a slave, sitting on a chair of light and the light emanated from his face and his image was like a full moon. I asked, 'Who is this young man, my brother Gabriel?' He said, 'This is Joseph, son of Jacob. God favoured him with goodness and beauty just as he favours the moon over all of the stars.' I approached him and greeted him. He greeted me in return. He congratulated me on the favour which my Lord Most High had bestowed on me and said, 'Greetings to the pious brother and the wise prophet.' The angels were lined up in rows and Gabriel introduced me, and I prayed two *rakʿa*s with them for the community of Abraham, the friend of God.

Then we went up to the fourth heaven in this night journey in the twinkling of an eye. Between it and the third heaven is five hundred years and its breadth is the same. Gabriel knocked on the door and they said, 'Who's there?' He said, 'Gabriel.' They said, 'Who is with you?' He said, 'Muḥammad.' They said, 'Welcome to you and to he who is with you.' Then they opened the door for us and we entered.

The heaven was silver white and it was called al-Zāhira ['the radiant']. Among the wonders of my Lord and the different types of angels, I saw a man from whose face came a luminous light. I asked humbly, 'Who is that, my brother Gabriel?' He said, 'Your brother Idrīs. God raised him to a high station. Draw near to him and greet him.' So I approached him and greeted him. He greeted me in return and sought God's forgiveness and blessings for me and my community.

V *The sixth heaven*

I said, 'Gabriel, who is this?' He said, 'This is an angel whom God created and entrusted with the regiment of heaven. He is the most faithful advisor among the angels for your community, the one who calls them to the day of resurrection.' So I drew near to him and greeted him and he returned my greeting. He said, 'Welcome, lover of the Lord of the worlds!'

I saw an old man with long, abundant hair who was wearing a thick garment of white wool. He was supporting himself with a staff. His hair almost covered his body and he had a white beard that rested on his chest. I said, 'Who is this, my brother Gabriel?' He said, 'This is your brother Moses ibn ʿImrān. God favoured him with His words and deeds and He made him His spokesman. Draw near to him and greet him.' So I approached him and greeted him. He looked at me and began saying, 'The tribe of Israel claims that I am the most noble of creation before God. But this one (in front of me) is more noble than I am before his Lord. This is the prophet of the Quraysh, the Meccan, the Hashemite Arab, the man from the open *wādī*. This is the lover; this is the great, noble one. This is Muḥammad the faithful, Ibn ʿAbd Allāh ibn ʿAbd al-Muṭṭalib. Welcome, pious brother and wise prophet.' Then he called out good tidings and blessings upon me and my community.

VI The seventh heaven

The angels were lined up in rows and I prayed two *rakʿa*s with them for the community of Abraham, the friend of God. Then we ascended to the seventh heaven in the twinkling of an eye. Between it and the sixth heaven is five hundred years and its breadth is the same. Gabriel knocked on the door and they said, 'Who's there?' He said, 'Gabriel.' They said, 'Who is with you?' He said, 'Muḥammad.' They said, 'Welcome to you and to he who is with you, for you are the two best of those who have arrived together.' They opened the door for us and we entered. The sky was made of white pearls and it was called al-ʿAjība ['the wondrous']. It is the highest heaven and I could not hear anything except the scratching of pens.

In it I saw some of the angels of my Lord who were called 'The Spiritual Ones'. I turned to the right and there beside me I saw an old man with a nice face and fine clothes sitting on a chair of light, the back of which supported the celestial house which is the heavenly counterpart of the divinely honoured Kaʿba. I said, 'My brother Gabriel, who is that?' He said, 'That is your father Adam, may the prayers of God be upon him. Draw near to him and greet him.' So I approached him and greeted him. He greeted me in return. He congratulated me on the favour which my Lord had bestowed on me and said, 'Welcome my pious son and wise prophet. Spread the good news, Muḥammad. The best of all creation are you and your community until the day of resurrection. Indeed, your Lord raised you up to Him in order to greet and honour you.' He said, 'You saw the celestial house and in it were candelabras of jewels with lights surrounding them, some yellow rubies, some green chrysolites and some fine pearls.'

The angels circumambulated around the house and I arose and circled with them seven times. I said to the angels, 'How long have you been visiting this house?' They replied, 'From 2000 years before the time that God created your father Adam.' Every day 170,000,000 angels visit the house and they will not get another chance to do so before the day of resurrection.

VII The number of prayers

I was just about to descend (from the seventh heaven) when my Lord called upon me, saying, 'Wait, Muḥammad! Indeed I have entrusted a religious obligation upon you and your community. Those who fulfil it will enter paradise; as for those who fail to attain it, if you desire, I will forgive them, or, if you desire, I will punish them. I have placed a religious duty on you and your community of fifty prayers every day and every night.' I said, 'We hear and we obey.' Then I descended and He blessed me. I continued the night journey until I came to my brother Moses ibn ʿImrān. When he saw me, he arose and said, ‘Welcome faithful loved one. Did you just return from your Lord?’ I said, ‘Yes.’ He asked, ‘What did He give you?’ I said, ‘He gave me something and the offer pleased me.’ He said, ‘What did He give your community?’ I said, ‘He gave them something and it pleased them. He placed a religious duty upon me and them of fifty prayers every day and every night.’ Moses said, ‘Return and ask Him to lighten this for your community, the final community of time. Their bodies are frail and their lives are short. They are not capable of that, so ask your Lord if He will lighten this burden for them.’ I said, ‘Brother, who can pass through these barriers which you passed through?’ Moses said, ‘Ask Him from here, for He is nearby and can answer.’ I swear by the summons from the Highest and Exalted, He said, “Ask what you will and I will answer you.” ’ I said, ‘Lord, my community is frail and is not in a position to perform fifty prayers. Reduce the number of prayers for me and my community by five.’ So I returned to Moses and I told him about this and he said, ‘Return to your Lord and ask him to lighten the burden for your community as they are still not capable of this.’ I did not cease asking my Lord and Moses did not cease talking to me about it, until He granted me release from forty-five prayers and made the duty upon me and my community to be only five prayers. Moses said, ‘Ask Him to lighten this burden.’ I said, ‘My brother, I am ashamed to face my Lord! My Lord called me saying, “Muḥammad, return! We will make it five deeds and it will be counted as fifty works in the scales. Every prayer is equal to ten prayers. The words are substituted in My presence as being equal to ten. Whoever does an evil act, I will write it against him as an equal sin.” ’

VIII The return to Mecca

When we concluded our journey in the heaven of the world it was still night, for time had not moved. I rode on and came to Mecca, which God has made noble and great, and I got off Burāq and Gabriel placed me on the ground. He said, ‘Muḥammad, when morning comes, tell your people about what you saw tonight and announce the good news of God’s mercy to them.’ I said, ‘Gabriel, my brother! I fear that they will think I am lying.’ Gabriel said, ‘If they say you are lying, your companion Abū Bakr will not pay attention to those who say that you lied (and he will support you).’

I slept on my cushions until the time of the morning prayer. Then I awoke and prayed the morning prayer. Afterwards I went out of the door of the mosque and there was, as usual, Abū Jahl, the evil one. When he passed by me, he said, ‘And what did you prophesy yesterday, Muḥammad?’ Whenever he passed by me he would ask me about various matters. I told him that I had travelled in a night journey. He asked, ‘To where?’ I said, ‘To the sacred house [in Jerusalem], and from there to the throne. I spoke to the Truth [God] and He spoke to me, gave me gifts and was generous to me. I also saw paradise and what God has promised to the people of eternal blessing. I saw the fire, the Zaqqūm [“the tree of bitter fruit” of Q 37/62, 44/43 and 56/52] and the pools of hot water which God promised to the people of hell.’ Abū Jahl said, ‘Muḥammad, conceal this statement and do not speak of it or they will think you a liar.’ I said to him, ‘Should I keep what was decreed and blessed by God a secret? God said to me, *You should speak of the good blessings of your Lord* (Q 93/11).’

Abū Jahl, may God curse him, said, ‘By God, the wonder of your words! Are you able to tell your community what you have reported to me?’ I said, ‘Yes.’ So Abū

Jahl called out to the people of the blessed community of Mecca, 'People of Mecca, gather round!' All of them did so.

IX Muḥammad's proof

The messenger of God rose to preach and he said, 'Assembly of Quraysh, know that God, may He be exalted, sent me travelling in the night to the sacred house and then made me ascend through the seven heavens. There I saw the prophets. I was raised up to the throne and I stepped on a carpet of light. I spoke to the Truth and He spoke to me. I saw paradise and the fire. I was instructed to describe all of this.'

Abū Bakr al-Ṣiddīq said, 'You are telling the truth, chosen one of God. Lover of God, you are telling the truth.' Abū Jahl, the evil one, said, 'You have described it nicely. However, I do not want a report of heaven from you, but rather a description of the sacred house. Depending on how you describe it, we will know if what you say is true and if your words are sincere.'

The prophet bowed his head to the earth disheartened, for he entered the sacred house in Jerusalem at night and he returned to Mecca in the same night, so he had been unable to see any distinctive elements. So God inspired Gabriel to descend to the sacred house and lift it up above the earth along with the surrounding mountains, hills, valleys, alleys, streets and mosques and to spread it all in front of His beloved, Muḥammad. So the faithful Gabriel brought the sacred house to the prophet and let the prophet view it. The prophet described it piece by piece and area by area such that the people bowed their heads and Abū Bakr said, 'Lover of God, you tell the truth.'

Then the prophet said, 'When my brother Gabriel and I were in the air, I saw some people from the clan of Makhzūm on Mount Arāk. An ash-coloured camel of theirs went astray. I called to them from the air that their camel was in Wādī 'l-Nakhl ["the valley of the palms"]. When the sun rises tomorrow, they will come to visit you. When they arrive, you may ask them about this.' When it was morning of the next day, however, the riders were still far away and they were unable to reach Mecca by sunrise. So God held back the sun and prevented it from rising until the riders reached Mecca in order to prove the noble and faithful words of the master of creatures, the lover of truth, and our master, Muḥammad. When the sun rose, the riders entered Mecca and they reported that, indeed, their camel had gone astray. They said, 'Someone summoned us from the air and told us the camel was in the valley of the palms and we found it, just as the voice indicated.'

When the Muslims heard that, they were very happy and they rejoiced in jubilation and glorification of God. The messenger of God left surrounded by the Muslims, just like the stars surround the moon. Four thousand people submitted to Islam on that day and the angels cried out in heaven rejoicing and glorifying God for the good news.

Abū Jahl acted hostilely towards him, disclaiming him and envying him. He said, 'This is great magic of yours, Muḥammad!' The prophet drew near and spoke to his companions about the amazing things which he had seen in heaven, at the throne, and of the gardens of the eternal blessings for the people who love him. He also told them of what he had seen in the fire, the boiling water and the painful torment for his enemies.

2.3 Al-Wāqidī on the raid of Biʾr Maʿūna

Muḥammad ibn ʿUmar al-Wāqidī was born in 130/747–8 and died in 207/822. A historian who lived in Medina and Baghdad, he is one of the major sources for information on the early Muslim community. His *Kitāb al-maghāzī* is his only major surviving book, although other works of his are frequently cited by later authors. As a chronology of the raids conducted during the time of Muḥammad in Medina, al-Wāqidī's work is a coherent and cohesive presentation which puts emphasis on establishing the sequence of events by providing a complete chronological framework. When confronted by contradictory sources, he frequently supplies his opinion as to the preferred version. Many of the accounts which he provides are reports formed by combining various sources and presenting the story as an overall coherent narrative.

Al-Wāqidī's account of the raid of Biʾr Maʿūna is representative of the composite accounts which present some details that are the same as in other known sources and some details that are independent and unknown elsewhere. Al-Wāqidī makes this clear at the very start (paragraph 1).

The purpose of recording such accounts was not so they could serve as a dispassionate chronicle. Certainly Muslims were eager historians, but here, as in other historical writing, there is a strong moral point to be made. God's guidance and its influence on Muslim destiny were being asserted and mapped out. The provision of material related to the revelation of the Qurʾān (*asbāb al-nuzūl*; see below section 4.4 from al-Wāḥidī) makes these connections explicit and provides a constant refrain in al-Wāqidī's work.

The raid of Biʾr Maʿūna revolves around an intra-tribal conflict between the chief of the Banū ʿĀmir, ʿĀmir ibn Mālik, and his nephew ʿĀmir ibn al-Ṭufayl, which led to the latter urging the Banū Sulaym to attack a contingent of Muslims who were under the protection of the chief. All the Muslims were killed. The story conveys certain principles about the relationship between clans and tribes in Arabia, and about the principles of justice that were prevalent. However, some of the very core facts of this story are presented quite differently in the variety of sources which are available to us. The portion of the account of the raid provided by al-Wāqidī as presented below may be compared with those of Ibn Isḥāq [Ibn Hishām], *Al-Sīra al-nabawiyya*, Cairo 1955, vol. 2, pp. 183–9, A. Guillaume (trans.), *The life of Muḥammad: a translation of [Ibn] Isḥāq's* Sīrat rasūl Allāh, Oxford 1955, pp. 433–6, al-Ṭabarī, *Taʾrīkh al-rusul waʾl-mulūk*, ed. M. J. de Goeje, Leiden 1879–1901, vol. 1, pp. 1441–8, and W. M. Watt, M. V. McDonald (trans.), *The history of al-Ṭabarī, volume VII: the foundation of the community*, Albany NY 1987, pp. 151–6.

Further reading

Martin Hinds, ' "Maghāzī" and "Sīra" in early Islamic scholarship,' in T. Fahd (ed.), *La vie du prophète Mahomet: Colloque de Strasbourg, Octobre 1980*, Paris 1983, pp. 57–66; reprinted in Uri Rubin (ed.), *The life of Muḥammad*, Aldershot 1998, pp. 1–10, and in M. Hinds, *Studies in early Islamic history*, Princeton 1996, pp. 188–98.

J. M. B. Jones, 'Ibn Isḥāq and al-Wāqidī: the dream of ʿĀtika and the raid to Nakhla in relation to the charge of plagiarism,' *Bulletin of the School of Oriental and African Studies*,

22 (1959), pp. 41–51; reprinted in Uri Rubin (ed.), *The life of Muḥammad*, Aldershot 1998, pp. 11–21.

M. J. Kister, 'The expedition of Biʾr Maʿūna,' in George Makdisi (ed.), *Arabic and Islamic studies in honor of Hamilton A. R. Gibb*, Cambridge MA 1965, pp. 337–57.

Source text

Al-Wāqidī, *Kitāb al-maghāzī*, ed. Marsden Jones, London 1966, pp. 346–8.

The raid of Biʾr Maʿūna, in the month of Ṣafar at the beginning of the thirty-sixth month after the **hijra**

1. Muḥammad ibn ʿAbd Allāh, ʿAbd al-Raḥmān ibn ʿAbd al-ʿAzīz, Maʿmar ibn Rāshid, Aflaḥ ibn Saʿīd, Ibn Abī Sabra, Abu Maʿshar, ʿAbd Allāh ibn Jaʿfar, and some people other than those named all told me parts of this report, some of them remembering about it better than others. I have gathered together all of what I have been told.

All these people report that ʿĀmir ibn Mālik ibn Jaʿfar, Abū ʾl-Barāʾ, the 'Player with Spears', came to the messenger of God and offered him a present of two riding horses. The messenger of God said, 'I cannot accept a gift from a polytheist!' So the messenger of God suggested that he become a Muslim. He would not submit, but neither was he far from doing so. He said, 'Muḥammad, I understand that this concern of yours is a good and noble one, and my people are behind me. If you were to send a group of your companions with me, I anticipate that they would respond to your call and follow your command. If they follow you, that would be great for you!' The messenger of God said, 'I fear for my companions with the people of Najd.' ʿĀmir said, 'Do not fear for them. I will be their surety against any of the people of Najd who would do anything to them.'

There were seventy young men called the Qurrāʾ ['pious ones'] among the Anṣār. One evening they started off in the direction of Medina. They studied together and prayed together. When morning came, they found some sweet water and they gathered firewood and took it to the rooms of the messenger of God. Their followers thought they were in the mosque while the people of the mosque thought they were with their followers. The messenger of God commissioned them to set off and they left and arrived at Biʾr Maʿūna. The messenger of God invoked God against their being killed for fifteen nights.

1.1. Abū Saʿīd al-Khudrī said that there were seventy of them while it is also said that there were forty of them. I consider the trustworthy report to be the one that says there were forty of them.

1.2. The messenger of God had sent a letter with them and he had made al-Mundhir ibn ʿAmr al-Saʿīdī commander over his companions. So they went out until they came to Biʾr Maʿūna. This was one of the springs of the Banū Sulaym which was between the regions of the Banū ʿĀmir and the Banū Sulaym, both tribes counting it as theirs.

2. Muṣʿab ibn Thābit told me on the authority of Abūʾl-Aswad on the authority of ʿUrwa who said that al-Mundhir went out with a guide from the Banū Sulaym named al-Muṭṭalib. When they arrived at the spring, they set up camp and sent their camels to pasture behind them. They sent al-Ḥārith ibn al-Ṣimma and ʿAmr ibn Umayya to the pasture. They also sent Ḥarām ibn Milḥān ahead with the letter from the messenger of God to ʿĀmir ibn Ṭufayl who was with some men of the Banū ʿĀmir. When Ḥarām reached them, they did not read the letter. ʿĀmir rushed at Ḥarām and killed him. ʿĀmir cried out for help from the Banū ʿĀmir against the Muslims, but they refused to do as he asked. Earlier, ʿĀmir ibn Mālik Abūʾl-Barāʾ had set out in the direction of Najd, leaving before the other people; he had informed them that the companions of Muḥammad were protected so they should not get in their way. They said that the protection of Abū ʾl-Barāʾ would never protect the Muslims. However, the Banū ʿĀmir refused to follow ʿĀmir ibn Ṭufayl's wishes. So when this happened, ʿĀmir asked for help against the Muslims from the Banū Sulaym – ʿUsayya and Riʿl – and they joined with him under his leadership.

ʿĀmir ibn Ṭufayl said, 'I swear by God that I will not do this alone!' So they followed the tracks of the Muslims until they located the group. The Banū Sulaym found their companion to be slow, so they followed the Muslims' tracks until they encountered al-Mundhir along with the group. The Banū Sulaym and ʿĀmir ibn Ṭufayl surrounded the Muslims, outnumbering them. They battled until the companions of the messenger of God were killed, leaving alive only al-Mundhir ibn ʿAmr. They said to him, 'If you wish, we will grant you safety.' He said, 'I will never be taken nor shall I agree to accept safety from you until I am taken to the body of Ḥarām and then your protection may be removed from me.'

So they granted him safety until they brought him to where Ḥarām had died. They then freed him from their protection and they battled until he was killed. That is what is meant by the messenger of God calling al-Mundhir, 'He who wished for death to be swift.'

3. Al-Ḥārith ibn al-Ṣimma and ʿAmr ibn Umayya returned from the pasture and they were alarmed by the birds who were hovering over and around their camping place. Suddenly they said, 'By God, our companions have been killed! It could only have been the people of Najd who killed them, by God!' From the high land they looked down at their dead companions whose horses were standing nearby. Al-Ḥārith ibn al-Ṣimma said to ʿAmr ibn Umayya, 'What do you think?' He replied, 'I think that I will return to the messenger of God and tell him what has happened.' Al-Ḥārith said, 'I do not want to tarry at a place in which al-Mundhir has been killed.' So the two of them approached the group from the Banū Sulaym and al-Ḥārith fought until he killed two of them. They then took him and ʿAmr ibn Umayya prisoner. They said to al-Ḥārith, 'What do you wish that we do to you, since we do not wish to kill you?' He said, 'Take me to the place where al-Mundhir and Ḥarām died. Then shedding your blood will be possible for me.' They said, 'We will do this.' So they went there with him and set him free. He then fought them and killed two of them; then he was killed. They did not kill him until many spears were aimed at him and they pierced him.

2.4 Ibn Saʿd on Muḥammad's wives

Abū 'Abd Allāh Muḥammad Ibn Sa'd (b. *c.* 168/784 in Basra, d. 230/845 in Baghdad) was a traditionalist and the compiler of one of the most important early Arabic biographical dictionaries, the *Kitāb al-ṭabaqāt al-kabīr*. The secretary to al-Wāqidī (see section 2.3), he lived in Baghdad and compiled his listing of some 4,250 people (including abut 600 women, separately classified) as a part of the process of cataloguing and defining Muslim tradition that was carried out in the early period.

The *Ṭabaqāt* covers the period from the time of Muḥammad up to the year 230/845. The first section of the work is devoted to Muḥammad and the rest provides biographies of transmitters of traditions organized in 'classes' or 'stages' (*ṭabaqāt*), first by region and then chronologically. The entries have been extracted from other works, each being preceded by an *isnād* providing attribution. Reports from Muḥammad ibn 'Umar, that is al-Wāqidī, predominate; Ibn Sa'd's work is sometimes spoken of as an expanded edition of al-Wāqidī's own work of the same title which has not survived. Al-Wāqidī is usually credited with the introduction of the classification scheme of *ṭabaqāt* which proved influential and lasting in every religious discipline; Ibn Sa'd's success is therefore seen to be in implementing al-Wāqidī's scheme fully and compellingly for later generations. Ibn Sa'd's work has been credited with having firmly established the basic structure of the life of Muḥammad for later generations through his extensive treatment of documents and, notably, through the emphasis he gives to the delegations which Muḥammad sent out in his efforts to spread Islam. The attention paid to Muḥammad's wives, as presented below, is integral to the overall presentation of the life of the prophet. The anecdotes reflect the fascination with the collection of as many details as possible about Muḥammad's life; any concern with the 'status of women' as it may be conceived in the twenty-first century is distant from the interests of Ibn Sa'd.

Further reading

Ruth Roded, *Women in Islamic biographical collections: from Ibn Sa'd to Who's who*, Boulder CO 1994.

Muḥammad Zubayr Ṣiddīqī, *Ḥadīth literature: its origin, development and special features*, revised edition, Cambridge 1993, pp. 96–100.

Barbara Freyer Stowasser, *Women in the Qur'an, traditions, and interpretation*, New York 1994.

W. Montgomery Watt, *Muhammad at Medina*, Oxford 1956, excursus L, pp. 393–9.

Source text

Ibn Sa'd, *Al-Ṭabaqāt al-kubrā*, Beirut 1957, vol. 1, pp. 131–3 (part I); vol. 1, pp. 499–501 (part II); vol. 2, pp. 231–3 (part III). These sections have been previously translated into English in S. Moinul Haq, H. K. Ghazanfar (trans.), *Ibn Sa'd's Kitab al-tabaqat al-kabir*, Karachi 1967–72; reference to that work has been made in translating these sections.

I *The account of the marriage of the messenger of God, peace be upon him, to Khadīja bint Khuwaylid*

1. Ibn Saʿd said that Muḥammad ibn ʿUmar ibn Wāqid al-Aslamī told him that Mūsā ibn Shayba told him on the authority of ʿUmayra bint ʿUbayd Allāh ibn Kaʿb ibn Mālik on the authority of Umm Saʿd bint Saʿd ibn al-Rabīʿ on the authority of Nafīsa bint Munya who said that Khadīja bint Khuwaylid ibn Asad ibn ʿAbd al-ʿUzzā ibn Quṣayy was a determined, patient and noble woman, for whom God willed blessings and goodness. She was, at that time, the most noble in descent in Quraysh, the greatest of them in distinction and the wealthiest of them. Every member of her tribe desired to marry her if that were possible, seeking her out and giving her gifts.

   Khadīja sent Nafīsa covertly to Muḥammad after he returned with her caravan from Syria, to say to him, 'Muḥammad, what prevents you from marrying?' He replied, 'I do not have anything to give in marriage.' She said, 'If you had the means and received a call from a beautiful, wealthy and noble woman of equal status, how would you respond?' He said, 'Who is she?' She said, 'Khadīja.' He replied, 'How would that be possible for me?' 'That's up to me,' she said. To this he agreed. So Nafīsa went to inform Khadīja. Khadīja then sent for him to come at a certain time and she sent for her uncle ʿAmr ibn Asad to give her away in marriage. ʿAmr arrived as did the messenger of God along with his uncles, one of whom married him to Khadīja. ʿAmr ibn Asad then said, 'This is the partnership untainted by any disdain.' The messenger of God married her when he was a young man, twenty-five years old, and Khadīja was, at the time, forty years old as she was born fifteen years before the 'Year of the Elephant'.

2. Muḥammad ibn ʿUmar informed us on the authority of Muḥammad ibn ʿAbd Allāh ibn Muslim who reported on the authority of his father who reported on the authority of Muḥammad ibn Jubayr ibn Muṭʿim and it was reported on the authority of Ibn Abi 'l-Zinād who reported on the authority of Hishām ibn ʿUrwa who reported on the authority of his father who reported on the authority of ʿĀ'isha and it was reported on the authority of Ibn Abi Ḥabība who reported on the authority of Dāwūd ibn al-Ḥuṣayn who reported on the authority of ʿIkrima who reported on the authority of Ibn ʿAbbās, all of whom said that her uncle ʿAmr ibn Asad married her to the messenger of God because her father had died before the battle of al-Fijār.

3. Hishām ibn Muḥammad ibn al-Sā'ib al-Kalbī informed us that his father informed him on the authority of Abu Ṣāliḥ who reported on the authority of Ibn ʿAbbās who said that ʿAmr ibn Asad ibn ʿAbd al-ʿUzzā ibn Quṣayy gave Khadīja bint Khuwaylid in marriage to the prophet and, at that time, he was an old man and his offspring had perished and no other members of the Asad family remained, and ʿAmr ibn Asad himself had no children.

4. Khālid ibn Khidāsh ibn ʿAjlān informed us that Muʿtamir ibn Sulaymān informed him that he had listened to his father recalling that Abu Mijlaz reported that Khadīja said to her sister, 'Dash off to Muḥammad and mention me to him!' or words to that effect. Her sister went and he replied to her according to God's

plan. They agreed that the messenger of God would marry her. The father of Khadīja was given wine to drink until it overcame him, and then he summoned Muḥammad and he married him to Khadīja. The old man was dressed in a vestment, and when sobriety returned to him, he said, 'What is this vestment?' They said, 'Muḥammad, your son-in-law, attired you in it.' He then became angry and took up his weapons, as did the tribe of Hāshim. They said, 'We have no desire to fight' and they compromised after that.

5. Muḥammad ibn ʿUmar informed us via another *isnād* that Khadīja gave wine to her father until he was intoxicated. She slaughtered a cow, and she perfumed her father and dressed him in a Yemeni vestment. When he recovered, he said, 'What is this slaughter? What is this fragrance? What is this Yemeni garment?' She said, 'You married me to Muḥammad.' 'I did not do that!' he replied. 'Would I do that and reject the notables of Quraysh (as marriage partners for you)?! I would never do that.'

6. Muḥammad ibn ʿUmar said that, according to him, all of this is in error and a source of consternation. The valid version, according to him, is what is preserved on the authority of the scholars that Khadīja's father, Khuwaylid ibn Asad, died before the battle of al-Fijār, and that her uncle ʿAmr ibn Asad married her to the messenger of God.

II The account of the houses of the messenger of God, peace be upon him, and the rooms of his wives

1. Muḥammad ibn ʿUmar informed us that ʿAbd Allāh ibn Zayd al-Hudhalī said that he saw the houses of the wives of the prophet when ʿUmar ibn ʿAbd al-ʿAzīz demolished them. The houses were made of brick and their rooms were separated by palm-tree stems plastered with mud. He counted nine houses with rooms, lying between the house of ʿĀʾisha and the door which was adjacent to the door of the prophet and the home of Asmāʾ bint Ḥasan ibn ʿAbd Allāh ibn ʿUbayd Allāh ibn al-ʿAbbās. He saw the house of Umm Salama, the room of which was made of bricks, and he asked her grandson about this. He said that when the messenger of God conducted a military raid (*ghazwa*) on Dūma, Umm Salama built her room with bricks. When the messenger of God came back, he looked at the bricks and went to her right away and said, 'What is this building?' She said, 'Messenger of God, I wanted to prevent people looking in.' He said, 'Umm Salama, the most iniquitous thing is the wealth of the Muslims going into buildings.'

2. Muḥammad ibn ʿUmar said that he communicated this *ḥadīth* to Muʿādh ibn Muḥammad al-Anṣārī who said that he heard ʿAṭāʾ al-Khurāsānī in a meeting at which ʿUmar ibn abī Anas, who was standing between the grave and the pulpit (of Muḥammad in Medina), said that he recalled the rooms of the wives of the messenger of God being made from palm-tree stalks with black hair draped on the doors. He was present for the reading of the decree of al-Walīd ibn ʿAbd al-Malik which ordered the entering of the rooms of the wives of the prophet in

the mosque of the messenger of God. He said that he had never seen more crying than on that day.

3. ʿAṭāʾ said that he heard Saʿīd ibn al-Musayyib saying at that time, 'By God, I wish that they had left them as it was.' The next generation of people in Medina and those who visit from distant lands would have been able to see what sufficed for the messenger of God during his life. Then people would have abstained from accumulating wealth and boasting about it. Muʿādh said that when ʿAṭāʾ al-Khurāsānī concluded his *ḥadīth*, ʿUmar ibn abī Anas said, 'Four of the houses were made of brick and their rooms were made from palm-tree stalks. Five houses were made of palm-tree stalks plastered with mud and they had no rooms within them. Curtains of hair covered the doors. I measured the openings and found them to be more or less three cubits. As for what I said about the weeping on that certain day, I myself saw in the meeting a group of the sons of companions of the messenger of God. Among them was Abū Salama ibn ʿAbd al-Raḥman ibn ʿAwf and Abū ʿUmāma ibn Sahl ibn Ḥunayf and Khārija ibn Zayd ibn Thābit. They were weeping such that their beards got wet. That day Abū Umāma said that he wished that the buildings had been left so that people would have abstained from building and they would have seen what pleased God about His prophet even when the keys to the treasuries of the world had been given to him.'

4. Muḥammad ibn ʿUmar informed us on the authority of ʿAbd Allāh ibn ʿĀmir al-Aslamī that Abū Bakr ibn Ḥazm said to him while in his prayer spot between the column which is adjacent to the end of the grave (of Muḥammad) and the nearby column which is on the way to the door of the messenger of God, that this was the house of Zaynab bint Jaḥsh. The messenger of God used to pray in it. All of this area which extended from the door of Asmāʾ bint Ḥasan ibn ʿAbd Allāh ibn ʿUbayd Allāh ibn al-ʿAbbās to the inner courtyard of the mosque at that time was where the houses of the prophet were. He said that he saw that they were made of palm-tree stalks plastered with mud and had curtains of hair.

5. Qabīṣa ibn ʿAqba informed us that Nijād ibn Farrūkh al-Yarbūʿī informed him on the authority of an elderly person from Medina who said that he had seen the rooms of the prophet before their demolition. They were made of palm-tree stalks covered with leather matting.

6. Khālid ibn Mukhallad informed us that Dāwūd ibn Shaybān told him, saying that he saw the rooms of the wives of the prophet and that they had curtains made of hair in the Bedouin style.

7. Muḥammad ibn Muqātil al-Marwazī informed us that ʿAbd Allāh ibn al-Mubārak informed him that Ḥurayth ibn al-Sāʾib heard al-Ḥasan saying that he used to enter the houses of the wives of the prophet during the time of the caliphate of ʿUthmān ibn ʿAffān and that he could reach the roofs with his hand.

III The account of the messenger of God seeking permission from his wives to be nursed in the house of ʿĀʾisha

1. Yaʿqūb ibn Ibrāhīm ibn Saʿd al-Zuhrī informed us on the authority of his father, who related it on the authority of Ṣāliḥ ibn Kaysān, who related it on the authority of Ibn Shihāb who said that when the ailment of the messenger of God became severe, he sought the permission of his wives to remain in the house of ʿĀʾisha. It is said that Fāṭima asked them about this, saying, 'The constant change is a burden for the messenger of God.' Permission was given to him and he left the house of Maymūna and went to the house of ʿĀʾisha, dragging his legs as he was carried between ʿAbbās and another man into ʿĀʾisha's house. It is claimed that Ibn ʿAbbās asked, 'Who is the other man?' to which the reply was, 'We do not know!' He said, 'He is ʿAlī ibn Abī Ṭālib.'

2. Aḥmad ibn al-Ḥajjāj informed us that ʿAbd Allāh ibn al-Mubārak informed him that Maʿmar and Yūnus informed him on the authority of al-Zuhrī that he was informed by ʿUbayd Allāh ibn ʿAbd Allāh ibn ʿAtba that ʿĀʾisha, the wife of the prophet, said, 'When the messenger of God fell ill and his ailment grew worse, he sought permission from his wives to be tended in my house. Permission was granted to him. He left dragging his feet on the ground while being carried between two men, Ibn ʿAbbās (known as al-Faḍl) and another man.' ʿUbayd Allāh said that he reported to Ibn ʿAbbās what ʿĀʾisha said and he said, 'Do you know who the other man was whom ʿĀʾisha did not name?' I said, 'No!' Ibn ʿAbbās replied, 'It was ʿAlī! ʿĀʾisha does not like to give him any credit for good deeds.' ʿĀʾisha said that the messenger of God, after he entered her house when his ailment grew worse, requested, 'Pour water on me from seven waterskins which are full when fastened. It may be that I will have to take a covenantal oath from the people.' So we sat him down in one of the vessels belonging to Ḥafṣa, the wife of the prophet, and began pouring water on him from these waterskins until he made a signal to us with his hand that we should stop. He then went out to the people and prayed with them and preached to them.

3. Yazīd ibn Hārūn informed us that Ḥammād ibn Salama informed him that Abū ʿImrān al-Jawnī informed him on the authority of Yazīd ibn Bābanūs who said that he sought permission for himself and one of his companions to meet with ʿĀʾisha and she granted it to them. When they entered, she drew the screen and gave them a pillow to sit on. She said, 'Whenever the messenger of God passed by my door he would say some words to me as a gift from God. One day he passed by and did not say anything. Then he passed by another day and did not say anything again. I said, "Handmaid, provide a pillow for me at the door!" When she had put it there, I sat on it so that I would be in his way and I wrapped up my head. When the messenger of God passed by me, he said, "What is the matter with you?" I replied that I had pain in my head and the messenger of God said, "Oh, and I too have a pain in my head." He then departed. He did not take long in his travels and he returned to me carrying a load of clothing. He entered my house and sent for his wives who gathered and to whom he said, "I am ill and will not be able to walk to your houses. If you wish, give me permission to

stay in ʿĀʾisha's house." They gave him permission and I began to nurse him although I had not tended to a sick person before him.'

4. Muḥammad ibn ʿUmar informed us that Ḥātim ibn Ismāʿīl told him on the authority of Jaʿfar ibn Muḥammad, who told him on the authority of his father, who said that when the illness of the prophet increased he said, 'Where am I supposed to be tomorrow?' They said, 'You will be with so-and-so.' He said, 'And where am I to be the day after tomorrow?' They said, 'With so-and-so.' Then his wives realized that he wanted to be with ʿĀʾisha and they said, 'Messenger of God, we give our turns to be with you to our sister, ʿĀʾisha.'

5. Muḥammad ibn ʿUmar informed us that al-Ḥakam ibn Qāsim told him on the authority of ʿAfīf ibn ʿAmr al-Sahmī, who told him on the authority of ʿUbayd Allāh ʿAbd Allāh ibn ʿUtba, who told him on the authority of ʿĀʾisha that she said that the messenger of God would go from house to house visiting his wives until he was overcome by it while he was in the house of Maymūna. The wives of the messenger of God knew that he preferred to be in her house. They said, 'Messenger of God, our days (with you) we bestow upon our sister!' by which they meant ʿĀʾisha.

Chapter 3

Ḥadīth

3.1 Mālik ibn Anas, selection from *al-Muwaṭṭa'* on *zakāt*

Mālik ibn Anas was a Muslim jurist from Medina and the eponymous patron of the Mālikī school of law (*madhhab*). He was born in about 93/711 and died in 179/795. During his life, Mālik's role was as the repository of local norms, and he was also involved in public and political judicial affairs. He has always been pictured as someone staunchly opposed to the governors of the time but able to act as a shrewd statesman in his interactions with them.

Mālik is portrayed as very strict in his judgement of the authenticity of *ḥadīth* reports. His legal text *al-Muwaṭṭa'*, therefore, has relatively few prophetic reports. As the representative of the Medinan practice, his work makes constant reference to that element, asserting it as a source of law. Mālik is also seen as not favouring intellectual speculation in matters of law; he deemed the answer 'I don't know' to a question an essential component of wisdom.

The *Muwaṭṭa'* became available in a number of different transmissions (nine are known today) and is, in its basic format, one of the earliest of Muslim legal texts. It represents an attempt to bring every aspect of Muslim life – from the most serious to the most mundane – under the framework of the divinely guided *sharī'a*. It foregrounds prophetic traditions but also contains much discursive material in Mālik's name. The section translated below, covering various aspects of the giving of charity, illustrates the ordering of material and the relative status of each type: prophetic *ḥadīth*, non-prophetic *ḥadīth*, Mālik's representation of the Medinan practice and the practice of the caliphs.

Further reading

Aisha Abdurrahman Bewley (trans.), *Al-Muwatta of Imam Malik ibn Anas: the first formulation of Islamic law*, London 1989; a full translation of the work of Mālik.
Norman Calder, *Studies in early Muslim jurisprudence*, Oxford 1993, chapter 2.
Yasin Dutton, *The origins of Islamic law: the Qur'ān, the* Muwaṭṭa' *and Madinan* 'amal, Richmond 1999.
A. Zysow, '*Zakāt*,' in *Encyclopaedia of Islam*, new edition.

Source text

Mālik ibn Anas, *Muwaṭṭa'*, ed. Muḥammad Fu'ād 'Abd al-Bāqī, Cairo 1951, vol. 1, pp. 268–70.

I *Chapter on prohibiting oppression of the people in the giving of charity*

1. Yaḥyā told me on the authority of Mālik from Yaḥyā ibn Saʿīd from Muḥammad ibn Yaḥyā ibn Ḥabbān from al-Qāsim ibn Muḥammad from ʿĀ'isha, wife of the prophet, that she said that ʿUmar ibn al-Khaṭṭāb passed by some sheep which were a part of charity. Among them he saw a sheep with a large udder flowing with milk. ʿUmar said, 'What is with this sheep?' They replied, 'This is a sheep which is part of charity (*ṣadaqa*).' ʿUmar said, 'The owners of this sheep did not give it willingly. Do not torment the people. Do not take the best animals of the Muslims, leaving them without food.'

2. Yaḥyā told me on the authority of Mālik from Yaḥyā ibn Saʿīd from Muḥammad ibn Yaḥyā ibn Ḥabbān who said that two men from the Ashjaʿ tribe informed him that Muḥammad ibn Maslamat al-Anṣārī used to come to them to collect their charity. To those who had possessions, he would say, 'Bring me charity from what you have!' He would accept a sheep as payment of the amount owed.

3. Mālik said, 'This is the *sunna* for us. What I have seen the people of knowledge doing in our region is that they would not create hardship for the Muslims in their payment of *zakāt* and that they would accept from them what they offered of their possessions.'

II *Chapter on taking charity and who is permitted to take it*

1. Yaḥyā told me on the authority of Mālik from Zayd ibn Aslam from ʿAṭā' ibn Yasār that the messenger of God said, 'Charity is not permitted to be given to a rich person except in five cases: someone fighting in the way of God; someone working collecting charity; someone who has suffered loss; someone who buys it with his own money; and someone who has a poor neighbour who is given charity and the poor person gives some to the rich one.'

2. Mālik said, 'For us, the dividing up of charity can only be done using individual judgement by the possessor of what is to be given. Whichever group of people has the most need and are most numerous are to be given preference as the giver decides is appropriate. It is possible that it could change to another group after one, two or more years. Preference is always given to the people who are in need and most numerous. This is the way the people of knowledge with whom I am pleased have acted.'

3. Mālik said that there is no set amount to be given to the collector of charity other than what the *imām* decides is appropriate.

III Chapter on taking charity and being firm in doing so

1. Yaḥyā told me on the authority of Mālik that it reached him that Abū Bakr al-Ṣiddīq said, 'If they hold back from me even a small portion of one year's charity, I will declare a *jihād* against them over it.'

2. Yaḥyā told me on the authority of Mālik from Zayd ibn Aslam that he said that ʿUmar ibn al-Khaṭṭāb drank some milk which he enjoyed, so he asked the person who had given it to him, 'Where did this milk come from?' He told him that he went to a water hole (which he named) and he found some livestock given in charity drinking there. He was given some of their milk which he put in his container, and that was the milk (he had given to ʿUmar). So ʿUmar ibn al-Khaṭṭāb made himself regurgitate it, using his own hand.

3. Mālik said, 'For us, if anyone refuses any of the obligations of God and the Muslims are unable to extract it from that person, *jihād* is a right which they have until such time as they get the obligation from that person.'

4. Yaḥyā told me on the authority of Mālik that it had reached him that one of the tax collectors under ʿUmar ibn ʿAbd al-ʿAzīz had written to him mentioning that a man had refused to give *zakāt* on his possessions. ʿUmar wrote to the tax collector telling him to leave the man alone and not take any *zakāt* from him along with that of the Muslims. Word of that reached the man and things became very difficult for him. After that he paid the *zakāt* on his possessions. The tax collector wrote to ʿUmar mentioning that to him. ʿUmar then wrote back saying that he could now take it from him.

3.2 Al-Bukhārī, selection from *al-Ṣaḥīḥ* on *zakāt*

Muḥammad ibn Ismāʿīl al-Bukhārī, who lived from 194/810 to 256/870, is the compiler of one of the six authoritative books of *ḥadīth* in Sunnī Islam. Born in Bukhara, he spent much of his life in Nishapur, returned to Bukhara and then went to Samarkand towards the end of his life.

Al-Bukhārī is said to have travelled throughout the Middle East in order to hear *ḥadīth* reports from as many sources as possible; he is said to have listened to some 1,000 transmitters. He is reported to have had an astounding memory which he cultivated from a young age and to have accumulated some 600,000 reports which he reduced down to about 2,762 distinct items (although there are 7,397 entries in the work when one includes the duplicated traditions) that he considered reliable enough according to his own strict criteria for inclusion in his book. Organized by subject matter, al-Bukhārī's *al-Ṣaḥīḥ* is considered to be the most reliable collection of authenticated reports along with that of Muslim ibn al-Ḥajjāj (d. 261/875); as a pair, these works are considered by Sunnī Muslims as second only to the Qur'ān in authority. The work, which took sixteen years to compile, is organized according to books (of which there are ninety-seven) and chapters (3,450 in total) following the established agenda of juristic and theological problems of the time. Some of the chapter headings have no *ḥadīth* reports under them, indicating that the structure of the work was pre-established.

The section translated below from the book on *zakāt* illustrates the organizational principles of the work as well as the way in which al-Bukhārī constructed his text to align the *ḥadīth* with the Qur'ān, and to privilege the Qur'ān as a source of Muslim practice. The topic of how charity is to be distributed clearly demanded close attention to both sources of authority in order to deal with what, given the structure and content of the chapter headings in al-Bukhārī's text, was bound by some well-established practices.

Further reading

Ignaz Goldziher, *Muslim studies*, London 1971, vol. 2, pp. 216–26.
Muḥammad Zubayr Ṣiddīqī, *Ḥadīth literature: its origin, development and special features*, revised edition, Cambridge 1993, pp. 53–8.

Source text

Al-Bukhārī, *Al-Ṣaḥīḥ*, Cairo 1981 (reprint), vol. 2, pp. 115–17.

I Chapter

1. Mūsā ibn Ismāʿīl told us that Abū ʿAwāna told him on the authority of Firās from al-Shaʿbī from Masrūq from ʿĀʾisha that some of the wives of the prophet said to him, 'Which of us will be the first to die after you?' He replied, 'Whichever of you has the longest hand.' So they began measuring their hands with a stick and discovered that Sawda had the longest hand. Later they came to know that giving charity was called 'the longest hand'. She was the first to die after him and she loved giving charity.

II Chapter on giving charity openly

1. This is as in the saying of God, *Those who give of their possessions at night and during the day in secret and openly . . . none of them will grieve* (Q 2/274).

III Chapter on giving charity secretly

1. Abū Hurayra reported on the authority of the prophet that he said that a person giving charity can do it secretly such that his left hand does not know what his right hand is doing. About this God said, *If you give charity openly it is good, but if you do it secretly and give it to the poor, that is better for you* (Q 2/271).

IV Chapter on giving charity to a rich person unknowingly

1. Abū ʾl-Yamān told me that Shuʿayb informed him that Abū Zinād told him on the authority of al-Aʿraj from Abū Hurayra that the messenger of God said that a man said, 'I will certainly give some charity!' So he took his charity and gave it to a thief. The next morning he was informed that he had given charity to a thief. He said, 'God, Praise be to You. I will certainly give charity (again)!' So he took his charity and gave it to an adulterer. The next morning he was informed that he had given charity to an adulterer the night before. He said, 'God, Praise be to You over an adulterer. I will certainly give charity (again)!' So he took his charity and gave it to a rich person. The next morning he was informed that he had given charity to a rich person. He said, 'God, Praise be to you over a thief, an adulterer and a rich person.' Someone came up to him and said, 'The charity you gave to a thief may make him abstain from stealing, and perhaps the adulterer will abstain from adultery. As for the rich person, perhaps he will learn a lesson from it and give of what God has given him.'

V Chapter on giving charity to one's son without realizing it

1. Muḥammad ibn Yūsuf told us that Isrāʾīl told him that Abū ʾl-Juwayriya told him that Maʿn ibn Yazīd told him that he, his father and his grandfather pledged allegiance to the messenger of God, who then proposed Maʿn in marriage and then

had him married. Maʿn said, 'I went to him with a problem concerning my father, Yazīd, who had taken some money to be given in charity and placed it with a man in the mosque. I then went and took it and brought it to my father.' His father said, 'By God, I did not wish to give it to you!' So Maʿn took the problem concerning this to the messenger of God who said, 'Yazīd, you will have what you intended in reward. Maʿn, what you took is yours!'

VI Chapter on charity given with the right hand

1. Musaddad told us that Yaḥyā told him on the authority of ʿUbayd Allāh who said that Khubayb ibn ʿAbd al-Raḥmān told him on the authority of Ḥafṣ ibn ʿĀṣim from Abū Hurayra from the prophet who said, 'Seven types of people will be shaded by God in His shadow on the day on which there will be no shade other than His: a just ruler; a young man raised in the worship of God; a man whose heart is attached to mosques; two people united in the love of God who join for Him and separate for Him; a man who is summoned by a noble and beautiful woman to whom he says, "I fear God"; a person who gives charity secretly such that his left hand does not know what his right hand is giving; and a person who remembers God in seclusion and whose eyes fill with tears.'

2. ʿAlī ibn al-Jaʿd told us that Shuʿba informed him saying that Maʿbad ibn Khālid said he heard Ḥāritha ibn Wahb al-Khuzāʿī saying that he heard the prophet saying, 'Give charity! A time will come when people will walk around with their charity and someone to whom it is offered will say, "If you had come yesterday, I would have taken it from you. Today, however, I have no need of it."'

3.3 Ibn Ḥajar, commentary on *Ṣaḥīḥ al-Bukhārī* on *zakāt*

Shihāb al-Dīn Aḥmad Ibn Ḥajar al-ʿAsqalānī (d. 852/1449) was one of the giants of Sunnī *ḥadīth* scholarship. He was born, in 773/1372, into a wealthy family of merchants based in Egypt. Though he was orphaned in childhood, his family's affluence enabled him to live comfortably and pursue his interests in religious scholarship. He began his career as a scholar and teacher at a relatively young age, and before reaching the age of forty became the head of the Baybarsiyya college, a position he was to hold for some thirty years. He also held the position of chief judge of Egypt for some twenty years in total. But it is his extraordinary literary output that has earned him the highest of reputations in Sunnī *ḥadīth* scholarship.

Ibn Ḥajar composed his first works on *ḥadīth* in his early thirties, before starting work on his *magnum opus,* his massive *ḥadīth* commentary entitled *Fatḥ al-bārī: sharḥ Ṣaḥīḥ al-Bukhārī,* which is widely regarded as the most important work of the *sharḥ al-ḥadīth* (*ḥadīth* commentary) genre. He completed it towards the end of his life, in 842/1438, some thirty years after starting. Its importance was immediately recognized, and it is even reported that, before the whole work was finished, powerful and wealthy individuals tried to acquire copies of the volumes he had already written. Ibn Ḥajar also wrote many other works in the *ḥadīth* sciences, including highly esteemed biography collections.

As a work of the *sharḥ al-ḥadīth* genre, the *Fatḥ al-bārī* presents the text of the *ḥadīth* collection on which it is based, segment by segment, in a way similar to that in which *tafsīr* works present the text of the Qur'ān. This format is in order to allow each segment to be followed by commentary, which, in the passage given below for instance, can range from variant readings and grammatical explanations to a consideration of the legal and ethical implications. He cites the opinions of previous commentators which he has collected from a rich variety of literary and oral sources. His task also includes justifying the arrangement of the text on which he is commenting, and taking into account variant transmissions of it. This enables Ibn Ḥajar to develop the argument that the donor's charity was accepted by God even though he repeatedly failed to give it to someone qualified to receive it. The overall effect of the form of this *ḥadīth* commentary can be seen as a broadening of the possible meaning of the text of al-Bukhārī's canonical *ḥadīth* collection through the historical experience of the Sunnī community.

Further reading

Norman Calder, 'History and nostalgia: reflections on John Wansbrough's *The sectarian milieu*,' in Herbert Berg (ed.), *Islamic origins reconsidered: John Wansbrough and the study of Islam*, special issue of *Method and theory in the study of religion: Journal of the North American Association for the Study of Religion*, 9 (1997), pp. 47–73.

Mohammed Fadel, 'Ibn Ḥajar's *Hady al-sārī*: a medieval interpretation of al-Bukhārī's *al-Jāmiʿ al-ṣaḥīḥ*: introduction and translation,' *Journal of Near Eastern studies*, 54 (1995), pp. 161–97.

Franz Rosenthal, 'Ibn Ḥadjar al-ʿAsqalānī,' in *Encyclopaedia of Islam*, new edition.

Source text

Ibn Ḥajar al-ʿAsqalānī, *Fatḥ al-bārī: sharḥ Ṣaḥīḥ al-Bukhārī*, Cairo 1978, vol. 4, pp. 39–41. The *ḥadīth*s on which the following commentary is based are presented in continuous form in section 3.2 above, parts III and IV; in this translation, the sections from al-Bukhārī have been italicized.

Commentary on: Chapter on giving charity secretly

1. *Abū Hurayra said on the authority of the prophet that he said that a person giving charity can do it secretly such that his left hand does not know what his right hand is doing. God said,* If you give charity openly it is good, but if you do it secretly and give it to the poor, that is better for you *(Q 2/271). Section: If one gives charity to a rich person unknowingly.*

   This is followed by the *ḥadīth* of Abū Hurayra about the person who took his charity and gave it to a thief, then to an adulterer and finally to a rich person. This is how the transmission by Abū Dharr reads.

   1.1. The latter is found in the transmissions of others under the separate rubric, 'Chapter on giving charity to a rich person unknowingly'. This is the way it is presented by al-Ismāʿīlī, followed by the citation of the *ḥadīth*. Its appropriateness is evident for the entry title 'giving charity secretly' was limited in direct relevance to that *ḥadīth* commenting on the citation from the Qurʾān.

   1.2. The content of Abū Dharr's transmission requires a link between the entry title 'giving charity secretly' and the *ḥadīth* about the person who gives charity. What is meant is that the acts of giving charity that are mentioned took place at night, as indicated by the words in the *ḥadīth*, *The next morning he was informed*. In *Ṣaḥīḥ Muslim* the explication of this fact can be found in the following words of the *ḥadīth*: 'I will certainly give some charity at night. . . .' This indicates that his giving of charity was secret, since if it were in broad daylight the identity of the rich person would not have been hidden from him, as it is most likely not to be hidden in daylight, unlike that of the adulterer and the thief. This is also why the rich person is singled out in the heading of this entry from amongst the three.

2. The *ḥadīth* of Abū Hurayra prior to this one actually forms a part of another *ḥadīth* which is presented in its entirety in another chapter 'Concerning someone who sat in the mosque in expectation of the ritual prayer'. It is the strongest evidence for the superiority of giving charity secretly.

   2.1. The Qurʾānic verse in that [*If you give charity openly it is good, but if you do it secretly and give it to the poor, that is better for you* (Q 2/271)] also ostensibly gives preference to giving charity secretly, but the majority hold the view that it was revealed only in relation to voluntary charity.

   2.2. Al-Ṭabarī and others report that the consensus is that in the giving of obligatory charity it is preferable to do it openly than secretly, while the opposite applies for voluntary charity.

2.3. Yazīd ibn Ḥabīb disagreed, saying that the verse was revealed in relation to the giving of charity to Jews and Christians; he said that the meaning is that if you give it openly to the people of the book there is a reward for you, but it is better for you if you give it secretly to your own poor brethren. He says also that the prophet used to command secrecy in all cases of the giving of charity, without exception.

2.4. Abū Isḥāq al-Zajjāj reports that in the time of the prophet giving *zakāt* secretly was preferable, but afterwards opinion went against those who gave it secretly, and thus openness in obligatory *zakāt* became preferable. Ibn ʿAṭiyya says that this is comparable with the fact that in our time secrecy in giving obligatory charity is preferable, for the obstacles to this have increased, and giving openly has become liable to ostentation and so forth. Moreover, the pious predecessors used to give their charity to the collectors and those who gave it secretly used to be accused of failing to pay up. Today, however, everyone has started to give *zakāt* openly for their own benefit, and so giving it secretly has become preferable. God knows best.

2.4.1. Al-Zayn ibn al-Munīr says that if it should be argued that it depends on the changing circumstances that would not be inconsistent, for if the governor should be a tyrant and the property of the person obliged to pay should be hidden, then secrecy is better. On the other hand, if he is a volunteer donor who is emulated and followed and concerns are expressed about his volunteering in accordance with the proper manner, but his intention is sound, then giving openly is better. God knows best.

3. *Section on giving charity to a rich person unknowingly.*
That is to say that his charity was acceptable nonetheless.

4. *On the authority of al-Aʿraj from Abū Hurayra.*
In Mālik's transmission given in al-Dāraquṭnī's *Gharāʾib Mālik* it is on the authority of Abū Zinād that ʿAbd al-Raḥmān ibn Hurmuz informed him that he heard it from Abū Hurayra.

5. *A man said*
I could not discover his name. According to Aḥmad, by way of Ibn Lahīʿa on the authority of al-Aʿraj, he was an Israelite.

6. *'I will certainly give some charity!'*
In Abū ʿAwāna's transmission on the authority of Abū Umayya, on the authority of Abū ʾl-Yamān with this *isnād,* it reads, 'I will certainly give some charity at night!' It is repeated in this form in three instances: Aḥmad expressed it like this (through Waraqāʾ), as well as Muslim (through Mūsā ibn ʿUqba) and al-Dāraquṭnī in *Gharāʾib Mālik,* each of them on the authority of Abū Zinād.

7. His saying, *I will certainly give some charity!* is binding, as in for example a vow. An oath is implied, as if he had said, 'By God, I will certainly give some charity!'

8. *He gave it to a thief*
That is to say that he did not know that he was a thief.

9. *The next morning he was informed that he had given charity to a thief*
Abū ʿUmayya's transmission reads, 'He gave charity to a thief at night,'while Ibn Lahīʿa's transmission reads, 'He gave charity at night to "such and such" a thief.'

9.1. I have not discovered from the sources the identity of any of the three recipients of charity [i.e., the thief, the adulterer and the rich man]. *Tuṣuddiqa* [given charity] is with a 'u' vowel (*ḍamma*) at the beginning according to the passive pattern.

10. *He said, 'God, praise be to You.'*
That is to say, 'I am not accountable for the fact that my charity fell into the hands of someone who did not deserve it, and *praise be to You* since this was carried out by your will, not by my own volition, and God's will is always for the best.'

10.1. Al-Ṭībī said, 'After he resolved to give charity to someone deserving he handed it to an adulterer. He praised God that he was unable to give charity to someone worse than that; or he praised God for using him as a witness to what causes amazement leading to the magnification of God, for when they were amazed by his actions, he too was amazed, and so he said, *God, praise be to You over an adulterer*,' meaning, by ellipsis, the one to whom he had given charity. . . .

10.2. So he praised God for that state because God is the one who deserves praise for all states. He did not praise the reprehensible deed rather than him. It has been established that the prophet used to say when he saw wealth that amazed him, '*God, praise be to You* over all states.'

11. *Someone came up to him and said,*
It is stated in al-Ṭabrānī's variant in the *Musnad* of the Syrians (on the authority of Aḥmad ibn ʿAbd al-Wahhāb, on the authority of Abū 'l-Yamān by the same *isnād*), 'That event tormented him, and someone came to him in his dream.'

11.1. Abū Nuʿaym also draws out this interpretation, and likewise al-Ismāʿīlī (through ʿAlī ibn ʿAyyāsh, on the authority of Shuʿayb) whose variant specifies one of the possibilities mentioned by Ibn al-Tīz and others. For instance, al-Kirmānī says, 'Its use of *came to him* means that he saw something in a dream, or he heard the voice of an angel or someone else, or a prophet informed him, or a scholar gave him a *fatwā*.' Others add, 'or an angel came and spoke to him, for angels would talk to some people about certain matters'.

11.2. It has emerged through a sound transmission that none of the above actually took place apart from the first version.

12. *The charity you gave to a thief.*
Abū Umayya adds, 'was accepted'. The variant of Mūsā ibn ʿAqaba and Ibn Lahīʿa reads, 'The charity which you gave was accepted.' Al-Ṭabrānī's variant reads, 'God has accepted your charity.'

12.1. The *ḥadīth* indicates that the charity was in the observers' view meant specifically for those in need from amongst the righteous, and consequently they were surprised by the giving of charity to the three different recipients.
12.2. It also suggests that if the intention of the donor was correct then the charity was accepted, even if the aim was not fulfilled.
12.3. The jurists are at variance regarding the permissibility of this for obligatory charity. There is nothing in the *ḥadīth* to indicate either permissibility or prohibition. That is why the *Muṣannaf* [of Ibn Abī Shayba] presents the passage in the form of a question without declaring the ruling.

13. It is said that the report applies only to a specific story, and that the information about it was presented here in relation to the issue of the acceptance of charity by means of a corroborative dream. So, how can there be general applicability for the ruling? The answer is that the point of this report is the hope of future abstention from sins on the part of the recipients, which serves as proof of the validity of the ruling, for the acceptance of the charity must be linked to these factors. The report expresses the preference for giving charity secretly and being sincere, as well as the recommendation to pay the charity again if it has not been carried out correctly (the ruling applies to the outward action, even if it ends up with the same result), the blessing of surrender and contentment with God's will, and the blameworthiness of anxiety over destiny. As one of the pious predecessors has said, 'Do not refrain from worship even if it seems obvious to you that it will not be accepted!'

3.4 Abū Dāwūd, selection from *al-Sunan* on *zakāt*

The compiler of one of the authoritative books of *ḥadīth* reports in Sunnī Islam, Sulaymān ibn al-Ash'ath Abū Dāwūd al-Sijistānī; was born in 202/817 in Sijistan, lived in Basra and died there in 275/889. He is reported to have travelled widely and learned in the process at least 500,000 *ḥadīth* reports, of which 4,800 were included in his collection. Devoted to juridical matters alone, Abū Dāwūd's *al-Sunan* is considered to have been less stringent in its criteria for inclusion of traditions than compilers such as al-Bukhārī, with the most attention being placed on the plausibility of the *isnād* transmission chain rather than the text (*matn*) of the report. Abū Dāwūd often includes explanatory comments supporting his decision to include less than totally authenticated reports and discussing the relative value of reports. He also adds remarks about the various transmissions of the reports, including variant readings and traditions.

The selection translated below illustrates both the organizational principles of Abū Dāwūd's work and the manner in which he provides comments, glosses and variant traditions. The main tradition is reported with variants, lexicographical explications and reports of supplementary transmission paths following in sequence afterwards.

Further reading

Ignaz Goldziher, *Muslim studies*, London 1971, vol. 2, pp. 229–34.
James Robson, 'The transmission of Abū Dāwūd's *Sunan*,' *Bulletin of the School of Oriental and African Studies*, 14 (1952), pp. 579–88.
Muḥammad Zubayr Ṣiddīqī, *Ḥadīth literature: its origin, development and special features*, revised edition, Cambridge 1993, pp. 61–3.

Source text

Abū Dāwūd, *Al-Sunan*, ed. Muḥammad Muḥyī 'l-Dīn 'Abd al-Ḥamīd, Tunis 1977, vol. 2, pp. 93–5 (parts I and II) and pp. 105–6 (part III).

I Kitāb al-zakāt

1. Qunayba ibn Saʿīd told us that Layth told him on the authority of ʿUqayl from al-Zuhrī that ʿUbayd Allāh ibn ʿAbd Allāh ibn ʿUtba informed him on the authority of Abū Hurayra saying that when the messenger of God died and Abū Bakr was made caliph after him and some among the Arabs disbelieved, ʿUmar ibn al-Khaṭṭāb asked Abū Bakr how he could fight the people when the messenger of God had said, 'I have been ordered to fight the people until they say, "There is no god but God." Those who say there is no god but God have protected their property and themselves from me other than what is due [in charity]. Their reckoning is with God.' Abū Bakr replied, 'By God, I will fight those who make a distinction between prayer and *zakāt*. *Zakāt* is due on

possessions. By God, if they hold back from me even a small portion of one year's charity which they used to give to the messenger of God, I will declare a *jihād* against them over its refusal.' ʿUmar ibn al-Khaṭṭāb said, 'By God, then I understood that God had opened the breast of Abū Bakr to fighting and I said, "I understand that this is right."'

1.1. Abū Dāwūd said that Rabāḥ ibn Zayd and ʿAbd al-Razzāq have transmitted this on the authority of Maʿmar from al-Zuhrī with its own *isnād*. Some transmitters have included the word *ʿiqāl*, 'a small portion of one year's charity [lit. "a rope used to hobble a camel"]', while Ibn Wahb transmits it from Yūnus with the word *ʿanāq*, 'a young female goat'.

1.2. Abū Dāwūd said that Shuʿayb ibn Abī Ḥamza and Maʿmar and al-Zubaydī say on the authority of al-Zuhrī that this report reads, 'if they hold back from me a young female goat'. ʿAnbasa transmits on the authority of Yūnus on the authority of al-Zuhrī that this report reads, 'a young female goat'.

Ibn Sarḥ and Sulaymān ibn Dāwūd told us that Ibn Wahb told them that Yūnus told him on the authority of al-Zuhrī that Abū Bakr said, 'The obligation is the payment of *zakāt*.' He also said, 'A young female goat.'

II Chapter concerning what necessitates zakāt

1. ʿAbd Allāh ibn Maslama told us that he repeated to Mālik ibn Anas on the authority of ʿAmr ibn Yaḥyā al-Māzinī from his father, who said that he heard Abū Saʿīd al-Khudrī report that the messenger of God said, 'There is no charity payable on less than five camels, less than five units of silver or on less than five camel loads (of agricultural produce).'

2. Ayyūb ibn Muḥammad al-Raqqī told us that Muḥammad ibn ʿUbayd told him that Idrīs ibn Yazīd al-Awdī told him on the authority of ʿAmr ibn Murrat al-Jamalī, from Abū ʾl-Bukhtarī al-Ṭāʾī, from Abū Saʿīd al-Khudrī, attributed to the prophet, the saying, 'There is no *zakāt* payable on less than five camel loads (of agricultural produce).' One camel load is sixty measures.

2.1. Abū Dāwūd said that Abū ʾl-Bukhtarī did not hear reports from Abū Saʿīd.

2.2. Muḥammad ibn Qudāma ibn Aʿyan told us that Jarīr told him on the authority of al-Mughīra, from Ibrāhīm, who said that a camel load is sixty measures as established by al-Ḥajjāj.

3. Muḥammad ibn Bashshār told us that Muḥammad ibn ʿAbd Allāh al-Anṣārī told him that Ṣadr ibn Abī Manāzil said that he heard Ḥabīb al-Mālikī reporting that a man said to ʿImrān ibn Ḥuṣayn, 'Abū Nujayd, you transmit reports for which we do not find any basis in the Qurʾān!' ʿImrān became angry and said to the man, 'Do you find that for every forty dirhams you must pay one dirham (in *zakāt*)? Or that for a certain number of goats one is due? Or that for a certain number of camels a certain number is due? Do you find this in the Qurʾān?' 'No,' he admitted. 'So,' ʿImrān said, 'where did you get this from? You got it from us and you got it from the prophet of God.' He mentioned many similar things.

III Chapter on pleasing the collectors of charity

1. Mahdī ibn Ḥafṣ and Muḥammad ibn ʿUbayd, agreeing in the sense of the report, told me that Ḥammād told them on the authority of a man called Daysam – Ibn ʿUbayd said he was from the tribe of Sudūs – from Bashīr ibn al-Khaṣāṣiyya – Ibn ʿUbayd said in his version that his name was not Bashīr but that the messenger of God had named him that – who said that they asked Muḥammad, 'If the collectors of charity act unjustly towards us [by taking more than is due], may we hide our possessions to the extent that they are unjust?' He said, 'No.'

    1.1. Al-Ḥasan ibn ʿAlī and Yaḥyā ibn Mūsā told us that ʿAbd al-Razzāq told them (this same report) on the authority of Maʿmar, from Ayyūb, with the same *isnād* and wording, except that Bashīr said that they said, 'Messenger of God, the collectors of charity act unjustly.'

    1.2. Abū Dāwūd said that ʿAbd al-Razzāq transmitted this report on the authority of Maʿmar.

2. ʿAbbās ibn ʿAbd al-ʿAẓīm and Muḥammad ibn al-Muthannā told us that Bishr ibn ʿUmar told them on the authority of Abū ʾl-Ghuṣn, from Ṣiḥr ibn Isḥāq, from ʿAbd al-Raḥmān ibn Jābir ibn ʿAtīk, from his father, that the messenger of God said, 'Riders who are disliked will come to you. When they come, you must welcome them and let them have what is necessary. If they are just, it will be to their credit. But if they are unjust, it will count against them. Satisfy them for the completion of your *zakāt* lies in satisfying them. They will seek a blessing for you.'

    2.1. Abū Dāwūd said that Abū ʾl-Ghuṣn is Thābit ibn Qays ibn Ghuṣn.

3. Abū Kāmil told us that ʿAbd al-Wāḥid, that is Ibn Ziyād, told him that ʿUthmān ibn Abī Shayba told him that ʿAbd al-Raḥīm ibn Sulaymān told him that this is the report of Abū Kāmil, transmitted on the authority of Muḥammad ibn Abī Ismāʿīl, who was told by ʿAbd al-Raḥmān ibn Hilāl al-ʿAbsī on the authority of Jarīr ibn ʿAbd Allāh, who said that some Bedouin came to the messenger of God and said that collectors of charity had come to them and acted unjustly. The messenger of God said, 'Satisfy those who collect charity from you.' They replied, 'Messenger of God, even if they act unjustly towards us?' He said, 'Satisfy those who collect charity from you.'

    3.1. ʿUthmān adds here, 'even if they act unjustly'.

    3.2. Abū Kāmil said in his version that Jarīr said, 'After I heard this from the messenger of God, every collector of charity who departed from me was satisfied with me.'

3.5 Ibn Bābawayh, selection from *Man lā yaḥḍuruh al-faqīh* on *khums*

Abū Jaʿfar Muḥammad ibn Abī ʾl-Ḥasan Ibn Bābawayh (or Ibn Bābūya), commonly referred to by the title al-Shaykh al-Ṣadūq, was born in Qum sometime after 305/917. His many surviving works indicate that he travelled extensively in Persia, Iraq and Transoxiana to collect Twelver Shīʿī *ḥadīth*, and died in Rayy in 381/991. His early works reveal him to have been a staunch traditionist among the leading representatives of the jurists in Qum. He was at first strongly opposed to the increasing influence of Muʿtazilite rationalism on Twelver Shiʿism in his time, but came under its influence himself, as his later works indicate.

The most famous of the hundreds of works traditionally attributed to Ibn Bābawayh is *Man lā yaḥḍuruh al-faqīh* ('He who has no jurist present'). This is considered to be one of the four canonical collections of Shīʿī *ḥadīth*, alongside Shaykh al-Ṭāʾifa Muḥammad ibn Ḥasan al-Ṭūsī's two collections, *Tahdhīb al-aḥkam* and *al-Istibṣār*, and al-Kulaynī's *Kitāb al-kāfī fī ʿilm al-dīn,* the latter being often considered to be the most authoritative of all. Ibn Bābawayh is reported to have written his collection during a period of residence in Balkh, in present-day northern Afghanistan, sometime before 372/983. The similarity of its title to that of the work by the famous physician and philosopher Abū Bakr al-Rāzī (d. 311/923 or 320/932), *Man lā yaḥḍuruh al-ṭabīb* ('He who has no doctor present') is accounted for by the tradition that Ibn Bābawayh compiled his *ḥadīth* collection after being asked specifically to prepare the juristic equivalent of al-Rāzī's work.

The passage presented here is the chapter on *khums,* a term which means literally 'one fifth', and is a religious tax acknowledged by both Sunnīs and Shīʿīs, albeit with significant differences in definition and procedure. The practice is based on the verse in the Qurʾān which is cited in paragraph 8 below. The Shīʿī jurists have interpreted this tax as having a much wider applicability than have their Sunnī counterparts such that, in addition to spoils of war, it includes minerals, treasure-trove, precious stones from the ocean, profits from trade, agriculture and crafts, land bought by a non-Muslim of protected status (*dhimmī*) from a Muslim, and lawful goods which have become mixed with unlawful goods. This chapter provides proof of the validity of this list by means of *ḥadīth*s about the Imāms. A number of these *ḥadīth*s also allude to the fact that this is not merely a fiscal issue (although it did eventually provide Shīʿī jurists with a considerable financial advantage over their Sunnī counterparts), but also a reflection of the Twelver Shīʿī world-view, in which the whole world belongs rightfully to the Imāms.

Further reading

Norman Calder, '*Khums* in Imāmī Shīʿī jurisprudence, from the tenth to the sixteenth century AD,' *Bulletin of the School of Oriental and African Studies*, 45 (1982), pp. 39–47.

Juan R. I. Cole, 'Khums,' in John L. Esposito (ed.), *The Oxford encyclopaedia of the modern Islamic world*, New York/Oxford 1995, vol. 1, pp. 431–2.

Martin McDermott, 'Ebn Bābawayh (Bābūya), Shaikh Ṣadūq,' in *Encyclopaedia Iranica*.

Abdulaziz Sachedina, '*Al-Khums:* the fifth in the Imāmī Shīʿī legal system,' *Journal of Near Eastern studies*, 39 (1980), pp. 276–89.

Source text

Ibn Bābawayh [Bābūya], *Kitāb man lā yaḥḍuruh al-faqīh*, ed. ʻAlī-Akbar al-Ghaffārī, Qum 1983, vol. 2, pp. 39–45.

1. Abū ʾl-Ḥasan Mūsā ibn Jaʿfar was asked, ‘Is *zakāt* to be paid on pearl, ruby and chrysolite extracted from the sea, and on mines of gold and silver?’ He answered, ‘If its value totals at least one dinar, then *khums* must be paid on it.’

2. ʿUbayd Allāh ibn ʿAlī al-Ḥulabī asked Imām Abū ʿAbd Allāh (Jaʿfar al-Ṣādiq) how much is to be paid on treasure-trove? He answered, ‘A fifth (*khums*).’ Then he asked about mines [of gold and silver]. Jaʿfar answered, ‘*Khums.*’ Then he asked about lead, zinc, iron and the contents of the mines. He answered, ‘The same amount is taken from them as is taken from mines of gold and silver.’

3. Al-Ḥasan ibn Maḥbūb related that ʿAbd Allāh ibn Sinān said that he heard Imām Abū ʿAbd Allāh (Jaʿfar al-Ṣādiq) say, ‘There is no *khums* except specifically on material profit.’

4. Aḥmad ibn Muḥammad ibn Abī Naṣr related on the authority of Imām Abū ʾl-Ḥasan al-Riḍā, saying that he asked him about how much treasure-trove is required in order for *khums* to be payable, and he replied, ‘The same amount that makes *zakāt* on such wealth obligatory.’

5. Muḥammad ibn Muslim asked Imām Abū Jaʿfar (Muḥammad al-Bāqir) what salt-mines are, to which he replied, ‘Salty marsh in which water has collected, turning it into salt. *Khums* is due on it just like other mines.’ Ibn Muslim then asked, ‘Sulphur and oil are extracted from the earth so [are they also liable for *khums*]?’ He answered, ‘*Khums* is due on them and other comparable things.’

6. Imām al-Ṣādiq said, ‘When God prohibited us from receiving alms, he sent down for us *khums*; for us, alms is forbidden while *khums* is obligatory, so favour to us is lawful.’

7. It is related that Abū Baṣīr said that he asked Imām Abū Jaʿfar (al-Bāqir), ‘What is the smallest thing for which a servant will enter hellfire?’ He said, ‘By spending one dirham of the property of orphans! We are the orphans!’

8. Zakariyā ibn Mālik al-Juʿfī asked Imām Abū ʿAbd Allāh (al-Ṣādiq) about God’s words, *Know that of whatever you acquire as material profit/booty a fifth* (khums) *belongs to God and the messenger, to those related to him, the orphans, the needy and the wayfarers* (Q 8/41). He replied, ‘God’s share goes to the messenger, the messenger’s share goes to his relatives in addition to their own share since they are “those related” to the messenger. The orphans are the orphans belonging to the messenger’s family. Thus God has determined that these four shares go to the family of the messenger. The shares of the poor and the wayfarers are met by their receipt of alms, since we do not receive that as it is not lawful for us.’

9. In the responses of Imām Riḍā to Ibrāhīm ibn Muḥammad al-Hamadānī, one finds: '*Khums* is calculated after the expenses for provisions are taken into account.'

10. Abū ʿUbayda al-Ḥadhdhāʾ related that Imām Abū Jaʿfar (al-Bāqir) said, 'Whichever *dhimmī* buys land from a Muslim must pay *khums* on it.'

11. Muḥammad ibn Muslim related that either Imām al-Bāqir or al-Ṣādiq said, 'The worst thing that can happen to people on the day of resurrection is for someone owed *khums* to stand up and say, "Lord, where is my *khums*?" We made the payment of *khums* agreeable for our Shīʿa in order that they should be pure.'

12. A man came to the commander of the faithful, ʿAlī, to ask, 'Commander of the faithful, I acquired wealth, the legitimacy of which I am uncertain; must I repent?' He answered, 'Bring me a fifth of it (*khums*).' So he brought him a fifth of it. Then he continued, 'The remainder belongs to you; if a man repents, so does his wealth.'

13. Imām Abū ʾl-Ḥasan (al-Riḍā) was asked about a man, the *zakāt* on whose wealth, or the *khums* on whose booty, or the *khums* on things extracted from mines for him was taken from him by those tyrants. Can it be counted as his *zakāt* and *khums*? He answered, 'Yes.'

14. It was related that Abū ʿAlī ibn Rāshid said that he said to Imām Abū ʾl-Ḥasan III, 'Something was brought to me with the message, "We consider this as having belonged to Imām Abū Jaʿfar (al-Bāqir)," so what should I do with it?' He answered, 'Whatever belonged to my father because of his Imamate now belongs to me, and anything besides is inherited according to the Qurʾān and the *sunna* of his prophet.'

15. ʿAbd Allāh ibn Bukayr related that Imām Abū ʿAbd Allāh (al-Ṣādiq) said, 'I take a dirham from each of you, even though I am one of the wealthiest people of Medina, simply in order to purify you.'

16. It was related that Yūnus ibn Yaʿqūb said that he was with Imām Abū ʿAbd Allāh (al-Ṣādiq) when one of the sheep-dealers entered before him to say, 'Profit, wealth and merchandise has come my way which I know includes your share, but I have overlooked that.' Al-Ṣādiq said, 'It would not be unfair of me to charge you today.'

17. It was related that ʿAlī ibn Mahziyār said, 'I read in one of Imām Abū Jaʿfar's (al-Bāqir) letters to a man who asked him to make his food and drink lawful with regards to *khums* that he wrote in response, in his own handwriting, "Whoever is in need of something rightfully belonging to me is allowed to use it."'

18. Abān ibn Taghlib related that Imām Abū ʿAbd Allāh (al-Ṣādiq) was asked about what happens when a man dies without an heir or client. He answered,

'He belongs to the category referred to in this verse, *They ask you about the anfāl* (Q 8/1) [i.e., spoils of war belonging to the prophet, or the Imām in his place].'

19. Dāwud ibn Kathīr al-Raqqī related that al-Ṣādiq said, 'People live off the surplus of what is rightfully ours and which has been taken unlawfully, apart from our Shīʿīs for whom we have made it lawful.'

20. Hafṣ ibn al-Bakhtarī related that Abū ʿAbd Allāh (al-Ṣādiq) said, 'The angel Gabriel dug out with his feet five rivers, and a gush of water flowed into them: the Euphrates, the Tigris, the Nile, Mihrān and Balkhāb. Whatever land is watered by them belongs to the Imām, as well as the sea that encircles the planet. The latter is called "Afsīkūn" [the Caspian Sea].'

3.6 Al-Kulaynī, selection from *al-Kāfī* on temporary marriage

Abū Jaʿfar Muḥammad ibn Yaʿqūb al-Kulaynī (or al-Kulīnī) came from a village called Kulayn, near Rayy in present-day Iran. Very little is known about his life. He eventually moved to Baghdad, where, apparently over the course of two decades, he compiled his only surviving work, the voluminous *Kitāb al-kāfī fī ʿilm al-dīn* ('The sufficient in the science of religion'). This is widely regarded by Shīʿī Muslims to be the most authoritative of their four canonical *ḥadīth* collections. Through this monumental work, al-Kulaynī has acquired a lofty status in Shīʿism, which is indicated by the fact that he is considered to have been the 'renewer' of the Shīʿī faith (*mujaddid*) for the fourth century after the prophet's lifetime. He died in about 329/940 in Baghdad, where his tomb is a major pilgrimage site for Shīʿīs from across the world.

As its title suggests, al-Kulaynī's *al-Kāfī* was meant to be a comprehensive account of the religious sciences through the traditions of the Imāms. It is divided into two parts, devoted to the sciences of theology and jurisprudence, respectively. There is also an appendix at the end, consisting of miscellaneous traditions. *Al-Kāfī*'s reputation as an authoritative source of traditions seems to have developed slowly, rising to prominence only after Muḥammad al-Ṭūsī, Shaykh al-Ṭāʾifa, made extensive use of it for his foundational works of Shīʿī jurisprudence. Since then it has attracted numerous commentaries and translations, especially during the Safavid period.

The passage presented here comes from the chapter of al-Kulaynī's *al-Kāfī* which offers juristic traditions about temporary marriage (*mutʿa*; lit. 'enjoyment') from the section of the work devoted to marital issues. The permissibility in Shiʿism of temporary marriage, which is forbidden in Sunnī Islam, is one of the most controversial differences between these two Muslim traditions. Shīʿī scholars point to sanction for this practice in the Qurʾān (Q 4/24; cited a number of times in the passage below) and the *sunna* of the prophet, and accuse the second caliph, ʿUmar ibn al-Khaṭṭāb, of innovation for forbidding what had been allowed during the prophet's life. In addition to *ḥadīth*s of the Imāms which prove the legitimacy of the practice for Twelver Shīʿīs, this passage also contains a typical polemical narrative, in which the Sunnī jurist Abū Ḥanīfa is outsmarted by his Shīʿī counterpart, whom he has approached specifically to refute the Shīʿī argument for the permissibility of temporary marriage.

On the variant reading of Q 4/24 in paragraph 3 below, attributed to Ibn ʿAbbās and Ibn Masʿūd, see Arthur Gribetz, *Strange bedfellows:* Mutʿat al-nisāʾ *and* Mutʿat al-ḥajj*: a study based on Sunnī and Shīʿī sources of* tafsīr, *ḥadīth and* fiqh, Berlin 1994, pp. 51–2. For Sunnī opinion of this variant reading, see al-Ṭabarī, *Tafsīr al-Ṭabarī*, ed. M. M. Shākir, A. M. Shākir, 16 vols, Cairo 1954–68, vol. 8, pp. 176–9.

Further reading

Shahla Haeri, *Law of desire: temporary marriage in Iran*, London/Syracuse 1989.
Willi Heffening, '*Mutʿa*,' in *Encyclopaedia of Islam*, new edition.
Ahmad Kazemi Moussavi, '*Ḥadīth* ii. In Shiʿism,' in *Encyclopaedia Iranica.*
Wilferd Madelung, 'Al-Kulaynī (or al-Kulīnī), Abū Djaʿfar Muḥammad,' in *Encyclopaedia of Islam*, new edition.

Andrew J. Newman, *The formative period of Twelver Shīʿism: ḥadīth as discourse between Qum and Baghdad*, Richmond 2000.

Source text

Al-Kulaynī, *Al-Furūʿ min al-Kāfī*, ed. M. al-Ākhundī, Tehran 1983, vol. 5, pp. 448–50.

Chapter: on temporary marriage

1. On the authority of a number of my associates, on the authority of Sahl ibn Ziyād and ʿAlī ibn Ibrāhīm, both on the authority of the latter's father, on the authority of Ibn Abī Najrān, on the authority of ʿĀṣim ibn Ḥamīd, on the authority of Abū Baṣīr, who said, 'I asked Imām Abū Jaʿfar (Muḥammad al-Bāqir) about *mutʿa*. He replied that it was revealed in the Qurʾān, *Since you enjoy them* (istamtaʿtum), *give them their recompense; but if you decide together on an alternative after the sum has already been prescribed, you will have done no wrong* (Q 4/24).'

2. On the authority of Muḥammad ibn Ismāʿīl, on the authority of al-Fadīl ibn Shādhān, on the authority of Ṣafwān ibn Yaḥyā, on the authority of Ibn Miskān, on the authority of ʿAbd Allāh ibn Sulaymān, who said that he heard Abū Jaʿfar (Muḥammad al-Bāqir) say that ʿAlī used to say, 'If it were not for what al-Khaṭṭāb [i.e., ʿUmar, the second caliph] did before me, there would have been little fornication committed.'

3. On the authority of ʿAlī ibn Ibrāhīm, on the authority of his father, on the authority of Ibn Abī ʿUmayr, from someone who mentioned it on the authority of Abū ʿAbd Allāh who said, 'It has been revealed, *Since you enjoy them* until an appointed time, *give them their recompense.*' [variant reading of Q 4/24]

4. On the authority of ʿAlī, on the authority of his father, on the authority of Ibn Abī ʿUmayr, on the authority of ʿUmar ibn Udhayna, on the authority of Zurāra who said that ʿAbd Allāh ibn ʿUmayr al-Laythī came before Imām Abū Jaʿfar (Muḥammad al-Bāqir) and said to him, 'What do you say concerning the *mutʿa* of women?' He replied, 'God made it lawful in His book and according to the words of his prophet: therefore it is lawful until the end of time.' ʿAbd Allāh said, 'Abū Jaʿfar, how can someone like you say this when ʿUmar forbade it?' Abū Jaʿfar responded, 'It makes no difference if he did that!' ʿAbd Allāh said, 'God forgive you for pronouncing legitimate what ʿUmar has prohibited!' Abū Jaʿfar said, 'You follow the opinion of your companion, while I follow the opinion of the messenger of God himself. Come here! May I be damned if the correct opinion is not that of the messenger of God, and the void opinion that of your companion.' Zurāra continued his narration saying that ʿAbd Allāh ibn ʿUmayr turned around and said, 'So you are happy that your women, daughters, sisters and cousins should do this.' Zurāra said that Abū Jaʿfar turned away when he mentioned them.

5. On the authority of Muḥammad ibn Yaḥyā, on the authority of ʿAbd Allāh ibn Muḥammad, on the authority of ʿAlī ibn al-Ḥukm, on the authority of Abān ibn ʿUthmān, on the authority of Abū Maryam, on the authority of Imām Abū ʿAbd Allāh (Jaʿfar al-Ṣādiq), who said, '*Mutʿa* was revealed in the Qurʾān, and was mentioned in the *sunna* of the messenger of God.'

6. On the authority of ʿAlī ibn Ibrāhīm, on the authority of his father, on the authority of Ibn Abī ʿUmayr, on the authority of ʿAlī ibn al-Ḥasan ibn Ribāṭ, on the authority of Ḥarīz, on the authority of ʿAbd al-Raḥmān ibn Abī ʿAbd Allāh, who said that he heard Abū Ḥanīfa ask Imām Abū ʿAbd Allāh (Jaʿfar al-Ṣādiq) about *mutʿa*, and he replied, 'About which of the two *mutʿa*s are you asking?' He said, 'I've already asked you about the *mutʿa* of *ḥajj* [the enjoyment of the freedom of normal life after the pilgrim's state of ritual consecration], so inform me about the *mutʿa* of women. Is this a man's right?' He replied, 'Glory be to God! Have you not read in the book of God, *Since you enjoy them, give them their recompense* (Q 4/24)?' Abū Ḥanīfa said, 'By God, it is as if I have never read that verse!'

7. On the authority of ʿAlī ibn Ibrāhīm, on the authority of his father, on the authority of Ibn Maḥbūb, on the authority of ʿAlī al-Sāʾī, who said that he said to Imām Abū ʾl-Ḥasan (ʿAlī al-Hādī), 'May I become your sacrifice! I used to have *mutʿa*s, but I began to dislike the practice and regarded it as wrong, and so I made a promise to God while between the Kaʿba and the Station of Abraham. I obliged myself to fast and make an offering, promising that I would not have any further *mutʿa*s. But then it became hard for me, and I regretted my vow, and not having the ability to marry openly again.' The Imām said to me, 'You made a vow to God that you would be disobedient to Him, and, by God, you were indeed extremely disobedient to Him!'

8. ʿAlī Rafʿa said that Abū Ḥanīfa asked Abū Jaʿfar Muḥammad ibn al-Nuʿmān Ṣāhib al-Ṭāq, 'What do you say, Abū Jaʿfar, concerning *mutʿa*? Do you consider it lawful?' He replied, 'Yes.' Abū Ḥanīfa then asked, 'What stops you from instructing your women to have *mutʿa*s on your authority?' Abū Jaʿfar answered him, 'Not all activities are desirable even if they should be lawful. People have different capacities and ranks, and they can increase their capacity. But what do you say, Abū Ḥanīfa, about (date) wine? Do you consider that lawful?' He answered, 'Yes.' Abū Jaʿfar countered, 'So what stops you from seating your women behind the liquor-stalls to drink on your authority?' Abū Ḥanīfa responded, 'It is one strike each, but your arrow has hit the mark! Abū Jaʿfar, the *āya* which is found in the *sūra* that opens with "The questioner asked" [i.e., Q 70] conveys the prohibition of *mutʿa* (Q 70/29–30), and the tradition about the messenger of God abrogates the permission for *mutʿa*.' Abū Jaʿfar responded to him, 'Abū Ḥanīfa, the *sūra* that opens with "The questioner asked" is Meccan, while the verse about *mutʿa* is Medinan, and your prophetic tradition is an unsound transmission.' Abū Ḥanīfa countered, 'The *āya* about inheritance also pronounces the abrogation of *mutʿa*.' Abū Jaʿfar responded, 'It is proven that there can be marriage without inheritance.' Abū Ḥanīfa asked, 'On what basis do you say this?' Abū Jaʿfar answered, 'If a Muslim man marries a Jewish or

Christian woman and then dies, what do you say should happen?' Abū Ḥanīfa said, 'She does not inherit anything from him.' Abū Jaʿfar concluded, 'Therefore the possibility of marriage without inheritance has indeed been proven!' Then they parted company.

Chapter: 'They have the same status as slave-girls and are not limited to a total of four'

1. ʿAlī ibn Ibrāhīm, on the authority of his father, on the authority of Ibn Abī ʿUmayr, on the authority of ʿUmar ibn Udhayna, on the authority of Imām Abū ʿAbd Allāh (Jaʿfar al-Ṣādiq), whom he asked, 'How many *mutʿa*s are lawful?' He replied, 'They have the same status as slave-girls.'

2. On the authority of al-Ḥasan ibn Muḥammad, on the authority of Aḥmad ibn Isḥāq al-Ashʿarī, on the authority of Bakr ibn Muḥammad al-Azdī, who said, 'I asked Imām Abū ʾl-Ḥasan (ʿAlī al-Hādī) about *mutʿa*, whether it is limited to a total of four, and he replied, "No."'

3. On the authority of Muḥammad ibn Yaḥyā, on the authority of Aḥmad ibn Muḥammad, on the authority of Ibn Maḥbūb, on the authority of Ibn Riʾāb, on the authority of Zurāra ibn Aʿyan, who said that he asked, 'What total is lawful for *mutʿa*?' He replied, 'As many as you like.'

4. On the authority of al-Ḥusayn ibn Muḥammad, on the authority of Muʿallī ibn Muḥammad, on the authority of al-Ḥasan ibn ʿAlī, on the authority of Ḥammād ibn ʿUthmān, on the authority of Abū Baṣīr, who said that Imām Abū ʿAbd Allāh (Jaʿfar al-Ṣādiq) was asked whether *mutʿa* is limited to a total of four, and he answered, 'No, and neither is it limited to seventy!'

5. On the authority of Muḥammad ibn Yaḥyā, on the authority of Aḥmad ibn Muḥammad ibn ʿĪsā, on the authority of al-Ḥusayn Saʿīd; also on the authority of Muḥammad ibn Khālid al-Barqī, on the authority of al-Qāsim ibn ʿUrwa, on the authority of ʿAbd al-Ḥamīd, on the authority of Muḥammad ibn Muslim, on the authority of Imām Abū Jaʿfar (Muḥammad al-Bāqir), who said concerning *mutʿa*, 'It is not limited to four because it does not involve divorce and inheritance, since it is merely something you lease.'

6. On the authority of ʿAlī ibn Ibrāhīm, on the authority of his father, on the authority of Ibn Abī ʿUmayr, on the authority of ʿUmar ibn Udhayna, on the authority of Ismāʿīl ibn al-Faḍl al-Hāshimī, who said that he asked Imām Abū ʿAbd Allāh (Jaʿfar al-Ṣādiq) about *mutʿa* and he said, 'Find ʿAbd al-Malik ibn Jurayj and ask him about it, for he has a lot of information about it.' So I met him, and he dictated to me a lot of material about its legitimacy, including the following. 'It does not have a specific duration, nor is it limited to a specific number of temporary wives; they have only the rank of slave-girls, so one can marry as many as one pleases, and a man with four wives can also marry as many as he pleases. No agent is required, nor witnesses. When the agreed termination point arrives, she parts from him without divorce and he gives her

something relatively small. Her period of abstinence (*ʿidda*) is two menstrual cycles, or, if she does not menstruate, then forty-five days.' I took what I had written down of this dictation to Abū ʿAbd Allāh (Jaʿfar al-Ṣādiq) and repeated it all to him. He responded, 'It is correct, and I personally confirm that.'

6.1. Ibn Udhayna said that Zurāra ibn Aʿyan used to say this and then swear that it is the truth, with only the following discrepancy: 'If she menstruates then her *ʿidda* should be one menstrual cycle, and if she does not menstruate, then a month and a half.'

7. On the authority of al-Ḥusayn ibn Muḥammad, on the authority of Aḥmad ibn Isḥāq, on the authority of Saʿdān ibn Muslim, on the authority of ʿUbayd ibn Zurāra, on the authority of his father, who said that he asked Imām Abū ʿAbd Allāh (Jaʿfar al-Ṣādiq) whether *mutʿa* is limited to a total of four, and he replied, 'Marry a thousand of them, for they are simply leased.'

Chapter 4

Religious history

4.1 Al-Ṭarafī on Mary, the mother of Jesus

The stories of the prophets were available in many different versions in the classical Muslim world but all served essentially the same purpose. They were designed to fill in the gaps in the Qur'ānic rendition of the stories, so it would not be necessary for Muslims to refer to the Bible or to ask Jews and Christians for clarification of the stories. Al-Ṭarafī provides one such version. Abū 'Abd Allāh Muḥammad ibn Aḥmad ibn Muṭarrif al-Ṭarafī was born in 387/997 in Cordova. Little is known of him other than that he was a religious scholar, especially devoted to the study of variant readings of the Qur'ān about which he wrote two books. He was famous among his contemporaries for his memory. He died in 454/1062.

Al-Ṭarafī's account of Mary and Jesus may be compared with those presented by al-Ṭabarī, al-Tha'labī and al-Kisā'ī (all of which are available in translation): al-Tha'labī, *'Arā'is al-majālis fī qiṣaṣ al-anbiyā'*, Cairo n.d., pp. 342–4, Arthur Jeffery (trans.), 'A prophet story,' in his *A reader on Islam*, S-Gravenhage 1962, pp. 560–9, al-Ṭabarī, *Ta'rīkh al-rusul wa'l-mulūk,* ed. M. J. de Goeje, Leiden 1879–1901, vol. 1, pp. 723–8, Moshe Perlmann (trans.), *The history of al-Ṭabarī, volume IV: the ancient kingdoms*, Albany NY 1987, pp. 112–16, al-Kisā'ī, *Qiṣaṣ al-anbiyā',* ed. I. Eisenberg, Leiden 1922–3, pp. 301–4, and W. M. Thackston Jr. (trans.), *The tales of the prophets of al-Kisa'i*, Boston 1978, pp. 326–30.

Al-Ṭarafī's stories are consistently exegetical, incorporating glosses of the Qur'ānic text, even to the extent that they can interrupt the flow of the narrative. The account of Mary and Jesus is extensively treated in the Qur'ān (as in section 1.6 above; it is also found in Q 3), which means that the storyteller's account is more frequently and obviously punctuated by scriptural reference. This feature is reinforced by the fact that the overall book is structured not according to the history of the prophets, but according to the exegetical usefulness of the characters: the twenty-four prophets named in the Qur'ān are dealt with first, followed by seven alluded to in scripture. Also notable is that there is little concern for the formalities of the *isnād*, with attributions such as 'some exegetes say' seeming sufficient.

Further reading

Loren D. Lybarger, 'Gender and prophetic authority in the Qur'ānic story of Maryam: a literary approach,' *Journal of Religion*, 80 (2000), pp. 240–70; analysis of the Qur'ānic story.

Jane Dammen McAuliffe, 'Chosen of all women: Mary and Fāṭima in Qur'ānic exegesis,' *Islamochristiana*, 7 (1981), pp. 19–28.

Jane I. Smith, Yvonne Y. Haddad, 'The Virgin Mary in Islamic tradition and commentary,' *The Muslim world*, 79 (1989), pp. 161–87.

Barbara Freyer Stowasser, *Women in the Qur'an, traditions, and interpretation*, New York 1994, pp. 67–82.

Roberto Tottoli, *Biblical prophets in the Qur'ān and Muslim literature*, Richmond 2002, pp. 155–7.

—— 'The *Qiṣaṣ al-anbiyā'* of Ibn Muṭarrif al-Ṭarafī (d. 454/1062): stories of the prophets from al-Andalus,' *Al-Qanṭara*, 19 (1998), pp. 131–60.

Source text

Roberto Tottoli, 'Le Qiṣaṣ al-anbiyā' di Ṭarafī,' PhD thesis, Naples 1996, pp. 330–6; Tottoli's edition of the Arabic text with notes and introduction in English is available in Klaus Schwarz Verlag's series Islamkundliche Untersuchungen 2003. Tottoli has also published his Italian translation of al-Ṭarafī: Roberto Tottoli (trans.), *Al-Ṭarafī: storie dei profeti*, Genoa 1997.

The story of the birth of Jesus

1. *The angels said, 'O Mary, God has selected you'*, that is chosen you, *and purified you*, that is, from menstruation and the blemishes which are a part of the nature of all women, *and chosen you above all women of the world* (Q 3/42), that is, chosen you for Jesus. No other woman in the world carried the like of Jesus.

2. It is said, He chose you over all women in the world during your time because of your obedience to Him.

3. It is related that the messenger of God said that the best of women was Mary, daughter of ʿImrān, and another was Khadīja daughter of Khuwaylid, that is, the best of the women of paradise. It is also related from him according to Anas ibn Mālik that he said that the best women of the world were four in number: Mary, the daughter of ʿImrān, Āsiya [the wife of Pharaoh], the daughter of Muzāḥim, Khadīja, the daughter of Khuwaylid, and Fāṭima, the daughter of Muḥammad.

4. Then God said to her, *O Mary, be dedicated to your Lord, prostrate and bow along with those who bow* (Q 3/43). She did not cease being in her state of dedication until her feet became swollen and pus began to flow from them because of the length of time she had been standing. When God intended to announce the birth of Jesus to Mary, He discovered that she had separated herself from her people and withdrawn from them to a place in the east where the sun did not set. That is in accord with the saying of God, *Mention in the book Mary, when she withdrew from her people to a place facing east* (Q 19/16).

5. Ibn ʿAbbās used to say that he knew best why the Christians have their *qibla* facing east; it is because of God's saying, *she withdrew from her people to a place facing east* (Q 19/16). So they took the birthplace of Jesus as their *qibla*. It is said that Mary went to the place close to the rising of the sun because what was close in the east was, for them, better than what was close in the west.

6. *She took a veil apart from them* (Q 19/17), that is, a screen of palm-leaf stalks or a veil to protect her from the sun. *So We sent to her Our spirit*, who was Gabriel, *who presented himself to her as a man without faults* (Q 19/17). That was after she had purified herself from her menstruation. She saw that, with her, there was a man who was perfect. She was afraid that he would want her. She said, 'I seek refuge with God from your getting from me what God has forbidden for you, *if you fear God!*' (Q 19/18), that is, if you have a fear of God, you will fear what He has forbidden and you will avoid those sins. Whoever is fearful of God avoids that. During this time she thought that he was a male human being. So Gabriel said to her, '*I am a messenger from your Lord, to give you a boy, pure*' (Q 19/19). Mary said to him, 'How can it be that I will have a child? Who is my spouse? Am I to be married so that I may be blessed with him? Or does God intend to create him afresh since *no mortal has touched me*' (Q 19/20), that is, a human creation by legal marriage? '*Nor have I been unchaste*' (Q 19/20), that is, a fornicator such that I would become pregnant as the result of an illicit relationship. Gabriel replied to her that, *It shall be so! Your Lord has said, 'It is easy for Me'* (Q 19/21). It is not difficult for Him to create him and grant him to you without a man to impregnate you. *We have appointed him as a sign to the people* (Q 19/21), that is, as a symbol and a proof of my creating him, *and a mercy from Us* (Q 19/21), to you and to those who believe in him and declare the truth of his breath in you. *It is a thing decreed* (Q 19/21); God decreed it and decreed it in His judgement and His prior knowledge. So God blew into her with His spirit and she became pregnant with Jesus. It is also reported that Gabriel blew into the opening of her cloak such that the breath went into her womb. He then departed from her.

7. Al-Suddī said that Mary went out wearing a robe, so Gabriel took her by her sleeves and breathed into the opening of her cloak such that it opened in the front and his breath entered her chest. So she became pregnant. Her sister, the wife of Zechariah, came to her one night to visit. When she opened the door, she clung to her. The wife of Zechariah said, 'Mary, look, I am pregnant!' Mary replied, 'I am pregnant too!' The wife of Zechariah said, 'I feel the baby in my belly bowing down to the child in your belly.' That is the meaning of the saying of God, *Confirming a word from God, noble* (Q 3/39).

8. Some of the exegetes say that Mary's nephew, Joseph by name, was with her in the temple (*miḥrāb*). He used to serve her and speak to her from behind a veil. He was the first one to learn about her pregnancy. He was disturbed by that, not understanding how it came about. Her state distracted him from everything else. He was a wise man, devoted to God, and Mary had always drawn her veil over herself when he was with her. When their stock of water was depleted, the two of them would take their cups to the cave in which there was water and fill their cups and then return. He used to hear the angels informing Mary that God had chosen her and purified her; he was amazed at what he heard. When her pregnancy became clear to him, he remembered the merits which God had bestowed on her and that Zechariah had protected her in the temple. Satan had no way in which to reach her, yet his mind was unsettled. He thought of him with her while her belly grew and he feared that sin had occurred. So, one day, he turned to her and said, 'Mary, does a plant grow without a seed?' She replied, 'Yes.' He said, 'So, does a tree grow without rain falling on it?' 'Certainly,' she replied. Joseph said, 'Can there be a child without a man involved?' 'Yes,' she said, 'Do you not know that God caused the plant to grow on the day He created it without a seed? Do you not know that God caused the tree to grow without rain and by His decree made rain give life to trees only after He had created each one of them separately? Or do you say that God is unable to make the tree grow until He has sought the aid of the water and, if it had not been for that water, He would have been unable to make it grow?' Joseph replied, 'No, I do not say this, but I know that God is able to do what He wishes. He says to something "Be!" and it is.' So Mary said to him, 'Do you not know that God created Adam and his wife, Eve, without a man and a woman?' 'Certainly,' Joseph replied. When she said that to him, he realized for himself that her child was something from God and it was inappropriate for him to question her about it. That was when he realized that she was concealing her situation.

9. When her labour pains became severe, she was called to, 'Leave the temple.' So she left and went far away from the sacred house. While she was walking, the pains came upon her and she took refuge in a donkey's manger built around a palm-tree, which she hugged. The angels surrounded her, encompassing her in ranks, encircling her. So, *She said, 'I wished I had died before this happened'* (Q 19/23) today, and I felt ashamed in front of the people. *'And had become a thing forgotten'* (Q 19/23), that is, that I am like something forgotten whose request and memory has been neglected. So Gabriel called out to her, *But he who was below her called to her, 'No, do not sorrow; see, your Lord has set below you a stream'* (Q 19/24), that is, a creek. She was thirsty and a river was caused to flow towards her out of the ground. The dry tree stump which was among the palms started to bear fruit even though over time it had lost all its leaves because of dryness. The fruit matured into *fresh, ripe fruit* (Q 19/25), that is, juicy and succulent. So Gabriel called to her, '*Shake the palm-trunk towards you and fresh, ripe fruit will tumble down on you* (Q 19/25) and *eat* from this palm-tree and *drink* from this river and *be comforted*' (Q 19/26). She said, 'What should I say when they ask me, "Where did this come from?"?' Gabriel said to her, *Say, 'I have vowed a fast to the All-merciful'* (Q 19/26), that is, be silent

about the matter of Jesus. *'And today I will not speak to any human being'* (Q 19/26) about him until he who comes forth from me is disclosed.

10. When the people could not find Mary in the temple, they went out looking for her. They heard the cry of a magpie from the top of the palm-tree under which Mary had been lying. Mary saw her people coming towards her as they hurried towards the magpie, so she took her child out to them. That is His saying, *Then she brought him to her folk, carrying him* (Q 19/27), because she was not suspicious of them. One of her nephews, whom she had named, came to her and they said to him, 'Mary has become pregnant as a result of fornication! Now the king will kill her!' So he went to her and took her and escaped with her. When he had travelled some distance, he intended to kill her but Gabriel told him that the child was from the holy spirit, so he held back from doing that and stayed with her.

11. When they saw her, her father ʿImrān rent his cloak and covered his head with dust. They said to her, *'Mary, you have surely committed an improper thing!'* (Q 19/27), that is, you have done a strange thing and provoked a great occurrence. They then said to her, *'Sister of Aaron'* (Q 19/28). This Aaron, to whom Mary was compared, was a righteous man; they used to name every righteous man Aaron. It is mentioned in the works of exegesis regarding this Aaron that 40,000 people escorted his funeral procession, all of them named Aaron. The family of Mary said to her, 'O resembler of Aaron in righteousness which we used to see from him in you, *Your father,* that is, ʿImrān, *was not an impure man*, committing impure acts, *nor was your mother an unchaste woman* (Q 19/28), that is, a fornicator who should be censured; that is, your parents were righteous and your people are righteous and you desire righteousness in such a way that you are excellent like Aaron the righteous man. So how can you be involved in this severe matter?'

12. Their censure of her increased and her ability to withstand it lessened, such that *she pointed to him* (Q 19/29), that is, to Jesus, indicating that they should speak to him. So they said to her, *'How can we speak to one who is still in the cradle, a child?'* (Q 19/29). The like of Jesus had not been known before and his ability to speak had not begun, so they thought that Mary was mocking them. That angered them substantially and they said, 'You were making fun of us when you suggested that we speak to this child; that makes your fornication even more significant a matter to us!' Then, at that moment, Jesus leaned over on to his left side and pointed with his finger, speaking about his mother and making clear his status, saying, *'Lo, I am God's servant; God has given me the book, and has made me a prophet. He has made me blessed, wherever I may be'* (Q 19/30–1), that is, He ordained it for me when I was in the belly of my mother.

4.2 Al-Thaʿlabī on Abraha and the expedition of the elephant

Aḥmad ibn Muḥammad ibn Ibrāhīm Abū Isḥāq al-Nīsābūrī al-Thaʿlabī was a Qur'ān exegete and collector of stories who died in 427/1035. Al-Thaʿlabī is famous today for two works. His massive *tafsīr, al-Kashf wa'l-bayān ʿan tafsīr al-Qur'ān*, is a landmark of intellectual achievement for the period. The work raised concerns in the past, however, for its reliability; its sources include those traditionally deemed untrustworthy within the Sunnī *tafsīr* tradition and this probably accounts for its being ignored for publication until recently, despite its significance. The second famous work by al-Thaʿlabī is his book on the stories of the prophets, *ʿArā'is al-majālis fī qiṣaṣ al-anbiyā'*, which gives a taste of the character of his *tafsīr*. Printed many times and available in numerous inexpensive mass market editions, it is a work of popular imagination designed for education and entertainment. It contains not only the history of the earlier prophets (especially biblical) but also various stories of pre-Islamic Arabian events which lead up to the arrival of Muḥammad, as in the passage translated here about the South Arabian leader Abraha and his attempt to invade Mecca in the year of the birth of Muḥammad.

Much of the account of this story about Abraha is derived from that of Ibn Isḥāq (d. 150/767), who provided the base text for the biography of Muḥammad for generations of later Muslims. After recounting the basic story of the invasion of Abraha with some editorial remarks, all in the form of a long explanation of a very allusive Qur'ān quotation, al-Thaʿlabī adds another version of the story from the *tafsīr* of Muqātil ibn Sulaymān (see section 5.3). This provides a wholly different, and much more fanciful, narrative explanation while still embedding the exegesis of the same Qur'ānic reference (the text is found in Muqātil ibn Sulaymān, *Tafsīr*, ed. A. M. Shihāṭa, Cairo 1988, vol. 4, pp. 850–3). Overall, the account is notable for the inclusion of poetry which serves as an additional witness to the events described by the narrative. Poetry is not cited as part of the events themselves, but as the vehicle for the transmission of the memories through later generations and for the glorification of the poets themselves, who are, as in this story, sometimes the heroes of the story as well. This story is included within this book dealing with the 'stories of the prophets' as the very last chapter. This emphasizes the point that the overall aim of the work is not simply to tell the stories of the past, but to see all of the past history as culminating in the coming of Muḥammad.

The historical events referred to in this text suggest the point at which the Muslim tradition of pre-Islamic times begins to overlap with contemporary external sources. It has, therefore, attracted a good deal of scholarly interest. For example, pre-Islamic South Arabian inscriptions and Procopius of Caesarea's *History of the Wars*, written in about 550 CE, provide a good deal of basic data which correlates to some degree with the memories transmitted in later Muslim sources.

Probably because no critical version of the text of al-Thaʿlabī is available, both the poetry and the spelling of some names in the text show variation from those found in the parallel sources such as Ibn Isḥāq [Ibn Hishām], *Al-Sīra al-Nabawiyya*, Cairo 1955, vol. 1, pp. 37–62, A. Guillaume (trans.), *The life of Muḥammad: a translation of [Ibn] Isḥāq's* Sīrat rasūl Allāh, Oxford 1955, pp. 18–30, al-Ṭabarī, *Ta'rīkh al-rusul wa'l-mulūk*, ed. M. J. de Goeje, Leiden 1879–1901, vol. 1, pp. 925–45, and C. E. Bosworth (trans.), *The history of al-Ṭabarī, volume V: the Sāsānids, the Byzantines, the Lakhmids, and Yemen*, Albany NY 1999, pp. 202–35. Occasionally, this translation has followed the better-edited texts of those other sources.

Further reading

Lawrence Conrad, 'Abraha and Muḥammad: some observations apropos of chronology and literary topoi in the early Arabic historical tradition,' *Bulletin of the School of Oriental and African Studies*, 50 (1987), pp. 225–40.

M. J. Kister, 'The campaign of Ḥulubān: new light on the expedition of Abraha,' *Le Muséon*, 78 (1965), pp. 425–36; reprinted in M. J. Kister, *Studies in Jāhiliyya and early Islam*, London 1980, chapter 18, and in F. E. Peters (ed.), *The Arabs and Arabia on the eve of Islam*, Aldershot 1999, chapter 18.

F. E. Peters, 'Introduction,' in his *The Arabs and Arabia on the eve of Islam*, Aldershot 1999, pp. xlii–xlviii; contains useful bibliographical material.

Sidney Smith, 'Events in Arabia in the 6th century AD,' *Bulletin of the School of Oriental and African Studies*, 16 (1954), pp. 425–68; includes translations of inscriptions and Greek sources.

Source text

Al-Thaʿlabī, *ʿArāʾis al-majālis fī qiṣaṣ al-anbiyāʾ*, Cairo n.d., pp. 396–402. The translations of the poems presented here are indebted to the partially parallel texts found in A. Guillaume (trans.), *The life of Muḥammad: a translation of [Ibn] Isḥāq's* Sīrat rasūl Allāh, Oxford 1955. A full translation of al-Thaʿlabī's work is available: W. M. Brinner (trans.), *ʿArāʾis al-majālis fī qiṣaṣ al-anbiyāʾ or 'Lives of the prophets' as recounted by Abū Isḥāq Aḥmad Ibn Muḥammad ibn Ibrāhīm al-Thaʿlabī*, Leiden 2002.

The story of the companions of the elephant along with an explanation of what occurred during it of benefit and distinction to our prophet Muḥammad

1. God said, *Have you not seen how your Lord acted with the companions of the elephant?* (Q 105/1) to the end of the chapter. Muḥammad ibn Isḥāq ibn Bashshār said that some of the people of knowledge transmit the story about the companions of the elephant on the authority of Saʿīd ibn Jubayr and ʿIkrima from Ibn ʿAbbās, and from other learned people from the Yemen as well as others. The story is as follows.

2. One of the kings of Himyar, named Zurʿa Dhū Nuwās, had adopted Judaism and all of Ḥimyar followed him in that except the people of Najrān who belonged to the Christian religion, following the rule of the Gospels. Their leader was ʿAbd Allāh ibn al-Thāmir. Dhū Nuwās summoned them to adopt Judaism but they refused. He let them choose (between that and death) and they chose death. So he dug trenches for them and he divided them up for different methods of

execution. Some were killed while captive and some were thrown into the fire. One man, named Daws Dhū Thaʿlabān from Saba', escaped, however, riding away on one of his own horses. He galloped away such that it was impossible for them to pursue him in the sand. He went to the Byzantine emperor ('Caesar') and told him what had happened to them and asked for help. The emperor said to him, 'Your land is far from us but I will write on your behalf to the ruler of Abyssinia, who also belongs to our religion, and he will help you.' So he wrote on his behalf to the ruler of Abyssinia, the Najāshī, ordering him to help Daws. When the letter reached the Najāshī, the king sent an Abyssinian named Aryāṭ with Daws, commissioning him saying, 'When you reach the Yemen, kill a third of the men, lay waste a third of the country and send me a third of the prisoners.' When they entered the Yemen, the armies engaged in battle. Dhū Nuwās became separated from his army and he plunged his horse into the sea. He and his horse died together. That was the end of him. Aryāṭ took the country and did as he had been commanded by the Najāshī.

3. Dhū Jadan al-Himyarī said the following about what happened to the people of Yemen.

> Leave me! May you have no father! You cannot turn me from my
> purpose. May God put shame on you; your scolding dries
> my spit.
> The music of singers in times past was pleasant when we drank our
> fill of excellent wine.
> Drinking the wine does not cause me shame, when no companion
> faults my behaviour.
> For no one can hold back death, though he drinks the perfumed
> potions of the remedy,
> And nor can the monk in his secluded cell on high where the
> vulture flies around its nest.
> You have heard of Ghumdān's towers which loom from the
> mountain top,
> Well carpentered, with stones for support, plastered with clean,
> damp, slippery clay.
> Oil lamps show within it in the evening like the lightning's glow;
> Beside its wall the palm-trees grow with ripening fruit in heavy
> clusters.
> This once new castle is in ashes today; the flames have eaten its
> beauty away.
> Dhū Nuwās, humbled, gave up his great castle and warned his
> people of their coming fate.

4. Aryāṭ held command in the Yemen and the Najāshī wrote to him saying, 'Remain there with your army and those with you.' He had been in command for some time when Abraha ibn al-Ṣabbāḥ became annoyed at him concerning the matter of the Abyssinians such that they split into two groups, one following Aryāṭ, the other Abraha. The two of them prepared to move against one another. When they were fairly close, Abraha sent a note to Aryāṭ saying, 'Don't do

anything! We Abyssinians should not fight one another. Come out and fight me alone. Whoever is killed, his army will unite with the other.' He replied, 'You have made a just suggestion.' They went out (to meet each other). Aryāṭ was a large, handsome man and held a spear in his hand. Abraha was short and fat and belonged to the Christian religion. Behind him was a helper named ʿAtawda. When they were close, Aryāṭ lifted his spear and hit Abraha on the head, striking his forehead, slashing his eye, brow, nose and lips. For this reason Abraha was called al-Ashram (the hare-lipped). When ʿAtawda saw that happen, he attacked Aryāṭ and killed him. So the armies were joined under the leadership of Abraha. When the news of what Abraha had done reached the Najāshī, he became angry and swore that he would not leave Abraha alone until he had cut off his forelock and trampled his country underfoot. So he wrote to Abraha saying, 'You attacked my commander and killed him without having received my command.' Abraha was a defiant person so when the Najāshī's letter reached him, he shaved his head and filled a bag with dirt from his land and wrote to the Najāshī saying, 'My King! Aryāṭ was your servant and I am your servant. We disagreed over your command. I was more knowledgeable and more firm in the affairs of the Abyssinians. I wanted to separate, so I killed him. When news of the oath of the king reached me, I shaved my head and I am sending my hair to you. I have also filled a bag with dirt from my land and I am sending it to you so that the king may trample on it and thus keep his oath.'

5. When that reached the Najāshī, he calmed down and he confirmed Abraha in his position, writing to him that he was in command of the soldiers who remained with him. Then Abraha built a church in Sanʿāʾ, calling it al-Qullays ['cathedral' from the Greek *ekklesia*]. He then wrote to the Najāshī saying, 'I have built a church for you in Sanʿāʾ, the like of which no king has ever built before. I shall not rest until the Arabs perform their pilgrimage to it.' A man from Banū Mālik ibn Kināna heard of this and went to al-Qullays and entered it one night, defiling it in a derogatory manner and praising the Kaʿba. When news of that reached Abraha, it is said that he went there to see it. He entered the church, and found that someone had defecated there, so he said, 'Who has had the nerve to do this?' He was told that an Arab from the people of that house to which the Arabs go for pilgrimage did it after he had heard what Abraha had said. Abraha swore as a result that he would go to the Kaʿba and demolish it. So the rest of the Abyssinians set out for Mecca, taking with them an elephant. News of this reached the Arabs who became alarmed and anxious when they saw that his effort was truly directed against them.

6. One of the Himyarite kings named Dhū Nafar set out with those of his people who would help him. They engaged Abraha in battle but they were routed and Dhū Nafar was captured and taken before Abraha. He said to him, 'O king, do not kill me! Your sparing me would be better for you than my death.' So he kept him alive but shackled him, for Abraha was a merciful man. The rest of the troops set out until they approached the territory of Khathʿam. Nufayl ibn Ḥabīb al-Khathʿamī went out against them with the two tribes of Khathʿam, Shahrān and Nāhis and some others from the Yemeni tribes who had joined them. They battled and were defeated, and Nufayl was taken prisoner. He said to Abraha,

'O king! I will be your guide in the land of the Arabs. Do not kill me! I will order my people to obey you.' So he spared him and they set out with him guiding them until they passed al-Ṭā'if, where Masʿūd ibn Muʿattib al-Thaqafī came out with troops from the tribe of Thaqīf. He said to him, 'O king! We are your servants and we have no quarrel with you. It is not our temple (that is, the temple of al-Lāt) that you want; rather you want the temple which is in Mecca. We will send someone to guide you there.' They sent Abū Righāl who was their client. They set out until they reached al-Mughammis, close to Mecca, where Abū Righāl died and later the Arabs would stone his grave.

7. Abraha sent an Abyssinian named al-Aswad ibn Mafṣūd out of al-Mughammis with a raiding party. He set about plundering and seized two hundred camels belonging to ʿAbd al-Muṭṭalib, grandfather of the messenger of God. Abraha sent Ḥunāṭa, the Himyarite, to the people of Mecca, telling him to ask about who their leader was and to tell them that they had not come to fight but to destroy the temple. On reaching Mecca, Ḥunāṭa met ʿAbd al-Muṭṭalib ibn Hāshim and said to him, 'The king has sent me to you to inform you that he has not come to fight you unless you attack him; rather, he has come in order to destroy this temple. He will then leave you alone.' ʿAbd al-Muṭṭalib said, 'We are powerless in front of him and what he brings. But this is God's sacred temple and the temple of His friend Abraham, upon whom may there be peace. If He defends it, then it is most certainly His temple and sacred place; if He lets him have it, then so be it for, by God, we do not have the strength (to do otherwise).' Ḥunāṭa replied, 'Come with me to the king.' Some of the learned ones claim that he sat him on one of his mules and he rode on that, and that some of his sons accompanied him to the camp. Dhū Nafar was a friend of ʿAbd al-Muṭṭalib, so he went to him and said, 'Dhū Nafar, do you have the ability to deal with this matter that has come upon us?' Dhū Nafar replied, 'A prisoner does not have any ability when he expects to be killed sooner or later. But I will send you to Unays, keeper of the elephant, who is a friend of mine. I will ask him to do whatever good he is able with the king on your behalf. That will strengthen your position and fortune with him.' So he wrote to Unays and he came to Dhū Nafar, who said, 'This is the lord of the Quraysh, master of the Meccan well, who has come; he feeds the people in the plain and the mountains as well as the wild animals and birds on the hilltops. The king has taken two hundred camels from him. If you are able to do something to his advantage with the king, please do so. He is my friend and I would like to see him rewarded.' Unays, accompanied by ʿAbd al-Muṭṭalib, went to Abraha and he praised ʿAbd al-Muṭṭalib to him, saying, 'We have come not to display antagonism nor to quarrel with you but to seek your permission for you to listen to him as we desire.' Permission was granted.

8. Now ʿAbd al-Muṭṭalib was an impressive, handsome man and, when he entered, he sat in front of Abraha, but Abraha got up and made him sit on his throne with him. He told his interpreter to ask what he wanted, to which ʿAbd al-Muṭṭalib replied that he wanted the return of the two hundred camels which were taken from him. Abraha replied through his translator, 'I was amazed when I saw you but I am displeased with you now!' He asked, 'Why?' The king replied, 'I have come to a temple which is at the centre of your religion and that of your fathers

in order to destroy it and you do not speak to me of that, but rather you speak of the two hundred camels which I have taken!' ʿAbd al-Muṭṭalib said, 'I am the owner of these camels and this temple has an owner who will defend it against you.' The king replied, 'It cannot be defended against me!' to which ʿAbd al-Muṭṭalib said, 'That's between you and Him!' Then he asked about his camels again and they were returned to him.

9. Muḥammad ibn Isḥāq said that some of the learned people have claimed that, when ʿAbd al-Muṭṭalib went to Abraha, he was accompanied by Yaʿmar ibn Nufātha ibn ʿAdī ibn al-Du'il ibn Bakr ibn ʿAbd Manāt ibn Kināna (who was at the time chief of the tribe of Kināna) and Khuwaylid ibn Wāthila al-Hudhalī (who was chief of the tribe of Hudhayl at that time). They offered to give Abraha a third of the property of Tihāma if he would withdraw and not destroy the temple. He refused to withdraw, however. When he returned the camels to ʿAbd al-Muṭṭalib, the latter went back and told the Quraysh of the news and ordered them to disperse into the hills and to keep a lookout on the mountaintops for fear of the large numbers of soldiers coming. They did that.

10. ʿAbd al-Muṭṭalib went to the Kaʿba and, seizing the door-knockers, began to say,

> Lord, I do not wish for them anyone against them but You! Lord,
> prevent them from entering Your sacred area!
> The enemy of the house is the one attacking You; so prevent them
> from destroying Your settlements.

and he said,

> O great God, the man defends his dwelling, so You must defend
> yours!
> Help Your people against the people of the cross and their servants
> today!
> Let not the cross and their crafts ever overcome Your craft.
> All of the people of their land and the elephant went into action in
> order to capture Your dependants.
> They attacked Your sacred area cunningly in ignorance and paid no
> need to Your majesty.
> If You had abandoned them and our place of worship, then the
> affair would have been of no concern to You.

11. Then ʿAbd al-Muṭṭalib let go of the knocker and went off with his people in various directions. In the morning Abraha prepared to enter Mecca with his troops and his elephant. The elephant's name was Maḥmūd and he had been sent by the Najāshī to Abraha. No one in the land had ever seen anything like it in size or strength. Al-Kalbī has said that only that one elephant had ever been there and therefore God said, *Have you not seen how your Lord acted with the companions of the elephant?* (Q 105/1)

11.1. Al-Daḥḥāk said that it was a huge elephant. It is also said that there were twelve other elephants with it, but there can only have been one in accordance with this interpretation of the beginning of the verse of the Qur'ān. It is also said that all these elephants were offspring of the one large elephant.

12. Nufayl approached the large elephant and took it by the ear and said to it, 'Kneel, Maḥmūd, or go back directly to where you came from. You are in God's holy land!' So the elephant knelt. The troops called it but it refused to get up. They beat it on the head but it still refused. They stuck hooks under it and lifted it up in order to make it stand up, but still it refused. So they turned it around in order to return to the Yemen, and then it got up and started off. They then turned it towards Syria and it did the same, as it did when they turned it to the east. But when they turned it towards the sacred area of Mecca, it knelt and refused to stand up. Nufayl, meanwhile, had left them and gone up into the hills. God sent some birds from the sea, various kinds of swallows, each of them carrying three rocks – two between their legs and one in their beak, just like lentils and peas. When they descended upon the people they had been sent to, everyone whom they hit with the rocks died, although not all the people were hit. That is what is referred to by God's saying, *birds in swarms* (Q 105/3), that is, scattered everywhere.

12.1. Ibn ʿAbbās said that they had beaks like fowl and claws like the paws of dogs. ʿIkrima said their heads were like those of lions, the likes of which had not been seen previously nor have they been seen since. Rabīʿ said that they had teeth like those of lions and Saʿīd ibn Jubayr said that they were green birds with yellow beaks. Abū 'l-Jawzā' said that God created them in the air at that time.

13. Ibn Masʿūd said that the birds screamed and pelted the troops with their rocks. God sent a wind which pushed the rocks and increased their strength; whenever a rock struck a man on the side, it would pass out the other side. If a rock struck someone's head, it would come out of his buttocks. He made those people resemble harvested plants, that is, like crops where the seed has been consumed and only the straw remains. When the Abyssinians saw this, they fled, rushing the way they had come.

14. They called for Nufayl ibn Ḥabīb to show them the way, but, when he saw the punishment God had sent down upon them, he said,

> Where can one go when God is the pursuer? Al-Ashram is the
> conquered, not the conqueror.

He also said about that,

> Greetings, Rudayna! Our eyes rejoice at you this morning!
> Rudayna, if only you had seen, but you will not see, what we saw
> near al-Muḥaṣṣab.
> Then you would have forgiven me and praised my action, and would
> not have been grieved at what has passed and gone between us.

I praised God when I saw the birds but I feared the stones would
fall on us.
All the people were asking for Nufayl, as though I owed the
Abyssinians a debt.

15. Ziyād mentioned on the authority of ʿAbd Allāh ibn ʿUmar that the *birds in swarms* (Q 105/3) had approached from the sea from the direction of India, pelting them with small rocks about the size of a man's head or somewhat bigger, such that what they threw hit its target, and what hit its target killed. Nufayl saw some of this from the hills. The people were leaving and some of them called to the others who then left, falling over each other via every route, but they were killed at every oasis at which they stopped. God caused Abraha to be injured on his body, and as he was being taken away, his fingertips fell off with pus and blood pouring out from their place. When he arrived in Sanʿāʾ he looked like a young bird in the midst of what remained of his followers. He did not die until his heart burst within his chest and then he was destroyed.

16. Muqātil ibn Sulaymān claims that the reason for the report about the companions of the elephant lies in the fact that a group of merchants from the Quraysh went to the country of the Najāshī. They travelled there and established an agreement with the Najāshī and the people of his land.

17. Some people, who settled in support of the agreement, gathered firewood and started a fire and cooked some meat. When they departed, they left the fire just as if it was a summer's day. However, a wind roared up and the temple caught on fire. The screaming reached the Najāshī and he was told what had happened. He fell into a rage at the agreement after that, and decided to send Abraha to destroy the Kaʿba. At that time Abū Masʿūd al-Thaqafī was in Mecca. Being blind, he spent the summer in al-Ṭāʾif and wintered in Mecca. He was a well-known, noble and intelligent man and a friend of ʿAbd al-Muṭṭalib. ʿAbd al-Muṭṭalib said, 'Abū Masʿūd! Today you have no need of your vision! What do you think?' He replied to him, 'Take one hundred camels and make them a gift to God. Adorn them with sandals hung around their necks and put them in the sacred area. Perhaps some of these black people will slaughter some of them and cause the Lord of this house to be angry.' So ʿAbd al-Muṭṭalib took them and did that. The people of Abraha came to the camels and mounted them, and they slaughtered some of them. ʿAbd al-Muṭṭalib began crying out and Abū Masʿūd said, 'There is a Lord of this house who will prevent these actions!' The followers of the king of Yemen stayed in the wasteland around the house which they wished to destroy. God prevented them from doing that by putting them to the test with three days of darkness. When ʿAbd al-Muṭṭalib saw that, he went out, draping a camel in fine white Egyptian cloth to enhance its greatness, and he slaughtered it as a sacrifice. Then Abū Masʿūd said to ʿAbd al-Muṭṭalib, 'Look towards the sea of Yemen. Do you see something?' He replied, 'I see white birds emerging out of the sea, circling over our heads.' Abū Masʿūd said, 'Do you understand it?' to which he replied, 'By God, I do not understand. They are not from the Najd or Tihāma, nor from the Arabian desert, nor Syria. They are flying over our land but are unfamiliar.' Abū Masʿūd said, 'How strong are they?' to

which he replied, 'They are like a swarm of bees; in their beaks they have little stones like stones from a slingshot.' They approached like the darkness of night, following one after the other. Leading in front of each group was a bird with a red beak, a black head and a long neck. This continued on until they faced the army of people, remaining motionless above their heads. When all of them had encircled the men, the birds dropped what was in their beaks on whoever was under them, the name of its victim being written on each stone. Then they returned to where they came from. When ʿAbd al-Muṭṭalib and Abū Masʿūd got up, they came down from atop the mountain and walked over the hill, but they met no one. They walked on and heard no sound at all. They said to each other, 'The people must have spent the night untroubled and must still be sleeping.' When they approached the army of the elephant they found they were all dying. The rocks had fallen on the helmets of every one of them and had smashed them, and the men's brains were split open. The elephant and the riding animals had all dispersed. The rocks had disappeared into the earth because of the force with which they had fallen.

. . .

18. There is disagreement concerning the date of the year of the elephant. Muqātil says that the affair of the elephant took place forty years before the birth of the prophet of God while ʿUbayd ibn ʿUmayr and al-Kalbī say it was twenty-three years before his birth. Everyone else says that it occurred in the year in which the messenger of God was born and, according to the opinion of the majority of the learned class, that is the sound opinion. What we are told from Abū Bakr al-Jawzaqī indicates this. He was told by ʿAbd al-Azīz ibn Abī Thābit al-Zubayr, who was told by Ibn Mūsā on the authority of Abū ʾl-Jawzāʾ, who said that he heard ʿAbd al-Malik ibn Marwān say to Ghayyāth ibn Usaym al-Kinānī, 'Ghayyāth! Who is older, you or the messenger of God?' He replied, 'The messenger of God is greater than me, but I am older than him. The messenger of God was born in the year of the elephant while my mother was with me in the dung [i.e., at the time] of the elephant.' A report from ʿĀʾisha also indicates this when she said, 'I saw the elephant's guide and its groom in Mecca, both of them blind, crippled and begging for food.'

After God had sufficed in the affair of the companions of the elephant, the Arabs exalted the Quraysh and they said that they were the people of God for whom God had fought and had sufficed them over their enemies. God is all-knowing and all-wise. May God grant us our final reckoning and the blessing of His representative. Amen.

4.3 Al-Wāḥidī on the occasions of revelation of *sūrat al-baqara* (2)

Abū'l-Ḥasan 'Alī ibn Aḥmad al-Wāḥidī al-Nīsābūrī was a philologist and Qur'ān scholar who died in 468/1076. A pupil of Abū Isḥāq al-Tha'labī, he stands out as one of the most prominent fifth-/eleventh-century interpreters of the Qur'ān, having written three commentaries of varying length – a short one for more popular consumption, a middle-length one and an expansive work full of grammatical and doctrinal excurses. His fame down to today has been primarily associated with his book on the 'occasions of revelation' of the Qur'ān, the *Kitāb asbāb al-nuzūl*. This book gathers together (and was probably the first to do so) all the traditions which indicate when or about what a verse was revealed.

The traditions on the 'occasions of revelation' provide a sense of the historical underpinnings of the Qur'ān, although in most cases they are quite vague about specific historical details such as date, time and place. Rather, the traditions convey a narrative interpretation of a given verse, usually embedded within the historical narrative through careful glosses. Notably, al-Wāḥidī, in gathering together these traditions, was not concerned to identify a single historical circumstance, but rather was quite prepared to accommodate rival accounts of the historical context within the text. This emphasizes the point that it is not history that is at stake in these traditions, but rather exegesis. A number of reports simply indicate to whom the verse was addressed or referring; such comments are crucial for interpretation but have little to do with a historical or chronological determination. The reports related to Q 2/26 also illustrate the flexibility of this audience motif between the Jews and the Arab hypocrites.

Overall, al-Wāḥidī's text is marked by variability in the completeness of the *isnād*s in the citation of traditions, which indicates that the provision of these chains of transmission is a mere formality. This aspect of al-Wāḥidī's book was addressed by Jalāl al-Dīn al-Suyūṭī (d. 911/1505) when he compiled his work on this topic some five centuries later, using al-Wāḥidī's text as his basis.

Further reading

A. Rippin, 'The exegetical genre *asbāb al-nuzūl:* a bibliographical and terminological survey,' *Bulletin of the School of Oriental and African Studies*, 48 (1985), pp. 1–15.

—— 'The function of *asbāb al-nuzūl* in Qur'ānic exegesis,' *Bulletin of the School of Oriental and African Studies*, 51 (1988), pp. 1–20.

—— 'Al-Zarkashī and al-Suyūṭī on the "occasion of revelation" material,' *Islamic culture*, 59 (1985), pp. 243–58.

—— *The Qur'ān and its interpretative tradition*, Aldershot 2001; includes reprints of the above three articles.

Source text

Al-Wāḥidī, *Kitāb asbāb nuzūl al-Qur'ān*, ed. A. Saqr, Cairo 1969, pp. 19–26.

Sūrat al-baqara (2)

The *sūra* was revealed in Medina; there is no disagreement about that.

1. Aḥmad ibn Muḥammad ibn Ibrāhīm informed us that ʿAbd Allāh ibn Ḥāmid informed him that Aḥmad ibn Muḥammad ibn Yūsuf informed him that Yaʿqūb ibn Sufyān the younger told him that Yaʿqūb ibn Sufyān the elder told him that Hishām ibn ʿAmmār told him that al-Walīd ibn Muslim told him that Shuʿayb ibn Zurayq told him on the authority of ʿAṭāʾ al-Khurāsānī who reported from ʿIkrima who said that the first *sūra* revealed in Medina was *sūrat al-baqara* (2).

Q 2/1–2: The saying of God, *Alif lām mīm. That is the book*

1. Abū ʿUthmān al-Thaqafī al-Zaʿfarānī told us that Abū ʿAmr ibn Maṭr told him that Jaʿfar ibn Muḥammad ibn al-Layth told him that Abū Ḥudhayfa informed him that Shibl informed him on the authority of Ibn Abī Najīḥ on the authority of Mujāhid who said that the first four verses of the *sūra* were revealed about the believers, the next two descended about the unbelievers, and thirteen after them were revealed about the hypocrites.

Q 2/6: The saying of God, *Indeed those who disbelieved alike it is to them*

1. Al-Ḍahhāk said it was revealed about Abū Jahl and five people from his immediate family. Al-Kalbī said (that *those who disbelieved*) were the Jews.

Q 2/14: The saying of God, *When they meet those who believe they say, 'We believe'*

1. Aḥmad ibn Muḥammad ibn Ibrāhīm told us that Shayba ibn Muḥammad told him that ʿAlī ibn Muḥammad ibn Qurra informed him that Aḥmad ibn Muḥammad ibn Naṣr informed him that Yūsuf ibn Bilāl informed him that Muḥammad ibn Marwān informed him on the authority of al-Kalbī on the authority of Abū Ṣāliḥ that Ibn ʿAbbās said that this verse was revealed about ʿAbd Allāh ibn Ubayy and those accompanying him. The story is that they set out one day and met with a group of the companions of the messenger of God. ʿAbd Allāh ibn Ubayy said to his companions, 'Look how I can make these people into fools in front of you.' He went and took the hand of Abū Bakr al-Ṣiddīq and said, 'Greetings, al-Ṣiddīq, elder of the tribe of Tayyim, shaykh of Islam, second in the cave with the messenger of God and sacrificer of himself and his property!' Then he took the hand of ʿUmar and said, 'Greetings to the elder of the tribe of ʿAdī ibn Kaʿb, the powerful distinguisher of truth from falsehood (al-Fārūq) in the religion of God, and the sacrificer of himself and his property to the messenger of God.' Then he took the hand of ʿAli, the Noble One of God, and said, 'Greetings to the cousin of the messenger of God and his son-in-law, elder of the tribe of Hāshim only exceeded by the messenger

of God himself!' They then separated and ʿAbd Allāh said to his companions, 'Did you see me do what I did? I did as I said I would do.' So they praised him greatly. The Muslims returned to the prophet and informed him about that meeting. God then revealed this verse.

Q 2/21: The saying of God, *O people, worship your Lord!*

1. Saʿīd ibn Muḥammad ibn Aḥmad al-Zāhid told us that Abū ʿAlī ibn Aḥmad al-Faqīh told him that Abū Turāb al-Quhistānī told him that ʿAbd al-Raḥmān ibn Bishr informed him that Rawḥ informed him that Shuʿba informed him on the authority of Sufyān al-Thawrī on the authority of al-Aʿmash on the authority of Ibrāhīm that ʿIlqama said that every verse which contains the phrase *O people* was revealed in Mecca, while those that state *O believers* were revealed in Medina. That means that *O people* is addressed to the people of Mecca, while *O believers* is addressed to the people of Medina. So, His saying, *O people, serve your Lord,* is addressed to the polytheists of Mecca and this address continues to His saying, *inform those who believe* (at the beginning of verse 25), which was revealed about the believers. That is God, after He mentions the punishment of the infidels in His saying, *The fire whose fuel is people and rocks, prepared for the unbelievers* (Q 2/24), mentions the reward of the believers.

Q 2/26: The saying of God, *Indeed, God is not ashamed to strike a similitude*

1. Ibn ʿAbbās, in the transmission from Abū Ṣāliḥ, said that when God coined these two similitudes for the hypocrites, that is, His words, *the likeness of the one who ignited the fire* (Q 2/17) and His saying, *like a rain cloud from the sky* (Q 2/19), the hypocrites said that God was too elevated and exalted to have coined these similitudes. So God revealed this verse.

2. Al-Ḥasan and Qatāda said that when God mentioned the fly and the spider in His book (Q 22/73 and 29/41 respectively) and coined this similitude for the hypocrites, the Jews laughed and said, 'This does not resemble the word of God!' So God revealed this verse.

3. Aḥmad ibn ʿAbd Allāh ibn Isḥāq al-Ḥāfiẓ told us in his book that Sulaymān ibn Ayyūb al-Ṭabarānī told him that Bakr ibn Sahl informed him that ʿAbd al-ʿAzīz ibn Saʿīd informed him on the authority of Mūsā ibn ʿAbd al-Raḥmān on the authority of Ibn Jurayj on the authority of ʿAṭāʾ on the authority of Ibn ʿAbbās who said concerning the saying of God, *Indeed, God is not ashamed to strike a similitude*, that God had mentioned the deities of the polytheists in *If the fly snatches away something from them* (Q 22/73) and had mentioned the deception of the deities, comparing it to the house of a spider [i.e., Q 29/41]. So, the polytheists said, 'Don't you see how God mentioned the fly and the spider in what was revealed to Muḥammad of the Qurʾān? What sort of thing is this?!' So God revealed this verse.

Q 2/44: The saying of God, *Do you command piety in the people but forget yourselves?*

1. Ibn ʿAbbās said the following, in the transmission from al-Kalbī on the authority of Abū Sāliḥ according to the *isnād* which has already been mentioned. The verse was revealed about the Jews of Medina. A certain man had said to his son-in-law and to his relatives and to those with him (and among them were some who were in a foster relationship with the Muslims), 'Be upright in your religion, and in what this man – meaning Muḥammad – orders you to do! Indeed, his commands are true.' So they had ordered the people to do that but they did not do it.

Q 2/45: The saying of God, *Seek help with patience and prayer!*

1. Most of the people of knowledge say that this verse is addressed to the people of the book, but it is, at the same time, a good practice for all worshippers. Others said that the passage here returns to being addressed to the Muslims. The first statement provides a more obvious interpretation.

Q 2/62: The saying of God, *Indeed those who believe and those who are Jews* to the end of the verse

1. Aḥmad ibn Muḥammad ibn Aḥmad al-Ḥāfiẓ told us that ʿAbd Allāh ibn Muḥammad ibn Jaʿfar al-Ḥāfiẓ told him that Abū Yaḥyā al-Rāzī informed him that Sahl ibn ʿUthmān al-ʿAskarī informed him that Yaḥyā ibn Abī Zāʾida informed him saying that Ibn Jurayj said on the authority of ʿAbd Allāh ibn Kathīr on the authority of Mujāhid who said that when Salmān told the prophet the story of the companions of the monasteries, the prophet said, 'They are in the fire.' Salmān said, 'The earth has become dark for me.' So, *Indeed those who believe and those who are Jews* up to *they will have no fear nor will they grieve* was revealed, to which Salmān responded, 'It was as if a mountain was lifted off me.'

2. Muḥammad ibn ʿAbd al-ʿAzīz al-Marwazī told us that Muḥammad ibn al-Ḥusayn al-Ḥaddādī told him that Abū Yazīd told him that Isḥāq ibn Ibrāhīm told him that ʿAmr told him on the authority of Asbāṭ on the authority of al-Suddī who said regarding *Indeed those who believe and those who are Jews* to the end of the verse, that it was revealed concerning the companions of Salmān al-Fārisī, on the occasion that Salmān drew near to the messenger and began reporting about their acts of worship and their struggles. He said, 'Messenger of God, they used to pray, fast and believe in you, and they used to testify that indeed you were sent as a prophet.' When Salmān finished his praise of them, the messenger of God said, 'Salmān, they are of the people of the fire.' So God revealed, *Indeed those who believe and those who are Jews* recited up to *nor will they grieve*.

3. Muḥammad ibn Aḥmad ibn Muḥammad ibn Jaʿfar told us that Muḥammad ibn ʿAbd Allāh ibn Zakariyāʾ told him that Muḥammad ibn ʿAbd al-Raḥmān

al-Daghūlī told him that Abū Bakr ibn Abī Khaythama told him that ʿAmr ibn Hammād informed him that Absāṭ informed him on the authority of al-Suddī on the authority of Abū Mālik on the authority of Abū Ṣāliḥ on the authority of Ibn ʿAbbās, and on the authority of Murra on the authority of Ibn Masʿūd on the authority of some of the companions of the prophet that *Indeed those who believe and those who are Jews* continuing to the end of the verse was revealed about Salmān al-Fārisī who was the most famous of the people of Jundaysābūr. What comes after this verse was revealed about the Jews.

Q 2/75: The saying of God, *Are you eager that they believe you to the end of the verse*

1. Ibn ʿAbbās and Muqātil said that this was revealed about the seventy whom Moses selected to go with him to God. They went with him, and they heard the speech of God and what he ordered and forbade. They then returned to their people. As for the true believers, they carried out what they heard. But a group of them said, 'We heard God say at the end of His speech, "If you are able to do these things, then do them; if you do not wish to, then do not do them, there is no harm in that."'

2. According to most of the exegetes this verse was revealed to those who altered the stoning verse and description of Muḥammad.

Q 2/79: The saying of God, *So woe to those who write the book with their own hands then say, 'This is from God' to the end of the verse*

1. This was revealed about those who changed the description of the prophet and altered his qualities. Al-Kalbī, according to the *isnād* which we have already reported, said that they changed the description of the messenger of God in their book, and they portrayed him as being dark, tall and having lank hair, whereas he really was of medium height with a brown complexion. They said to their companions and followers, 'Look at the description of the prophet who will be sent at the end of time! His qualities do not resemble those of this man.' The rabbis and the learned ones used to receive provisions from the rest of the Jews and they feared that they would not receive them if they revealed the (true) description; therefore they changed it.

Q 2/80: The saying of God, *They say, 'The fire shall touch us only for some numbered days'*

1. Ismāʿīl ibn Abī ʾl-Qāsim al-Ṣūfī told us that Abū ʾl-Ḥusayn Muḥammad ibn Aḥmad ibn Ḥāmid al-ʿAṭṭār told him that Aḥmad ibn al-Ḥasan ibn ʿAbd al-Jabbār told him that Abū ʾl-Qāsim ʿAbd Allāh ibn Saʿd al-Zuhrī told him that his father and his uncle informed him that their father told them on the authority of Ibn Isḥāq that Muḥammad ibn Abī Muḥammad informed him on the authority of ʿIkrima on the authority of Ibn ʿAbbās who said that the messenger came to

Medina and the Jews were saying, 'The duration of the world is 7,000 years. God will punish the people in the fire for a single day in the hereafter for each 1,000 years of the existence of this world. So, there will be seven days of punishment.' So God revealed about their saying that, *They say, 'The fire shall touch us only for some numbered days.'*

2. Abū Bakr Aḥmad ibn Muḥammad al-Tamīmī told us that ʿAbd Allāh ibn Muḥammad ibn Ḥayyān told him that Muḥammad ibn ʿAbd al-Raḥmān al-Rāzī informed him that Sahl ibn ʿUthmān informed him that Marwān ibn Muʿāwiya informed him that Juwaybir informed him on the authority of al-Ḍaḥḥāk on the authority of Ibn ʿAbbās who said concerning *They say, 'The fire shall touch us only for some numbered days'* that the people of the book found that it would take forty years to cross between the extremities of hell. So they said, 'We will be punished in the fire for only the period which we find in the Torah.' So, when it is the day of resurrection, they will jump into the fire. They will remain in the punishment until they finish the journey, arriving at the Zaqqūm tree on the last of the numbered days. Then the keepers of the fire will say, 'Enemies of God! You claimed that you would be punished in hell for only some numbered days and then the period would be completed. But eternity still remains!'

Q 2/89: The saying of God, *They had prayed for victory over those who disbelieve*

1. Ibn ʿAbbās said that the Jews of Khaybar used to fight with Ghaṭafān. Whenever they met, the Jews of Khaybar were put to flight. So the Jews sought protection with this prayer, saying, 'O God, we ask you by the truth of Muḥammad, the *ummī* prophet whom you have promised that you will send to us at the end of time, help us against them!' So when they next met them, they prayed this prayer and Ghaṭafān fled. But when the prophet was sent they disbelieved in him, and so God revealed, *They had prayed for victory over those who disbelieve*, that is, in you, Muḥammad, up to His saying, *The curse of God is on the disbelievers!*

2. Al-Suddī reported that the Arabs used to pass by the Jews and cause them injury. The Jews found the description of Muḥammad in the Torah and they asked God to send him so that the Arabs would be fighting him (instead of them). When Muḥammad came, they disbelieved in him out of envy and said, 'The messengers are from the tribe of Israel. Why is it that this one is from the tribe of Ishmael?!'

Q 2/97: The saying of God, *Say: Whoever is an enemy of Gabriel, to the end of the verse*

1. Saʿīd ibn Muḥammad ibn Aḥmad al-Zāhid told us that al-Ḥasan ibn Aḥmad al-Shaybānī told him that al-Muʾammil ibn al-Ḥasan ibn ʿĪsā told him that Muḥammad ibn Ismāʿīl ibn Sālim informed him that Abū Nuʿaym informed him that ʿAbd Allāh ibn al-Walīd informed him on the authority of Bukayr on the authority of Ibn Shihāb on the authority of Saʿīd ibn Jubayr on the authority of Ibn ʿAbbās who said that the Jews approached the prophet and said, 'Abū

'l-Qāsim, we want to ask you about some things! If you answer them for us, we will follow you. Tell us about the angel which has come to you. No one can be a prophet unless an angel comes from his Lord with the message and the revelation. So, who is your companion?' He said, 'Gabriel.' They replied, 'This is the one who descends with war and killing. This is our enemy. If you had said that it was Michael, he who descends with land and mercy, we would have followed you.' So God revealed, *Say: Whoever is an enemy of Gabriel* until His saying, *Indeed God is an enemy of the disbelievers.*

4.4 Ibn ʿAṭiyya on the collection of the Qurʾān

Abū Muḥammad ʿAbd al-Ḥaqq ibn ʿAṭiyya was born in Granada in 481/1088 and died in the small Spanish city of Lorca in 541/1147. His father was a famous traditionist who travelled widely and initiated his son into discussions with the most learned people of his era. Ibn ʿAṭiyya wrote a full commentary on the Qurʾān called *al-Muḥarrar al-wajīz fī tafsīr al-kitāb al-ʿazīz*; the introduction to that work is a summary of many issues related to the study of the Qurʾān. While the main body of his commentary is devoted to legal matters, grammar, language, meaning, and reading/recitation, his introduction provides a summary of what previous scholars had reported on more theoretical issues or topics of broad significance related to the fundamental assumptions and procedures of what the commentary itself deals with (for example, the presence of foreign words and the use of concision in the text). It is within this context that Ibn ʿAṭiyya then provides a concise statement on the historical processes through which the Qurʾān came to look the way it does in its written form.

Ibn ʿAṭiyya's account is a compressed one, but this represents the late consensus on how the Qurʾān became the text that it is today. Certain aspects of the account may be profitably compared with those found in *ḥadīth* literature, for example in al-Bukhārī's *al-Ṣaḥīḥ* which is often presented as the consensus view of the community on these events. The reconciliation and consolidation of all the various accounts in creating such a cohesive and coherent presentation of a sequence of events demonstrates the power of community consensus (*ijmāʿ*) to establish history.

Further reading

Ismail Albayrak, 'Isrāʾīliyyāt and classical exegetes' comments on the calf with a hollow sound Q. 20: 83–98/7: 147–155 with special reference to Ibn ʿAṭiyya,' *Journal of Semitic studies*, 47 (2002), pp. 39–65; one of the few studies of Ibn ʿAtiyya's exegesis.

John Burton, *The collection of the Qur'ān*, Cambridge 1977.

Abu Ameenah Bilal Philips, *Usool at-tafseer: the methodology of Qur'aanic explanation*, Sharjah 1997, pp. 147–91; a summary of basic Muslim sources on questions of the text of the Qurʾān.

Source text

Arthur Jeffery (ed.), *Two muqaddimas to the Qur'anic sciences*, second edition, Cairo 1972, pp. 273–5.

Chapter regarding the collection of the Qurʾān and its form

1. At the time of the messenger of God, the Qurʾān was dispersed in the hearts of people. People wrote some of it on sheets, on palm-leaf stalks, on pumice stone, on baked clay, and on other items like that. When the killing of the Qurʾānic reciters intensified one day during the battle of al-Yamāma, ʿUmar ibn al-Khaṭṭāb

suggested to Abū Bakr al-Ṣiddīq that the Qurʾān should be collected. He feared that the important Qurʾān reciters like Ubayy, Zayd, Ibn Masʿūd and others like them might die. So the two of them delegated that task of collection to Zayd ibn Thābit. He collected it with great difficulty, without organizing the *sūras*. It is reported that, in this collection, verses from the end of *sūrat al-barāʾa* (9) were omitted until they were found in the possession of Khuzayma ibn Thābit.

1.1. Al-Ṭabarī related that it is true that verses were omitted from both collections.
1.2. That is also what al-Bukhārī relates, except that he says the verses were found with Abū Khuzayma al-Anṣārī and that in the second collection, Zayd failed to find a verse from the *sūrat al-aḥzāb*, *Among the believers were people* . . . (Q 23/33), which was later found with Khuzayma ibn Thābit.

2. The sheets remained in the possession of Abū Bakr and were transferred to ʿUmar ibn al-Khaṭṭāb after him. Then Ḥafṣa, his daughter, kept them during the rule of ʿUthmān. It is well known that, during this time, sheets were also written in distant lands on the authority of the companions of Muḥammad, such as the codex of Ibn Masʿūd, what was written on the authority of the companions in Syria, the codex of Ubayy, and others like them. That is the source of differing opinions about the seven forms (*aḥruf*) in which the Qurʾān was revealed.

When Ḥudhayfa returned from the military expedition in Armenia, he also considered the factors just mentioned. ʿUthmān authorized the collection of the codex and appointed Zayd ibn Thābit to the task of collecting it.

2.1. According to what al-Bukhārī related, he brought together three men from the Quraysh with Zayd, Saʿīd ibn al-ʿĀṣ, ʿAbd al-Raḥman ibn al-Ḥārith ibn Hishām and ʿAbd Allāh ibn al-Zubayr. This is what al-Tirmidhī and others say also.
2.2. Al-Ṭabarī said in the account he transmitted that ʿUthmān brought together only Abān ibn Saʿīd ibn al-ʿĀṣ with Zayd. This is unfounded.
2.3. Al-Ṭabarī also said that the pages which were in the possession of Ḥafṣa served as the standard in this final collection.

3. It is reported that ʿUthmān said to this group collecting the Qurʾān that if they disagreed about something, they should write it in the dialect of the Quraysh. They differed about whether the word should be *al-tābūh* or *al-tābūt* (Q 2/248, 20/39). Zayd ibn Thābit read it with the *hāʾ* whereas those from the Quraysh read it with the *tāʾ* and so it was written that way. The original codex had been written in whatever manner it had been written but the copy of ʿUthmān was written for distant parts of the world. He ordered that *taḥriqa* and *takhriqa* (in Q 17/37) be considered the same in the codex. Thus you see it written with a *ḥāʾ*, without the dot, or with *khāʾ*, with the dot, both with the same meaning of 'bury' or 'conceal'. The transmission with the *ḥāʾ* without the dot is best.

4. Qāḍī Abū Bakr ibn al-Ṭayyib said that the arrangement of the *sūras* today is that of Zayd and the associates of ʿUthmān who were with him. Makkī [Ibn Abī Ṭālib

al-Qaysī] mentioned that in his *tafsīr* on *sūrat al-barā'a* (9). He mentioned that the arrangement of the verses in the *sūra*s and the placement of the *basmala* (*In the name of God, the All-merciful, the All-compassionate*) at the beginning of the *sūra*s is derived from the prophet. Muḥammad did not command the writing of the *basmala* at the beginning of *sūrat al-barā'a* (9) so this is how things were left in that *sūra*. That will be fully examined in its place in this *tafsīr*, if God wills. It is apparent from tradition that the *mathānī* [the seven long *sūra*s], the *sūra*s which start with *Ḥā'-mīm* and the *mufaṣṣal sūra*s [usually those between *sūra* 49 and 114] were arranged in the time of the prophet and that the arrangement of the other *sūra*s was done at the time of the writing down of the book.

5. As for the vowelling and diacritical markings of the codex, it is reported that ʿAbd al-Malik ibn Marwān [ruled 65–86/685–705] ordered this to be done, and worked on it. Al-Ḥajjāj was devoted to this task in Wāsiṭ where he was located. However, his involvement in wars increased while he was governor of Iraq [75–95/694–714], and so he ordered al-Ḥasan and Yaḥyā ibn Yaʿmar to do it. Immediately after that, he wrote a book in Wāsiṭ about the variant readings of the Qur'ān, gathering together the differences among the people in cases where the writing of the text was the same but the pronunciation varied. The people continued to follow that text for a long time until Ibn Mujāhiḍ [d. 324/936] wrote his book about the variant readings.

    5.1. Al-Zubayrī, in *Kitāb al-ṭabaqāt*, attributes to al-Mubarrad the report that the first person to provide the codex with diacritical markings was Abū 'l-Aswad al-Du'alī. He also mentions that Ibn Sīrīn had a codex which had diacritical markings from Yaḥyā ibn Yaʿmar.
    5.2. Abū 'l-Faraj mentioned that Ziyād ibn Abī Sufyān ordered Abu 'l-Aswad to provide the diacritical markings to the codex.
    5.3. Al-Jāḥiẓ mentioned, in *Kitāb al-anṣār*, that Naṣr ibn ʿĀṣim was the first to provide diacritical markers in the codex and that he was thus called Naṣr al-Ḥurūf ('The helper with the letters').

6. As for the placement of the markers for every ten verses in the codex, it has come to my attention that in some books of history it is said that the ʿAbbasid caliph al-Ma'mūn ordered that done, but it is also said that al-Ḥajjāj did it.

    6.1. Abu ʿAmr al-Misrāfī mentioned, on the authority of Qatāda, that he said that they began with the collected text. They then provided diacritical markings. Next, they numbered every five verses, and then they numbered every ten verses. This was a new development.

4.5 Al-Suyūṭī on the assassination of ʿUthmān

A prolific polymath, Jalāl al-Dīn al-Suyūṭī (849/1445–911/1505) may well be considered to be an author right on the chronological edge of the historical period of classical Islam. Certainly, his period represents an era of consolidation and careful definition of the boundaries of Islam, as the life work of al-Suyūṭī himself suggests. In his attempt to encapsulate almost every aspect of Islamic learning, al-Suyūṭī proliferated works (some five hundred in total, the most attributed to any author in the Islamic world), often re-using the same material in slightly altered frameworks in order to address different concerns. Born and resident for most of his life in Cairo, he was also very active as a jurist in providing researched *fatwā*s to those who sought his legal opinion.

Al-Suyūṭī's *Ta'rīkh al-khulafā'*, 'History of the caliphs', provides, as do many of his other works, extracts from a wide variety of sources, brought together into one cohesive, authoritative account. Given this, it is possible to view him as being unoriginal and even a plagiarist, but in this act of compiling, the strong editorial hand that is being employed in making decisions about what to include and what to exclude must still be noted. The very attempt to distil and encapsulate history reveals something of an era, its concerns and its goals. But al-Suyūṭī's work may also be read for its value in providing access to earlier sources, perhaps not as reflective of their original author's conception of the task at hand, but as a way of summarizing the known facts of history that can be used to reconstruct an overall narrative. Indeed, al-Suyūṭī expresses this desire to maintain the legacy of the achievements of the past as one of his prime goals, in response to the tendency which he saw in the world around him to gradually lose possession of, or ignore, those treasures. Al-Suyūṭī's *Ta'rīkh al-khulafā'* follows the structure which has informed most later historical pictures of Islamic society: it provides a chronological account of the four 'rightly guided' caliphs, followed by the caliphs of the Umayyad family and then the general ʿAbbāsids, the ʿAbbāsid caliphs of Egypt, the Umayyad caliphs of Spain, the ʿAlawīs, the second Umayyad dynasty in Spain, the Fāṭimids, and two little-known Persian dynasties.

The section translated here, on the assassination of the caliph ʿUthmān, focuses on an event of tremendous significance for Islamic identity and theology, creating the paradigmatic events by which the notion of rightful membership in the community would be discussed. The account may be compared with those found in al-Ṭabarī, *Ta'rīkh al-rusul wa'l-mulūk*, ed. M. J. de Goeje, Leiden 1879–1901, vol. 1, pp. 2980–3025 and R. Stevens Humphreys (trans.), *The history of al-Ṭabarī, volume XV: the crisis of the early caliphate*, Albany NY 1990, pp. 181–223.

Further reading

Martin Hinds, 'The murder of the caliph ʿUthmān,' *International journal of Middle East studies*, 3 (1972), pp. 450–69; reprinted in his *Studies in early Islamic history*, Princeton 1996, pp. 29–55.

Wilferd Madelung, *The succession to Muḥammad: a study of the early caliphate*, Cambridge 1997.

Source text

Al-Suyūṭī, *Ta'rīkh al-khulafā'*, ed. Muḥammad Abū 'l-Faḍl Ibrāhīm, Cairo 1976, pp. 251–8; an antiquated translation of the entire book is available: H. S. Jarrett (trans.), *History of the caliphs*, Calcutta 1881.

1. In the year 35 the murder of ʿUthmān occurred. Al-Zuhrī said that ʿUthmān administered the caliphate for twelve years. For six years he governed and the people did not have any negative feelings towards him for anything. Indeed, he was considered preferable to ʿUmar Ibn al-Khaṭṭāb by the Quraysh since ʿUmar was harsh towards them. While ʿUthmān was their ruler, he was lenient to them and connected with them. However, he became neglectful of their affairs and installed his relatives and people of his house during the last six years. He gave Marwān one-fifth of the revenue from Africa and gave gifts to his relatives and his family from the property of the state. He justified this by saying that it was a gift which God had commanded, saying, 'Indeed, Abū Bakr and ʿUmar neglected what they were required to do. So, I have taken it and divided it among my relatives.' The people did not approve of his action. I took this from Ibn Saʿd.

2. Ibn ʿAsākir states on the authority of al-Zuhrī according to another line of transmission that he said to Saʿīd ibn al-Musayyab, 'Will you please tell me how ʿUthmān was killed. What was his situation with the people? Why did the companions of Muḥammad abandon him?' Ibn al-Musayyab said, '"ʿUthmān was killed unjustly. He who killed him did wrong, but those who abandoned him are to be absolved.' I said, 'How is that?' He said, '"ʿUthmān was despised as a leader by some of the companions because he acted preferentially towards his own tribe. He ruled the people for twelve years and during that time entrusted matters to members of the tribe of Umayya who were not companions of the messenger of God. Things were done by his commanders which were disapproved of by the companions of Muḥammad. ʿUthmān continued to be pleased with them and did not dismiss them. That was in the year 35. During the last six years, ʿUthmān held in high esteem the children of his uncle and appointed them to rule without anyone sharing in the power; he did not command them to fear God. He appointed ʿAbd Allāh ibn Abī Sarḥ governor of Egypt and he remained in that position for two years. The people of Egypt complained about him and were angry with him. Before that there was a disagreement between ʿUthmān and ʿAbd Allāh ibn Masʿūd, Abū Dharr and ʿAmmār ibn Yāsir. Banū Hudhayl and Banū Zuhra felt in their hearts that anger because of the situation of Ibn Masʿūd. Banū Ghafār and their allies who supported Abū Dharr felt anger in their hearts as well. Banū Makhzūm were annoyed with ʿUthmān over the situation of ʿAmmār ibn Yāsir.

   The people of Egypt complained about Ibn Abī Sarḥ. ʿUthmān wrote a letter threatening him in it, but Ibn Abī Sarḥ refused to accept the ruling on what ʿUthmān had forbidden him. He attacked those who came to him from ʿUthmān and the people of Egypt who had complained to ʿUthmān, and he killed them. Then 700 people departed from Egypt on foot and they descended on the mosque in Medina and complained to the companions in the places of prayer about what

Ibn Abī Sarḥ had done to them. Ṭalḥa ibn ʿUbayd Allāh arose and spoke harshly to ʿUthmān, and ʿĀʾisha was sent to him, saying, 'The companions of Muḥammad have drawn near to you and asked you to remove this man and you have refused. This person killed one of them! Seek justice against your governor!' Then ʿAlī ibn Abī Ṭālib went to him and said, 'They are asking you for the life of one man in place of another. They claim it as blood revenge. Remove him from rule over them and decree a settlement between them! The obligation is a duty for him, so you must act justly regarding it.' ʿUthmān replied to them, 'Select a man to rule over you in his place.' And the people indicated Muḥammad ibn Abī Bakr, saying, 'Place Muḥammad ibn Abī Bakr over us!' So he decreed his obligation as governor and appointed him. A number of the emigrants (*muhājirūn*) and the helpers (*anṣār*) went out with them to see what would happen between the people of Egypt and Ibn Abī Sarḥ.

Muḥammad ibn Abī Bakr and those who were with him went out. After three days of travel away from Medina, they saw a black slave on a camel galloping quickly as if he was seeking something or being sought. Those accompanying Muḥammad said to him, 'What is your story and your status? It is as if you flee or seek!' He said to them, 'I am the slave of the commander of the faithful (ʿUthmān) and he has sent me to the governor of Egypt.' A man said to him, 'This is the governor of Egypt!' He said, 'This person is not the one I want.' Muḥammad ibn Abī Bakr was informed about him, and he sent someone after him. He caught the slave and brought him to Muḥammad. Muḥammad said, 'Slave, who are you?' He repeated himself, saying, 'I am the slave of the commander of the faithful,' and then another time said, 'I am the slave of Marwān.' Finally someone recognized him as belonging to ʿUthmān. Muḥammad said to him, 'To whom have you been sent out?' He said, 'To the governor of Egypt.' He said, 'With what?' He replied, 'A letter.' 'Do you have the letter with you?' Muḥammad asked. 'No,' he said. They searched him but did not find the letter but they did find a ewer which contained something crushed. They shook it so as to move it and get it out, but it did not come out. So they broke the ewer and found in it a letter from ʿUthmān to Ibn Abī Sarḥ. Muḥammad gathered those who were with him from the emigrants and the helpers and others. He opened the letter in their presence, and it read, 'When Muḥammad and so-and-so and so-and-so reach you, set a plan to murder them. Declare his appointment as governor nullified, and continue your governorship until my advice reaches you. Detain in prison those who have come to me complaining about you. My advice about that will reach you, if God wills.'

When they read the letter they were afraid and confused and they returned to Medina. Muḥammad sealed the letter with the seal of the party which was with him and gave the letter to a certain man among them and they returned to Medina. There they gathered Ṭalḥa, al-Zubayr, ʿAlī and Saʿd and other companions of Muḥammad. They opened the letter in their presence and informed them of the story of the slave. They read the letter to them. Not a soul among the people of Medina was without anger at ʿUthmān and it served to increase the anger of those who were already enraged at the situation of Ibn Masʿūd, Abū Dharr and ʿAmmār ibn Yāsir. The companions of Muḥammad returned to their homes and all of them were saddened by what they had read in the letter. So, in the year 35, the people besieged ʿUthmān, and Muḥammad ibn Abī Bakr, aligned with Banū Tayyim and others, moved against him. When ʿAli saw that, he sent for Ṭalḥa, al-Zubayr, Saʿd and ʿAmmār and the party of the companions, all of whom had been at the battle of Badr. He then went to ʿUthmān, taking with him the letter, the slave and the camel, and said to him, 'Is this your slave?' He replied, 'Yes.' ʿAlī said, 'Is this your camel?' He replied, 'Yes.' ʿAlī said, 'So you wrote this letter?' ʿUthmān replied, 'No,' and he swore by God that he did not write this letter, saying, 'I did not command that it be written, and I have no knowledge of it.' So ʿAli said to him, 'So, is this your seal?' He said, 'Yes.' ʿAlī replied, 'Then how could your slave leave with your camel and this letter which has your seal on it, without you knowing of it?' But ʿUthmān swore to God saying, 'I did not write this letter, I did not command it written, and I did not send this slave to Egypt.'

As for the writing in the letter, they knew it was the handwriting of Marwān, but they were suspicious of ʿUthmān. They asked him to give Marwān over to them but he refused even though Marwān was there with him. ʿAlī and his companions departed from him angrily and still suspected his involvement. They knew that ʿUthmān would not swear on his faith falsely, although one group said, "ʿUthmān will not be forgiven in our hearts unless he gives over Marwān to us so that we may question him, learn of his involvement with the letter and how he commanded the killing of one of the companions of Muḥammad without just cause! But if it was ʿUthmān who wrote the letter, we will depose him; if Marwān wrote it from the dictation of ʿUthmān, we will see what to do with Marwān.' They then waited in their houses. ʿUthmān declined to release Marwān to them, fearing that he would be killed. The people besieged ʿUthmān and prevented him from obtaining water. He looked down on the people from above and said, 'Is ʿAlī among you?' They replied, 'No.' He said, 'Is Saʿd there?' They said, 'No.' He was quiet and then said, 'Is there not one of you who will contact ʿAlī so he can provide us with water to drink?'

ʿAlī was informed of this and he sent him three waterskins brimming with water. They nearly did not reach him, a number of the clients of Banū Hāshim and Banū Umayya having been injured on account of them. Finally the water arrived. ʿAlī learned that they wanted to kill ʿUthmān. He said, 'We want Marwān from him but not the murder of ʿUthmān!' So he said to al-Ḥasan and al-Ḥusayn, 'Go with your swords until you come close to the door of ʿUthmān and do not allow anyone to join him.' Al-Zubayr, Ṭalḥa and a number of the companions of the messenger of God sent their sons to prevent the people from attacking ʿUthmān and to ask ʿUthmān to release Marwān. When the people saw that, they shot arrows at the door of ʿUthmān until al-Ḥasan ibn ʿAlī was splattered with blood at the door. An arrow reached Marwān inside the house. Muḥammad ibn Ṭalḥa was splattered with blood and the head of Qanbar, client of ʿAlī, was split open.

Muḥammad ibn Abī Bakr was scared that the Banū Hāshim would be furious at the condition of al-Ḥasan and al-Ḥusayn and that they would provoke a revolt. He took the hands of two men and said to them, 'If the Banū Hāshim come and see the blood on the face of al-Ḥasan, the people will be dispersed from around ʿUthmān and we will not achieve what we want. Come with us and scale the house so that we can kill him without anyone knowing.'

So Muḥammad and his companions scaled the house of a man from the helpers so they could enter upon ʿUthmān without anyone knowing. All who were with ʿUthmān were on top of the houses and he was alone with his wife. Muḥammad said to the two men, 'Stay here! His wife is with him. I will enter first. When I seize him, you two come in and attack him until you have killed him.'

So Muḥammad entered and seized ʿUthmān by his beard. ʿUthmān said to him, 'By God, I wish your father could see you now! He would disapprove of your behaviour with me!' His hand relaxed but the other two men entered and attacked him until he was dead. They escaped via the route they came in. ʿUthmān's wife screamed but her screams were not heard because of the uproar in the house. She screamed again to the people, saying, 'The commander of the believers has been killed!' The people entered and found him murdered. The news reached ʿAlī, Ṭalḥa, al-Zubayr, Saʿd and the others who were in Medina and they fled – their good sense having left them at the shock of the news – until they returned and entered upon ʿUthmān and found him killed. They returned and ʿAlī said to his sons, 'How is it that the commander of the believers was killed while you were at the door?!' He raised his hand and struck al-Ḥasan in the face and he hit al-Ḥusayn in the chest. He scolded Muḥammad ibn Ṭalḥa and ʿAbd Allāh ibn al-Zubayr.

He went out very angry and returned home. The people hurried towards him saying, 'We swear allegiance to you, so stretch out your hand to us, for it is essential that we have a commander.' ʿAlī said, 'That is not up to you. That is up to the people of Badr, for whoever the people of Badr are satisfied with is the one who should be caliph.'

Everyone of the people of Badr without exception came to ʿAlī and said to him, 'We do not know of anyone more entitled to it than you. Stretch out your hand and we will pay homage to you.' They swore allegiance to him, and Marwān and his son fled. ʿAlī then came to the wife of ʿUthmān and said to her, 'Who killed ʿUthmān?' She said, 'I don't know. Two men entered upon him whom I did not know. Muḥammad ibn Abī Bakr was with them.' She informed ʿAlī and the people of what Muḥammad had done and ʿAlī called Muḥammad and asked him about what ʿUthmān's wife had alleged. Muḥammad said, 'She is not lying. By God, I entered upon him and I wanted to kill him, but he made me remember my father and I turned away from him, repenting to God. By God, I did not kill him.' ʿUthmān's wife said, 'He is being truthful but he did allow the other two to enter.'

4.6 Al-Yaʿqūbī and al-Muqaddasī on building the Dome of the Rock

Aḥmad ibn Abī Yaʿqūb al-Yaʿqūbī (d. 284/897) wrote one of the earliest Arabic universal histories. Starting with creation and continuing as far as his own time (ending in 259/872), the work, simply called *Taʾrīkh*, 'History', was written in Khurasan, in the Muslim east. Concise and clearly reflecting his own moderate Shīʿī views, the book has a focus on pre-Islamic history and the prophets as well as cultural history in general. Following a chronological framework, he includes information about many groups of people outside the central Islamic world (including those in India, China and Ethiopia), reflecting the way in which the various cultures were becoming part of the Muslim empire. The framework follows the rule of the caliphs but also gives prominence to the activities of the Shīʿī Imāms.

Shams al-Dīn Abū ʿAbd Allāh Muḥammad ibn Aḥmad al-Muqaddasī wrote *Aḥsān al-Taqāsīm fī maʿrifat al-aqālīm* ('The best divisions for knowledge of the regions') in 375/985. This provides some of the earliest records of Jerusalem, the author having been born there in the decade of 330/941. Al-Muqaddasī travelled widely, pursuing his interest in geography which becomes manifested in this book. He notes physical features, economic conditions, and the social and religious make-up of the inhabitants of each of the areas he details. He shows a special interest in the aesthetic qualities of architecture.

Guy Le Strange (*Palestine under the Moslems,* London 1890, pp. 116–18) drew attention to these texts in trying to contextualize the construction of the Dome of the Rock in Jerusalem. That topic has attracted extensive scholarly attention, involving a close reading of every available text which might provide some insight into the matter. The examination of these texts, therefore, takes one straight to the heart of the efforts to reconstruct history from sources which themselves come from several centuries after the events they narrate. The accounts given in each of these sources clearly reflect the interests and perspective of their respective writers; all such accounts must be put into the context of a broader picture of the rise of Islam for them to make sense fully.

Further reading

A. A. Duri, *The rise of historical writing among the Arabs*, Princeton 1983, pp. 64–7; on al-Yaʿqūbī.

Raya Shani, 'The iconography of the Dome of the Rock,' *Jerusalem studies in Arabic and Islam*, 23 (1999), pp. 158–207; contains a full bibliography of the scholarly discussion on the building of the Dome of the Rock.

Source texts

Al-Yaʿqūbī, *Taʾrīkh*, ed. M. T. Houtsma, Leiden 1883, vol. 2, p. 11.

Al-Muqaddasī, *Aḥsān al-taqāsīm fī maʿrifat al-aqālīm,* ed. M. J. de Goeje, Leiden 1906, p. 159; the entire work is translated as al-Muqaddasī, *The best divisions for knowledge of the regions*, trans. Basil Anthony Collins, Reading 1994.

I Al-Yaʿqūbī

Then ʿAbd al-Malik forbade the people of Syria from going to Mecca on pilgrimage. The reason for this was that ʿAbd Allāh ibn al-Zubayr used to attack them during the pilgrimage and force them to pay him allegiance. ʿAbd al-Malik knew of this and forbade the people to journey to Mecca. The people were disturbed by this and said, 'How can you forbid us to make the pilgrimage to God's house, when it is a commandment of God that we should do so?' The caliph answered them saying, 'Have you not heard that Ibn Shihāb al-Zuhrī reported that the messenger of God had said, "People should journey only to three mosques: the holy mosque in Mecca, my mosque in Medina, and the mosque of the sacred city, Jerusalem." So, Jerusalem is now appointed for pilgrimage instead of the holy mosque in Mecca. This rock, upon which the messenger of God is reported to have set his foot when he ascended to heaven, will serve in place of the Kaʿba for you.' Then ʿAbd al-Malik built a dome above the rock and hung curtains of brocade around it and instituted doorkeepers for it. People began circumambulating the rock just as they had walked around the Kaʿba. The practice continued throughout the days of the Umayyads.

II Al-Muqaddasī

One day, I [al-Muqaddasī] was speaking to my father's brother. 'Uncle, surely it was inappropriate for the caliph al-Walīd to spend so much of the wealth of the Muslims on the mosque in Damascus! If he had spent the money on roads or caravanserais or in the restoration of fortresses, it would have been more fitting and more excellent of him.' My uncle replied to me, 'My little son, you do not understand! Al-Walīd was right and he undertook a worthy project. He saw that Syria had been occupied for a long time by the Christians, and he noticed the beautiful churches that still belonged to them, so fair and so renowned for their splendour, especially the Church of the Holy Sepulchre at Jerusalem and the churches of Lydda and Edessa. So he built a mosque for the Muslims that would divert them from looking at these Christian buildings, one that would be unique and a wonder to the world. In a like manner, is it not apparent how the caliph ʿAbd al-Malik, seeing the greatness and magnificence of the Church of the Holy Sepulchre, was afraid that it would dazzle the Muslims and so erected the dome above the rock which is now seen there?'

4.7 ʿUmar II and the 'protected people'

Legal texts also function as historical documents for historians. The following text is a generic treaty with Christians, setting out a common set of restrictions to be placed upon non-Muslim communities living in the Islamic context. As such, it displays the processes which lay behind the assimilation and integration of various groups to create Islamic society. The text below is a version of one which is widely known as the 'Covenant of ʿUmar'. That designation may simply be a name which came to be applied to documents such as this one as a result of juristic attempts to consolidate various legal decisions regarding the *dhimmī* communities.

This text comes from al-Shāfiʿī, *Kitāb al-umm*, a work which is itself a composite document, representing the early tradition of the Shāfiʿī legal school with uncertain direct connection to al-Shāfiʿī himself. The document suggests that it has been constructed from several layers, given the differences in structure in various places. Other versions of the pact which may be compared with the one presented below are readily available. Several examples are available on the Web, for example in the Medieval Sourcebook ('Pact of Umar, 7th century?') and the Jewish History Sourcebook ('Islam and the Jews: the pact of Umar, 9th century CE'). Both are notable, in contrast to the one translated here, for being expressed in the voice of the Christians.

Further reading

Norman Calder, *Studies in early Muslim jurisprudence*, Oxford 1993, chapter 4; on al-Shāfiʿī's *Kitāb al-umm*.

Mark R. Cohen, 'What was the pact of ʿUmar? A literary-historical study,' *Jerusalem studies in Arabic and Islam*, 23 (1999), pp. 100–57.

R. Stephen Humphreys, *Islamic history: a framework for inquiry*, revised edition, Princeton 1991, chapter 11.

A. S. Tritton, *The caliphs and their non-Muslim subjects: a critical study of the covenant of ʿUmar*, London 1970; this version of the pact is translated on pp. 12–16, a rendering to which this translation is indebted.

Source text

Al-Shāfiʿī, *Kitāb al-umm*, ed. M. al-Najjār, Beirut n.d., vol. 4, pp. 197–8.

1. When the leader wishes to write a peace treaty according to the rules of *jizya*, he should write as follows:

2. This treaty has been written by ʿAbd Allāh So-and-so, commander of the faithful, on the second night of Rabīʿ I in such-and-such a year with the Christian So-and-so, son of So-and-so, from the tribe of such-and-such, inhabitants in such-and-such land, and the Christians dwelling in such-and-such land.

3. You have asked me to establish peace with you and the Christian people of such-and-such land and to covenant with you and them as has been covenanted with the protected communities, setting out what shall be given to me, and to stipulate the conditions on both sides involving you and them. So I reply to you that I covenant with you and them that providing security is incumbent upon me and all Muslims, as long as you and they keep the conditions we impose upon you.

4. Those conditions are that you shall be under Muslim law and no other, being under the conditions it allows you, and you will not resist anything which we consider that you are required to do by it.

4.1. If any of you says of Muḥammad or God's book or His religion something which is inappropriate for him to say, the protection of God, the commander of the faithful and all Muslims is removed from him; the conditions under which security was given will be annulled and the commander of the faithful will put that person's property and life outside the protection of the law, like the property and lives of enemies.

4.2. If one of you commits adultery with or marries a Muslim woman, or robs a Muslim on the highway, or turns a Muslim away from his religion, or helps their enemies as a soldier or as a guide to Muslim weaknesses, or shelters their spies, he has broken this agreement, and his life and property are outside the protection of the law. Whoever does harm in other ways than this to the goods or honour of a Muslim (or to those under his protection who have been kept from the status of unbeliever by covenant or surety) shall be punished. We shall examine your every dealing between yourself and Muslims, and if you have had a part in anything that is unlawful for a Muslim, we shall undo it and punish you for it. If you have sold to a Muslim any forbidden thing, such as wine, pigs, blood from carrion or anything else, we shall annul the sale, take the price from you (if you have received it) or withhold it from you (if it is still pending); we shall pour it out if it is wine or blood, and we shall burn it if it is carrion. If the Muslim wishes it to be destroyed, we shall do nothing to him, but we shall punish you. You will not give a Muslim any forbidden thing to eat or drink, and you will not allow him to marry in the presence of your witnesses, nor to partake in a marriage we consider illegal. We shall not scrutinize nor inquire into a contract between you and any other unbeliever. If either party wishes to annul the contract, and brings a request to us, if it should be annulled in our opinion, then we shall annul it; if it is legal, we shall allow it. But if the object has been taken and lost, we shall not restore it, for a sale between unbelievers has been finished. If you or any other unbeliever asks for judgment, we shall give it according to Muslim law; if we are not approached, we shall not interfere between you.

4.3. If you kill accidentally a Muslim or an ally, Christian or not, then the relatives of the homicide culprit shall pay blood money, as it is among Muslims. For you, the liable relatives are those on the father's side. If a homicide culprit has no relatives, then his estate must pay. A murderer shall be killed unless the heirs wish to take blood money, which shall be paid at once. Whoever is a thief among you, if his victim complains, shall have his hand cut off, if this is the punishment, and shall pay a fine. The slanderer shall be punished if that is the appropriate punishment; but if the punishment is not stipulated, then he shall be punished according to Muslim law in accordance with what is customary among you depending on what was and was not heard of the slander.

4.4. You shall not display the cross nor parade your idolatry in any Muslim town, nor shall you build a church or place of assembly for your prayers, nor sound your bells. You will not use your idolatrous language about Jesus, son of Mary, or anyone else to any Muslim. You shall wear your sash outside of all your clothing, cloaks and anything else, so that it is not hidden. You shall use your saddles and your manner of riding, and you shall make your head coverings different from those of the Muslims by putting a mark on them. You shall not take the high side of the road nor the chief seats in assemblies if it puts you over Muslims.

4.5. For every free adult male of sound mind, there will be on his head a poll-tax of one dinar of full weight, payable at new year. He will not leave his land until he has paid the tax, nor will he appoint as a substitute someone who pays no *jizya* until the beginning of the year. A poor man is liable for his *jizya* until it is paid; poverty does not cancel any of your obligations nor annul the protection which is due to you. However, when you do have something, we shall take it. The *jizya* is the only burden on your property as long as you stay in your land or travel in Muslim lands (unless you are there as a merchant). You may not enter Mecca under any conditions. If you travel with merchandise, you must pay one-tenth of all your merchandise to the Muslims. You may go where you like in Muslim lands, except to Mecca, and you may stay in any Muslim land you like except the Hijaz, where you may only stay for three days and then you must depart.

4.6. These terms are binding on him who has hair under his clothes, is adult, or is fifteen years old before this, if he agrees to them; if he does not accept them, then no treaty exists with him. No *jizya* is payable by your young sons, those who have not reached puberty, those who have lost their minds, and slaves. If an insane person becomes sane, a boy grows up, a slave is set free and follows your religion, then he will pay the *jizya*.

5. These terms are binding on you and those who accept them; we have no treaty with those who reject them. We will protect you and your property which we deem lawful against anyone, Muslim or not, who tries to wrong you, just as we protect ourselves and our own property. Our decisions about it will be the same as those about our own property and ourselves. Our protection does not extend to forbidden things, like blood, carrion, wine and pigs, but we will not interfere with them unless you display them in Muslim towns. If a Muslim or someone else buys them, we will not force him to pay, for they are forbidden and have no price; but we will not let him pester you for them, and if he does it again, we will punish him, but we will not force him to pay.

6. You must fulfil all the conditions we have imposed on you. You must not attack a Muslim nor help their enemies by word or deed. The treaty of God and His promise and the most complete fulfilment of promise He has imposed on any of

His creatures is in this covenant. You have the treaty of God and His promise and the protection of so-and-so, the commander of the faithful, and of the Muslims to fulfil their obligations towards you. Your sons, when they grow up, will have the same obligations as you. If you alter or change them then, the protection of God, of so-and-so, the commander of the faithful, and of the Muslims is removed from you. For those who are absent yet receive this document and approve of it, these are the terms that are binding on them and on us, if they accept them; if they do not accept, then we do not have a treaty with them.

PART TWO

Elaboration of the tradition

Chapter 5

Qurʾānic interpretation

5.1 Al-Qurṭubī on interpretation of the Qur'ān

Muḥammad ibn Aḥmad Abū 'Abd Allāh al-Anṣārī al-Qurṭubī was a Mālikī jurist born in Spain who seems to have travelled widely and lived a good deal of his life in upper Egypt, where he died in 671/1272. His Qur'ān commentary is his most famous work, and is considered one of the great works in its field. Its scope is enormous but it focuses tightly on the Qur'ān itself, following the text through verse by verse, and celebrating its status in the community. Al-Qurṭubī's commitment to the text is made clear by his emphasis on the merits and responsibilities of those who devote themselves to explicating it. Purity and sincerity are required of those who attempt the task and all hypocrisy must be put aside: devotion to the text means implementing what it says as well. The primary resource which he brings to the text is *ḥadīth*, although he is not so much interested in determining the authenticity of individual reports, but gathers them all together with little attention to the *isnād*. Grammar and stylistics play an important role as well, all being used towards the ultimate aim of extracting as much law as possible from the text in all its variations and permutations.

In the introduction to his commentary, al-Qurṭubī covers a wide selection of topics designed to produce the correct attitude and procedure in the commentator as well as the reader. The topics covered include:

1. the superior qualities (*faḍā'il*) of the Qur'ān;
2. the manner of reading the book of God, in which he discusses the chanting and setting to music of the Qur'ān (which he says are not required);
3. the inward dispositions of men who pursue knowledge of the Qur'ān;
4. the *i'rāb* of the Qur'ān, and the need to read and recite it correctly;
5. the value of commentary and commentators;
6. the respect due for the Qur'ān and its sacred character as an obligatory requirement of the reader and of the 'bearer' of the Qur'ān;

7. his opposition to commentary based on personal point of view (*ra'y*);
8. the interpretation (*tabyīn*) of the Qur'ān through the *sunna* of the prophet;
9. how to study and understand the Qur'ān and the *sunna*;
10. the meaning of the saying of the prophet: 'This Qur'ān has been revealed according to seven letters [or 'readings']; therefore read according to that which is the easiest for you';
11. the unity (*jamʿ*) of the parts of the Qur'ān, providing a precise and concise history of the text as far as the recension of 'Uthmān, with a study of the arrangement (*tartīb*) of the *sūra*s and verses;
12. definitions of the words *sūra, āya, kalima, ḥarf*;
13. the question of whether there are words foreign to the Arabic language in the Qur'ān;
14. the inimitability of the Qur'ān (*iʿjāz al*-Qur'ān), with an examination of ten aspects;
15. reflections on the *istiʿādha* and the *basmala*.

The translation below comes from section seven of al-Qurṭubī's introduction (some repetitive material has been omitted as indicated by the ellipses). The text may be profitably compared with the principles set out in Ibn Taymiyya (d. 728/1327), *Muqaddima fī uṣūl al-tafsīr*, translated by Muhammad 'Abdul Haq Ansari under the title *An introduction to the interpretation of the Qur'ān*, Birmingham 1993.

Further reading

R. Arnaldez, 'Al-Ḳurṭubī, Abū 'Abd Allāh Muḥammad,' in *Encyclopaedia of Islam*, new edition.
Norman Calder, 'Tafsīr from Ṭabarī to Ibn Kathīr: problems in the description of a genre, illustrated with reference to the story of Abraham,' in G. R. Hawting, Abdul-Kader A. Shareef (eds), *Approaches to the Qur'ān*, London 1993, pp. 101–40.

Source text

Al-Qurṭubī, *Al-Jāmiʿ li-aḥkām al-Qur'ān*, Cairo 1967, vol. 1, pp. 31–7.

Chapter: On the warnings relating to interpretation of the Qur'ān by opinion; and on the ranks of the exegetes.

1. It is related from ʿĀ'isha that she said that the messenger of God never used to interpret the book of God except a limited number of verses, as taught to him by Gabriel. Ibn ʿAṭiyya said that the purport of this *ḥadīth* relates to the hidden matters of the Qur'ān, the interpretation of its obscure passages and other things which cannot be ascertained except through God's favour. Amongst these hidden matters are things of which God has provided no knowledge, such as the precise time of the resurrection and other matters susceptible to inquiry on the basis of the Qur'ān's words, for example, the number of blasts on the trumpet [at the final resurrection], or the order of creation of the heavens and the earth.

2. Al-Tirmidhī relates from Ibn ʿAbbās from the prophet that he said, 'Beware of attributing *ḥadīth* to me, save what you know. He who lies about me, deliberately, let him take up his seat in Hell; and he who speaks on the Qur'ān on the basis of opinion, let him take up his seat in Hell.' Al-Tirmidhī also relates from Jundub that the messenger of God said, 'He who speaks on the Qur'ān on the basis of opinion, and is correct, still has erred.' According to al-Tirmidhī, this latter *ḥadīth* is unusual. It is also recorded by Abū Dāwūd, but there has been some criticism of one of its transmitters. Zarīn adds the following [to what Muḥammad said], 'And he who, speaking on the basis of opinion, errs, he is an unbeliever.'

Muḥammad ibn al-Qāsim ibn Bashshār al-Anbārī, the linguist and grammarian, says in his *Kitāb al-radd* that the *ḥadīth* of Ibn ʿAbbās has two explanations. Firstly, one who speaks on difficult parts of the Qur'ān, basing himself on something other than that which is known from the early generations, the companions and the successors, is exposed to God's anger. Secondly – and this is the firmer and the more correct of the two explanations – one who speaks on the Qur'ān, uttering opinions that he knows to be untrue, let him take up his seat in Hell. . . .

2.1. About the *ḥadīth* of Jundub, al-Anbārī said that some of the learned have interpreted this *ḥadīth* on the assumption that 'opinion' here means desire or whim. One who speaks on the Qur'ān, uttering views that accord with his desire – views which he has not derived from the leaders of preceding generations – and is correct, has nevertheless erred. This is because he has passed judgement on the Qur'ān without secure knowledge and has not based himself on the established traditions of those who transmit in this field.

2.2. Ibn ʿAṭiyya says the following concerning this *ḥadīth*. This means that a man asks concerning the significance of some part of God's book; he then plunges into an answer based on opinion without consideration of what the learned have said, and without consideration of the requirements of the scientific disciplines, such as grammar and the principles of interpretation. This *ḥadīth* does not relate to linguists who explain its language, or grammarians who explain its grammar, or scholars who explain its significances, each one basing his view on *ijtihād* founded on the rules of science and debate. One who speaks in this manner is not speaking merely on the basis of opinion.

2.3. I (al-Qurṭubī) agree that this is correct. It is a view that has been chosen by many of the learned. For one who utters whatever strikes his imagination or springs to mind, without sound deduction based on principles, is indeed in error; but one who deduces the meaning of the Qur'ān by relating it to principles that are established and agreed on, he is worthy of praise.

3. One of the learned has said that *tafsīr* is based solely on revelation because of *If you dispute on anything, refer it to God and his prophet* (Q 4/59). This is false. For to deny *tafsīr* of the Qur'ān either must mean to restrict oneself to transmission and revelation, abandoning deduction, or it must mean something else (i.e., the opposite). Now, it is false to claim that one may not talk about the

Qur'ān except on the basis of transmitted knowledge. For the companions read the Qur'ān and were at variance on its interpretation. Clearly it is not the case that all the views they expressed had been heard from the prophet. Indeed the prophet prayed for Ibn ʿAbbās, saying, 'God, grant him learning in religion, grant him knowledge of interpretation.' Now, if interpretation were a transmitted matter like revelation, then what would be the point of this prayer? More will be said on this matter when we discuss *sūrat al-nisā'* (4).

4. Denial of *tafsīr* may be based on two suppositions.

4.1. A man, having an opinion on a matter – an inclination arising out of his nature and his desires – interprets the Qur'ān in accord with this opinion and desire, in order to provide an argument for the correctness of his own views. If he did not have that opinion and desire, that meaning of the Qur'ān would not occur to him.

4.1.1. This type of argument may be adduced by a person fully aware of his actions, such as one who argues, on the basis of certain verses, for the correctness of some heretical innovation, while knowing full well that the intention of the verses is not so.

4.1.2. Or it may be adduced by one who does not know what he is doing. This happens in the case of a polyvalent or uncertain verse when a man's understanding inclines him to the interpretation that agrees with his objectives. In this case, preferring a certain view on the basis of opinion and desire, he has interpreted by opinion; it is mere opinion that has made him prefer that interpretation. . . .

4.1.3. Or, in a third case, one may have a valid objective and, seeking evidence for it in the Qur'ān, one may discover proofs in a verse that one knows is not intended for that purpose. This is like the person who, summoning his listeners to struggle with the obdurate heart, cites, *Go to Pharaoh for he has sinned* (Q 20/24), and points to his heart at the same time. He thereby implies that the heart is meant by 'Pharaoh'. This type of argument is practised by many preachers for valid ends, as an adornment of speech or an incitement to the listener; but it is forbidden, being an analogical use of language which is illegitimate. Such practices are also used by the Bāṭiniyya for invalid ends, in order to delude the people and induce them into their false beliefs in matters which they know for sure are not intended by the Qur'ānic text.

4.2. Some rush into the interpretation of the Qur'ān, relying on a plain reading of the Arabic language and ignoring the help provided by revelation and tradition in respect to rare words, or obscure and difficult expressions, or such rhetorical devices as abbreviation, omission, ellipsis and transposition. One who, not having mastered the main tradition of *tafsīr*, hastens to deduce meanings based merely on his understanding of the Arabic language will make many mistakes. Such a one is counted amongst the number of those who interpret the Qur'ān by opinion. Revelation and tradition are indispensable within the discipline of *tafsīr*, firstly in order to avoid the occasions of error, and subsequently for the broadening of under-

> standing and deductive capacity. Many are the rare words that cannot be understood except through revelation. There is no hope of attaining the inner meaning without mastering the main tradition (of *tafsīr*). . . .

Except in these two aspects, the denial of *tafsīr* is not accepted.

5. Ibn ʿAṭiyya said that a group of the pious ancestors, such as Saʿīd ibn al-Musayyib, ʿĀmir al-Shaʿbī and others, used to so revere the practice of exegesis that they abstained from it, out of fear and caution, in spite of their understanding and their status. Al-Anbārī said that certain leaders of the past generations used to abstain from exegesis of difficult passages in the Qurʾān. Some considered that their interpretation might not coincide with God's intention and so they desisted from all utterance in the field. Others feared that they might become an *imām* – a model to be followed in matters of exegesis; they feared that their techniques might be built on and their methodology adopted. In such a case, a later thinker, interpreting a phrase on the basis of opinion, and erring in his interpretation, might say, 'My *imām* in interpreting the Qurʾān by opinion is so-and-so.' Ibn Abī Malīka said that Abū Bakr al-Ṣiddīq, when asked about the interpretation of a word in the Qurʾān, said, 'What sky will shelter me and what earth will support me and where shall I flee and how shall I manage, if I speak on a single word of the Qurʾān and deviate from what God intended?'

5.1. Ibn ʿAṭiyya also said that there was a further group amongst the early generations, large in number, who used to practise *tafsīr* and they commended this practice to the Muslims. The leader of the exegetes, their prop, was ʿAlī ibn Abī Ṭālib, who was followed by ʿAbd Allāh ibn ʿAbbās. The latter devoted himself to this activity and perfected it. He was followed by certain scholars such as Mujāhid, Saʿīd ibn Jubayr and others. In fact, more has been preserved from him than from ʿAlī. Ibn ʿAbbās said, 'Whatever I have adopted as *tafsīr* of the Qurʾān, I have taken from ʿAlī.' And ʿAlī used to praise Ibn ʿAbbās's *tafsīr* and urge that he be listened to. About Ibn ʿAbbās, ʿAlī used to say, 'What a fine interpreter of the Qurʾān Ibn ʿAbbās is.' ʿAlī commended him thus: 'It is as if Ibn ʿAbbās looks into the invisible world through only a thin veil.' Ibn ʿAbbās was followed by ʿAbd Allāh ibn Masʿūd, Ubayy ibn Kaʿb, Zayd ibn Thābit and ʿAbd Allāh ibn ʿAmr ibn al-ʿĀṣ. All that is taken from the companions is a good to be accepted, because they witnessed revelation and it was revealed in their language. . . .

5.2. Ibn ʿAṭiyya further said that among the outstanding exegetes in the generation of the Successors were al-Ḥasan al-Baṣrī, Mujāhid, Saʿīd ibn Jubayr and ʿAlqama. . . . They were followed by ʿIkrima and al-Ḍaḥḥāk; the latter did not meet Ibn ʿAbbās but was instructed by Ibn Jubayr. As to al-Suddī and Abū Ṣāliḥ, they were criticized by ʿĀmir al-Shaʿbī because he considered them to be deficient in reasoning. Yaḥyā ibn Māʾin said that al-Kalbī is nothing. . . . And Ḥabīb ibn Abī Thābit said of Abū Ṣāliḥ, 'We used to call him (in Persian) the liar.' . . .

5.3. Subsequently, the upright of every succeeding generation were bearers of *tafsīr*, as is reflected in the words of the prophet, 'The upright of every generation will bear this knowledge, preserving it from the distortions of extremists, from the partisanship of false believers, and from the interpretations of the ignorant.' This *ḥadīth* is found in Abū ʿAmr and others. According to al-Khaṭīb al-Baghdādī, this *ḥadīth* shows the messenger of God bearing witness that they are the guides of this religion and the *imāms* of all Muslims because they preserve the *sharīʿa* from distortion and partisanship, and they refute the interpretations of the ignorant. It is incumbent to turn to them and to rely on them.

5.4. Ibn ʿAṭiyya said that people composed books within the discipline, including people such as ʿAbd al-Razzāq, al-Mufaḍḍal, ʿAlī ibn Abī Ṭalḥa, al-Bukhārī and others. Later Muḥammad ibn Jarīr al-Ṭabarī gathered the scattered segments of *tafsīr*, explained what was difficult and dealt with *isnād*s. Amongst the outstanding recent authorities are Abū Isḥāq al-Zajjāj and Abū ʿAlī al-Fārisī. As to Abū Bakr al-Naqqāsh and Abū Jaʿfar al-Naḥḥās, they have frequently had to be rectified; and Makkī ibn Abī Ṭālib followed their practices. Abū 'l-ʿAbbās al-Mahdawī perfected the art of composition. But every one of them is a *mujtahid*, a recipient of divine reward for his intellectual effort [i.e., even if he is not demonstrably and securely correct in his views]. May God have mercy on them and preserve their reputations.

5.2 Al-Qummī on Shīʿī alternative readings in the Qurʾān

ʿAlī ibn Ibrāhīm al-Qummī is one of the most important of the early Shīʿī Qurʾān commentators. Little is known of the person himself; he was a legal scholar and the author of perhaps a dozen books. His dates are uncertain but contextually it is possible to determine that he died early in the fourth/tenth century, sometime after 307/919. Al-Qummī's Qurʾān commentary is his only extant book, although the text as it exists today has been subject to editorial intrusion and reformulation by later generations. Al-Qummī is fully involved in his exegetical task; he expresses his opinion as to the validity of the material he provides and he emphasizes the Shīʿī doctrinal elements, such as devotion to the family of the prophet and the role of the Imāms in interpreting the Qurʾān. The commentary extends beyond verses of specifically Shīʿī interest which suggests that we witness, in reading this text, the emergence of a more developed and separate Shīʿī identity.

The section translated here comes from the introduction to the text dealing with a contentious issue which has provided, during certain historical eras, one of the marking points of Shīʿī versus Sunnī identity. The introduction to the *tafsīr* provides what is a common set of topics and terminology that are summarized in many such works: abrogated and abrogating verses, the distinction between the 'clear' and the 'ambiguous' verses, those verses which are of 'general' versus 'specific' application. As a part of this preamble, the section concerning verses 'which are different from what was revealed' provides a specifically Shīʿī aspect to the material. The section does not fully summarize all the relevant examples of what have become known as the 'alterations' to the text from the Shīʿī perspective because elsewhere throughout his work, al-Qummī points out other places where words have been 'removed' from the Qurʾānic text as well as where words have been 'substituted'. Such examinations and attitudes towards the text mark Shīʿī identity at this particular point in its history; later Shīʿī exegetes, especially in the fifth/tenth and sixth/eleventh centuries, played down this sort of approach to the Qurʾānic text and did not wish to differentiate themselves from the majority definition of Islam. This supported a generalized Muslim notion of a unified text of the Qurʾān. The desire of the Shīʿa for acceptance by the broader Sunnī community in these later centuries seems to have influenced significantly the de-emphasizing of the doctrine suggested in this passage from al-Qummī.

Further reading

Meir M. Bar-Asher, *Scripture and exegesis in early Imāmī Shiism*, Leiden 1999.

—— 'Variant readings and additions of the Imāmī-šīʿa to the Quran', *Israel Oriental studies*, 13 (1993), pp. 39–74.

Etan Kohlberg, 'Some notes on the Imāmite attitude to the Qurʾān,' in S. M. Stern, A. Hourani, V. Brown (eds), *Islamic philosophy and the classical tradition. Essays presented by his friends and pupils to Richard Walzer on his seventieth birthday*, Oxford 1972, pp. 209–24.

Source text

Al-Qummī, *Tafsīr al-Qummī*, Beirut 1991, vol. 1, pp. 22–3.

1. Among what is in the Qur'ān which is different from what was revealed is His saying, *You are the best community* [umma] *which has emerged from humanity. You command good and forbid evil and believe in God* (Q 3/110). Abū ʿAbd Allāh [Jaʿfar al-Ṣādiq] said to someone who recited *the best community*, 'Have the Commander of the Believers, and al-Ḥasan and al-Ḥusayn, the sons of ʿAlī, been killed?' He was then asked, 'How was it revealed, descendant of the messenger of God?' He said, 'It was revealed as *You are the best of Imāms* [a'imma] *who have emerged from humanity*. Do you not see that God praised them at the end of the verse (in saying), *You command good and forbid evil and believe in God*?

2. Likewise is the case of a verse which was read to Abū ʿAbd Allāh, *Those who say, 'Our Lord, grant us from our wives and our offspring comfort in our eyes and make us a model* [imām] *to the God-fearing'* (Q 25/74). ʿAbū ʿAbd Allāh said, 'They were asking God something important, that He make them an *imām* from the God-fearing.' He was asked, 'Descendant of the messenger of God, how was the verse revealed?' He said, 'It was revealed as *Those who say, 'Our Lord grant us from our wives and our descendants comfort in our eyes and give to us a model* (imām) *from among the God-fearing*.'

3. Likewise, regarding His saying, *He has attendant angels before him and behind him, watching over him by God's command* (Q 13/11), Abū ʿAbd Allāh said, 'How can one watch over something by God's command and how can the attendant angels be before him?' He was asked, 'How is that, descendant of the messenger of God?' He replied, 'It was revealed as *He has attendant angels behind him and a guardian before him, watching over him by God's command*. There are many more examples of this.

4. Among the passages in which words have been corrupted [by omitting words which are here inserted] is God's saying, *But God bears witness to that which He sends down to you*, concerning ʿAlī. *He has sent it down with His knowledge and the angels bear witness also* (Q 4/166). Another instance is His saying, *O messenger, deliver what has been sent down to you from your Lord*, regarding ʿAlī, *for if you do not, you will not have delivered His message* (Q 5/67). Another instance is His saying, *Indeed the unbelievers who have done wrong* to the family of Muḥammad in their rights, *God will not be forgiving to them* (Q 4/168). Another instance is His saying, *Those who do wrong* to the family of Muḥammad in their rights, *will surely know by what overturning they will be overturned* (Q 26/227). Another instance is His saying, *If only you could see those who do wrong* to the family of Muḥammad in their rights, *in the agonies of death* (Q 6/93). There are many other instances of this which we will mention in their place in this commentary.

5.3 Muqātil ibn Sulaymān on *sūrat al-bayyina* (98)

Muqātil ibn Sulaymān, traditionist and commentator on the Qur'ān, was born in Balkh and lived in Marw, Baghdad and Basra, where he died in 150/767 at an old age according to some biographers. He is also said to have taught in Mecca, Damascus and Beirut. Muqātil's prestige as a traditionist is low; he is reproached for not being accurate in his use of the *isnād*. His exegesis enjoys even less respect among his critics, who cite his deceptiveness and his professing to know everything as less than worthy characteristics. Stories are frequently told of ludicrous questions which were put to him about the most impossible things, to which he either gave fantastic answers or could make no reply. His elaborations of biblical elements in the Qur'ān and his tracing every allusion back to the Jews and the Christians led to his disrepute in later centuries, and resulted in his exegetical work being cited only infrequently by later authors. The major fourth-/tenth-century exegete al-Ṭabarī, for example, makes no use of the work. Muqātil is also associated with sectarian movements and deviant theology (e.g., extreme anthropomorphism). These attributions are likely further condemnations of his authority and may not have any historical basis. Certainly, there is little or no evidence for any of these stances in his extant works.

Three texts of Qur'ānic interpretation ascribed to Muqātil still exist and have been published; they are of great significance because of their likely (although not undisputed) early date. *Tafsīr Muqātil ibn Sulaymān* provides an interpretation of the entire text of the Qur'ān; the work is characterized by its desire to elaborate as fully as possible all the scriptural narrative elements with very little emphasis on issues of text, grammar or the like. It is likely that it presents versions of the stories told by the early storytellers. *Kitāb tafsīr khams mi'at āya min al-Qur'ān al-karīm* organizes Qur'ānic verses under legal topics and provides some basic exegesis of them; the content of the book suggests a direct relationship to the larger *Tafsīr*. *Al-Ashbāh wa'l-naẓā'ir fī'l-Qur'ān al-karīm* studies Qur'ānic vocabulary by providing the number of meanings or aspects (*ashbāh*) of each word, and a gloss for each meaning, followed by the provision of parallel passages, or analogues, in which the word is used in that sense (*naẓā'ir*).

Notable within the *tafsīr* of Muqātil are the techniques of gloss and completion which are incorporated in a manner that conveys the continuous and consistent narrative of the Qur'ānic text as Muqātil saw it. Some editorial interference in the form of interruptions to the narrative are to be noted at the end of this section, and perhaps also at the beginning, indicating most probably the editing which the text went through in subsequent generations.

Further reading

Claude Gilliot, 'Muqātil, grand exégète, traditionniste et théologien maudit,' *Journal asiatique*, 279 (1991), pp. 39–92.

C. M. H. Versteegh, *Arabic grammar and Qur'ānic exegesis in early Islam*, Leiden 1993.

Kees Versteegh, 'Grammar and exegesis: the origins of Kufan grammar and the *Tafsīr Muqātil*,' *Der Islam*, 67 (1990), pp. 206–42.

John Wansbrough, *Quranic studies: sources and methods of scriptural interpretation*, Oxford 1977, part 4.

Source text

Muqātil ibn Sulaymān, *Tafsīr Muqātil ibn Sulaymān*, ed. A. M. Shiḥāta, Cairo 1979–88, vol. 4, pp. 779–81.

1. His saying, *The unbelievers of the people of the book*, that is, the Jews and the Christians; *and the idolaters,* that is, the idolaters among the Arabs; *would not leave off,* that is, they would not renounce disbelief and idolatry. In that regard the people of the book said, 'When will he whom we find in our book be sent?' The Arabs said, 'If only we knew of a mention of him by our ancestors, then we would be sincere slaves of God.' So, *The unbelievers of the people of the book*, that is, the Jews and the Christians; *and the idolaters*, that is, the idolaters among the Arabs; *would not leave off*, that is, they would not finish with disbelief and idolatry. *Until the clear sign comes to them*, Muḥammad. So he explained their error and idolatry to them. Then God informed (them) about the prophet by saying, *a messenger from God, reading aloud pages purified*, that is, he will recite purified pages, that is, a book, because its pages, which gather many qualities of every kind, are purified from disbelief and idolatry. So, He is saying he will recite a book in which there is neither disbelief nor idolatry. Everything in it is a decree and it is named 'pages'. Then He said, *therein*, that is, in the pages of Muḥammad; *true books*, that is, a book which establishes truth, in which there is no crookedness and no disagreement. It is called 'books' because it contains many diverse matters which God mentioned in the Qur'ān.

2. Then He said, *And those who were given the book did not separate*, that is, the Jews and the Christians in the matter of Muḥammad; *except after the clear sign came to them*, that is, the explanation. God informed us saying that those who disbelieve never ceased agreeing on the truth of Muḥammad until he was sent, because they had his description in their books. When God designated him from the offspring of someone other than Isaac, they disagreed about him. Some of them believed including ʿAbd Allāh ibn Salām and his companions from the people of the Torah, and forty men from the people of the Gospel including Baḥīrā. But the rest of the people of the book told lies about him. So God says, *They were commanded*, He is saying that Muḥammad commanded them; *only to serve God, making the religion His sincerely*, meaning by that belief in one God; *men of true faith*, that is, Muslims not idolaters; *and*, He ordered them *to establish prayer*, the five decreed (daily prayers) *and pay the alms* that are obligatory; *and that is the religion of the true*, that is, the upright community.

3. Then God mentioned the idolaters on the day of resurrection. So He said, *The unbelievers of the people of the book and the idolaters will be in the fire of Gehenna, therein dwelling forever*, He is saying they will remain in it, not dying. Then He said, *Those are the worst of creatures*, that is, the worst of the created beings among the people of the earth.

4. Then He mentioned the abode of those who declare the truth of the prophet by saying, *But those who believe and do righteous deeds, those are the best of*

creatures, that is, the best of the created beings among the people of the earth; *Their recompense*, that is, their reward; *is with their Lord* in the hereafter; *gardens of Eden, underneath which rivers flow, therein dwelling forever and ever*, not dying; *God is well pleased with them*, by (their) pious deeds; *and they are well pleased with Him*, by (their) reward; *that is for him who fears his Lord* in the world.

5. Everything which is created from dust is called *al-bariyya*, 'creatures' [suggesting an etymology that relates the meaning to a root sense of 'dust', *barā*].

5.4 Al-Farrā' on *sūrat al-bayyina* (98)

Abū Zakariyyā Yaḥyā ibn Ziyād al-Farrā' was a prominent grammarian from Kufa who died in 207/822. Author of perhaps a dozen books (most of which are now lost), he distinguished himself as a formative figure in the development of the study of Arab grammar as well as lexicography. His commentary on the Qur'ān, *Ma'ānī al-Qur'ān*, provides a rigorous explanation of the difficult points of grammar in the text. In doing so, al-Farrā' does not explain every verse but only those which need attention. The aim of the work is clearly to establish that grammar is the key to all understanding of the Qur'ān, and that the grammarians are, therefore, the most important of the scholarly élite in Islamic society. Knowledge of correct Arabic (a language which certainly was not al-Farrā''s mother tongue, not that the Qur'ānic form of Arabic was anyone's mother tongue) was seen as a mark of the élite; this was not a concern for the literacy of the masses, but necessary for the right to interpret and convey the meaning of the Qur'ān to the masses. Accusations of incorrect grammar, therefore, became a way of excluding people from power. Although grammar may be used to support theological and legal arguments as well, it can also be used to resolve differences and maintain the unity of the community.

Parts of al-Farrā''s commentary as it exists today indicate that the work is likely to be the product of a student of al-Farrā' who wrote down the master's comments. The passage translated below does not, however, display any editorial intrusions which might make that evident. The citation of poetry to illustrate grammatical and lexical points is noteworthy; the verses cited here became standard pieces of illustration for later generations and are repeated in many texts.

Further reading

Edmund Beck, 'Die dogmatisch religiöse Einstellung des Grammatikers Yaḥyā b. Ziyād al-Farrā',' *Le Muséon*, 64 (1951), pp. 187–202, translated as 'The dogmatic religious stance of the grammarian Yaḥyā ibn Ziyād al-Farrā',' in A. Rippin (ed.), *The Qur'an: formative interpretation*, Aldershot 1999, pp. 137–58.

C. M. H. Versteegh, *Arabic grammar and Qur'ānic exegesis in early Islam*, Leiden 1993.

John Wansbrough, *Quranic studies: sources and methods of scriptural interpretation*, Oxford 1977, part 4.

Source text

Al-Farrā', *Ma'ānī 'l-Qur'ān*, Cairo 1972, vol. 3, pp. 281–2.

Concerning sūra lam yakun:

In the name of God, the All-merciful, the All-compassionate.

1. Concerning the saying of God, *The unbelievers of the people of the book and the idolaters would not leave off until the clear sign comes to them*, He means, the prophet. There is a reading from ʿAbd Allāh [ibn Masʿūd] that reads, 'The idolaters and the people of the book would not leave off.' Interpretation of this verse varies, with some saying (it means), 'They will not leave off renouncing until the clear sign comes to them', meaning the sending of Muḥammad and the Qurʾān. The others say that it means, 'they will not renounce the description of Muḥammad as found in their book', that is, that he is a prophet, until he actually appears. When he appears, they will separate and disagree. Confirming that (interpretation) is the saying of God, *And those who were given the book did not separate except after the clear sign came to them* (Q 98/4).

   1.1. Perhaps this points to a meaning of 'leaving off' in the sense of 'abandon'. It would have to be the 'leaving off' of someone whom you know. If the meaning is in the sense of 'ceasing', it must have a verb following it and it must be attached to a negative particle. One says, 'I did not leave off mentioning you,' meaning, 'I did not cease mentioning you.' For it to have the other meaning, that is of 'abandon', you would say, 'I am leaving you/abandoning you' and 'I left off/abandoned something for something else.' [In the latter sense] there would not be negation nor would it be followed by a verb. The poet Dhū ʾl-Rumma said:

   > Youthful female camels which you only abandon lying down
   > In a state of hunger, or with which you direct your course to a
   > desert region.

   The only negative aspect here is suggested in the word 'only' by which is intended the completion of the act and this is the opposite of 'ceasing', because one cannot say, 'I only cease standing.'

2. In the saying of God, *a messenger from God*, 'messenger' is an indefinite noun starting a new sentence, linked to *the clear proof* [in the previous verse, such that 'the clear proof' is the same as 'a messenger']. This is a well-known phenomenon, just as in His saying, *Lord of the throne, the All-glorious, performer of whatever He wishes* (Q 85/15–6). In the reading of Ubayy this is read as 'a messenger from God' in the accusative case, separated from 'the clear proof' [such that it might be understood as 'the clear proof who will be a messenger'].

3. Concerning the saying of God, *They were commanded only to serve God*, the Arabs use a *lām* [the letter 'l' which comes before the verb 'to serve'] in the place of *an* [to form the infinitive] in many expressions of commands and intentions. Another example of that is in the saying of God, *God wishes to make clear to you* (Q 4/26) and *They desire to put out* (Q 61/8). He also uses it in other

places in the revelation in cases of commands, as in, *We have been ordered to submit to the Lord of the worlds* (Q 6/71). In the reading of ʿAbd Allāh [ibn Masʿūd] [*an* replaces the *lām* before 'to serve' in this verse].

4. In the reading of ʿAbd Allāh [ibn Masʿūd] (the text reads) *the religion, the true*, but in our reading it is *the religion of the true.* This is an instance of using the possessive case to join something to itself when there is a difference [in gender] between the words being used. This has been explained in another place in this commentary.

5. Concerning the saying of God, *those are the best of creatures*, there is no *hamza* in *al-bariyya* ('creatures') although some people of the Hijaz do provide it with a *hamza* as if it was derived from the word in the saying of God, 'He created (*baraʾa)* you' and 'He created (*baraʾa*) the creation' [neither of which actually occurs in the Qurʾān]. However, those who do not put a *hamza* on the word might reckon that it is derived from this meaning anyway. But it is agreed that the *hamza* is left off, as in *yarā*, *tarā* and *narā* [all of which are derived from the root *raʾā*, 'to see', but from which the *hamza* has been dropped in forming the imperfect of the verb]. However, if the word is derived from *al-barā*, then it would not have a *hamza*. *Al-barā* means 'dirt'. I have heard the Arabs say,

> In his mouth be dust,
> And may the fever of Khaybar befall him,
> And evil be that which he shall see,
> For he is the one who goes astray.

[These verses are formed out of a number of words ending in *ā* (including *barā*, 'dust') which serve as epithets.]

5.5 Furāt al-Kūfī on *sūrat al-bayyina* (98)

Little is known of Furāt ibn Furāt al-Kūfī. Judging by his name, he was associated with Kufa in Iraq. On the basis of the authorities cited in his work, he lived around the end of the third/ninth century; the date of 310/922 is sometimes suggested for his death but there is no definitive evidence for that. His commentary on the Qur'ān, his only extant work, consists entirely of *ḥadīth* reports and his reputation as a *ḥadīth* scholar of his time seems credible. The traditions which he cites usually are those related by the two Shī'ī Imāms, Muḥammad al-Bāqir and Ja'far al-Ṣādiq, although other prominent early authorities are cited as well.

The commentary is a selective one, only providing explanations for certain verses and always concentrating on those verses which can have a special meaning within the Shī'ī context. A broad spectrum of ideas is covered within the commentary as a whole, covering especially the special nature and qualities of the Imāms. The passage translated below on *sūrat al-bayyina* (98) provides comment only on one section of a single verse which is seen as a reference to 'Alī ibn Abī Ṭālib and his followers as the 'best of creation'.

Further reading

Mahmoud Ayoub, 'The speaking Qur'ān and the silent Qur'ān: a study of the principles and development of Imāmī Shī'ī *tafsīr*,' in Andrew Rippin (ed.), *Approaches to the history of the interpretation of the Qur'ān*, Oxford 1988, pp. 177–98.

Meir M. Bar-Asher, *Scripture and exegesis in early Imāmī Shiism*, Leiden 1999.

Source text

Furāt, *Tafsīr Furāt al-Kūfī*, Najaf 1354 AH, pp. 218–20. The version edited by M. al-Kāẓim, Tehran 1990, Beirut 1992, vol. 2, pp. 583–7 was also consulted.

1. Abū 'l-Qāsim al-ʿAlawī told him that Furāt ibn Ibrāhīm al-Kūfī transmitted to him on the authority of Abū Jaʿfar Muḥammad ibn ʿAlī that he said that the messenger of God said, 'Something good was addressed to ʿAlī ibn Abī Ṭālib which was not said to anyone else. God said, *But those who believe and do righteous deeds, those are the best of creatures* (Q 98/7), that is you and your party (*shīʿa*), ʿAlī, the best of creation. By God, ʿAlī is the best of creation after the messenger of God.'

2. Furāt said that al-Ḥusayn ibn Saʿīd transmitted to him on the authority of Muʿādh that with regard to *But those who believe and do righteous deeds, those are the best of creatures*, the commander of the believers, ʿAlī ibn Abī Ṭālib, said, 'No one disagrees concerning it.'

3. Furāt said that Ismāʿīl ibn Ibrāhīm al-ʿAṭṭār transmitted to him the authority of Abū Jaʿfar who said that the messenger of God said, '*Those are the best of creatures,* that is you and your party, ʿAlī!'

4. Furāt said that Aḥmad ibn ʿĪsā ibn Hārūn transmitted to him on the authority of Jābir ibn ʿAbd Allāh al-Anṣārī who said that they were sitting with the messenger of God when the commander of the believers, ʿAlī ibn Abī Ṭālib, approached. When the prophet saw him, he said, 'My brother is coming towards you.' Then he turned towards the Kaʿba and said, 'Lord of this house, this one and his party, they will be the victors on the day of resurrection!' He then turned his face towards us and said, 'By God, he is the foremost of you in faith in God, the most upright of you in maintaining the command of God, the most faithful of you in keeping the covenant of God, the most steadfast of you in keeping the rules of God, the most just of you in maintaining equality, the fairest of you in providing protection, and the highest rank of you with God.' Jābir then said that God revealed this verse, *But those who believe and do righteous deeds, those are the best of creatures*. Jābir said that when ʿAlī would come, his companions would announce, 'Here comes the best of creation after the messenger of God!'

5. Furāt said that al-Ḥusayn ibn al-Ḥakam transmitted to him on the authority of Abū Jaʿfar that the prophet said, "ʿAlī, *But those who believe and do righteous deeds, those are the best of creatures*, they are you and your party. You will return to me, you and your party who are satisfiers and satisfying.'

6. Furāt said that Jaʿfar ibn Muḥammad ibn Saʿīd al-Aḥmasī transmitted to him on the authority of Abū Jaʿfar Muḥammad ibn ʿAlī who said that the messenger of God said, "ʿAlī, the verse which God revealed, *But those who believe and do righteous deeds, those are the best of creatures*, that is you and your party, ʿAlī!'

7. Furāt said that Jaʿfar transmitted to him on the authority of Abū Jaʿfar who said that the messenger of God said to ʿAlī concerning 'the best' on more than one occasion, '*Those are the best of creatures*, they are you and your party, ʿAlī!'

8. Furāt said that ʿAlī ibn Muḥammad al-Zuhrī transmitted to him on the authority of Abū Ayyūb al-Anṣārī who said that the messenger of God said that when he journeyed by night to heaven and arrived at the distant lotus tree, he heard a wind stirring in it, so he said to Gabriel, 'What is that?' who replied, 'This is the distant lotus tree which yearns for your cousin when it sees you.' Muḥammad said, 'I heard someone calling from near my Lord, "Muḥammad is the best of the prophets, and the commander of the believers, ʿAlī, is the best of all the saints (*awliyāʾ*), and his family and followers (*ahl wilāyatihi*) are the best of creatures. *Their recompense is with their Lord* in heaven *underneath which rivers flow, therein dwelling forever and ever* (Q 98/8). May God be pleased with ʿAlī and the members of his family. They are special recipients of the mercy of God; they are covered by the light of God; they are close to God. *Paradise is for them* (Q 13/28). Creatures will envy them on the day of judgement for their place close to their Lord."'

9. Furāt said that ʿUbayd ibn Kathīr transmitted to him on the authority of Abū Jaʿfar Muḥammad ibn ʿAlī that when God revealed to his prophet Muḥammad,

We are giving you al-Kawthar (Q 108/1), the commander of the believers, ʿAlī ibn Abī Ṭālib, said, 'Messenger of God, God has glorified and ennobled this river. Describe it to us!' He said, 'All right, ʿAlī! Al-Kawthar is a river which God causes to run under the throne. Its water is whiter than milk and sweeter than honey and softer than butter. Its pebbles are like pearls, sapphires and coral. Its soil is like pungent musk and its herbs are like saffron. The grounding of its supports are the throne of the Lord of the worlds. Its fruits are like the finest of green crystals, rubies and white pearls whose insides may be clearly seen from the outside and the outside from the inside.' The prophet and his companions wept and he struck ʿAlī with his hand, saying, "ʿAlī, by God, this does not relate to me and my limits, but it relates to me and to you and to your coming after me.'

10. Furāt said that ʿUbayd ibn Kathīr transmitted to him on the authority of Jābir ibn ʿAbd Allāh al-Anṣārī that the messenger of God said to Fāṭima, during his final illness, 'By my father and mother, send for your husband and summon him to me!' So Fāṭima said to al-Ḥasan, 'Hurry to your father and say to him, "My grandfather has summoned you!"' So al-Ḥasan hurried to him and summoned him. The commander of the believers, ʿAlī ibn Abī Ṭālib, came and went in to see the messenger of God. Fāṭima, who was with him, was saying, 'I am worried about you, father!' The messenger of God said to her, 'You will not have to worry about your father after today, Fāṭima! Do not cry your heart out for the prophet nor lament nor wail in affliction. Rather, say the same as your father did regarding Ibrāhīm, "Eyes cry and hearts ache but we will not say things to annoy the Lord and I am with you, Ibrāhīm, saddened." If Ibrāhīm had lived, he would have been a prophet.' He then said, 'Come close to me, ʿAlī!' He came closer and Muḥammad said, 'Put your ear near my mouth.' He did that and then Muḥammad said, 'Have you not heard the saying of God in His book, *But those who believe and do righteous deeds are the best of creatures*?' 'Of course, messenger of God,' replied ʿAlī. Muḥammad then said, 'That is you and your party who are honourable, unique, satisfied and elevated. Have you not heard the saying of God in His book, *The unbelievers of the people of the book and the idolaters will be in the fire of Gehenna, therein dwelling forever. Those are the worst of creatures* (Q 98/6)?' 'Of course, messenger of God,' said ʿAlī. Muḥammad then said, 'They are the enemies of you and your party who will come to the day of judgement the most thirsty and the most miserable of those who will be punished of the disbelieving hypocrites. That is how it is for you and your party, and that is how it is for the enemies of you and your party.' Thus Jābir ibn ʿAbd Allāh transmitted it.

5.6 Al-Ṭabarī on *sūrat al-bayyina* (98)

The first landmark in the vast library of books providing comprehensive interpretations of the Qur'ān was written by Abū Ja'far Muḥammad ibn Jarīr al-Ṭabarī, who died in 310/923. Born in the area near the Caspian sea, al-Ṭabarī studied first in Iran and then went to Baghdad where he spent most of his life. He developed a sufficient following as a teacher and a jurist to have a law school named after him, the Jarīriyya, although it disappeared within a couple of generations after his death. He left behind several books dealing with aspects of law. Al-Ṭabarī also achieved considerable fame as a historian, writing a universal history which has been translated into English in thirty-nine volumes.

Al-Ṭabarī's commentary on the Qur'ān, *Jāmi' al-bayān fī ta'wīl āy al-Qur'ān*, has stood the test of time as a comprehensive and astute reading of the text. By means of a verse-by-verse analysis, al-Ṭabarī provides a detailed discussion of every major interpretational trend (generally without detailing sectarian tendencies, although some exceptions may be noted as in the text translated below). Almost every idea is documented by the transmission of the opinions said to derive from Muḥammad or his closest companions, who are pictured as having the best information regarding the understanding of the text. However, al-Ṭabarī is certainly willing to express his own opinion when there is a lack of reports or even when faced with contradictory reports. It also becomes clear that grammar, along with theological perspective, was his main guiding tool for constructing a mature exegesis of the Qur'ān. Grammar served to assert the scholar's status and authority within the whole discipline of *tafsīr*, such that the ability to pursue the minutiae of Arabic constructions became a focal point of argumentation over how a meaning of the text could be derived. Theology tended to play a lesser role, usually subsumed under grammatical or legal wrangling. The very methodical approach of al-Ṭabarī leaves the reader fully confident that all ambiguity or uncertainty can be removed by a knowledgeable exegete and thus that Islam, as the manifestation of God's will and word, can be fully implemented as the divine will intends it to be.

Further reading

Herbert Berg, *The development of exegesis in early Islam: the authenticity of Muslim literature from the formative period*, Richmond 2000.

Norman Calder, 'Tafsīr from Ṭabarī to Ibn Kathīr: problems in the description of a genre, illustrated with reference to the story of Abraham,' in G. R. Hawting, Abdul-Kader A. Shareef (eds), *Approaches to the Qur'ān*, London 1993, pp. 101–40.

J. Cooper (trans.), *The commentary on the Qur'ān by Abū Ja'far Muḥammad b. Jarīr al-Ṭabarī*, Oxford 1987; translation of the introduction and the commentary through *sūrat al-baqara* (2), verse 103.

Claude Gilliot, *Exégèse, langue, et théologie en Islam. L'exégèse coranique de Tabari (m. 311/923)*, Paris 1990.

Yvonne Haddad, 'An exegesis of sura ninety-eight,' *Journal of the American Oriental Society*, 97 (1977), pp. 519–30; provides an overview of the interpretation of the *sūra* by exegetes from al-Ṭabarī to modern times.

Source text

Al-Ṭabarī, *Jāmiʿ al-bayān fī taʾwīl āy al-Qurʾān*, Bulaq 1905–12, vol. 30, pp. 169–71.

In the name of God, the All-merciful, the All-compassionate.

The sayings on the interpretation of His word, *The unbelievers of the people of the book and the idolaters would not leave off until the clear sign comes to them, a messenger from God, reading aloud pages purified, therein true books. And those who were given the book did not separate except after the clear sign came to them*, are as follows.

1. The interpreters differ in the interpretation of *The unbelievers of the people of the book and the idolaters would not leave off until the clear sign comes to them*. Some of them say the meaning of that is that those unbelievers from the people of the Torah and the Gospel and the idolaters who worship idols will not leave off, that is to say, will not renounce their disbelief until this Qurʾān comes to them. The interpreters who support what we have said about that say the following.

   1.1. Muḥammad ibn ʿAmr told me that Abū ʿĀṣim told him ʿĪsā told him, and also al-Ḥārith told me that al-Ḥasan told him that Warqāʾ told him, both reporting on the authority of Ibn Najīḥ on the authority of Mujāhid about His word, *leave off*, that he said, renounce what they are doing.

   1.2. Bishr told us that Yazīd told him that Saʿīd told him on the authority of Qatāda concerning His saying, *not leave off until the clear sign comes to them*, that is, this Qurʾān.

   1.3. Yūnus told me that Ibn Wahb informed him that Ibn Zayd said concerning God's saying, *and the idolaters would not leave off*, they will not renounce what they are doing until that one who causes them to leave off comes to them.

2. The others say that instead the meaning of that statement is that the people of the book are those who are the idolaters, and they will not ignore the description of Muḥammad as found in their book until he is sent to them. When he is sent, however, they will split up into groups over him.

3. The first of these interpretations concerning that verse which is sound is the one which says that the meaning of that is those who disbelieve among the people of the book and the idolaters will break into groups concerning the matter of Muḥammad until the clear sign comes to them, which is God's sending of him to His creation as a messenger from God. And *leave off* in this place, according to me, means 'separating one thing from another'. That is why it is possible for the word not to have a verb following it. If it had the meaning of 'did not cease', it would need a verb following it to complete it.

4. His saying, *a messenger from God*, is an indefinite noun in apposition with *the clear proof* (a definite noun); this is a known phenomenon as is found in *Lord*

of the throne, the All-glorious, performer [of whatever He wishes] (Q 85/15–6). So it is as if He said, 'Until there comes to them the evidence in the matter of Muḥammad that he is the messenger of God, by God's sending him to you.'

5. Then He explicated *the clear sign* by saying 'This clear sign is *a messenger from God, reading aloud pages purified*, by which He means reciting the pages which are purified of falsehood. *Therein true books*, He is saying that in the purified pages there are books from God which are true, just and sound. There are no errors in them because they are from God. The interpreters who support what we have said about that say the following:

    5.1. Bishr told us that Yazīd told him that Saʿīd told him on the authority of Qatāda, *a messenger from God, reading aloud pages purified*, God cites the Qur'ān in the best manner, and praises it highly.

6. Concerning His saying, *And those who were given the book did not separate except after the clear sign came to them*, He is saying that the Jews and Christians did not split into groups concerning the matter of Muḥammad. However, they told lies about him only after the clear sign came to them, that is, after the clear sign came to these Jews and Christians. *The clear sign* was the evidence in the matter of Muḥammad that he was a messenger whom God had sent to His creation. He is saying that when God sent him, they split into groups in their opinions about him. Some of them told lies about him and some of them believed. Before he was sent, they had not split into groups concerning his status as a prophet.

7. The sayings on the interpretation of His saying, *They were commanded only to serve God, making the religion His sincerely as men of true faith, and to establish prayer and pay the alms; and that is the religion of the true.* God is saying that He only ordered these Jews and Christians, who are the people of the book, to worship God; *making the religion His sincerely*, He is saying, devoted to Him in obedience without mixing their obedience to their lords in a polytheistic fashion. The Jews worshipped their lord when they said, 'Ezra is the son of God' and the Christians likewise when they said the same about the Messiah. Both of them denied the prophethood of Muḥammad.

8. *As men of true faith*, our explanation of the meaning of *ḥanīfiyya* has come before in this book with many statements of support. We did not previously mention the following among the traditions on this topic.

    8.1. Muḥammad ibn Saʿd told me that his father informed him that his uncle informed him that his father informed him on the authority of his father on the authority of Ibn ʿAbbās, concerning His saying, *making the religion His sincerely as men of true faith*, that he said, 'as pilgrims who are Muslims and not as idolaters'. He said, *and to establish prayer and pay the alms,* and to perform the pilgrimage; *that is the religion of the true.*

    8.2. Bishr told us that Yazīd told him that Saʿīd told him on the authority of Qatāda regarding His saying, *They were commanded only to serve God, making the religion His sincerely as men of true faith*: the creed of true faith (*ḥanīfiyya*) is the requirement of circumcision, observing the prohibitions of marriage to mothers, daughters, sisters, paternal aunts and maternal aunts, and following the rites of the pilgrimage.

9. Regarding His saying, *and to establish prayer and pay the alms*, He is saying, in order to establish prayer and in order to pay the alms.

10. Regarding His saying, *and that is the religion of the true*, He means: that which He mentions as that which He orders those who disbelieve from among the people of the book and the idolaters to do is the true religion. By *true* He means sound and just. *Religion* is in a grammatically possessive relationship with *true,* thus meaning the religion is the true one. It is understood as an attribute of *religion* because of the difference between its two spellings [i.e., in the masculine and the feminine]. In the reading of ʿAbd Allāh [Ibn Masʿūd], among those readings which I think have been mentioned to me, is 'And that is the true religion' with the word 'true' grammatically feminine because it is understood to be a description of the community [*milla*, which is grammatically feminine]. It is as if one said, 'That is the true community' without it including the Jews and the Christians [i.e., it is the community of Abraham].

11. The interpreters who support what we have said about that say the following.

    11.1. Bishr told us that Yazīd told him that Saʿīd told him on the authority of Qatāda regarding His saying, *The religion of the true*, that it is the religion which God sent the messenger with and a law of its own.
    11.2. Yūnus told me that Ibn Wahb informed him that Ibn Zayd said regarding His saying, *true books and that is the religion of the true*, in both cases this means they are sound and just.

12. Concerning the interpretation of the word of the Most High, *The unbelievers of the people of the book and the idolaters will be in the fire of Gehenna therein dwelling forever. Those are the worst of creatures. But those who believe and do righteous deeds, those are the best of creatures*, He is saying that all of those from among the Jews, Christians and idolaters who disbelieve in God and His messenger Muḥammad, and thus reject his prophethood, *will be in the fire of Gehenna therein dwelling forever*. By this He is saying they will be residing and staying there forever, and that they will never come out of it; nor will they die in it. *Those are the worst of creatures*: He is saying that those who disbelieve from among the people of the book and the idolaters are the worst part of what God has created and made.

13. The Arabs do not put a *hamza* in the word *bariyya* [meaning 'creatures'] although in the readings of the Amṣār it is left in except in the case of a report from Nāfiʿ ibn Abī Nuʿaym about whom some report on his authority that it should have a *hamza*. For evidence he cites the saying of God, *before we bring it into existence* [*nabraʾa*] (Q 57/22) such that *barīya* [*bariyya*] is a noun of the form *faʿīla* derived from that. As for those who say that it is not spelled with a *hamza*, they explain the omission of the *hamza* in two ways.

13.1. One opinion is that the *hamza* will be omitted just as it is omitted from *al-malak* [meaning 'angels'] which is of the form *mafʿal* from either the root *hamza-lām-kāf* or *lām-hamza-kāf*. This is the same as *yarā, tarā* and *narā* which is the imperfect verbal form of the verb *raʾytu* ['I saw'].

13.2. The other opinion is that it is derived from *al-barā* in the form *faʿīla* with the meaning of 'dust'. A generally accepted usage transmitted from the Arabs is, 'In his mouth be *al-barā*', meaning thereby 'dust'.

14. And His saying, *But those who believe and do righteous deeds, those are the best of creatures*, He is saying that those who believe in God and His messenger Muḥammad and who act *to serve God, making the religion His sincerely as men of true faith, and to establish prayer and pay the alms*, and obey God in what He commands and forbids, they are *the best of creation*, by which He is saying those among the people who do all this are the best of creation.

14.1. Ibn Ḥamīd told us that ʿĪsā ibn Farqad told him on the authority of Ibn Jārūd on the authority of Muḥammad ibn ʿAlī regarding *those are the best of creation*, that the prophet said, 'You, ʿAlī, and your party [*shīʿa*].'

15. The sayings on the interpretation of His word, *their recompense is with their Lord; gardens of Eden, underneath which rivers flow, therein dwelling forever and ever; God is well pleased with them and they are well pleased with Him; that is for him who fears his Lord.*

He is saying that the reward of those who believe and do good works will be with their Lord on the day of resurrection. By *gardens of Eden* He means the ever-lasting gardens in which nothing is transitory. *Underneath which rivers flow, therein dwelling forever and ever*, He is saying that they will reside in it forever, they will not get out of there and they will not die in it. *God is well pleased with them* in the way they obey Him in the world and in the way they work for their deliverance from His punishment thereby. *And they are well pleased with Him* in the way He gives them rewards in the here-and-now for their obedience to their Lord in the world in the way He recompenses them for their actions with blessings.

16. In His saying, *that is for him who fears his Lord*, He is saying that this is what describes those who believe and do good works and that which is promised to them on the day of resurrection. *For him who fears his Lord*: He is saying that it is for those who fear God in the world both secretly and openly and who fear Him in the performance of their obligations and in their avoidance of sinful acts. May God grant success!

5.7 Al-Zamakhsharī on *sūrat al-bayyina* (98)

Abū ʾl-Qāsim Maḥmūd ibn ʿUmar al-Zamakhsharī (467/1075–538/1144) was a philologist, theologian and Qurʾān commentator. For most of his life al-Zamakhsharī lived in the region of his birth, Khwarazm in Central Asia, although he did spend some time studying in Bukhara and Baghdad, and twice he visited Mecca. Motivated by a great appreciation of Arabic (although he was a native Persian speaker) and influenced by rationalist Muʿtazilī theology, al-Zamakhsharī wrote one of the most widely read commentaries on the Qurʾān called *al-Kashshāf ʿan ḥaqāʾiq ghawāmid al-tanzīl*, 'The unveiler of the realities of the sciences of the revelation'. Despite what came to be regarded as its heretical theological slant, the work has been an essential part of the curriculum of religious education throughout the Muslim world for centuries. It attracted many super-commentaries which attempted to explain its terse style and intricacies, as well as refutations (e.g., by Fakhr al-Dīn al-Rāzī; see section 5.8) and bowdlerized versions (e.g., by al-Bayḍāwī, d. *c.* 691/1292). Al-Zamakhsharī comments on each phrase of the Qurʾān in sequence, providing philosophical, lexicographical and philological glosses while displaying a concern for the rhetorical qualities of the text. His text is also imbued with his theological vision which is characterized by a thorough-going de-anthropomorphization and support for the doctrines of human free will and the created Qurʾān. Among al-Zamakhsharī's numerous other works are books on Arabic grammar, rhetoric and lexicography, and a collection of proverbs.

Further reading

Lutpi Ibrahim, 'Al-Zamakhsharī: his life and works,' *Islamic studies*, 19 (1980), pp. 95–110.
Jane Dammen McAuliffe, *Qurʾānic Christians: an analysis of classical and modern exegesis*, Cambridge 1991, pp. 49–54.
Sabine Schmidtke, *A Muʿtazilite creed of az-Zamakhsharī (d. 538/1144): al-Minhāg fī uṣūl ad-dīn*, Abhandlung für die Kunde des Morgenlandes 51/4, Stuttgart 1997.

Source text

Al-Zamakhsharī, *Al-Kashshāf ʿan ḥaqāʾiq ghawāmid al-tanzīl*, Cairo 1966, vol. 4, pp. 274–5.

1. The unbelievers are of two types, the people of the book and the worshippers of idols. Before the mission of the prophet they all used to say, 'We will not leave off from what we have in our religion. We will not leave it until the prophet who is promised and described in the Torah and the Gospel is sent.' He is Muḥammad. God reported what they used to say. Then He said, *And those who were given the book did not separate*, meaning that they promised in the agreement of their words and in conforming with the truth that when they were sent the messenger, then they would not separate from the truth. Then they established themselves in disbelief at the coming of the messenger.

2. This is parallel to what is said in speech, as in when a poor and corrupt person says to someone who admonishes him, 'I will not be stopped from my evil actions until God bestows wealth upon me.' When God does bestow wealth on him, his corruption only increases. So, his admonisher says to him, 'You have not left off from your corruption even though you are able to. You slip your head into corruption even after the situation has eased.' This was said as a rebuke and a rejection of the argument.

3. Separating something from something else means that something leaves something else after having adhered to it. This is like a bone which becomes separated from the joint. So the meaning is that they are those who cling to their religion and do not leave it until the time of the coming of the clear sign.

4. *The clear sign* means the evident proof; *a messenger* is in apposition with *the clear sign*; in the reading of ʿAbd Allāh [ibn Masʿūd] it reads *rasūlan* and is a circumstantial phrase related to *the clear sign*. *Pages*, sheets of paper, *purified* of impurity. *Books,* things written; *true*, endowed with truth and justice.

5. The sense of 'their separating' is that they separated and scattered from the truth. Or, it could mean that they separated into groups, among whom some believed and some rejected the truth. It could not be, however, that there were those who were stubborn and resistant [and some who were not]. If you say, why did He bring together the people of the book and the idolaters at the beginning and then separate out the people of the book in His saying, *And those who were given the book did not separate*, I would say that they had knowledge of Muḥammad since he appeared in their books. If the idolaters were described as separating from him, then the verse would have suggested that those who did not have a book were included in this description.

6. *They were commanded only*, that is, in the Torah and the Gospel and, except for the *ḥanīfī* aspects, they altered and changed their scriptures. *That is the religion of the true*, that is, the religion of the true community. This is also read, 'That is the true religion' by understanding 'religion' as 'community' [i.e., in order to explain the feminine ending on 'true']. If you ask, 'What is the meaning of His saying, *They were commanded only to serve God*?', I would reply that its meaning is that they were only commanded by what is in the two books to worship God in this way. Ibn Masʿūd reads this, 'except that they worship' with the meaning, '(they were commanded) in the service . . .'. Nāfiʿ reads *al-barīʾa* with a *hamza* while the (majority of the) readers have it with a doubled *yāʾ*. This is the same as *al-nabī* in that it utilizes the doubling of the letter rather than following the root. There is also a reading 'best of creation' using the plural *khiyār* of 'best' [*khayr*, as in the standard text] as in the plural forms of 'outstanding' (*jiyād*) and 'good things' (*ṭiyāb*) from the singulars *jayyid* and *ṭayyib*.

7. It is reported on the authority of the messenger of God that he said, 'Whoever reads *lam yakun* [i.e., Q 98] in the evening in his resting place will be with the best of creation on the day of resurrection.'

5.8 Fakhr al-Dīn al-Rāzī, selections on *sūrat al-bayyina* (98)

The intellectual renewer of the sixth/twelfth century, Muḥammad ibn ʿUmar Fakhr al-Dīn al-Rāzī was born in Rayy near modern Tehran in either 543/1149 or 544/1150. He travelled widely in Central Asia and attracted many students to his study circles; he finally settled in Herat in Afghanistan and died there in 606/1210. He aggressively defended Ashʿarī dogma against the Muʿtazilīs, as is evident in his *tafsīr* work, *Mafātīḥ al-ghayb*, 'The keys of the unseen'. The work itself is al-Rāzī's greatest accomplishment, although he did write a number of other works; it is written on a massive scale and full of philosophical and theological argumentation. It makes constant reference to the authorities of the past, but it is not held back by them, nor does it simply reproduce earlier thought.

Al-Rāzī's approach is clear. He states what the perceived problem in the text is and then addresses it, usually in a variety of ways. Frequently, the issues are separated into questions with multiple answers fully explored. In dealing with some aspects, al-Rāzī discloses the fundamental principle that every piece of the Qur'ānic text must have meaning; things are stated by God the way they are for a reason. Even omitted words have meanings which can be deduced. Overall, the exegesis may be viewed as a theological reading with a spiritual/mystical tinge, performed through the traditional exegetical tools of grammar, semantics and narrative. There is little appeal to the actual authority of tradition; polyvalency is allowed but a preference in terms of meaning is always indicated.

Further reading

Yasin Ceylan, *Theology and tafsīr in the major works of Fakhr al-Dīn al-Rāzī*, Kuala Lumpur 1996.

Jacques Jomier, 'The Qur'anic commentary of Imam Fakhr al-Din al-Razi: its sources and its originality,' in A. H. Johns (ed.), *International congress for the study of the Qur'an. Australian National University, Canberra 8–13 May 1980*, Canberra n.d., pp. 93–111.

Jane Dammen McAuliffe, *Qur'ānic Christians: an analysis of classical and modern exegesis*, Cambridge 1991, pp. 63–71.

Source text

Al-Rāzī, *Al-Tafsīr al-kabīr: mafātīḥ al-ghayb*, reprint Beirut n.d., vol. 32, pp. 38–40, 49–50. Because of the length of al-Rāzī's analysis, it has only been possible to provide an excerpt of the section dealing with this *sūra*.

> *The unbelievers of the people of the book and the idolaters would not leave off until the clear sign comes to them, a messenger from God, reading aloud pages purified, therein true books. And those who were given the book did not separate except after the clear sign came to them.*

Know that concerning these verses a number of problems arise.

1. Problem one. Al-Wāḥidī says in his *Kitāb al-basīṭ* ('The expansive commentary') that this verse is one of the most difficult in terms of structure and interpretation. Many members of the *ʿulamāʾ* have stumbled in dealing with it. May God Most High have mercy on whoever attempts to summarize the nature of the difficulty in the verse.

   One aspect of the difficulty occurs in re-expressing the verse, *The unbelievers . . . would not leave off until the clear sign comes to them*, which is the messenger. The Most High does not mention what it is that they 'left off' from. This, however, is known; it is the disbelief which they once had. So, one can re-express the verse in the following way. Those who disbelieve did not leave off their disbelief until the clear sign came to them which is the messenger. Thus the word *until* is used to indicate their reaching the end of what they were doing. So, this verse then demands that they began to leave off disbelieving when the messenger came. However, after that He said, *And those who were given the book did not separate except after the clear sign came to them*. This then demands that their disbelief increased at the time of the coming of the messenger. So, between the first verse and the second is a contradiction in the apparent sense of the verse. This results in the difficulty in these considerations.

   The response to this has a number of aspects.

1.1. The first and the best is what is given by the author of *al-Kashshāf* ('The unveiling') [al-Zamakhsharī]. That is that the unbelievers are of two types, the people of the book and the worshippers of idols. Before the mission of Muḥammad, they all used to say, 'We will not leave off from what we have in our religion. We will not leave it until the prophet who is promised and described in the Torah and the Gospel is sent.' He is Muḥammad. God reported what they used to say. Then He said, *And those who were given the book did not separate*, meaning that they promised in the agreement of their words and in conforming with the truth that when they were sent the messenger, then they would not separate from the truth. Then they established themselves in disbelief at the coming of the messenger.

1.1.1. This is parallel to what is said in speech, as when a poor and corrupt person says to someone who admonishes him, 'I will not be stopped from my evil actions until God bestows wealth upon me.' When God does bestow wealth on him, his corruption only increases. So, his admonisher says to him, 'You have not left off from your corruption even though you are able to. You slip your head into corruption even after the situation has eased.' This was said as a rebuke and a rejection of the argument.

The essence of this response rests on a single expression which is His saying, *Those who disbelieve would not leave off* – from disbelief – *until the clear sign comes to them* which mentions a story which they told among themselves. However, His saying, *Those who were given the book did not separate* is the notification of an actual outcome. The meaning is thus that what will occur is the contrary of what they claimed.

1.2. The second aspect in response to this problem is that one should re-express the verse as follows. Those who disbelieve will not leave off from their disbelief even though the clear sign has come to them. The ambiguity is removed in this re-expression and this is the way the Qāḍī deals with it, although this explanation of the word *until* does not have any support in the Arabic language.

1.3. The third aspect in response to this problem is that we do not connect His saying *leave off* to disbelief but rather to their leaving off mentioning Muḥammad and his virtues and merits. The meaning then would be that those who disbelieve would not leave off from mentioning the virtues and merits of Muḥammad until the clear sign comes to them. Ibn ʿUrfa said this means 'until it came to them', such that even though the verb is in the imperfect tense, the meaning is of the perfect. That is like the saying of the Most High, *[They follow] what the devils recite [over Solomon's kingdom]* (Q 2/102) meaning 'what they recited'. So the meaning is that they did not leave off mentioning his virtues; but when Muḥammad came to them, they separated into groups regarding him. Every one of them said something about him that was incorrect. This is parallel to the saying of the Most High, *Previously they implored [God] for victory over those who disbelieve. But when there came to them what they recognized, they disbelieved in it* (Q 2/89).

The preferred answer in this is the first one.

1.4. There is a fourth aspect concerning this verse. The Most High decreed that the unbelievers would not leave off from their unbelief until the time of the coming of the messenger. The word *until* demands that it refer to a subsequent state which opposes what came before. This was the state of affairs because that specific group did not remain in unbelief but rather they separated. Among them were some who became believers while others became unbelievers. Since the state of those in the group did not remain the same after the coming of the messenger as it was before he came, that justifies the use of the word *until*.

1.5. A fifth aspect is that the unbelievers, before the sending of the messenger, had left off all hesitation about their unbelief. They were firmly convinced of it, believing in its truth. That conviction ceased at the coming of the messenger although they remained doubtful and confused about that and all other religions. This is similar to His saying, *The people were a single nation; then God sent forth the prophets as good tidings bearing warnings* (Q 2/213). The meaning of this is that the religion to which they belonged had become like the mixture of their flesh and blood. So, the Jews were firmly convinced in their Judaism, and likewise with the Christians and the idol worshippers. When Muḥammad was sent, their ideas and thoughts became troubled and all of them doubted their own religion, their teachings and their creeds. So God said, *leave off*, that is, knowing this, because 'leaving off' something for something else is being separated from the first. So the meaning is that their hearts were not freed from those creeds nor were they separated from their sound convictions. Thus, after the sending of Muḥammad, the matter did not remain in the same condition.

2. Problem two. The unbelievers are of two types. One consists of the people of the book, such as groups within the Jews and the Christians who are unbelievers because of their creation of their religion with elements of unbelief, as in His saying, *Ezra is the son of God* (Q 9/30) and, *The Messiah is the son of God* (Q 9/30) and their alteration of the book of God and His religion. The second type are the idolaters who do not hold to a scripture. God mentioned these two types in His statement, *Those who disbelieve*, as a summation, which He then followed by a differentiation which is *of the people of the book and the idolaters.* This then provokes two questions.

    2.1. One, the verse may be re-expressed as, 'The unbelievers of the people of the book and from among the idolaters. . . .' This necessitates that the people of the book be composed of some who disbelieve and some who do not. This is true. But it also suggests that the idolaters are composed of some who disbelieve and some who do not, and it is known that this is not true.

    2.1.1. The answer to this has a number of possibilities. One is that the word 'from' is not to be taken as a distributive here but as an explanation as in His saying, *So avoid the abomination (which comes) from idols* (Q 22/30). Another would be that of those who disbelieve in Muḥammad, some are members of the people of the book and some are of the idolaters. So, this would be the reason for the insertion of the word 'from'. Third is that His saying *the idolaters* is a description of the people of the book. This is because Christians are tri-theists and Jews are generally anthropomorphists; both of these are forms of idolatry. Someone may say, 'The intelligent ones and elegant ones came to me', meaning thereby a single group of people whose importance is indicated by these two characteristics. God has also said, *Those who bow, those who prostrate themselves, those who bid to honour and forbid dishonour, those who keep God's bounds* (Q 9/112); this is a description of a single group of people. There are many examples of this in the Qur'ān where a group of people is described by various qualities connected by the conjunctive particle. All of them describe a single entity.

    2.2. The second question is in regards to the Majūs: are they a part of the people of the book? Some of the *ʿulamāʾ* state that they are a part of the people of the book due to Muḥammad saying, 'We will entrust them to the practice of the people of the book', while others reject this because when God mentioned the disbelievers, He was speaking of the people in the land of the Arabs and they were the Jews and the Christians. God related a story about them, *If you say that the book was revealed to two groups before you* (Q 6/156), and the *two groups* are the Jews and the Christians.

3. The third problem relates to why the people of the book are given precedence in disbelief over the idolaters when He says, *Those who disbelieve of the people of the book and the idolaters*. The answer here is that the connective *and* does not indicate an ordering. There are several merits to this structure, however. First, the *sūra* was revealed in Medina and the aim of the passage was to address the

people of the book. Second, those knowledgeable in the scriptures had within their power the most complete knowledge of the sincerity of Muḥammad. Their persistence in disbelief is the most shameful aspect. Third, because they were learned, others copied them; so, their disbelief was the source of the disbelief of others. Thus they were mentioned first. Fourth, because they were learned and more noble than the others, they were mentioned first.

4. Problem four. Why does He say, *of the people of the book*, and not 'of the Jews and the Christians'? The answer to this is because His saying, *of the people of the book*, indicates that they are learned. Either this emphasizes a magnificent attribute which surely must describe more than just the Jews and the Christians, or it is because they are learned that this emphasizes the extent of the shamefulness of their disbelief. They are described in this way to emphasize their penalty in the hereafter as well.

. . .

> *They were commanded only to serve God, making the religion His sincerely as men of true faith, and to establish prayer and pay the alms; and that is the religion of the true. The unbelievers of the people of the book and the idolaters will be in the fire of Gehenna, therein dwelling forever. Those are the worst of creatures.*

5. Know that when God mentioned the condition of the unbelievers first in His saying, *The unbelievers of the people of the book and the idolaters*, He followed this with a mention of the condition of the believers in His saying, *They were commanded only to serve God*. He returns at the end of this *sūra* to the mention of both groups; so, He began with the condition of *the unbelievers*, those who disbelieve. Know that God mentions only two of their conditions, one, existing in the fire of Gehenna, and two, that they are the worst of creation. Questions arise here.

6. Problem one. Why are the people of the book given precedence here over the disbelievers? The answer here has several aspects.

    6.1. One is that Muḥammad gave precedence to the truth of God over the truth of himself. Do you not see that when the community reached its fifth year, Muḥammad said, 'God, guide my community for they do not know!' When the *ʿaṣr* prayer was decreed on the day of Khandaq, he said, 'God, fill their bellies and their graves with fire!' It is as if Muḥammad had himself spoken of punishment first as an illustration, and then, on the day of Khandaq, as a way of proper conduct which is prayer. Subsequently, God decreed that. God said, 'You give My truth precedence over your truth. So also I give precedence to your truth over My own. Whoever forgets prayer for all of his life does not commit disbelief, but whoever speaks evil of even one of your hairs commits disbelief. You knew that, so We say that the people of the book do not speak evil of God but only of the messenger. However, the idolaters speak evil of God.' When God wished in this verse to mention the evil of the unbelievers' condition, He began first with the offence of speaking evil of Muḥammad – and that is the offence of the people of the book. Second, He mentioned those who speak evil of Himself, and they are the idolaters.

6.2. The second point is that the crime of the people of the book in denying the truth of the messenger was greater because the idolaters saw him as a small child and he grew up among them. He then called them foolish and declared their religions corrupt. This was a difficult matter for them. The people of the book, on the other hand, started out with his coming as a prophet and they acknowledged his mission. When he came to them, however, they rejected him even though they had the knowledge. This is a serious crime.

7. Problem two. Why does He say, *the unbelievers* (lit.: '*those who disbelieve*'), using a verb but then say, *the idolaters*, using a noun? The answer is that this draws attention to the fact that the people of the book were not unbelievers from the beginning, because they believed in the Torah and the Gospel. They confirmed the mission of Muḥammad but then they disbelieved in that after his mission began. This is contrary to the idolaters who were born into the worship of idols and rejected the ideas of the assembly and the resurrection at the end of time.

8. Problem three. The idolaters rejected the ideas about the Maker, prophethood and resurrection. As for the people of the book, they accepted all of these matters but they rejected the prophethood of Muḥammad. Therefore, the disbelief of the people of the book is less than that of the idolaters. If that is so, why is the punishment of the two groups the same? The answer is as follows. One may say, 'The spring of Gehenna' when meaning a spring which comes from great depth. Thus it is as if God is saying they are proud of their search for height but they become the lowest of the low. The two groups are formed into a partnership, but their partnership in this fate is not inconsistent with there being a difference in the degree of punishment. Know that there are two aspects to sin in the appropriateness of this punishment. One is the sin of someone who does evil to you, and the other the sin of someone who benefits you. This second type is the more detestable. Benefit is likewise of two types: the benefit to the one who benefits you, and the benefit to one who does evil to you.

8.1. This benefit is of two types. The benefit of God to those disbelievers is of a greater type of benefit, and their sin and disbelief is of a more severe kind of sin. It is known that the punishment is in proportion to the crime. So, for abuse there is censure; for defamation, a *ḥadd;* for stealing, amputation; for adultery, stoning; for killing, retaliation. So, the abuse of property necessitates censure, and a nasty glance at the messenger necessitates death. The crimes of these disbelievers are great, so surely they are entitled to a great punishment which is the fire of Gehenna. This fire is in a deep, dark dreadful place from which there is definitely no escape. It is as if someone said, 'Assuming there is no hope of escape, is there any hope of getting out?' So He said, 'No, they will remain in it forever.' Then it is as if someone said, 'Isn't there someone there who will have pity on them?' and He said, 'No. They blame and curse them because they are the worst of creation.'

9. Problem four. What is the reason that He does not say here, 'therein residing forever and ever'. He said in the description of the people who will be rewarded in paradise that they will be *therein residing forever and ever* (Q 98/8). The answer has several aspects, one of which is that it draws attention to the fact that God's mercy is greater than His wrath. The second is that the judgements, punishments and atonements of Hell are intertwined. As for the reward, its various aspects are not intertwined. Third, an account is related from God that He said, 'David, make me acceptable to My creation!' 'How can I do that?' he replied. He said, 'Mention the extent of My mercy to them.' This is of the same type of expression.

10. Problem five concerns the readings of the word *al-bariyya* ('creatures'). Nāfiʿ read this as *al-barīʾa* with a *hamza* while everyone else read it without a *hamza*. It would be related to 'God formed [*baraʾa*] creation' with the *hamza* considered to have been left out, as in the words *nabī, dhariyya* and *khābiyya*. The *hamza* is present in the original root of the word in common usage, just as one can add the *hamza* to *nabī* although leaving it out is better. If *hamza* is considered a part of the root and is understood as something which was originally discarded, then this would indicate that it is false to consider that *bariyya* is from *barā* in the sense of 'dust'.

11. Problem six. What is the benefit of His saying, *the worst of creatures*? The answer is that it allows their expulsion and bears witness against them such that they are alone. Know that the worst of creatures as a whole extends its details into many aspects, for example that he is worse than a thief because he steals the description of Muḥammad from the book of God, and worse than the highway robber because he takes the way of truth from creation, and worse than the most ignorant or the boor because he pretends to have knowledge but it is really disbelief and stubbornness. And that is the absolute worst.

5.9 Ibn Kathīr on *sūrat al-bayyina* (98)

In the wake of the Mongol invasion of the Islamic heartlands and the fall of Baghdad in 656/1258, a close definition of Islam was felt by many to be needed as a method of Muslim self-preservation in the face of an external threat. 'Imād al-Dīn Ismā'īl ibn 'Umar ibn Kathīr was born in Basra in 700/1300 and moved to Damascus when he was six, where he studied with some of the most famous scholars of his time, including the Ḥanbalī theologian, jurist and reformer Taqī al-Dīn Aḥmad ibn Taymiyya (d. 729/1328). Ibn Kathīr became known as a scholar of law and a teacher of *ḥadīth*, and was also praised as one of the most respected preachers and lecturers in Damascus. He died in 774/1373.

Ibn Kathīr's major work, a commentary on the Qur'ān entitled simply *Tafsīr al-Qur'ān*, provides a synopsis of earlier material in a readily accessible form, a factor which gave the work much popularity in subsequent generations. However, he relies totally upon *ḥadīth* material; the era of Ibn Kathīr marks the final submersion of rationalism under the powers of traditionalism. No longer did even the measure of personal opinion displayed in the work of al-Ṭabarī or al-Zamakhsharī have any substantial place in the understanding of the Qur'ān. Ibn Kathīr frequently structures his commentary around extracts from the classical books of *ḥadīth*, citing those reports relevant to the passage in question. In this way, the tradition of *tafsīr* was being contracted severely; no longer were the intellectual disciplines of grammar, law and theology being brought into dialogue and debate with the text.

Ibn Kathīr's text is structured consistently to deal with the 'merits' of each *sūra* at the beginning of his treatment before entering into a verse-by-verse discussion.

Further reading

Norman Calder, 'Tafsīr from Ṭabarī to Ibn Kathīr: problems in the description of a genre, illustrated with reference to the story of Abraham,' in G. R. Hawting, Abdul-Kader A. Shareef (eds), *Approaches to the Qur'ān*, London 1993, pp. 101–40.

Jane Dammen McAuliffe, 'Quranic hermeneutics: the views of al-Ṭabarī and Ibn Kathīr,' in Andrew Rippin (ed.), *Approaches to the history of the interpretation of the Qur'ān*, Oxford 1988, pp. 46–62.

Source text

Ibn Kathīr, *Tafsīr al-Qur'ān al-'aẓīm,* Beirut 1987, vol. 4, pp. 573–5.

1. Imām Aḥmad [ibn Ḥanbal] said that ʿAffān told him that Ḥammād, that is Ibn Salama, told him that ʿAlī, that is Ibn Zayd, informed him on the authority of ʿAmmār ibn Abī ʿAmmār who said that he heard Abū Ḥibbat al-Badrī, that is Mālik ibn ʿAmr ibn Thābit al-Anṣārī, say that when *The unbelievers of the people of the book* to the end, was revealed, Gabriel said, 'Messenger of God, Your

Lord is commanding you to recite this to Ubayy.' So the prophet said to Ubayy, 'Gabriel ordered me to recite this *sūra* to you.' Ubayy said, 'Was I mentioned again, messenger of God?' He said, 'Yes.' So Ubayy wept.

1.1. Another report says that Imām Aḥmad said that Muḥammad ibn Jaʿfar told him that Shuʿba told him that he heard Qatāda reporting that Anas ibn Mālik said that the messenger of God said to Ubayy ibn Kaʿb, 'God has ordered me to recite to you, *The unbelievers of the people of the book*.' Ubayy replied, 'He named me?' 'Yes,' he said. So Ubayy wept. Al-Bukhārī, Muslim, al-Tirmidhī, and al-Nasāʾī transmit the report of Shuʿba.

1.2. Another report says that Imām Aḥmad said Muʾammil told him that Sufyān told him that Aslam al-Munqarī told him on the authority of ʿAbd Allāh ibn ʿAbd al-Raḥmān ibn Abzā on the authority of his father on the authority of Ubayy ibn Kaʿb who said that the messenger of God said to him, 'I have been ordered to recite *sūra* such-and-such to you.' He said, 'Messenger of God, was I actually mentioned in that regard?' He said, 'Yes.' [Ubayy was asked,] 'Abū ʾl-Mundhir, were you gladdened by that?' He said, 'And why not? God has said, *Say: in the glory of God and His mercy, let them rejoice. That is better than what they gather* (Q 10/58).' Muʾammil said that he asked Sufyān about the reading of this report. He said that it was unique.

1.3. Another transmission has Imām Aḥmad say that Muḥammad ibn Jaʿfar and Ḥajjāj both say that Shuʿba told them on the authority of ʿĀṣim ibn Bahdala on the authority of Zarr ibn Hubaysh on the authority of Ubayy ibn Kaʿb who said that the messenger of God said to him, 'God ordered me to recite the Qurʾān to you.' So he recited, *The unbelievers of the people of the book*, and in it he recited, 'If the son of Adam asks for a valley full of wealth and I give it to him, he will ask for another. And if he asks for another, I will give it to him and he will ask for a third one. Only dirt can fill the belly of the son of Adam. God forgives those who repent. The nature of religion according to God is *ḥanīfiyya*, not idolatry nor Judaism, nor Christianity. Those who do good will never be ungrateful towards Him.' Al-Tirmidhī transmitted the report of Ubayy on the authority of Dāwūd al-Ṭayālisī from Shuʿba. It is a solid, sound report.

1.4. Another transmission has the *ḥāfiẓ* Abū ʾl-Qāsim al-Ṭabarānī reporting that Aḥmad ibn Khalīd al-Ḥalabī told him that Muḥammad ibn ʿĪsā al-Ṭabbaʿ told him that Muʿādh ibn Muḥammad ibn Muʿādh ibn Ubayy ibn Kaʿb on the authority of his father on the authority of his grandfather on the authority of Ubayy ibn Kaʿb said that the messenger of God said, 'Abū ʾl-Mundhir, I have been ordered to offer the Qurʾān to you.' He said, 'By God, I believe and on your hand I submit, and by you I will be taught.' The prophet repeated the statement. Ubayy said, 'Messenger of God, was I really mentioned in this regard?' 'Yes,' he said, 'by name and by your ancestry among the heavenly host.' Ubayy responded, 'So, recite it to me, messenger of God!' This is a rare report.

1.5. It has been demonstrated in these previous reports that the prophet recited this *sūra* to Ubayy as a proof and to strengthen him in his faith. That is how Aḥmad and al-Nasāʾī have transmitted it from Anas, and Aḥmad and Abū Dāwūd from Sulaymān ibn Ṣadr, and Aḥmad from ʿAffān ibn Ḥammād from Ḥamīd from Anas from ʿIbāda ibn al-Ṣāmit, and Aḥmad and Muslim and Abū Dāwūd and al-Nasāʾī from Ismāʿīl ibn Abī Khālid from ʿAbd Allāh ibn ʿĪsā from ʿAbd al-Raḥmān ibn Abī Layla.

1.6. ʿAbd Allāh ibn Masʿūd was rebuked by Ubayy for reading something from the Qurʾān contrary to how the messenger of God had recited it. So he took him to the prophet who asked the two of them to recite it and to each of them he said that he was right. Ubayy said that this created doubt in him as in the days of the *jāhiliyya*. The messenger of God struck Ubayy's breast and Ubayy said that he sweated profusely as if he was fearfully gazing at God. The messenger of God informed Ubayy that Gabriel had come to him and said, 'God has ordered you to recite the Qurʾān to your community in one set way.' I said, 'I ask God for forgiveness and pardon!' He said, 'All right, in two ways then!' That did not cease until he said, 'God orders you to recite the Qurʾān to your community in seven ways (*aḥruf*).' We mentioned this report in many transmissions and wordings at the beginning of the commentary. When this glorious *sūra* was revealed, saying, *a messenger from God, reading aloud pages purified, therein true books*, the messenger of God recited it to him in various ways he had not heard previously. God knows best.

1.7. This is similar to when ʿUmar ibn al-Khaṭṭāb asked the messenger of God many questions on the day of Ḥudaybiyya. Among those questions was, 'Did you not tell us that we would go to the house and circumambulate it?' He replied, 'Of course I did, but I did not tell you that it would be this year.' 'That's true,' ʿUmar responded. He said, 'The time will come when you will circumambulate it.' When they returned from Ḥudaybiyya, God revealed *sūrat al-fatḥ* (48) to the prophet. So, he called ʿUmar ibn al-Khaṭṭāb and recited it to him, including the verse, *God will confirm his messenger with a vision in truth. You will certainly enter the holy mosque in safety, if God wills* (Q 48/27), just as has been explained earlier.

2. The *ḥāfiẓ* Abū Nuʿaym transmitted in his book, *The names of the companions* in the transmission of Muḥammad ibn Ismāʿīl al-Jaʿfarī al-Madanī that ʿAbd Allāh ibn Salama ibn Aslam reported on the authority of Ibn Shihāb on the authority of Ismāʿīl ibn Abī Ḥakīm al-Muzanī that Fuḍayl heard the messenger of God saying that when God hears the recitation of *sūrat al-bayyina* (98), He says, 'I will bless My servant, and, by My glory, I will give to you a firm position in paradise that will please you.' This is a very rare report. The *ḥāfiẓ* Abū Mūsā al-Madīnī and Ibn al-Athīr report it in the transmission of al-Zuhrī from Ismāʿīl ibn Abī Kaltham from Maṭar al-Muzanī from the messenger of God in which the report says, 'I will bless My servant, and, by My glory, I will not forget you in any situation in the world or the hereafter and I will give you a firm position in paradise that will please you.'

The unbelievers of the people of the book and the idolaters would not leave off until the clear sign comes to them, a messenger from God, reading aloud pages purified, therein true books. And those who were given the book did not separate except after the clear sign came to them. They were commanded only to serve God, making the religion His sincerely as men of true faith, and to establish prayer and pay the alms; and that is the religion of the true.

3. As for *the people of the book* they are the Jews and the Christians while *the idolaters* are the idol worshippers and fire worshippers from among the Arabs and the non-Arabs. Mujāhid said, they will never *leave off*, that is, cease until the truth is made clear to them. Likewise Qatāda said, *until the clear sign comes to them*, that is, this Qur'ān. Because of this, the Most High said, *The unbelievers of the people of the book and the idolaters would not leave off until the clear sign comes to them.*

4. Then He explained *the clear sign* by His saying, *a messenger from God, reading aloud pages purified*, that is, Muḥammad and what he recites of the glorious Qur'ān which is written in heaven most high in *pages purified* just as in His saying, *Upon pages honoured, lifted up, purified, by the hands of scribes, noble, pious* (Q 80/13–5).

5. Regarding His saying, *therein true books*, Ibn Jarīr [al-Ṭabarī] said that among the purified pages are some of God's books which are true, full of justice and righteousness; there are no errors in them because they are from God, Most High.

   5.1. Qatāda said concerning, *a messenger from God, reading aloud pages purified*, that He is mentioning the Qur'ān in the best way and He praises it highly.
   5.2. Ibn Zayd said concerning *therein true books*, establishing righteousness and justice.

6. The Most High said, *And those who were given the book did not separate except after the clear sign came to them* which is just like His saying, *Be not as those who are separated and differed after the clear signs came to them. For those people there will be a mighty punishment* (Q 3/105). By this He means that the people of the revealed books among the communities before us, after God had established for them the proofs and evidence, divided into groups and differed in understanding what God meant in their books. They differed greatly as is illustrated by the widely transmitted report, 'The Jews differed in seventy-one ways and the Christians differed in seventy-two ways. This community will divide into seventy-three groups all of which will be in the fire of hell, except one. They asked, "Which group is this, messenger of God?" He replied, "Those who follow me and my companions."'

7. Concerning His saying, *They were commanded only to serve God, making the religion His sincerely,* this is like *We have not sent a messenger before you without revealing to him that there is no god but Me, so worship Me!* (Q 21/25). About this He mentioned the *men of true faith*, that is, those inclined away from polytheism towards monotheism, as in His saying, *We sent a messenger to each community (saying) 'Worship God and avoid falsehood!'* (Q 16/36).

The meaning of 'man of pure faith' (*ḥanīf*) has been stipulated in the treatment of *sūrat al-an'ām* (6) and I am able to dispense with repeating that here.

8. *And to establish prayer*, that is, the best of bodily actions of worship. *And pay the alms*, that is, benevolence towards the poor and the needy. *And that is the religion of the true*, that is, the true, just congregation (*milla*), or the righteous, just community (*umma*). Many of the *imāms* such as al-Zuhrī and al-Shāfiʿī have argued on the basis of these glorious verses that works are a part of faith. God has said, *They were commanded only to serve God, making the religion His sincerely as men of true faith, and to establish prayer and pay the alms; and that is the religion of the true.*

> *The unbelievers of the people of the book and the idolaters will be in the fire of Gehenna, therein dwelling forever. Those are the worst of creatures. But those who believe and do righteous deeds, those are the best of creatures, their recompense is with their Lord; gardens of Eden, underneath which rivers flow, therein dwelling forever and ever; God is well pleased with them and they are well pleased with Him; that is for him who fears his Lord.*

9. The Most High is speaking of the consequences for the liars among the unbelievers of the people of the book and the idolaters who reject the revealed books of God and the prophets whom God has sent. After the day of judgement they *will be in the fire of Gehenna, therein dwelling forever*, that is, remaining there without departing from there, and they will not cease being there. *Those are the worst of creatures*, that is, the worst of creation whom God created and produced.

10. Then the Most High spoke of the pious ones *who believe* in their hearts and *do righteous deeds* with their bodies. They are *the best of creatures*. Abū Hurayra and a group of the *ʿulamā'* have argued on the basis of this verse for the merits of the believers from among all the creatures over the angels, due to God's saying, *Those are the best of creatures.*

11. Then the Most High said, *their recompense is with their Lord*, that is, on the day of judgement. *Gardens of Eden, underneath which rivers flow, therein dwelling forever and ever*, that is, never ending, unceasingly, without termination. *God is well pleased with them and they are well pleased with Him*: the station of His being pleased with them is higher than that which they are given of grace. *And they are well pleased with Him*: in what He grants them of general merit.

12. Concerning the Most High's saying, *that is for him who fears his Lord*, that is, this is the reward which is for the one who fears God completely and serves Him, as if he thinks and knows that, even though he does not see Him, He does see him [i.e., that he does everything as if God was watching].

13. Imām Aḥmad said that Isḥāq ibn ʿĪsā told him that Abū Maʿshar told him on the authority of Abū Wahb, the client of Abū Hurayra, on the authority of Abū Hurayra that he said that the messenger of God said, 'Should I tell you about

> the best of creatures?' They said, 'Why, yes, messenger of God!' He said, 'He is the man who holds the reins of his horse in the way of God, waiting for the call to be mounted on it. Should I tell you about the best of creatures?' They said, 'Why, yes, messenger of God!' He said, 'He is the man who, while guarding his flock of sheep, performs the prayer and gives *zakāt*. Should I tell you about the worst of creatures?' They said, 'Why, yes!' 'He is the one who asks for something in the name of God but does not give in the same manner'.

That is the end of the interpretation of *sūrat al-bayyina* (98), by the praise and grace of God.

Chapter 6

Theology and philosophy

6.1 Abū ʿUbayd on faith

A group of Muslim scholars, generally termed the 'Traditionalists', called themselves the *ahl al-sunna*, 'the people of the *sunna*'; the name 'Traditionalist' refers to the use of *ḥadīth* materials in preference to the independent powers of reason. One prominent early representative of this approach was Abū 'Ubayd al-Qāsim ibn Sallām. Born in about 154/770 in Herat, he studied in Kufa, Basra and Baghdad, lived in Khurasan and Baghdad, and ended his life in Mecca, where he died in 224/838. He was a scholar with broad intellectual interests whose influence on many fields of knowledge was significant and lasting. Works on the Qur'ān, *ḥadīth*, lexicography, law and theology are attributed to him.

The nature of early Muslim theological writing is displayed in the *Kitāb al-īmān* of Abū 'Ubayd translated here. In dealing with the controversial but very pressing question of the relationship between faith and works, the book presents an argument based upon direct readings of the Qur'ān and *ḥadīth* reports structured in such a manner as to suggest an origin in the context of popular preaching or rudimentary instruction. The book is likely a transcript of such a session written by a student, as evidenced by the presence of the name of Abū 'Ubayd himself within the text.

Given the controversy surrounding the topic itself, it may be observed that the conclusion arrived at by Muslim consensus was that works do count towards one's status in the community although one can still be a believer and commit sin; there are, therefore, what may be termed 'degrees of faith'. This position, that favoured by traditionalists such as Abū 'Ubayd, then became the position firmly embodied in the books of *ḥadīth* which emerged in the following generations.

The Arabic word *īmān* is commonly translated as 'faith'; the person who has 'faith' is commonly called a 'believer', a *mu'min.* In order to keep the issue clear, that latter word is translated here as 'person of faith'; this helps keep the common sense of 'believe' as an intellectual assent to certain statements separate from the argument of Abū ʿUbayd that faith is saying the *shahāda*, doing the actions required by Islamic law and 'believing' (as commonly understood in English) in one's heart.

Further reading

Toshihiko Izutsu, *The concept of belief in Islamic theology*, reprint, New York 1980.

Wilferd Madelung, 'Early Sunnī doctrine concerning faith as reflected in the *Kitāb al-īmān* of Abū ʿUbayd al-Qāsim b. Sallām (d. 224/839),' *Studia Islamica*, 32 (1970), pp. 233–54; reprinted in his *Religious schools and sects in medieval Islam*, London 1985, chapter 1.

J. Meric Pessagno, 'The Murji'a, īmān and Abū ʿUbayd,' *Journal of the American Oriental Society*, 95 (1975), pp. 382–94.

A. J. Wensinck, *The Muslim creed: its genesis and historical development*, London 1932.

Source text

Abū ʿUbayd, *Kitāb al-īmān*, in Muḥammad Nāṣir al-Dīn al-Albānī (ed.), *Kitāb al-īmān: min kunūz al-sunna, rasāʾil arbaʿ*, Kuwait 1985, pp. 53–66.

Chapter on the characteristics of faith with regards to its perfection and its stages

1. You have asked me about faith (*īmān*) and the disagreement in the community regarding faith's perfection, increase and decrease. You mentioned that you wish to know what the *ahl al-sunna* think about this and what their proofs are against those who differ with them. Indeed, may the mercy of God be upon you, the pious ancestors (*salaf*) discussed this issue during the formative times of this community as did the generation of the followers and all those after them down to this time. I have thus written to you what knowledge I have in this short treatise. All success comes from God!

2. Know, may God have mercy on you, that the people of knowledge and those who are concerned for the religion have divided into two groups on this matter. One of them says that faith is sincerity towards God in the heart, verbal witnessing and bodily actions. The other group says rather that faith is of the heart and the tongue, but actions are a part of God-fearing and piety, and are not a part of faith.

3. When we examined the differences between these two, we found that the book and the *sunna* confirmed those who understood faith as intention, statement and action together, and the statement of the others was not supported by the book and the *sunna*.

3.1. The basis by which we have arrived at this proof follows what the Qur'ān says on the subject. God has said in the unequivocal part of His book, *If you quarrel about anything, refer it to God and the messenger, if you believe in God and the last day. That is better and fairer in the resolution* (Q 4/59).

3.2. We traced the matter back to what God sent to His messenger. God revealed His book to him. We found that He made the beginning of faith to lie in witnessing that 'There is no god but God' and that 'Muḥammad is the messenger of God'. The prophet remained in Mecca for ten or more years after the start of his prophethood, calling everyone to this witnessing only. Nothing else at all was prescribed as a part of faith for the worshippers at that time. Whoever answered the call was one with faith (*mu'min*) and it was not necessary to call him anything else within the religion. Neither *zakāt* nor fasting nor anything else related to the requirements of the religion was required of that person.

3.3. According to what the scholars have reported, this lightening of responsibility on the people at that time was a mercy and kindness from God to his servants. This was necessary because they had only recently left the state of *jāhiliyya* and its harshness. If God had imposed all the duties upon them at one time, their hearts would have turned away from Him and their bodies would have been burdened. So affirmation (*iqrār*) by their tongues was made the only duty of faith for the people at that time. That was so for their entire stay in Mecca as well as for ten or so months in Medina after the *hijra*.

3.4. When the people were established firmly in Islam, God increased them in their faith by changing the direction of prayer to the Kaʿba after it had been towards Jerusalem. He said, *We have seen you turning your face about in the heavens; now We will certainly turn you to a direction that will satisfy you. Turn your face to the holy mosque and wherever you are, turn your face towards it* (Q 2/144). He then addressed them while they were in Medina, speaking to them in the name of faith, just as they had previously been addressed whenever He had ordered them to do something or forbidden them from doing something. Thus He said, *O you who believe, bow down and prostrate!* (Q 22/77) and *O you who believe, when you stand up to pray, wash your faces and your hands up to your elbows* (Q 5/6). He also forbade them, saying, *O you who believe, do not devour usury, doubled and redoubled* (Q 3/130), and *O you who believe, do not kill game while in the sacred state of the pilgrim* (Q 5/95).

3.5. Thus, in every address to them after the *hijra* in which there was a command or prohibition, He called them by this name ('You who believe') on account of their affirmation of the *shahāda* alone. There was nothing else obligatory for them at that time. When the laws were revealed, they were obligatory for them in the same way that the first obligation of the *shahāda* was obligatory; no differentiation was made between them because they were all from God, by His command and His obligation. So if, at the time of the changing of the *qibla* (from Jerusalem to the Kaʿba), they had refused to pray towards the Kaʿba, and had kept following the faith which had previously been given the designation of 'faith' and continued to face the *qibla* which had been commanded [i.e., Jerusalem], that would not have helped them at all. They would have been in violation of their affirmation of the *shahāda* because their first act of obedience was not more deserving of the term 'faith' than the second act. When they responded to God and His messenger in establishing the prayer just as they had responded in affirming (the *shahāda*), then these two came together from that time as being called 'faith' because prayer was added to the affirmation.

4. God's statement, *God would never leave your faith to waste; indeed God is gentle towards the people and compassionate* (Q 2/143), demonstrates that prayer is a part of faith. This was revealed about those companions of the messenger of God who died while the direction of prayer was still towards Jerusalem. The messenger of God was asked about them and this verse was revealed. What more proof could be needed after this verse to be able to say that prayer is a part of faith?

5. They remained this way for a period of time, they hastened to prayer and their hearts accepted it. Then God revealed the obligation of *zakāt* as a part of their faith, adding to what had come before. He said, *Establish prayer and give* zakāt (Q 2/83 and 2/110) and *Take of their wealth a freewill offering to purify them and cleanse them thereby* (Q 9/103). If they had refused to give *zakāt* while giving affirmation of their faith, or had provided affirmation of their faith verbally and established prayer but refused to give *zakāt*, that would have eliminated what had come before and nullified their affirmation of faith and prayer, just as the refusal to accept the imposition of prayer before that would have nullified their affirmation of faith which had preceded it. Confirmation of that is seen in the *jihād* of Abū Bakr al-Ṣiddīq along with the emigrants and the helpers against the Arabs who objected to paying the *zakāt*, just like the *jihād* of the messenger of God against the idolaters. There is no difference between them in terms of the shedding of blood, taking children as captives and the taking of booty. The Arabs had objected to paying *zakāt*, but they had not repudiated the obligation.

6. All the laws of Islam became established in the same way. Whenever a law was revealed, it became a part of what had already been established before. All of them became a part of what was called 'faith' and those who followed them were called 'people of faith'. This is where those who follow those who say that faith is by speech alone err. When they heard God call them 'people of faith' (the first time), they attributed to them complete, perfect faith. They make the same error in the interpretation of the *ḥadīth* report of the prophet of God when he was asked what faith was. He replied that it is that you have faith in God and so forth. Also, when he was asked by someone who had a slave girl who was a person of faith whom he wished to free, Muḥammad ordered that she be freed and he called her a 'person of faith'. These reports are, as I have told you, about their entering into faith, their acceptance of it and their declaring the truth of what had been revealed of the conditions of faith at that time. The contents of faith were revealed in stages just like the revelation of the Qurʾān.

6.1. The witness and evidence for what we say is in the book of God and in the *sunna* of the messenger of God. From the book of God is His saying, *Whenever a* sūra *is sent down, some of them say, 'Which of you has this increased in belief?' As for those who believe, it has increased them in belief and they are joyful* (Q 9/124), and *Those are only the ones who believe who, when God is mentioned, their hearts quake, and when His signs are recited to them it increases them in faith and they put their trust in their Lord* (Q 8/2). There are other passages in the Qur'ān that are similar.

6.2. Do you not see that God did not reveal faith to them as a single entity just as He did not reveal the Qur'ān as a single entity? This is the proof from the book, for if faith was complete by that affirmation, there would be no meaning to the idea of 'increasing' [as in Q 9/124] and it would not have been mentioned in this passage.

7. As for the proof from the *sunna* and the fully authenticated reports (*āthār*) concerning this concept of the increase in the precepts of faith in which some of them come after others, we find that in one *ḥadīth* there are four requirements, in another, five, in the third, nine, and in the fourth, even more.

7.1. A *ḥadīth* transmitted by Ibn ʿAbbās from the prophet containing four precepts is as follows. A delegation from ʿAbd al-Qays came to him and said, 'Messenger of God, we are a tribe from Rabīʿa and the unbelievers of Maḍr reside between us and you. We are only safe in the sacred month to come to you. So command us with an order which we can do and we will pass it on to those we left behind.' So, Muḥammad said, 'I command you with four precepts and I forbid you with four precepts. One is faith,' which he explained was the *shahāda*, witnessing that there is no god but God and that Muḥammad is the messenger of God; 'the others are establishing prayer, giving *zakāt* and giving one-fifth of whatever you take in booty. And I forbid you from four actions associated with pagan times.'

7.1.1. Abū ʿUbayd said that ʿAbbād ibn ʿAbbād al-Muhallabī told him this report, saying that Abū Jamra told him on the authority of Ibn ʿAbbās on the authority of the prophet.

7.2. A *ḥadīth* transmitted from Ibn ʿUmar containing the five precepts reports that he heard the messenger of God saying, 'Islam is built upon five precepts: the *shahāda* (that there is no god but God and that Muḥammad is the messenger of God), the establishment of prayer, the giving of *zakāt*, the fast in Ramaḍān and the pilgrimage to the house in Mecca.'

7.2.1. Abū ʿUbayd said that Isḥāq ibn Sulaymān al-Rāzī told him this report on the authority of Ḥanẓala ibn Abī Sufyān on the authority of ʿIkrima ibn Khālid on the authority of Ibn ʿUmār on the authority of the prophet.

7.3. A *ḥadīth* transmitted from Abū Hurayra containing the nine precepts reports on the authority of the prophet that he said, 'Islam has waymarks (*ṣuwā*) and lights just like the lights of a road.' Abū ʿUbayd said that *ṣuwā* are things which come up and out of the ground; the singular is *ṣuwa*. They are that you believe in God and not believe in any partners to Him, that you establish prayer, give *zakāt*, fast during Ramaḍān, go on the pilgrimage to the house, command good, forbid evil, and that you greet your family with the *taslīm* when you enter among them, and that you greet people with the *taslīm* when you go by them. Whoever neglects any of that has left a portion of Islam and whoever leaves them all has put Islam behind him.

7.3.1. Abū ʿUbayd said, 'Yaḥyā ibn Saʿīd al-ʿAṭṭār told me this report on the authority of Thawr ibn Yazīd on the authority of Khālid ibn Miʿdān on the authority of a certain man who transmitted it on the authority of Abū Hurayra on the authority of the prophet.'

7.4. Ignorant people have thought that these reports were contradictory because of the variance in the number of precepts among them. However, it is a glory to God and because of His mercy that these are, in fact, not at all contradictory. As I have indicated to you, the revelation of the requirements of faith was in stages. Every time one was revealed, the messenger of God joined it to the precepts of faith. Whenever God revealed to him another of them, he would add it to the number such that it eventually became seventy items, just as it says in the *ḥadīth* authenticated by Muḥammad in which he said, 'Faith has seventy-odd parts of which the most excellent is the *shahāda* that there is no god but God and the lowest is removal of harmful things from the road.'

7.4.1. Abū ʿUbayd said that Abū Aḥmad al-Zubayr told us this report on the authority of Sufyān ibn Saʿīd on the authority of Suhayl ibn Abī Ṣāliḥ on the authority of ʿAbd Allāh ibn Dīnār on the authority of Abū Ṣāliḥ on the authority of Abū Hurayra.

8. Even though the number in this report is greater, there is no disagreement with those which came before since they refer to the pillars and roots of faith while these are its requirements, which are greater in number in the edifice of faith than those pillars. On the basis of the number as stated and the characteristics provided, we consider, and God knows best, that this other statement in which the messenger of God described faith is confirmed as the summation of Islam by the saying of God, *Today I have perfected your religion for you and have completed My favour to you* (Q 5/3).

8.1. Abū ʿUbayd said that ʿAbd al-Raḥmān told him on the authority of Sufyān on the authority of Qays ibn Muslim on the authority of Ṭāriq ibn Shihāb that the Jews said to ʿUmar ibn al-Khaṭṭāb, 'You recite a verse which, if it had been revealed about us, indeed we would have made that occasion a festival day.' This verse was then mentioned. ʿUmar said, 'Indeed, I know where and on which day it was revealed. It was revealed at ʿArafa and the messenger of God was performing the standing at ʿArafa.' Sufyān said, 'I do not know whether he said that it was on the day of gathering of the *ḥajj* or not.'

8.2. Abū ʿUbayd said that Yazīd told him on the authority of Ḥammād ibn Salama on the authority of ʿAmmār ibn Abī ʿAmmār that he said that Ibn ʿAbbās repeated this verse in the presence of a Jew who then said, 'If this verse had been revealed about us, indeed we would have made that occasion a festival day.' Ibn ʿAbbās said, 'It was revealed on a festival day, the day of the gathering, and the day of ʿArafa.'
8.3. Abū ʿUbayd said that Ismāʿīl ibn Ibrāhīm told him on the authority of Dāwūd ibn Abī Hind on the authority of Saʿbī who said that it was revealed to Muḥammad while he was standing on ʿArafa when idolatry had faded away and the lights of the *jāhiliyya* had been demolished and no statues decorated the house [i.e., the Kaʿba].
8.4. God declared the perfection of the religion in this verse [i.e., Q 5/3]. According to what has been transmitted, it was revealed eighty-one days before the death of the prophet of God.
8.5. Abū ʿUbayd said that Ḥajjāj told him that on the authority of Ibn Jurayj.
8.6. If faith was perfected by affirmation (alone) when the messenger of God was in Mecca at the beginning of his prophetic mission just as these reports say, then what would the meaning be of 'perfection' (in Q 5/3)? How can something be perfected that already contains perfection and comes in its final form?

9. Abū ʿUbayd said the following. Someone may say to you, 'What are these seventy-three aspects?' The reply would be as follows. They have not been named for us as a grouping to be named individually. However, knowledge indicates that they are (aspects of) obedience to, and fear of, God. Even though they have not been reported to us in any single *ḥadīth*, if you should search the reports, you would find them scattered throughout. Did you not listen to his saying about removal of harm, which was one aspect of faith? Similar is his statement in another *ḥadīth*, 'Modesty is a branch of faith', and in a third, 'Shame is from faith', and in a fourth, 'Abstemiousness is from faith', and in a fifth, 'fulfilling covenants is from faith'. All these are precepts of faith. Among them is the *ḥadīth* of ʿAmmār which says, 'Three things are from faith: spending for charity, being truly just and spreading peace throughout the world.'

10. There are also the well-known *ḥadīth* reports mentioning the perfection of faith, as when Muḥammad asked, 'Which part of creation has the greatest faith?' It was said, 'The angels.' Then it was said, 'We do, O messenger of God.' He then replied, 'No, it is a nation which will come after you,' and then he described them. Another instance is Muḥammad's saying, 'The most perfect in faith, or among the most perfect of the people of faith, is the best of them in character.' Also, there is his saying, 'A man will not have complete faith until he ceases lying in jest and arguing, even if he is truthful.' ʿUmar ibn al-Khaṭṭāb and Ibn ʿUmar transmitted a report like this or one similar to it.

11. Even more apparent than that, as I shall explain, is the report from the prophet concerning intercession. He said, 'The one in whose heart is a grain or speck of faith shall come out of hell fire.' There is also the report about when he was asked about whispering and said, 'That is manifest faith.' Also, there is the report

of ʿAlī, 'Faith starts as a white spot in the heart. As faith increases, that white spot gets bigger.' There are many other reports in this vein that could be mentioned to you to lengthen this explanation of the relationship between the heart and actions in matters of faith. Most, if not all, of them strengthen the notion that works of piety are a part of faith. How could these reports be opposed except by falsehood and mistruth?

12. Among the aspects which confirm the relationship between works and faith is the statement of God, *Only those are the ones who believe who, when God is mentioned, their hearts quake, and when His signs are recited to them it increases them in faith and they put their trust in their Lord, and those who perform the prayer, and expend of what we have provided them, those in truth are the believers* (Q 8/2–4). God did not give to faith a reality other than with actions according to these conditions. Whoever claims that a statement specifically makes one a person of faith in reality, without there being any action with it, is rejecting the book of God and His *sunna*.

12.1. Among the statements which explain the relationship (between faith and works) in the heart are, *O you who believe, when believing women come to you as emigrants, test them* (Q 60/10). Do you not see that there is a level referred to here that is different from another level [as is suggested by the need to 'test them']? *God knows very well their faith. Then, if you know them to be believers (return them not to the unbelievers)* (Q 60/10). Likewise, in a similar way, is His saying, *O you who believe, believe in God and His messenger* (Q 4/136). If this were not a place of increase, what would be the meaning of His ordering them to faith? He also said, *Alif, lām, mīm, Do the people think that they will be left to say 'We believe' and will not be tried? We certainly tried those who were before them, and assuredly God knows those who speak truly and assuredly He knows the liars* (Q 29/1–3); and He said, *There are some men who say, 'We believe in God' but when such a man is hurt for God, he treats the trial of humanity as if it were God's punishment* (Q 29/10); and He said, *God may prove the correctness of those who believe and destroy those who are unbelievers* (Q 3/141).

12.2. Do you not see that God is subjecting them to a test of the sincerity of their statement by an act and that He is not pleased with them solely on the basis of affirmation of the *shahāda* without action, such that He puts one of them after the mention of the other? What else is there to follow after the book of God and the *sunna* of His messenger and, after him, the way of the pious ancestors who are our models and leaders?

13. So, the position which is the *sunna* in all that our scholars have stipulated is what we have reported in this book of ours, and that is that faith consists of intention, statement and actions together. It has levels in which some are above others, except that the beginnings of it and the highest point of it are the verbal utterance of the *shahāda*, just as the messenger of God said in the *ḥadīth* which stipulated seventy-odd aspects (to faith). So, if someone enunciates the *shahāda*, and accepts what has come from God, the name of 'faith' is incumbent for him

because he has entered into it; its perfection will be with God and not in his own purifying himself of desires. As his obedience to, and fear of, God increases, God increases him in faith.

6.2 Al-Nawawī on faith and the divine decree

Born in the village of Nawa, 100 kilometres to the south of Damascus, in 631/1233, Yaḥyā ibn Sharaf Muḥyī ʾl-Dīn al-Nawawī moved to Damascus, where he spent most of the rest of his life, as a student and teacher of the religious sciences. He studied at various *madrasas*, including the Rawāḥiyya and the Dār al-Ḥadīth al-Ashrafiyya. He gained a minor post in the Iqbāliyya in 649/1251, and six years later added to it the major post of 'rector' at the Ashrafiyya, which he held until the year of his death. His lifetime saw the brief Mongol occupation of Damascus (658/1260), the Battle of ʿAyn Jālūt, and the energetic activity of the Mamluk sultan Baybars to lay the foundation of Mamluk power (centred in Cairo), and to rid the province of Syria of Christian and other independent powers. Baybars and al-Nawawī died in the same year, 676/1277.

Through his post in the Ashrafiyya and his learning, al-Nawawī was an influential figure who occasionally came into conflict, it is said, with Baybars. He was a Shāfiʿī jurist, and a famous commentator on *ḥadīth*. He produced an important introductory text on the law, the *Kitāb minhaj al-ṭālibīn*, a number of other juristic works, a multi-volume commentary on the *Ṣaḥīḥ* of Muslim, and other works of commentary. His *Kitāb al-arbaʿīn* or *Forty ḥadīth* is a small collection of *ḥadīth*, belonging to an established genre of such works. Such collections might be specialized or general. His was general, with the intention of serving as a fundamental collection whose implications covered all the basic principles of the Muslim religion. He wrote a commentary on the *Forty ḥadīth*, which is short, fairly accessible and clearly intended for a wide audience. The following passage includes the second *ḥadīth* in the collection and a part of the commentary on it.

Further reading

W. Heffening, 'al-Nawawī,' in *Encyclopaedia of Islam*, new edition.
Ezzeddin Ibrahim, Denys Johnson-Davies (trans.), *An-Nawawi's forty hadith. An anthology of sayings of the prophet Muhammad*, Damascus 1976.

Source text

Louis Pouzet, *Une hermeneutique de la tradition islamique: le commentaire des Arba'un al-Nawawiyya de Muhyi al-Din Yahya al-Nawawi*, Beirut 1982, pp. 17–19 of the Arabic text.

Ḥadīth 2

From ʿUmar. While we were sitting with the prophet one day suddenly we were approached by a man, whose clothes were exceedingly white and whose hair was exceedingly black. There was nothing about him to suggest he had been travelling, and none of us knew him. He sat in front of the prophet, setting his knees against the prophet's, and placing his hands upon the prophet's thighs. 'Prophet of God,' he said,

'Tell me about Islam.' 'It is that you should bear witness that there is no god but God, and that Muḥammad is the prophet of God. That you should perform the prayer, give *zakāt*, fast in the month of Ramaḍān and make the pilgrimage to Mecca if you find the means.' 'Correct,' said the stranger. And we were amazed that he should ask the prophet and then pass judgement on the answer. 'Tell me', he said, 'about *īmān*.' 'It is that you should believe in God, his angels, his books, his prophets and the last day. And that you should believe in the divine decree (*qadar*), both the good and the evil of it.' 'Correct. Tell me now about *iḥsān*.' 'It is that you should worship God as if you see him, for though you see him not, he still sees you.' 'Tell me then', said the stranger, 'about the Hour.' 'The one questioned knows no more than the questioner,' said the prophet. 'Tell me of its signs.' 'That the slave girl gives birth to her mistress; that the barefoot, the naked, the destitute, the herders of flocks, will compete in building high houses.' The stranger went off. The prophet waited for a short time, then said, 'ʿUmar, do you know who that was?' 'God and His prophet know best.' 'It was the angel Gabriel. He came to give you instruction in your religion.'

1. 'Tell me about *īmān*.' *Īmān*, linguistically, means assent. In the law, it is an expression for a special type of assent, namely assent to God, His angels, His books, His messengers, the last day and the divine decree, both the good and the evil of it. Islam is an expression for doing what is mandatory, that is participation in the externals of practice. God distinguishes in the Qurʾān *īmān* and *islām* as they are distinguished in this *ḥadīth*. *The bedouin say, We have* īmān. *Say, You do not have* īmān*; affirm rather that you have* islām (Q 49/14). This verse relates to the hypocrites. They used to pray, fast and give alms, while in their hearts there was rejection. Hence, when they claimed *īmān*, God accused them of lying because of the rejection that was in their hearts. But God acknowledged their claim to *islām* because of their practice. Further, God says, *When the hypocrites come to you, they say, We testify that you are God's messenger; God knows that you are his messenger. But God testifies that the hypocrites are liars* (Q 63/1). They are liars in claiming that they testify to Muḥammad's status as messenger, since their hearts dispute this. For their tongues do not match their hearts. And that tongues should match hearts is a condition of this testimony. Since they lied in their claim, God explained their lie.

2. Since *īmān* is a condition for the validity of [the acts that constitute] *islām*, God has also mentioned the category of *muslims* [those with *islām*] as coinciding with the category of *muʾmins* [those with *īmān*]. God says, *We brought out those* muʾmin*s who were there. And we found there only a single tribe of* muslims (Q 51/35–6). This is a rhetorical figure known as the 'linked exclusion'. It depends on the continuity or linking of the condition and that which is conditioned. On the same ground we find that God calls prayer *īmān* [i.e., on the grounds that *īmān* is a condition of valid prayer]. Hence God says, *God does not neglect your* īmān (Q 2/143), and *You do not know what the book is, nor* īmān (Q 42/52), meaning, in both cases, prayer.

3. 'And that you should believe in the divine decree (*qadar*), both the good and the evil of it.' The word for divine decree may be spelled *qadar* or *qadr*. It is the tradition amongst true believers to affirm the divine decree. The meaning of

this is that God has decreed things from eternity, and He knows that they will happen at times and in places known to Him. Also, that they will happen in accord with His decree.

4. Know that divine decrees are of four kinds.

   4.1. The decree subsisting in divine knowledge. Because of this it is said, 'Outcome is prior to appointment; happiness is prior to birth; proceedings are built on what precedes.' God says, *They are deflected from it, those who were deflected* (Q 51/9). This means that those people are turned away from listening to the Qur'ān and giving assent to it who were turned away in pre-eternity. The prophet said that God destroys only those on the way to destruction. He meant those about whom it is inscribed in God's eternal knowledge that they will be destroyed.
   4.2. The decree inscribed on the preserved tablet. Decrees of this type are susceptible to change. God says, *God erases whatever he desires, and he affirms. The mother of the book is his* (Q 13/39). Further, there is a report from Ibn ʿUmar that he used to pray thus, 'O God, if You have written my name as one who will perish, wipe it out, and write me down as one who will prosper.'
   4.3. The decree in the womb. This refers to the fact that the angel is commanded to write down for a foetus its provision, its life-span and its miserable or prosperous end.
   4.4. The decree which consists in driving human fates to their appointed times. For God creates both good and evil, and He decrees their impingement on humans at known times. The evidence for God's creation of both good and evil is in His words, *The wicked are in error, and in madness. On the day they are dragged on their faces to hellfire – Taste the touch of Hell! We have created all things according to the decree* (Q 54/47–9). These verses were revealed about the Qadariyya. They will be addressed thus in hell. Further, God says, *Say, I seek refuge with the Lord of dawn from the evil he created* (Q 113/1–2). This category of decree may be averted from man before the time of its arrival, if divine grace supervenes. In a *ḥadīth*, it is said, 'Alms and the provision for relatives may cancel a death that is evil and change it into a death of prosperity.' In another *ḥadīth*, 'Between heaven and earth, prayer and misfortune struggle, and prayer may cancel misfortune before it occurs.'

5. The Qadariyya used to claim that God did not decree things in pre-eternity, and that His knowledge does not precede events. They said that events are initiated by people and that God knows them after their occurrence. They lie about God, may He be blessed and exalted beyond their lying words. But this group have died out, and the Qadariyya in recent times claim rather that good comes from God and that evil comes from another source. True, then, are the words of the prophet, 'The Qadariyya are the Zoroastrians of this community.' He called them Zoroastrians because their beliefs correspond to those of the Zoroastrians. The dualist Zoroastrians claim that good is the work of light and that evil is the work of darkness, and hence they are dualists. Likewise are the Qadariyya; they

attribute good to God and evil to something else. But He is the creator of both good and evil.

6. The Imām al-Ḥaramayn, al-Juwaynī, in his *Kitāb al-irshād*, relates the words of one of the Qadariyya. 'We are not *qadarī*', he said, 'but you are *qadarī* because you believe in the reports about *qadar*.' Al-Juwaynī refuted the claims of these ignoramuses, by pointing out that they attribute *qadar* [i.e., power over their actions] to themselves. Those who claim evil for themselves and attribute it to themselves are more reasonably associated with it than those who attribute it to another and reject it from themselves.

6.3 Ibn Qutayba on the partisans of theological reasoning

ʿAbd Allāh ibn Muslim Abū Muḥammad Ibn Qutayba was a central figure in formative Islamic theology and literature (*adab*). He was born in Kufa in 213/828 and he studied with some major theologians, philologists and traditionists in the area. He died in Baghdad in 276/889. His works range from philological commentaries on the Qur'ān and *ḥadīth* to works on poetry, from a brief encyclopaedia dealing with the known world to a manual for secretaries. His *Kitāb ta'wīl mukhtalif al-ḥadīth* is, on the surface, an attempt to interpret (that is, apply *ta'wīl* to) problematic portions of the *sunna*. Its overall argument, however, provides an opportunity for him to set out his ideas on the theological and political issues of his time. In this way, Ibn Qutayba provides a definition of what was, to him, the true Muslim community.

In the introduction to this book Ibn Qutayba identifies two groups of whom he disapproves, namely the *aṣḥāb al-kalām* and the *aṣḥāb al-ra'y*. The former are those who indulge in (excessive) theological speculation and can probably be identified largely (perhaps not exclusively) with the Muʿtazila. The latter are the jurists, the followers of the major early masters like Mālik ibn Anas and some secondary masters like Sufyān al-Thawrī and al-Awzāʿī. Ibn Qutayba identifies himself with a third group, the *aṣḥāb al-ḥadīth*. This is the group which, according to him, cling to prophetic *ḥadīth* and the Qur'ān, and so avoid error and dispute. They are, however, accused by their opponents of lies, confusion and contradiction. The bulk of Ibn Qutayba's book is concerned with apparent contradictions between *ḥadīth* and *ḥadīth* or between *ḥadīth* and the Qur'ān. These he undertakes to resolve. His resolutions are designed to enunciate an anti-rationalist position, in which consensus is the only supplement to the Qur'ān and the *sunna* for the community. The use of *ra'y* by the Ḥanafīs and *qiyās* by the Shāfiʿīs is condemned, and he clearly supports the political position of the anti-Muʿtazilī ʿAbbāsid regime.

Further reading

Norman Calder, *Studies in early Muslim jurisprudence,* Oxford 1993, pp. 223–33.
I. M. Husayni, *The life and works of Ibn Qutayba*, Beirut 1950.
Gérard Lecomte, *Ibn Qutayba (mort en 276 (889)): l'homme, son oeuvre, ses idées*, Damascus 1965.

Source text

Ibn Qutayba, *Kitāb ta'wīl mukhtalif al-ḥadīth*, Beirut 1393/1972, pp. 13–17. A French translation of the entire work is available: Gérard Lecomte (trans.), *Le traité des divergences du ḥadīṯ d'Ibn Qutayba*, Damascus 1962.

1. I have considered the talk of the *ahl al-kalām* and I have found that they say things concerning God that they do not truly know. They try the people with their words. They detect the speck in the eyes of the people while their own eyes are closed to beams. They cast aspersions on others in matters of transmission (*naql*, 'revelation') while not criticizing their own opinions in matters of *taʾwīl*. The meanings of the book [i.e., the Qurʾān] and *ḥadīth*, the subtleties of wisdom and of language which these contain, cannot be understood by reference to 'the leap' or 'generation' or 'accidents' or 'essences', nor by reference to 'how-ness' or 'how much-ness' or 'where-ness'. If they would refer the difficulties of the book and *ḥadīth* to those who have knowledge of these materials, the path would become clear and the solution evident. But they are held back from this by desire for status, and love of followers, and the faith of the brotherhood in intellectual discussion. For people are like flocks of birds: they follow one another. If there appeared amongst them a man claiming prophecy – though they know that the prophet is the seal of prophets – or a man claiming divinity, such a one would find followers and believers.

2. Considering their claim to know logical deduction and to have prepared the tools of rational discourse, they should not differ amongst themselves. Mathematicians, geometrists and engineers do not differ amongst themselves. This is because the tools of their science lead to a single number or a single shape. And skilled doctors do not differ on the nature [or function] of water, nor on the pulse of the arteries, because the ancients have taught them one doctrine. But what about them? They are the most contentious of people, no two of their leaders agreeing on any one thing in the field of religion. Abū ʾl-Hudhayl al-ʿAllāf disagrees with al-Naẓẓām; and al-Najjār disagrees with both of them; and Hishām ibn al-Ḥakam opposes all three. And so also with Thumāma, Muways, Hāshim al-Awqāṣ, ʿUbayd Allāh ibn al-Ḥasan, Bakr al-ʿAmmī, Ḥafṣ, Qubba and so on and so forth. There is not one of them who does not have his own religious system – adopted on a basis of opinion – and not one of them who does not have his own followers.

3. If their differences were in the fields of *furūʿ* and *sunan* [i.e., in details of legal prescription], they would, in our view, be absolved from guilt – though there is no excuse for them in view of what they claim for themselves – just as the jurists are absolved from guilt in their differences. The jurists would constitute a model for them. But their differences are on the questions of God's unity, his attributes, his power, on the felicity of the inhabitants of paradise and the punishment of the inhabitants of hell, on limbo between life and death, on the tablet, and on other matters which even a prophet does not know except through revelation from God.

4. This difference will not disappear by referring these principles to preference, or rational consideration or the result of analogical thinking because of the differences of mankind in their intellects and wills and choices. You can scarcely find two men in agreement, such that each one favours what the other favours, or rejects what the other rejects, except it be a result of submission to authority. He who differentiated between their capacities for rational thought, and between

their shapes and colours and languages and voices; between their handwritings and their tracks – such that a skilled tracker can distinguish one from another – and between male and female, he differentiated too their opinions. And he who differentiated their opinions, he willed the dispute amongst them. Wisdom and power will not be perfect except through the creation of a thing and its opposite, so that each may be known through the other. For light is known through darkness and knowledge through ignorance, and good is known through evil, benefit through loss and sweetness through bitterness. As God has said, *Praise be to him who has created pairs, all of them; in what the earth produces, and in themselves and in what they do not know* (Q 36/36). *Pairs* here means opposites and categories such as male and female, dry and moist. He also said, *He created the pair, male and female* (Q 53/45).

5. If we wished to abandon the *aṣḥāb al-ḥadīth* and turn from them to the *aṣḥāb al-kalām*, and to follow them, then we would pass from unity to disunity, from order to dispute, from civility to barbarity, from agreement to difference. For the *aṣḥāb al-ḥadīth* are agreed on the following points:

   (a) that whatever God wills is and whatever he does not will is not
   (b) that he is the creator of good and of evil
   (c) that the Qur'ān is the word of God, uncreated
   (d) that God will be seen on the day of resurrection
   (e) on the priority of the two *shaykh*s [i.e., Abū Bakr and ʿUmar]
   (f) on belief in the punishment of the grave.

   On these principles, they have no disputes. Whoever departs from them on these matters is opposed, despised, accused of heresy and abandoned. However, they differ on the question of the pronunciation of the Qur'ān, because of an obscurity pertaining to that matter. But all of them are agreed that the Qur'ān in whatever state – recited, written, heard, memorized – is uncreated. This is *ijmāʿ*.

6. As to the establishment of authority for these principles, it is based on the outstanding *ʿulamā'*, the *fuqahā'* of earlier generations, the pious who strove, who could not be kept up with, whose achievement cannot be matched. They are the like of Sufyān al-Thawrī, Mālik ibn Anas, al-Awzāʿī, Shuʿba and Layth ibn Saʿd; also the *ʿulamā'* of the great cities like Ibrāhīm ibn Adham, Muslim al-Khawwāṣ, al-Fuḍayl ibn ʿIyāḍ, Dāwūd al-Ṭāʾī, Muḥammad ibn al-Naḍr al-Ḥārithī, Aḥmad ibn Ḥanbal, Bishr al-Ḥāfī and others of similar stature who lived near to our time. As to the ancients, they are more than can be counted.

7. Further, authority is derived from the masses of the people, the common people, the generality in every town and in every age. For one of the signs of truth is the agreement and satisfaction of their hearts. If a man were to stand up in their meeting places and their market places proclaiming the doctrines of the *aṣḥāb al-ḥadīth*, those concerning which we have mentioned their agreement, there would be no opponent in their midst, none to deny these beliefs. But if he stood up to proclaim what the *aṣḥāb al-kalām* believe, which is opposed to these beliefs, he would scarcely last for the twinkling of an eye.

6.4 Al-Ghazālī on theological reasoning

Muḥammad ibn Muḥammad Abū Ḥāmid al-Ghazālī was born at Tus near the modern city of Mashhad in 450/1058. He went to Nishapur, where he was a pupil of al-Juwaynī, traditionally referred to as Imām al-Ḥaramayn, until the latter's death in 478/1085. In that year he came to the attention of Niẓām al-Mulk, and in 484/1091 he became a professor at the Niẓāmiyya *madrasa* in Baghdad. He privately pursued the study of philosophy and wrote several books. In 488/1095, he withdrew from teaching and made the pilgrimage to Mecca, but in reality he was abandoning his professorship and his whole career as a jurist and theologian. He returned to teaching at Nishapur in 499/1106, in the meantime having lived as a Ṣūfī, and written his most significant work, his *Iḥyāʾ ʿulūm al-dīn* ('The revival of the religious sciences'). He died in 505/1111.

It was not long after returning to Nishapur that he wrote *al-Munqidh min al-ḍalāl* ('Deliverance from error') which appears to be, and has usually been interpreted as, a spiritual or intellectual autobiography. It is probably better understood as a work of epistemology. Right knowledge is that which, in the end, is shown to deliver one from error. In the course of coming to that conclusion al-Ghazālī portrays the major epistemological categories of his day. He begins with radical doubt and its cure. He then considers, in turn, the achievements of the theologians (the *mutakallimūn*), the philosophers, the Ismāʿīlīs (the Taʿlīmiyya) and the mystics (the Ṣūfīs). The last two sections of his book are entitled 'The truth of prophecy' and 'The return to teaching'. In the first of these, he denies that the intellect is the highest faculty of the soul and puts forward a theory of a higher faculty that is concerned with the unseen. This, in brief, is his reply to the philosophers; for him, prophecy is a faculty of perception grounded in this part of the soul. The essential characteristics of the prophetic experience can be understood by non-prophets through 'taste' (i.e., direct experience) by following the path of the Ṣūfīs. In the last section al-Ghazālī defends his decision to return to teaching, a process he sees as one of correcting the errors of those who deviate from truth (i.e., Ismāʿīlīs, philosophers, etc.) and guiding people to the truth of prophetic knowledge.

The discussion of *kalām*, which is presented here, reveals that al-Ghazālī considered its primary function to be defending the religion from innovation, perhaps referring to the Muʿtazilites, and that he found it inadequate for the discovery of knowledge of necessary truths.

Further reading

Richard M. Frank, *Al-Ghazālī and the Ashʿarite school*, Durham NC 1994.

Richard Joseph McCarthy, *Freedom and fulfillment. An annotated translation of al-Ghazālī's* al-Munqidh min al-ḍalāl *and other relevant works of al-Ghazālī*, Boston 1980; contains an extensive bibliography, pp. 383–92.

Farouk Mitha, *Al-Ghazālī and the Ismailis: a debate on reason and authority in medieval Islam*, London 2001.

Source text

Farid Jabre, *Al-Munqid min aḍalāl (Erreur de délivrance)*, Beirut 1959 (Collection UNESCO d'oeuvres representatives, série Arabe), pp. 16–17 of the Arabic text.

Chapter: The science of **kalām***: its aims and achievement*

1. I began with the science of *kalām*, gathering it and considering it. I studied the works of the adepts of this science, and composed works on it according to my desire. I found it a science adequate to its own aims, but not adequate to mine.

2. The aim of this science is to defend the creed of the orthodox and to guard it from the confusion of the innovators. For God has given to his servants, through the words of his prophet, a creed which is the truth. Upon it depends the welfare of their spiritual and secular life. Qur'ān and *akhbār* articulate knowledge of it. Subsequently the devil introduced, through the murmurings of the innovators, matters opposed to orthodoxy (*sunna*). They became besotted with these matters and almost corrupted the true creed of those who possessed it. Hence God sent the group known as *mutakallims* (or theologians) and He moved them to defend the *sunna* through systematic theology which revealed the contrived obscurities of the innovators that were in opposition to the established *sunna*. Thus the science of *kalām* and its practitioners grew up.

3. A group of them undertook the task to which they had been appointed by God: they skilfully defended the *sunna*, struggled on behalf of the creed received through acceptance from prophecy, and changed what the innovators had introduced. But they relied, in all this, upon principles which they had accepted from their adversaries, being compelled to do so by either *taqlīd*, or consensus of the community, or simply acceptance from Qur'ān and *akhbār*. Most of their activities were concerned with demonstration of the contradictions of their adversaries or with criticism of the conclusions which necessarily followed from their (adversaries') assumptions.

4. This was of little use to one who accepts only necessary truths; and so *kalām* was of little use to me and constituted no cure for my malady.

5. When the skills of *kalām* developed, and the practice of it increased and time passed, the *mutakallimūn* developed a taste for defending [the *sunna*] through investigating the true nature of things. They plunged into discussion of 'essences' and 'accidents' and their attendant rules. However, since this was not the aim of their science, their investigations did not achieve their ultimate target. And they did not achieve [an understanding] which could completely remove the darkness of confusion that lies in human dispute.

6. I do not consider it impossible that this was achieved for others, indeed I do not doubt that for a certain group of people it was achieved; but it was an achievement mixed with *taqlīd* in areas other than first principles. My aim at present is to tell of my own state, and not to contradict those who look for a cure in *kalām*.

6.5 ʿAbd al-Jabbār on knowledge

Qāḍī al-Quḍāt ʿAbd al-Jabbār ibn Aḥmad Abūʾl-Ḥasan was a major Muʿtazilī thinker of medieval Islam. Born around 325/936, he lived in Baghdad until he was appointed as judge in Rayy in 367/978. He died in 415/1025. His main work is entitled *al-Mughnī*, and is an extensive treatment of all aspects of Muʿtazilī dogma. In his work, *al-Muḥīṭ*, as preserved in the paraphrase/commentary compiled by his student Ibn Mattawayh (d. 469/1076), ʿAbd al-Jabbār provides a fairly concise survey of the main principles and arguments that constitute Muʿtazilī theology. The organizing principle and *raison d'être* of the book is the notion of *taklīf* and the role of the human to be a *mukallaf*: it is an explanation of what must be known in order for a person to fulfil the divine commission (*taklīf*) and truly become a *mukallaf*.

The translated passage is taken from an introductory chapter in which ʿAbd al-Jabbār gives a pre-emptive survey of the material he intends to cover. In the immediately preceding chapter he had set out the basic divisions of knowledge that human beings were charged (*taklīf*) to acquire. Here, he justifies the structure and organization of his book. That organization is based on the five principles of the Muʿtazila: divine unity (*tawḥīd*), divine justice (*ʿadl*), the promise and the threat, commanding what is good and prohibiting what is evil, and the intermediate position. ʿAbd al-Jabbār's concern to demonstrate the integrity, coherence and sufficiency of his organization is not simply a matter of aesthetics. The way in which Muʿtazilī beliefs lent themselves to a systematic and orderly structure of classification and argument was also a sign of their validity (see below in paragraph 10).

Further reading

Binyamin Abrahamov, 'ʿAbd al-Jabbār's theory of divine assistance (*luṭf*),' *Jerusalem studies in Arabic and Islam*, 16 (1993), pp. 41–58.

Margaretha Heemskerk, *Suffering in the Muʿtazilite theology: ʿAbd al-Jabbār's teaching on pain and divine justice*, Leiden 2000; see especially pp. 142–51 on *taklīf* and *luṭf*.

Richard Martin, Mark R. Woodward, Dwi S. Atmaja, *Defenders of reason in Islam. Muʿtazilism from medieval school to modern symbol*, Oxford 1997.

Source text

ʿAbd al-Jabbār, *Kitāb al-majmūʿ fīʾl-muḥīṭ biʾl-taklīf*, ed. J. I. Houben, Beirut 1965, vol. 1, pp. 11–12. On the authorship of the work itself see the 'Note annexe' by Daniel Gimaret in vol. 2, pp. 19–32 of the text (published under the name of Abū Muḥammad ibn Mattawayh), Beirut 1981.

Chapter: On the organization of these branches of knowledge

1. The aim of this chapter is to establish the manner of organizing the branches of knowledge which we have asserted are necessary for the *mukallaf*; it is also to establish which knowledge is of primary rank and which is of secondary rank.

2. The fundamental principle here is that affirmation of God's unity (*tawḥīd*) comes first and the question of divine justice (*ʿadl*) is subordinate to it. There are two reasons for this:

   (a) Knowledge of divine justice relates to knowledge of God's actions. In order that we may validly discuss His actions, knowledge of His essence must precede, for discussion of His actions is discussion of something which is other than Him.
   (b) We infer His justice by reference to His being knowing and self-sufficient. But these last points are part of the subject matter of *tawḥīd*. Hence *tawḥīd* must come first so that the discussion of justice can be built on it.

3. Just as justice is subordinate to *tawḥīd*, so also *tawḥīd* is based on certain principles without which there can be no understanding of *tawḥīd*. Consider: the aim of *tawḥīd* is to identify God as uniquely possessed of attributes to which no other being can lay claim. But this aim cannot be achieved without knowledge of the origination of bodies and their dependence on an originator, together with the establishment of God as their sole originator. Subsequent to this comes the explanation of the attributes affirmed of His essence, and of that which is impossible in reference to Him. We must acquire knowledge of all this first. When it has been established, then *tawḥīd* has been understood.

4. The discussion of divine justice is built on this foundation. But justice, too, is based on principles from which the purpose of divine justice is deduced. Consider: the aim of (affirming) divine justice is to establish that God commits no evil and neglects no duty. That being the case, we must first know the moral status of acts and the factors which influence their moral status, that is, what is good, what is evil and what is incumbent, and what influences good, evil and incumbency. Indeed we must understand also those acts which have no moral attribute additional to their origination, such as reflex movements and automatic speech, whether they occur in a sleeping or in a waking agent. Knowledge of these things is necessary because we desire to affirm of Him that He does what is incumbent on Him and we wish to deny that any evil results from His actions. We further deny that His actions can be of that type which have no moral quality additional to their origination, that is, actions which cannot be described as either good or evil.

5. Once we have established these fundamentals, denying that His actions may encompass evil, and affirming that He will do what is incumbent and what is good, then, under the same heading [i.e., that of divine justice] comes discussion of revealed duties which are associated with prophecy. This is because of the following. If God knows that the welfare of His servants depends upon a particular matter which they cannot know through the intellect alone, then He

must send to them one who will inform them of this. It is a matter of removing the cause [of injustice, etc.], and so comes under the general heading of divine justice. We know of the person sent by God that what he commands is good and what he prohibits is evil, and that the information he provides is true.

6. If prophecy and revealed laws come under the heading of divine justice, so too does the question of the promise and the threat. This is because such knowledge as we have of these matters at present is derived from revelation.

7. Likewise, if it is necessary for God to inform us of what is conducive to our welfare, then, by that token, He is responsible for explaining the 'intermediate position'. This is because we are subject to a duty in relation to the moral judgements we pass on others and the names we call them by. These too are for us varieties of benefit and welfare.

8. Likewise, God is responsible for imposing upon us (*taklīf*) the duty of commanding what is good and prohibiting what is evil; this too is part of our welfare.

9. All of these principles and attendant notions come under the general headings of *tawḥīd* and justice according to the structure we have elaborated above.

10. No dispute belonging to the discussion of justice falls outside the structure we have given. For we deny that God may commit evil actions, whereas the Mujbira [who hold that humans do not have a free will] attribute such actions to Him; and we affirm of many actions that they – in so far as they belong to the category of the good – are His, whereas the dualists – believing these actions to be evil – deny they are His. Further, we affirm that it is incumbent upon God to act with grace (*luṭf*) towards the *mukallaf*, whereas the *aṣḥāb al-luṭf* [likely the Ashʿariyya] deny this incumbency. And, contrariwise, whereas the partisans of the 'greater good' (*al-aṣlaḥ*) affirm that it is incumbent on God to do what constitutes the greater good, we deny this incumbency. If you consider all these problems you will realize that there are no problems related to divine justice which fall outside our structure.

6.6 Al-Nasafī and al-Taftāzānī on God's speech

Abū Ḥafṣ ʿUmar al-Nasafī was a Ḥanafī jurist who died in 537/1142. Little is known of him beyond his creedal statement which provides the viewpoint of the Māturīdī school of theology, one which proved to be among the most successful of all such attempts. The creed is structured in what became the standard formulation in the fifth and sixth Muslim centuries. It starts with the sources of knowledge, and then proceeds to describe the world composed of substances and accidents. God as creator of that world is then described, His attributes are investigated and the possibility of a vision of God discussed. The relationship between God and his creation is raised, especially with regards to issues such as freewill, and then the concept and content of belief are outlined (prophets, messengers, angels, the acts of the saints). The work concludes with a consideration of leadership in the state and various other general considerations.

Saʿd al-Dīn al-Taftāzānī was a renowned scholar and author on grammar, rhetoric, theology, logic, law and Qur'ānic exegesis. Born in 722/1322 in Taftazan, a village in Khurasan, he lived mainly in the area of Herat and became famous as a commentator on earlier texts. His works have continued to be used extensively in educational settings down to today. He died in 793/1390.

Al-Taftāzānī's commentary on al-Nasafī's creed, written in 768/1367, has been a standard work of Muslim theological learning from the time it was written, attracting to itself a good number of super-commentaries. The work itself follows standard commentarial form, by quoting a few words at a time from al-Nasafī and then glossing them. Dialectic form provides a good deal of the comment, investigating other possible views and the appropriate response to them. Some of the comments reveal the different theological perspective of al-Taftāzānī: he was a member of the Ashʿarī school of theology. This, however, did not create a situation of conflict or the accusation of 'heresy' because both schools were accepted as valid expressions of Islam, especially in the trans-Oxus area in which al-Taftāzānī was writing, which was heavily populated by followers of the Māturīdī school. Furthermore, al-Taftāzānī himself appears to have tried to forge some consolidation of the two positions, sometimes abandoning the Ashʿarī position in favour of the more moderate Māturīdī one, which was true in general of followers of the Ashʿarī school in medieval times.

Further reading

Zafar Ishaq Ansari, 'Taftāzānī's views on *taklīf, ǧabr* and *qadr*: a note on the development of Islamic theological doctrines,' *Arabica*, 16 (1969), pp. 65–78.

Duncan Black Macdonald, *The development of Muslim theology, jurisprudence and constitutional theory*, London 1902; contains a translation of al-Nasafī's creed, pp. 308–15.

Wilferd Madelung, 'Al-Taftāzānī,' in *Encyclopaedia of Islam*, new edition.

Source text

Al-Taftāzānī, *Sharḥ ʿalā 'l-ʿaqā'id al-Nasafiyya*, Cairo 1916, pp. 77–84. Section I below is the original text of al-Nasafī; section II is al-Taftāzānī's commentary with the text of al-Nasafī (which is being subjected to commentary) being italicized. The full work is available in English translation: E. E. Elder (trans.), *A commentary on the creed of Islam. Sa'd al-Dīn al-Taftāzānī on the creed of Najm al-Dīn al-Nasafī*, New York 1950.

I Al-Nasafī on God's attributes

He has attributes; they are eternal and subsist in His essence. They are not He, nor are they other than He. They are knowledge, power, life, strength, hearing, seeing, will, desire, doing, creating, sustaining and speech (*kalām*). He speaks by means of a *kalām*, which is an attribute of His, an eternal attribute which is not of the genus of letters and sounds. It is an attribute opposed to silence and defect. Through it God speaks, ordering, prohibiting and informing. The Qur'ān, the speech of God, is uncreated. It is written in our volumes, recited by our tongues, heard by our ears, but it is not incarnate (*ḥāll*) in them.

II Al-Taftāzānī's commentary, specifically on the aspect of the divine attribute of speech [picking up at the end of the third sentence of al-Nasafī's statement above; the italicized text is quoted from al-Nasafī]

1. *Speech*: this is an eternal attribute to which [God] has given expression, by that ordered speech which is called the Qur'ān and is composed of letters. Everyone who commands or prohibits or informs finds an idea (*ma'nā*) in his soul (*nafs*), and then indicates it by expression, or by writing, or by gesture. This attribute is not knowledge; for a man may give information concerning things of which he has no knowledge, or of which he knows the contrary. Nor is it will; for a man may order what he does not will, such as a man who orders his slave, intending thereby to demonstrate his disobedience and recalcitrance. This [speech found in the soul] is called speech of the soul. . . .

2. The evidence for the establishment of the attribute of speech is the *ijmā'* of the community and the *tawātur* transmission from the prophets both of which confirm that God speaks, granted also the certain knowledge of the impossibility of speaking without the attribute of speech.

3. It is established then that God has eight attributes: knowledge, power, life, hearing, seeing, will, creativity and speech. Since there is on the last three a great deal of dispute and obscurity, al-Nasafī in his creed repeated the affirmation of their being established, and presented them in some detail.

4. *He*: that is, God; *speaks by means of a* kalām *which is an attribute of His*, because it is necessarily impossible to establish a derivative in a thing without establishing also the source of the derivative in that thing [i.e., if God speaks (derivative), He must possess speech (source)]. This constitutes a refutation of the Mu'tazila who claim that He speaks, by means of a *kalām* which subsists

in something other than Him and is not an attribute of His. *An eternal attribute*: because it is necessarily impossible that originated things should subsist in His essence. *Which is not of the genus of letters and sounds*, because these are necessarily accidents subject to origination, the origination of some of them being conditional upon the completion of others. The impossibility of pronouncing the second letter of a word without finishing the first letter is evident. This constitutes a refutation of the Ḥanābila and the Karrāmiyya who claim that God's *kalām* is an accident of the genus of sounds and letters, and yet, in spite of this, is eternal.

5. *It*, that is, speech; *is an attribute*, that is, an idea existing in the essence; *opposed to silence*: which is not speaking yet having the power to speak; *and defect. . . . Through it God speaks, ordering, prohibiting and informing.* This means that it is one attribute [implying simple, undivided] which becomes many in the form of commands, prohibitions and propositions, through a variety of connections. So also with knowledge, power and the other attributes; each one of them is a single eternal attribute. Multiplicity and origination take place through connections and relationships. This is more fitting to the perfection of God's oneness; and also there is no evidence for multiplicity [division] within each attribute.

   Someone may object, saying that these [i.e., multiplicity and originations and so forth] are divisions of speech; the existence of speech without them is inconceivable. We reply that it is not so. Rather, any one of these divisions only comes into existence as a result of connections. That of course relates only to things that are ongoing. In eternity there is no division whatsoever. . . .

6. When al-Nasafī spoke of the eternity of God's speech, he tried also to show that the term 'the Qur'ān' is applied to the eternal speech of the soul just as it is applied to the ordered speech which is recited and originated. And so he said, *the Qur'ān, the speech of God, is uncreated.* He followed the term, 'the Qur'ān', with the words, 'the speech of God', because of what the early shaykhs said, namely, that it is acceptable to say that the Qur'ān, the speech of God, is uncreated; but it is not acceptable to say that the Qur'ān is uncreated. This is so that it should not occur to the mind that the thing composed of sounds and letters is eternal. This, however, is the position taken up by the Ḥanābila, out of ignorance and obstinacy. . . . The evidence for our position is what has been already stated, namely, that it is established by *ijmāʿ* and by *tawātur*, from the prophets, that God speaks; and there can be no meaning to this statement except that He has the attribute of speech. And since the subsistence of verbal, originated speech in His essence is impossible, it is sure that His speech is of the soul and eternal. . . .

7. The Muʿtazila, since they were unable to deny that God speaks, claimed that He speaks only in the sense of bringing into existence sounds and letters in their places; or He speaks in the sense of bringing into existence the forms of writing on the preserved tablet, though they are not read there. There is some dispute amongst them on the last point. But you are aware that the concept 'one who moves' refers to one in whom movement subsists and does not mean

one who brings movement into existence. If the Muʿtazilī argument were correct, it would be correct to attribute to God all the accidents created by Him. May He be exalted above such an idea.

8. That is among the strongest arguments of the Muʿtazila. You are agreed that the Qurʾān is a name given to what is transmitted to us between the covers of the volumes, by *tawātur*. This belief requires that it be written in the volumes, recited on the tongues, heard by the ears; and all of these things are necessarily signs of origination. So, al-Nasafī indicated the answer by saying, *It*, that is, the Qurʾān, the *kalām* of God; *is written in our volumes*, that is, by the forms of writing and the shapes of letters, which signify it; *preserved in our hearts*, that is, by verbal expressions which are imagined; *recited on our tongues*, with sounds uttered and heard; *heard by our ears*, in the same manner; *not incarnate in them*, this means that, in spite of all this, the eternal *kalām* of God is not incarnate in the volumes, nor in the hearts, tongues or ears. For it is an eternal idea subsisting in God's essence. This idea is uttered and heard by means of ordered speech which signifies the eternal speech. It is preserved [i.e., in memory] by means of ordered speech which is imagined. And it is written by signs, forms and characters which represent sounds indicating it [i.e., signifying the eternal speech].

9. It is like this. Fire is a burning substance which is mentioned by means of an utterance, and written by means of a pen. But it does not follow from this that the reality of fire is a sound and a letter. The truth is that a given thing has an existence in substances, and an existence in expressions, and an existence in writing. The writing signifies the expression, and the expression signifies what is in the mind, and this signifies what is instantiated in substances. So, wherever the Qurʾān is described as necessarily linked to the eternal, as in our saying that the Qurʾān is uncreated, the meaning is its true nature, existent outside the world of created things. But when it is described as necessarily linked to created and originated things, then it is the words which are uttered or heard that are meant, as when we say, 'I have recited half the Qurʾān.' Or it is the imagined words of the Qurʾān that are meant as when we say, 'I have memorized the Qurʾān.' Or it is the written letters that are meant, as when we say, 'It is forbidden for a person in a state of ritual impurity to touch the Qurʾān.'

Since the guide to the legal judgments is the verbal form and not the eternal idea, the *imām*s in the field of theological truths have defined it as written in the volumes and transmitted by *tawātur*. They made it a name both for the ordered speech (*naẓm*) and for the eternal idea. That is, it refers to the ordered speech in so far as it signifies the eternal idea; it is not applied solely to the eternal idea.

6.7 Ibn al-Jawzī on the edicts of the caliph al-Qādir

ʿAbd al-Raḥmān ibn al-Jawzī was a jurist, traditionist and historian who lived in Baghdad. Born in 510/1116, he was one of the major intellectual figures of his time; he died in 597/1200. During a lifetime spent teaching and preaching, he wrote many books and was extremely influential in the court of the caliph in Baghdad; he became famous for the examination of the faith of his contemporaries, being especially fervent in seeking out Shīʿīs in their midst whom he accused of impugning the reputation of Muḥammad's companions.

One of Ibn al-Jawzī's major works is his *al-Muntaẓam fī taʾrīkh al-mulūk waʾl-umam*, which is a biographical dictionary of Baghdadi notables, covering the years 257/871 to 574/1179. Works such as these conveyed the sense of pride that people had in a place and its scholarly reputation but also served as a means to check the scholarly credentials of those involved in the transmission of religious knowledge. Establishing the trustworthiness of the élite and their students was a necessary part of the legitimization of authority. The *Muntaẓam* is structured in an annalistic style, written as chronologically sequenced obituary notices. It also provides a chronicle of events especially in the introductions given before all the death notices in a given year. Those chronicles often pay attention also to statistical data and the changing topography of Baghdad through the ages.

Within this context, Ibn al-Jawzī provides a record of a theological decree issued by the caliph al-Qādir biʾllāh and then proclaimed by his son, the subsequent caliph al-Qāʾim bi-Amr Allāh in the year 430/1039. Starting in the year 408/1017, al-Qādir was active in demanding that the jurists renounce all Muʿtazilī or Shīʿī doctrines and forbade the teaching of those subjects. In 409/1018 he proclaimed a profession of faith which served to define the official dogma of the state. Veneration of the companions of Muḥammad was the prime obligation of all Muslims, and many aspects of speculative theology, even those associated with Ashʿarī doctrine, were denounced. Further proclamations were given in 420/1029 against the Muʿtazilīs, on the doctrine of the created Qurʾān, on the status of the first caliphs and on the need to proclaim good and denounce evil. The profession of faith was then renewed by al-Qādir's successor, al-Qāʾim, and this is the text which Ibn al-Jawzī reports.

Further reading

George Makdisi, *Ibn ʿAqil. Religion and culture in classical Islam*, Edinburgh 1997, section 1.

—— *Ibn ʿAqīl et la résurgence de l'Islam traditionaliste au XIe siècle (Ve siècle de l'hégire)*, Damascus and Paris 1958, pp. 303–10; includes a French translation of Ibn al-Jawzī's text.

Adam Mez, *The renaissance of Islam,* London 1937, chapter 13; includes an English translation of Ibn al-Jawzī's text.

Source text

Ibn al-Jawzī, *Al-Muntaẓam fī taʾrīkh al-mulūk waʾl-umam*, ed. F. Krenkow, Hyderabad 1938, vol. 8, pp. 109–11.

1. Muḥammad ibn Nāṣir al-Ḥāfiẓ informed us that Abū'l-Ḥusayn Muḥammad ibn Muḥammad ibn al-Farrā' reported to him saying that the Imām al-Qā'im bi-Amr Allāh, the commander of the faithful Abū Jaʿfar ibn al-Qādir bi'llāh, announced, in about the year 430 [1039], the Qādirī creed which al-Qādir had proclaimed. It was read in the chancery in the presence of the ascetics and the learned people. Among those present was the *shaykh* Abū'l-Ḥasan ʿAlī ibn ʿUmar al-Qazwīnī. He signed his name at the bottom of it, before any of the other jurists wrote theirs. The jurists signed their names, agreeing to the statement, 'This is the profession of faith for Muslims. Whoever is at variance with it is corrupt and an unbeliever.'

2. It is incumbent on the people that they know that God is one and He has no associate. He neither begets nor was begotten. There is no equal to Him and He has not taken a companion or a son. There is not an associate with Him in the dominion. He is the first and has always been and He is the last and will not cease. He is powerful over all things, in need of nothing. When He wishes something, He says to it, 'Be,' and it is. He has everything and needs nothing. His is the everlasting life; He does not age and He does not sleep. He provides food but does not eat. He does not feel lonely on account of His solitary life. He is not on familiar terms with anything. He has wealth above all things. The ages and time have no affect on Him. Indeed, how could the ages and time change Him? He is the creator of the eras and time, of night and day, of light and darkness, of the heavens and the earth and what is in it of the species of creatures and the open lands, and the sea and what is in it of all things living, dead or inanimate.

3. Our Lord is alone, nothing is with Him. There is no space which encloses him. He created everything with His decree. He created the throne not out of need, but He is on it because He so wills it and not because He wants to be settled in the manner of creatures who seek comfort. He is the leader of the heavens and the earth and of what is in it, what is on the open land and in the sea; there is no leader other than Him and no protector except Him. He provides sustenance for them, makes them sick and makes them well. He makes them die and makes them live. All of creation is weak, even the angels, the prophets, the messengers, and every created being. He ordains by His decree and He is knowing by His knowledge. He is eternal and incomprehensible. He is the hearer who hears and the seer who sees. He is known by these two attributes but no created being can attain the essence of the two of them. He speaks, but not with organs of created beings. He should only be described by those attributes He has described Himself with, or those which His prophet has described Him with. Every attribute with which He has described Himself or His prophet has described Him is a real attribute and not meant metaphorically.

4. Know that the word of God is not created. He has spoken and revealed it to His messenger through the voice of Gabriel after Gabriel had heard it from Him and then repeated it to Muḥammad. Muḥammad then repeated it to his companions and his companions repeated it to the community. The repetition of the word of God by created beings does not make it created because that speech is in its

essence still the speech of God and it is uncreated. So, in every situation, repeated or memorized or written or heard, it remains that way. Anybody who says it is created in any way is an unbeliever whose blood may be shed after he has been called on to repent [and refused].

5. Know also that faith is conveyed by speech, action and intention. Speech is via the tongue, action via the members and the limbs, and intention is the honest affirming of it. Faith increases by obedience and decreases by sin, and it may be divided into parts and portions. The highest part is the confession of faith, 'There is no god but God' which brings its reward. Restraint is a part of faith and patience is a part of faith in the way the head is a part of the body. People cannot know of what is written in the book that is with God, nor what knowledge He keeps sealed with Him. So, one must say that 'I am a believer, if God wills', and 'I hope that I am a believer'. Hoping will not be harmful. Doubt and despair will not occur just because he wishes for something in the future. Everything returns to God. So, he should carry out all acts sincerely, acting in accord with the laws, practices and meritorious acts. All of this is a part of faith; there is no end to faith since there is no limit to meritorious acts and nothing above them.

6. It is necessary that one love all the companions of the prophet. We know that they are the best of creation after the messenger of God and that the best and most meritorious of them after the messenger of God is Abū Bakr al-Ṣiddīq, then ʿUmar ibn al-Khaṭṭāb, then ʿUthmān ibn ʿAffān, then ʿAlī ibn Abī Ṭālib. One will testify to their association in paradise. One must invoke the mercy of God on the wives of the messenger of God and whoever slanders ʿĀ'isha has no share in Islam. One should only say good things about Muʿāwiya and not enter into any argument concerning him. One should invoke the mercy of God on everyone. God has said, *Those who came after them, they say, 'My Lord, forgive us and our brothers who preceded us in faith. Do not put rancour in our hearts towards those who believe. Our Lord, indeed You are the All-gentle, the All-compassionate'* (Q 59/10). He also said about them, *We shall remove the rancour that is in their chests; as brothers they will be on couches facing each other* (Q 15/47).

7. Disbelief is not associated with the omission of any of the required acts other than proscribed prayer. Whoever abandons prayer without an excuse while being able to do it, even if he intends to do it at another time, is an unbeliever. He cannot deny this because of the saying of the prophet, 'The difference between the worshipper and the disbeliever is neglecting prayer. Whoever neglects it is an unbeliever and will remain an unbeliever until he repents and returns to performing it. If he dies before repenting and returning to it or if he keeps a secret of his return to prayer, then it is as if he had not prayed and he will be gathered (in hell) with Pharaoh, Haman and Korah.'

8. Rejecting a political leader and neglecting other duties does not make one an unbeliever even if one is so corrupt as to reject their obligation. These are the statements of the people of the *sunna* and the community. Those who hold with them are following the clear truth, the well-proven path of religion, and the evident path. For them there is hope of rescue from the fire and for entrance into

paradise, if God wills. The prophet said, ‘Knowledge of religion is good advice.’ ‘For whom, messenger?’ he was asked. He said, ‘For God, for His book, for His messenger, and for the community of Muslims, and for people at large.’ The messenger of God said, ‘If an exhortation comes to a worshipper from God in His religion, it is a blessing from God sent to him, as long as he gives thanks before that. Otherwise, it is testimony against him. God will increase his sin and God’s anger with him will increase.’

9. May God make us one of those who are thankful for His favours and mindful of His blessings! May He make us protectors of the *sunna*. May He forgive us and all Muslims.

6.8 Al-Nawbakhtī on the Imāmiyya

Abū Muḥammad al-Ḥasan ibn Mūsā al-Nawbakhtī was a scholar and theologian of Imāmī Shi'ism who died sometime between 300/912 and 310/922. He was one of the formative figures in the development of Shī'ī theology, fusing Mu'tazilī theology with Imāmī teachings. The Mu'tazilī doctrines of divine attributes and justice, denial of the beatific vision of God, and rejection of the view that God creates human acts were upheld by al-Nawbakhtī. However, he opposed the Mu'tazilī version of the doctrine of the imamate, arguing strenuously for the infallibility and necessity of the Imāms.

The work *Firaq al-Shī'a* is the best known of the approximately forty books attributed to Nawbakhtī although the ascription of the work to him is not undisputed. After recounting the history of the Imāms and the differences which developed among the Shī'a, he lists thirteen groups who were active at his time, the era in the wake of the death of the eleventh Imām, al-Ḥasan al-'Askarī, in 260/874 (a fourteenth group may have been lost from extant manuscript copies). Each group is described according to its doctrines, especially as related to the issue of who can legitimately hold the title of Imām. The twelfth group, called the Imāmiyya, described in the section translated below, is clearly the favoured group in the opinion of the author. Such heresiographical listings are popular in Islam and are clearly designed not only to catalogue various opinions but also, and most importantly, to establish the definition of the community and its limits.

Further reading

Etan Kohlberg, 'From Imāmiyya to Ithnā-'Ashariyya,' *Bulletin of the School of Oriental and African Studies*, 39 (1976), pp. 521–34.

Wilferd Madelung, 'Bemerkungen zur imamitischen Firaq-Literatur,' *Der Islam*, 43 (1967), pp. 37–52; reprinted in his *Religious schools and sects in medieval Islam*, London 1985, chapter 15.

—— 'Imāmism and Mu'tazilite theology,' in T. Fahd (ed.), *Le Shi'isme imāmite*, Paris 1979, pp. 13–29; reprinted in his *Religious schools and sects in medieval Islam*, London 1985, chapter 7.

William Montgomery Watt, 'The reappraisal of Abbasid Shi'ism,' in George Makdisi (ed.), *Arabic and Islamic studies in honor of Hamilton A. R. Gibb*, Cambridge MA 1965, pp. 638–54; the article provides an overview of the contents of al-Nawbakhtī's work and its significance.

Source text

Al-Nawbakhtī, *Firaq al-Shī'a*, ed. H. Ritter, Istanbul 1931, pp. 90–3. A French translation of the entire work is available: *Les sectes shiites an-Nawbakhti; traduction annotée avec intro. par M. Javad Mashkour*, second edition, Tehran 1980.

The Imāmiyya

1. The twelfth division of the Shīʿa, which is the Imāmiyya, denies the claims of all of the other groups. Rather, they say that God has placed on the earth a proof (*ḥujja*) who is a descendant of al-Ḥasan ibn ʿAlī al-ʿAskarī. The command of God will remain such that this person is designated as the trustee (*waṣī*) of his father in accordance with the first way of selection and past practices. After al-Ḥasan and al-Ḥusayn, the imamate cannot again be given to two brothers. Such a thing is not possible again. There have been no Imāms among the descendants of al-Ḥasan ibn ʿAlī according to God's decree. If there were only two people on the earth, one of them must be the proof of God so that the command of God would persist. If one of them died, the one who survived would be the proof so that the commands and prohibitions of God would continue to be maintained in His creation. It is not possible that the imamate should go to the offspring of someone who has not established his imamate. It is not imperative to accept a person as the proof when he dies during the lifetime of his father or during his offspring's lifetime. If all of that were possible, then the claims of the followers of Ismāʿīl ibn Jaʿfar and their school would be sound; it would allow for the imamate of Muḥammad ibn Jaʿfar and it would allow them to lay claim to the line of Imāms after the death of Jaʿfar ibn Muḥammad.

   1.1. That which we have said here is from the traditions of the Truthful Ones among which there are no contradictions. Given their soundness, their strength of support and their excellence in *isnād*, there can be no doubt in the matter.

2. It is not possible for there to be no proof in the world. If he were absent even for an hour, then the earth would perish along with all those on it. Nothing of what any of these other groups says is possible to believe in this regard. We follow the traditions of the past and we believe in the imamate of al-Ḥasan al-ʿAskarī and his death. We recognize that he has a successor who is his proper son and the Imām. He will be proclaimed and he will display his power just as his forefathers were proclaimed and became known. God allows it because the matter belongs to God Himself. The appearance and concealment of the Imām follows His wishes and it is commanded as He intends with regards to it. This follows what the commander of the believers indicated when he said, 'By God, You will not leave the world without a proof, whether he be visible and known or hidden and protected. Thus Your proof and Your signs will not be rendered worthless.'

   2.1. This is how we have been commanded and this is the information we have received from the past Imāms. It is not appropriate for people to discuss divine affairs nor to judge without true knowledge and without researching the roots of what is concealed from them.

3. It is not possible to mention the name of the *mahdī* nor to ask about his location until the divinely established time comes for him to become active. He is being protected, hidden and concealed under the guard of God. It is not incumbent

upon us to discuss his affair; in fact, it is forbidden, not permitted and impossible. If he who is hidden to us were to be discovered, then it would be permitted for his blood and our blood to be shed. His existence and his protection depends upon his being concealed and silent.

4. It is not possible for us, nor for any believer, to choose an Imām by rational thought and choice. Rather, God must make him arise and must choose him. He will make him appear when He wishes, for He knows best His overall plan for creation and He understands best the situation of His creation. The Imām also knows better than us about himself and the era of his appearance.

    4.1. Abū ʿAbd Allāh Jaʿfar al-Ṣādiq whose manifestation of the affair is known, whose lineage is not denied, who was not hidden at birth, and whose name became well known both in select circles and by the masses, said, 'God will curse whoever calls me by my name!' One of his followers met him and averted his glance from him. (It was also reported on his authority that one of his followers met him on the road and averted his glance and declined to greet him.) The Imām thanked him for that and praised him, saying, 'If a person meets me and greets me pleasantly, there is nothing better than blaming him for this and attacking him with disgust!'
    4.2. Similarly, reports come from Abū Ibrāhīm Mūsā ibn Jaʿfar that he said such things concerning not mentioning his name.
    4.3. Abū ʾl-Ḥasan al-Riḍā said, 'If I had known what people would wish of me, I would have killed myself, given that my religion now puts faith in playing with pigeons, roosters and similar entertaining things.'
    4.4. So how is this possible in our time with the total surveillance of us and the tyranny of the ruling powers and the lack of respect shown to al-Ḥasan al-ʿAskarī by [the ʿAbbasid general] Ṣāliḥ ibn Waṣīf, and his naming of he who had not yet been announced and whose name and birth had been concealed?

5. A good deal of information is reported regarding the fact that al-Qāʾim hid his birth from the people and that mention was not made of him. Nothing is known of him other than he will arise when he is manifested. It is known that he is the son of an Imām and the designated trustee who is the son of a designated trustee. He can be accepted as Imām before he is manifested. People can trust him and his father even though only a few people know of his affairs. The imamate which was passed on by al-Ḥasan ibn ʿAlī al-ʿAskarī cannot be altered because it is one of the affairs of God. It is not possible for it to return to his brothers. The designation by the Imām, a part of his legacy given to someone, is not less valuable because it is not known by two witnesses.

6. This is the path of the imamate; it is the clear, certain and necessary one which the true Imāmī Shīʿa will never abandon.

6.9 Al-Ṭūsī and al-ʿAllāma al-Ḥillī on prophecy

The remarkable thirteenth-century polymath Naṣīr al-Dīn al-Ṭūsī was primarily a philosopher, often considered on a par with Avicenna and al-Fārābī. Born in 597/1201 in Tus near Mashhad, he studied in Iran and Iraq, and died in Baghdad in 672/1274. Particularly significant in his life in this context is his report that he became dissatisfied with traditional theology and turned to philosophy. One of his major works is a refutation of Fakhr al-Dīn al-Rāzī's critical commentaries on Ibn Sīnā.

Al-Ṭūsī's *Tajrīd al-iʿtiqād*, however, has attained the status of a Shīʿī creed, primarily as a result of the commentary written upon it by al-ʿAllāma al-Ḥillī, who was born in 648/1250 in al-Ḥilla (midway between Baghdad and Kufa, a stronghold of the Shīʿa when the Sunnīs held power in Baghdad) and died there in 726/1325. Al-Ḥillī initially studied Qurʾān, *ḥadīth*, theology and law with his father and with his maternal uncle, Muḥaqqiq al-Awwal (d. 676/1277), but later he became a pupil of al-Ṭūsī. Among more than five hundred works ascribed to him, al-Ḥillī's commentary on the theological work of his teacher was written after several of his own books of theology. It was the first commentary composed on al-Ṭūsī's work, and it remained the main interpretive reading and served as the basis for many later commentaries. Al-Ḥillī, as compared with al-Ṭūsī, was primarily a theologian; his position is usually quite conservative compared with his teacher's and, ultimately, more representative of the broad streams of thought among the Shīʿa; his works are in general considered to be the authoritative expression of Shīʿī thought. This particular work is the standard text taught in Shīʿī religious schools (*madrasas*).

Al-Ṭūsī's work is organized in the following manner, providing a typical argumentative structure as the foundation of his theological position:

Section 1, On general principles: (a) On existence and non-existence; (b) On substances and their properties; (c) On causes and their results.

Section 2, On essences and accidents: (a) On essences; (b) On bodies; (c) On bodies, continued; (d) On essences which are free from matter; (e) On accidents, of which there are nine types.

Section 3, Demonstrating the qualities of the Creator: (a) On His existence; (b) On His attributes; (c) On His actions.

Section 4, On prophecy.

Section 5, On the Imamate.

Section 6, On the return (eschatology).

The passage presented below is taken from the fourth section, on prophecy. It explains how the sending of prophets by God, which is denied by the Barāhima, is beneficial for creation and incumbent on God.

Further reading

Al-'Allāma al-Ḥillī, *Al-Babu 'l-hadi 'ashar*, trans. W. M. Miller, London 1958.
Hamid Dabashi, 'Khwājah Naṣīr al-Dīn al-Ṭūsī: the philosopher/vizier and the intellectual climate of his times,' in Seyyed Hossein Nasr, Oliver Leaman (eds), *History of Islamic philosophy*, London 1996, pp. 527–84.
Sabine Schmidtke, *The theology of al-'Allāma al-Ḥillī (d. 726/1325)*, Berlin 1991.

Source text

Al-Ṭūsī, *Tajrīd al-i'tiqād*, with the commentary by al-'Allāma al-Ḥillī, *Kashf al-murād fī sharḥ Tajrīd al-i'tiqād*, Qum n.d., pp. 271–3. In the commentary, paragraphs 1 to 11 relate to the first paragraph of the base text, entitled 'On prophecy', while paragraph 12 relates to the second paragraph.

Section 4: On prophecy

1. God's sending of prophets is good, because it involves benefits, such as: supporting the intellect in matters accessible to the intellect, providing rulings on matters not accessible to the intellect, removing fear, providing knowledge of good and evil and of what is beneficial and harmful, preserving the human species and perfecting human individuals according to their varied abilities, teaching them hidden crafts, morals and politics, and informing them of the punishment and the reward. Through all of this, divine bounty (*luṭf*) is provided to the *mukallaf*. The doubts of the Barāhima [who deny the need for prophets] are false, on the basis of the arguments just adduced.

   God's sending of prophets is incumbent on Him because it comprises a bounty in relation to rational obligations (*al-takālīf al-'aqliyya*).

Commentary

1. People are at variance on this. But all the leaders of the religious sects and some of the philosophers agree that sending prophets is good. The Barāhima deny it. The evidence lies in the fact that sending prophets comprises benefits, while being free from any bad effects. Hence it is a good, without doubt. The author [i.e. Naṣīr al-Dīn al-Ṭūsī] mentioned a number of the benefits.

2. For example, that the intellect should be supported by revelation in judgements that are accessible to the intellect. These include the unity of the Creator and so forth. Also that judgements may be derived from the sending of prophets in matters not accessible to the intellect, like religious laws and other principles.

3. Further, removal of the fear that accrues to the *mukallaf* as a result of his exploitation of the world. For he knows through the intellect that the material world is owned by another, and that usufruct of another's property without his permission is evil. If it were not for the sending of prophets, he would not know that his

usufruct of material things is good, and there would be fear both with such usufruct and without it. For the intellect recognizes that it is permissible for an owner to demand an action from his slave which cannot possibly be effected without sending a messenger; hence fear arises [until such time as a messenger arrives].

4. Some actions are good and some are evil. Of the category of good, there are some which the intellect can by its own independent activity know to be good; and some which it cannot know through its own independent activity. It is the same with evil actions. Through the sending of prophets comes knowledge of those aspects of good and evil which cannot be known independently.

5. Some things are beneficial for us, such as many foods and drugs, while some are harmful, such as poisons and damaging drugs. The intellect cannot attain knowledge of all these things; hence this great benefit comes into being as a result of sending prophets.

6. Humankind is a species differing from all other animals, being 'political' [city-dwelling] by nature. Man requires many things in life, things indispensable for social activity, which he cannot contrive except by common activity and co-operation. Further the impetus to domination is naturally present in humankind, so there arises internecine violence which is opposed to the wisdom of community. Hence there is need for a uniting factor which forces them into community: this factor is the law and *sunna*. But the *sunna* requires a law-giver to establish it and to lay down its sanctions. This person must be distinguished from others of his species, because of the absence of any [natural] hierarchy. The distinction may not arise out of anything intrinsic to the species because of the possibility of mutual violence in recognizing it; hence it must come from God, in the form of a miracle which leads men to believe its perpetrator, making them afraid to oppose him, and inducing them to follow him. In this way a social system is formed and the human species is preserved in that degree of perfection which is possible for it.

7. Individual humans are varied in their achievement of perfections, in their acquisition of knowledge and in their participation in virtues. Some are without need of any helper because of the strength of their soul, the perfection of their understanding and their extreme readiness to achieve contact with higher matters. Others are completely incapable of these things. Still others are in a middle position, their degrees of perfection varying as they are nearer or further from the two extremes. The benefit of the prophet lies in this, that he perfects those individuals in the species who fall short, according to their varied aptitudes.

8. The human species requires implements and other practical things for its survival, such as clothes, dwellings and so forth, and the achievement of these things demands a practical knowledge of which human power is incapable. The benefit of the prophet is that he teaches these hidden practical crafts.

9. The various degrees and the variety of morals is known, and is of such kinds that there is a need for a perfecting agent who will teach morals and political

policies so that man's affairs can be ordered both in his city and in his household.

10. Prophets know the reward and the punishment that belongs to obedience and to failure of obedience. Hence there accrues to the *mukallaf*, through the sending of prophets, a bounty. For these reasons the sending of prophets is binding (*wājib*) on God.

11. The Barāhima argue for the uselessness of sending prophets on the following grounds. A prophet, they say, brings either a message that conforms to the intellect or a message that is opposed to it. In the former case, there is no need for him, and no benefit in sending him. In the latter case, it is incumbent to reject his words. This argument is false for the reasons given at the beginning of the list of benefits. That is, we ask why should He not bring a message that conforms to the intellect, so that the benefit lies in the confirmation he provides for intellectual evidence? Or, we could ask why should he not bring a message neither required by nor accessible to the intellect, but not opposed to it either, [by which we] mean things [or actions] not rejected by the intellect, such as many ritual obligations, the details of which cannot be derived from the intellect.

12. [*Sending prophets is incumbent because it comprises a bounty in relation to intellectual obligations.*] People are at variance on this. The Muʿtazila say that the sending of prophets is a binding duty (*wājib*). The Ashʿarīs say it is not *wājib*. The Muʿtazila argue that revealed obligations constitute bounties in relation to intellectual obligations. Further, that bounties are *wājib*, so revealed obligations are *wājib*. These cannot be known except through a prophet. So the existence of prophets is *wājib*, for that without which a binding duty (*wājib*) cannot be completed is itself *wājib*. They argue that revealed obligations are a bounty in relation to intellectual obligations in the following manner. Man, if he is persistent in carrying out revealed obligations and in avoiding legal prohibitions, is brought closer to the carrying out of intellectual obligations and to the avoidance of intellectual prohibitions. This is known of necessity to all rational beings.

6.10 Al-Fārābī on the soul

Little is known of the life of Abū Naṣr al-Fārābī. He was of Turkish origin, was born in Turkestan and spent many years of his life in Baghdad. He died in 339/950. He appears to have been an independent intellectual who did not allow his views to become altered by patronage although he did enter the court circle of Sayf al-Dawla in Aleppo in the final eight years of his life.

The work presented here, *Mabādi' ārā' ahl al-madīna al-fāḍila* ('The essential features of the views of the citizens of the best state'), was written by al-Fārābī shortly before he died. It is a mature work of independent philosophy (that is, it is neither a commentary on a Greek work nor an adaptation of another work) directed to a Muslim audience which attempts to answer the pressing religious and political questions of his age. The basis of the work is fully Greek, but the arguments are such that they are said to apply universally; the book presupposes a good deal of knowledge and acceptance of ancient Greek philosophy.

The work is divided into six sections comprising a total of nineteen chapters overall: on the eternal world (in two sections), the sub-lunar world of 'coming to be and passing away', human physical and moral nature, the structure of human society, and the faulty views of inhabitants of 'misguided' states (that is, those of al-Fārābī's time). The emphasis on political philosophy and the philosopher-king was uncommon in writings of the time, having become less significant after the classical philosophical works of Plato and Aristotle, but the question of the authority of the caliph was still a vital one and the relevance of ancient answers is clearly being expressed in this work. The passage presented below exemplifies al-Fārābī's work as a philosopher in the Greek tradition but within an Islamic context. He describes the faculties of the soul, including the senses, reason and the faculty of representation. Al-Fārābī's discussion of the latter provides a rational explanation of revelation as being received by those with the most highly developed faculties of representation. The highest level of humanity, that of the ruler, is characterized as a perfect combination of both philosopher and prophet. In addition to a perfected faculty of reason this ideal ruler must also have a perfected faculty of representation. The ideal ruler would therefore, like Muḥammad, be able both to receive revelation and to convey intelligibles in the form of accessible symbolic representations for the benefit of the masses.

Further reading

Deborah L. Black, 'Al-Fārābī,' in Seyyed Hossein Nasr, Oliver Leaman (eds), *History of Islamic philosophy*, London 1996, pp. 178–97.

—— Thérèse-Anne Druart, Dimitri Gutas, Muhsin Mahdi, 'Al-Fārābī,' in *Encyclopaedia Iranica*.

Muhsin Mahdi, *Alfarabi and the foundations of Islamic political philosophy*, Chicago 2001.

Richard Walzer, 'Aspects of Islamic political thought: al-Farabi and Ibn Xaldun,' *Oriens*, 15 (1963), pp. 40–60.

—— 'Al-Fārābī', in *Encyclopaedia of Islam*, new edition.

Source text

Al-Fārābī, *Mabādi' ārā' ahl al-madīna al-fāḍila*, in R. Walzer (ed. and trans.), *Al-Farabi on the perfect state*, Oxford 1985; selected portions of the Arabic text found on pp. 164–74 (chapter 10), 196–210 (chapter 13), 210–26 (chapter 14), 240–6 (chapter 15); the numbering of the paragraphs does not follow that of the edition of the Arabic text in every instance.

Chapter 10: The faculties of the soul

1. When a man comes into being, the first thing to come into being in him is the faculty whereby he takes nourishment: this is the nutritive faculty. Subsequent to that is the faculty whereby he 'senses' tangibles, such as heat, cold, etc.; and whereby he senses [sequentially] tastes, smells, sounds, then colours and all visible objects such as rays of light. There comes into being along with the senses another faculty, through which there is appetition towards what is sensed, such that he feels desire or dislike for what is sensually perceived. Subsequently there comes into being in man another faculty; through this faculty he preserves the sensibles which are imprinted in his soul, after they have ceased to be immediate objects of sense perception. This is the faculty of representation [or imagination]. In this faculty he composes and separates sensibles by diverse processes of composition and separation, some of which are false and some true. Accompanying this faculty too there is an appetition towards what is represented [or imagined]. Subsequently there comes into being in man the rational faculty whereby he is able to apprehend intelligibles, whereby he distinguishes good and evil, and through which the crafts and sciences become possible. Accompanying this faculty too is an appetition towards what is apprehended intellectually.

2. The nutritive faculty consists of a single ruling faculty and other faculties which are auxiliaries and subordinates to the ruling faculty. The ruling faculty of nutrition is situated in the heart while the auxiliaries and subordinates are distributed in the other bodily members. . . .

3. The sensory faculty consists of a ruler and auxiliaries. The auxiliaries are the five senses, familiar to all, and distributed to the eyes, the ears and so forth, each one of them apprehending its own special type of sensible. . . . The ruling faculty is like a king: the news from the various districts of his kingdom, gathered by his spies, is united in his presence. The ruling faculty here too is situated in the heart.

4. The faculty of representation has no auxiliaries distributed to other senses; it is a single faculty, situated likewise in the heart . . .

5. The rational faculty has no auxiliaries or subordinates of its own kind in the various organs of the body. But it has rulership over the other faculties, namely the representative faculty, and the ruling faculties of every class in which

there are a ruler and subordinates. So it is the ruling faculty, ruling over the representative faculty and over the ruling faculties of the sensory and nutritive faculties.

6. The appetitive faculty, that whereby a thing is either desired or disliked, is composed of a ruling faculty and subordinates. This is the faculty through which the will comes into existence . . . Appetition comes into existence in the ruling faculty of appetition, but bodily acts [the results of appetition] come into existence through faculties which serve the appetitive faculty . . . The ruling faculty of appetition is situated in the heart . . .

7. Knowledge of a thing may come into existence either through the rational faculty or through the representative faculty or through the sensory faculties . . .

8. These then are the faculties of the soul: the nutritive . . . , the sensory . . . , the representative . . . , the rational. As to the appetitive faculty it is related to the ruling faculty of sense and to the faculties of representation and reason in the same way as heat exists in fire, being related to the essential nature of fire.

Chapter 13: The faculty of reason

1. It remains to discuss the imprints of various types of intelligibles which are imprinted in the rational faculty. The intelligibles which are of such a kind that they can be imprinted in the rational faculty are:

   (a) those intelligibles which are by their substantial nature intellects *in actu* and intelligibles *in actu*; these are the immaterial things;

   (b) those intelligibles which are not by their substantial nature intelligibles *in actu*, such as stones, plants and, in general, everything which is a body, or is in a material body, or matter itself along with everything which subsists in matter. These things are neither intellects *in actu* nor intelligibles *in actu*.

   The human intellect, however, which develops in man by nature from the beginning [of his existence], is a structure in matter specially prepared to receive the imprints of the intelligibles. It is an intellect *in potentia*; it is also an intelligible *in potentia*. All other things which are in matter, or are matter, or possess matter are not intellects either *in actu* or *in potentia*. But they are intelligibles *in potentia* and can become intelligibles *in actu*. They do not, however, have by virtue of their own substances the capacity to become, of their own accord, intelligibles *in actu*. Likewise, neither the rational faculty nor any quality given [to man] by nature possesses the capacity to become of its own accord an intellect *in actu*. In order to become an intellect *in actu*, it needs something else which transfers it from potentiality to actuality. It becomes intellect *in actu* only when intelligibles arise in it.

   Likewise intelligibles *in potentia* become intelligibles *in actu* when they become intelligibles in [intelligized by] an intellect *in actu*. But they too require something else which transfers them from potentiality to actuality.

2. The agent which transfers these things from potentiality to actuality is an essence which is, by its substantial nature, intellect *in actu*, and which is separate from matter. This intellect provides to the material [i.e., human] intellect, which is an intellect *in potentia*, something corresponding to the light which the sun provides to the faculty of sight. It is related to the material [human] intellect as the sun is related to the faculty of sight. Sight is a faculty and a structure in matter. Prior to actually perceiving, it is sight *in potentia*. And colours, prior to being perceived, are perceptible and visible *in potentia*. But the faculty of sight, situated in the eye, does not, of itself, possess the capacity to become sight *in actu*, nor do colours, of themselves, possess the capacity to become perceptible or visible *in actu*. But the sun gives light to the faculty of sight, linking the one to the other; and it gives the colours light, linking it to them. Thus the faculty of sight, through the light which it acquires from the sun, becomes seeing *in actu* and sight *in actu*. And the colours, by virtue of that same light, become seen and visible *in actu* after having been seen and visible only *in potentia*.

In the same way, this intellect *in actu* provides the material [human] intellect with something which it imprints on it. The relationship of this thing to the material intellect corresponds to that of light to the faculty of sight.

The faculty of sight, by virtue of the light itself, sees the light which is the cause of its seeing, and sees the sun which is the cause of the light, and sees too the things which were potentially seen and visible, so that they become actually seen and visible. In the same way, the material [human] intellect, by virtue of that thing which corresponds to light in relation to the faculty of sight, perceives intellectually the thing itself, perceives too the intellect *in actu* which is the cause of providing that thing to the material intellect. Further, those things which were intelligible *in potentia* become actually intelligible. And the [human] intellect itself becomes an intellect *in actu*, after having been only an intellect *in potentia*.

The action of this separate [immaterial] intellect on the material [human] intellect resembles the action of the sun on the faculty of sight. Hence it is called the Active Intellect. It is, in fact, of those immaterial things previously mentioned and subordinate to the First Cause, the tenth ranking. The material [human] intellect is called the passive intellect [because it is acted upon by the Active Intellect].

When that which corresponds to light in relation to sight arises in the rational faculty as a result of the action of the Active Intellect, it happens too that the sensibles which are preserved in the faculty of representation give rise to intelligibles in the rational faculty, such as that the whole is greater than the part, and that measurements equal to one thing are equal to one another. . . .

3. The emergence of the first intelligibles in man is his first perfection. But these intelligibles are only granted to him so that he might use them in order to attain his final perfection. This is 'felicity'. Felicity means that the human soul reaches such a degree of perfection in its existence that it no longer needs matter in which to subsist. That is, it becomes one of the incorporeal things, one of the substances that are separate from matter, and it remains in this state forever. But its rank is below that of the Active Intellect.

4. The soul reaches this position only through certain willed actions, some of them mental, some physical; not through any actions at all which happen, but through specific determined actions, arising out of specific and determined structures and dispositions. This is because there are willed actions which are opposed to felicity. Felicity is the good which is sought for its own sake and is not sought at all or at any time as a means to the acquisition of something else. There is nothing beyond it, that a man can obtain, which is greater than it. Willed actions which promote the attainment of felicity are good actions; and the structures and dispositions from which these actions emerge are virtues. These are good [actions], not for their own sake but for the sake of felicity. The actions which are opposed to felicity are bad [actions]; they are evil [actions]. The structures and dispositions from which these actions emerge are deficiencies, vices and meannesses.

Chapter 14: The faculty of representation

1. The representative faculty is intermediate between the faculties of sense and reason. When the auxiliaries of the faculty of sense are actually in the process of sensing and carrying out their tasks, the representative faculty is acted upon by them and is busy with the perceptibles which the senses bring to it and imprint on it. It is further busy in serving the rational faculty; and in supplying the appetitive faculty. But if the faculties of sense, reason and appetition revert to their state of first perfection [that is, their lowest level of being] and cease carrying out their characteristic tasks, as happens in a state of sleep, then the representative faculty is left alone. It is free from the imprints of perceptibles which the senses constantly bring to it; it is relieved of service to the rational and appetitive faculties; and so it turns to the imprints of perceptibles which it finds preserved and enduring in itself. It acts upon these, joining some parts to others and separating some parts from others.

2. In addition to the activities of (a) preserving the imprints of sensibles and (b) composing [and separating] their parts, the representative faculty has a third activity. This is imitation ['mimesis']. Amongst all the faculties of the soul, this one is unique in possessing the power to imitate the sensually perceived things which remain preserved in it. Sometimes it imitates the things perceived by the five senses by composing [and separating] the perceptibles preserved in it which are themselves imitations of things perceived. Sometimes it imitates the intelligibles; sometimes the nutritive faculty and sometimes the appetitive faculty. It also imitates the 'temperament' in which it happens to find the body. . . .

3. The faculty of representation imitates the rational faculty in this sense, that it imitates the intelligibles which arise in it, by means of things whose characteristic is that the intelligibles can be imitated by them. Thus, it imitates intelligibles which possess the utmost perfection, such as the First Cause, the immaterial things and the heavens, by the most superior and perfect of sensibles, like things beautiful to see. It imitates imperfect intelligibles by the meanest and most imperfect of sensibles, like things ugly to see. The former category it likewise imitates by all sensibles which are pleasant to the eye.

4. The Active Intellect is the cause whereby things which are intelligible *in potentia* become intelligible *in actu*, and things which are intellect *in potentia* become intellect *in actu*. Now that which can become intellect *in actu* is [only] the rational faculty of the soul. And this faculty has two aspects: a theoretical and a practical aspect. The function of the practical aspect is to act on present and future particulars; the function of the theoretical aspect is to grasp those intelligibles which cannot be made the object of action. Now, the representative faculty is joined to these two aspects of the rational faculty. Hence that which the rational faculty derives from the Active Intellect – which is to it as light is to sight – may well emanate from the Active Intellect into the representative faculty and thus the Active Intellect may have a certain effect on the representative faculty. Sometimes it provides it with intelligibles whose nature it is to occur in the sphere of theoretical reason; sometimes with sensible particulars whose nature it is to occur in the sphere of practical reason. The representative faculty receives the intelligibles in mimetic form, derived from sensibles which it composes; and receives the particulars sometimes by representing them as they really are and sometimes mimetically by imitating them with other sensibles. These particulars are things which practical reason acts upon through deliberation, some of them being present and some of them arising in the future. However, those which arise in the representative faculty do so without the mediation of deliberation. Thus it is that things arise in the representative faculty without having been inferred through deliberation. In respect of the particulars which the Active Intellect provides to the representative faculty in sleep, these are true visions. And in respect of the intelligibles provided by the Active Intellect and received by the representative faculty in the form of imitations which it receives in their place, these are divinations concerning divine things.

5. These things may occur in sleep or in a state of wakefulness. However, those which occur in a state of wakefulness are rare, and restricted to a minority of people. Even in sleep most of these occurrences relate to particulars; the perception of intelligibles is rare. [In so far as they occur in a state of wakefulness] these occurrences are due to the fact that when a man's representative faculty is strong and perfectly developed such that it is not completely overwhelmed by the sensibles which reach it nor by its service to the rational faculty, but rather its occupation with these two activities leaves a great surplus [of power] to carry out its special activities, then its waking state when it is occupied with these activities is like its sleeping state when it is free from them. Now, much of what the Active Intellect provides to the representative faculty it represents mimetically by visual sensibles. These representations [formed in the representative faculty] may return and be imprinted in the common faculty of sense. And if these imprints arise in the common faculty, the faculty of sight will be affected by those imprints and they will be imprinted on it, in such a way that the imprints of those things that are in the faculty of sight will manifest themselves in the shining air that is joined to the sight by rays of vision. When these things arise in the air, they are re-imprinted in the faculty of sight which is in the eye and reflected thence in the common faculty of sense and finally in the representative faculty. All of these activities are continuous and through them that which the

Active Intellect has provided to the faculty of representation becomes visible to [perceived by] a man of this kind.

6. If it happens that the sensibles whereby the representative faculty imitates these things are of the utmost beauty and perfection, then the man who sees them will experience a great and remarkable pleasure; he will see astonishing things such that of necessity no aspect of them can possibly be found in other existents. It is not impossible that a man whose representative faculty has reached the utmost perfection may receive from the Active Intellect, while awake, present and future particulars or sensory imitations of them; or he may receive imitations of the separate [immaterial] intellects and other noble existents, actually seeing them. In so far as he receives particulars and actually sees them this man possesses prophecy of present and future events. In so far as he receives the intelligibles he possesses prophecy of divine things. This is the most perfect rank to which the representative faculty can attain.

7. Inferior to this rank are those who see all of these things, partly during sleep and partly in a waking state. . . . And below these are those who see all of these things only in sleep, etc.

Chapter 15: The perfect ruler

1. [The perfect man and ruler of the perfect state] is one who has achieved perfection in becoming intellect *in actu* and intelligible *in actu*; further, his representative faculty has by natural development achieved the highest perfection as we have explained. It is ready to receive, either in a waking or a sleeping state, from the Active Intellect, particulars, either as they are or through imitation; and also to receive intelligibles through imitation. His passive [material, human] intellect has achieved perfection through apprehension of the intelligibles in such manner that none is withheld from him. His intellect has become intellect *in actu* and intelligible [i.e., object of intellection] *in actu*. If any man achieves perfection in this manner through apprehension of all the intelligibles, and through becoming intellect *in actu* . . . there emerges in him a further intellect *in actu*, whose status relative to the passive intellect is higher, more perfect and more free from matter. This is called the acquired intellect. It is intermediate between the passive intellect and the active intellect. . . .

2. When this occurs in relation to both parts of the rational faculty, and subsequently in relation to the representative faculty, this man is the recipient of revelation and God grants him revelation through the medium of the Active Intellect. That which emanates from God to the Active Intellect is emanated from the Active Intellect to the passive intellect through the intermediary of the acquired intellect; then it emanates to the representative faculty. This man is a philosopher by virtue of that which emanates from the Active Intellect to the passive intellect . . . and he is, by virtue of that which emanates into the representative faculty, a prophet, a warner of particular events that will happen or are happening, and an informer of divine things [in mimetic form].

3. This man is at the highest level of humanity; he has reached the furthest degree of felicity; his soul is, as it were, united to the Active Intellect, in the manner we have explained. He understands all the actions whereby felicity can be reached and this is the first of the conditions of being a ruler.

Chapter 7

Law and ritual

7.1 Ibn ʿAbd al-Barr on the status of the *sunna*

Ibn ʿAbd al-Barr Abū ʿUmar Yūsuf al-Namarī was born in Cordoba in 368/978. He studied in his home city with the most respected local scholars, but he also travelled throughout Spain and corresponded with prominent authorities further afield in his thirst for knowledge. He was considered an outstanding scholar of traditions and biographies as well as a significant jurist, holding the position of judge in Lisbon and Santarem. Ibn ʿAbd al-Barr was affiliated to the Mālikī school of jurisprudence although his works also reveal influence from both the Ẓāhirī and Shāfiʿī schools. He died in 463/1070.

About a dozen works of Ibn ʿAbd al-Barr have survived. They include works of jurisprudence, *ḥadīth*, biographies, genealogies and *belles lettres*, demonstrating his wide range of interests and expertise. The *Jāmiʿ bayān al-ʿilm wa-faḍlihi* explores the nature of knowledge from a Muslim perspective. Its component chapters explore various aspects, such as how to acquire knowledge, its virtues and the ethics that should be followed by those who possess it. *Ḥadīth* are prominent throughout the work, and in the final portion, where the following passage is found, Ibn ʿAbd al-Barr underlines their importance a final time. The high frequency of verse citations in this work is an indication of the author's literary predilections.

The chapters presented below are concerned with the relationship between the Qur'ān and the *sunna,* which both became regarded as forms of prophetic revelation (*waḥy*) in Islam. The former, distinguished in al-Shāfiʿī's *Risāla* as 'revelation recited [in worship]' (*waḥy matlū*), is considered superior in status, but the latter, termed 'revelation not recited [in worship]' (*waḥy ghayr matlū*), outnumbers it in sheer quantity. Ibn ʿAbd al-Barr argues that the *sunna* should be accepted as authoritative independently of the Qur'ān: there should be no need to find confirmation in the Qur'ān before acceptance of a *sunna.* Moreover, the *sunna* explains and, according to some jurists, can even abrogate the Qur'ān. Ibn ʿAbd al-Barr's presentation of this issue reveals a range of viewpoints in what remains in many Muslim circles a contentious issue.

Further reading

Shahab Ahmed, 'Ḥadīth: i. A. General introduction,' in *Encyclopaedia Iranica*.
Ch. Pellat, 'Ibn ʿAbd al-Barr,' in *Encyclopaedia of Islam*, new edition.
Joseph Schacht, *The origins of Muhammadan jurisprudence*, Oxford 1950, pp. 40–81.

Source text

Ibn ʿAbd al-Barr, *Jāmiʿ bayān al-ʿilm wa-faḍlihi*, ed. ʿAbd al-Raḥmān Ḥasan Maḥmūd, Cairo 1975, pp. 491–6 (part I) and 498–9 (part II).

I *Chapter: On the status of the* sunna *in relation to the book and its [function as] clarification of the book*

1. God said, *We have revealed to you the remembrance that you might explain to the people what has been revealed to them* (Q 16/44). Also, *Let him warn those who turn away from his command that they will be stricken with dissension and stricken with painful punishment* (Q 24/63). Also, *You lead to a straight path, the path of God* (Q 42/52). God has laid down obedience to his prophet in several verses of the book, and joined this requirement to that of obedience to himself. He has also said, *What the prophet brings you, take it; what he prohibits you from, avoid* (Q 59/7).

2. Saʿīd ibn Naṣr told us that Qāsim ibn Aṣbagh said that Muḥammad ibn Ismāʿīl told him that al-Ḥamīdī told him that Sufyān told him on the authority of Manṣūr from Ibrāhīm from ʿAlqama that a woman of the Banū Asad tribe came to ʿAbd Allāh ibn Masʿūd and said, 'I have heard that you curse such-and-such and such-and-such, and women who tattoo and women who receive tattoos. But I have read what is between the covers and I have not found what you say. What's more, I suspect your wife of this practice.' ʿAbd Allāh said, 'Come in and look.' She entered, looked and saw nothing. 'Did you not read', said ʿAbd Allāh, 'the verse, *What the messenger brings you, take it; what he prohibits you from, avoid* (Q 59/7)?' 'Yes.' 'That is the one [that supports this ruling],' he said.
   2.1 It is related from ʿAbd al-Razzāq, who said that al-Thawrī informed him on the authority of Manṣūr from Ibrāhīm from ʿAlqama who said that ʿAbd Allāh ibn Masʿūd said, 'God curse these women: those who tattoo and those who receive tattoos, those who pluck their hair and those who cut their skin for beauty's sake. They are changers of God's creation.' A certain woman of the Banū Asad tribe heard this. Her name was Umm Yaʿqūb. She said, 'Hey, ʿAbd Allāh, I have heard that you curse such-and-such and such-and-such.' 'Why shouldn't I curse those whom God's messenger has cursed, those mentioned in God's book?' 'But I have read what is between

the covers and I have never found this.' 'If you have read, you have found it. Did you never read, *What the messenger brings you, take it; what he prohibits you from, avoid*?' 'Yes.' 'It was prohibited by the messenger of God,' said ʿAbd Allāh. 'I think your wife does this kind of thing.' 'Go, look.' And she went, and looked, but saw nothing. ʿAbd Allāh said, 'If she had been like that I wouldn't have married her.'

3. Muḥammad ibn Khalīfa told us that Muḥammad ibn al-Ḥusayn al-Baghdādī told him in Mecca that Abū al-ʿAbbās Aḥmad ibn Sahl al-Ashnānī told him that al-Ḥusayn ibn ʿAlī ibn al-Aswadī told him that Yaḥyā ibn Ādam told him that Quṭba ibn ʿAbd al-ʿAzīz and Abū Bakr ibn ʿAyyāsh told him on the authority of Abū Isḥāq from ʿAbd al-Raḥmān ibn Yazīd that he saw a *muḥrim* [a pilgrim within the boundaries of Mecca] wearing ordinary clothes, and he forbad the *muḥrim* to do so. 'Bring me a verse from the book of God', said the *muḥrim*, 'and I will take off these clothes.' ʿAbd al-Raḥmān recited, *What the messenger brings you, take it; what he prohibits you from, avoid.*

4. Muḥammad ibn ʿAbd al-Malik told us that Ibn al-Aʿrābī told him that Saʿdān ibn Naṣr told him that Sufyān ibn ʿUyayna told him on the authority of Hishām ibn Ḥajīr that he said that Ṭāwūs was praying two *rakʿa*s just after the afternoon prayer when Ibn ʿAbbās told him to abandon them. Ṭāwūs said that what was forbidden was that these extra *rakʿa*s should be adopted as a *sunna*. Ibn ʿAbbās replied, 'The messenger of God prohibited prayer after the afternoon prayer. I don't know whether you will be punished or rewarded for these; for God said, *No believer, man or woman, has the right, if God and his prophet have decreed something, to choose freely in the matter* (Q 33/36).'

5. Khalaf ibn al-Qāsim told us that Ibn al-Mufassir said that Aḥmad ibn ʿAlī ibn Saʿīd al-Qāḍī told him that Dāwūd ibn Rashīd told him that Baqiyya ibn al-Walīd told him on the authority of Maḥfūẓ ibn al-Musawwar al-Fahrī from Muḥammad ibn al-Munkadar from Jābir that he said that the messenger of God said, 'Any one of you may be on the verge of saying, "This is the book of God; what is designated here as *ḥalāl*, we recognize as *ḥalāl*; what is designated *ḥarām*, we recognize as *ḥarām*." Beware. He who hears a *ḥadīth* related from me, and denies it, he has denied God and His messenger and His own words.'

6. Saʿīd ibn Naṣr told us that Qāsim ibn Aṣbagh told him that Muḥammad ibn Ismāʿīl told him that al-Ḥamīdī told him that Sufyān told him that Abū al-Naḍr Mawlā ʿUmar ibn ʿUbayd Allāh ibn Maʿmar told him on the authority of ʿUbayd Allāh ibn Rāfiʿ from his father who said that Sufyān told him (with a report via Ibn al-Munkadar that is incomplete) that the messenger of God said, 'Let me not find any one of you reclining on a soft couch, and saying, when a command reaches him from me – something I have ordered or prohibited – "I don't know this: what we find in the book of God, that is what we follow."'...

7. Aḥmad ibn ʿAbd Allāh ibn Muḥammad informed us that his father informed him that Aḥmad ibn Khālid said that ʿAlī ibn ʿAbd al-ʿAzīz told him that Ḥajjāj told him that Ḥammād ibn Salama told him on the authority of Muḥammad ibn Isḥāq from Sālim al-Makkī from Mūsā ibn ʿAbd Allāh ibn Qays from ʿUbayd Allāh or

ʿAbd Allāh ibn Abī Rāfiʿ from his father Abū Rāfiʿ that he said he heard the prophet of God say, 'Let me never know that a *ḥadīth* reached one of you, concerning something I have commanded or prohibited, in which I am reported to have said, while reclining on my couch, "This Qurʾān, what we find in it we accept; what we do not find in it we have no need of."'

8. Saʿīd ibn Naṣr told us that Qāsim told him that Ibn Waḍḍāḥ told him that Abū Bakr ibn Abī Shayba told him that Zayd ibn al-Ḥabbāb told him on the authority of Muʿāwiya ibn Ṣāliḥ who told him that al-Ḥasan ibn Ḥāritha told him that he heard Miqdām ibn Maʿdī Karīb say that he said that the messenger of God said, 'One of you, reclining on a soft couch, on hearing a *ḥadīth* related from me, may be on the verge of saying, "We have the book of God. Whatever we find in it to be *ḥalāl*, we consider *ḥalāl*. And whatever we find in it to be *ḥarām*, we consider *ḥarām*." Beware. Whatever the messenger of God has declared *ḥarām* is like what God has declared *ḥarām*.'

9. ʿAbd al-Wārith ibn Sufyān told us that Qāsim ibn Aṣbagh told him that Aḥmad ibn Zuhayr told him that Abū Nuʿaym told him that Jaʿfar ibn Burqān told him on the authority of Maymūn ibn Mihrān [regarding] *If you dispute on a matter refer it to God and the messenger . . .* (Q 4/59). He said that referring to God is a matter of referring to His book. Referring may be directly to the messenger when he is alive; and when he is dead, referring is to his *sunna*.

10. Abū ʿUmar [Ibn ʿAbd al-Barr, author of this work] says that the prophet of God said, 'I have omitted nothing of what God has commanded you: I have commanded all. And I have omitted nothing of what God has prohibited to you: I have prohibited all.' This is related from al-Muṭṭalab ibn Ḥinṭab and others. Further, God has said, *He does not utter mere whims; it is revelation revealed* (Q 53/3–4). Also, *By your lord, they will not believe till they set you up as arbitrator; then they will find in their souls no doubts about your decree, and submit willingly* (Q 4/65). Also, *No believer, man or woman, has the right, if God and his messenger have decreed something, to choose freely in the matter* (Q 33/36).

11. Clarification from the prophet is of two kinds.

    11.1. Clarification of a general (or comprehensive) statement in the holy book. For example, the prophet clarified the five prayers, their specific times, their bowings and prostrations and the other detailed rules of prayer; *zakāt*, its limits, timing and what goods are subject to it; the rituals of *ḥajj*, as in when the prophet performed the *ḥajj* with the people, and he said, 'Take your rituals from me.' The Qurʾān offers only a general (or summary) injunction to prayer, *zakāt* and *ḥajj*, but gives no details. The *ḥadīth* provide details.

    11.2. An addition to the laws that are in the book. For example, the prophet stipulated the prohibition of a woman's marrying her maternal or paternal uncles; recognizing the domestic donkey as *ḥarām*, as well as all predatory animals possessed of a canine tooth; and other things which it would take too long to mention here and which I have summarized elsewhere.

12. God has commanded us to obey and follow the prophet, with a command which is absolute, comprehensive and unconditional, just as he has commanded us to follow the book of God. God did not add, 'If he agrees with God's book', as some have claimed who deviate [from the truth]. ʿAbd al-Raḥmān ibn Mahdī said that the Zindīqs and the Khawārij fabricated that *ḥadīth*. He was referring to the words related from the prophet, 'Whatever you hear related from me, compare it with the book of God. If it agrees with the book of God, I said it. If it opposes the book of God, I did not say it. I am only ever in agreement with the book of God; through it God guided me.' These words are not recognized by the people of knowledge as soundly transmitted from him, by sound as opposed to faulty transmission. Indeed, some of the people of knowledge have dealt with this *ḥadīth*. They say they have compared it with the book of God before anything else and they have relied upon the results of this comparison. They say that when they compared it they found it opposed to the book of God. They have said that they did not find in the book of God that a *ḥadīth* should only be accepted when it agrees with the book of God. Indeed they found the book of God absolute in setting up the prophet as a model, in commanding obedience to him, and in warning against opposition to his commands. This is total and under every circumstance.

13. Muḥammad ibn Khalīfa told us that Muḥammad ibn al-Ḥusayn told him that Aḥmad ibn al-Ḥusayn ibn Sahl al-Ishbānī told him that al-Ḥusayn ibn ʿAlī ʾl-Aswad told him that Yaḥyā ibn Ādam told him that Ibn al-Mubārak reported on the authority of Maʿmar from ʿAlī ibn Zayd from Abū Naḍra from ʿImrān ibn Ḥaṣīn that he said to a man, 'You are a fool. Do you find in the book of God that the noon-prayer is four *rakʿa*s, or that you must not recite out loud during this prayer?' Then he enumerated the rules of prayer, *zakāt* and so forth, and said, 'Do you find anything to explain these rules in the book of God? The book of God gives these things in a vague fashion. The *sunna* explains.'

14. ʿAbd al-Wārith ibn Sufyān told us that Qāsim ibn Aṣbagh told him that Ismāʿīl ibn Isḥāq al-Qāḍī told him that Sulaymān ibn Ḥarb told him that Ḥammād ibn Zayd told him on the authority of Ayyūb that a certain man spoke to Muṭarrif ibn ʿAbd Allāh ibn al-Shakhīr, saying, 'Do not talk to us except of the Qurʾān.' Muṭarrif replied, 'By God, we have no desire to propose a substitute for the Qurʾān. But we have a desire for someone who knows the Qurʾān better than us.'

15. Al-Awzāʿī related from Ḥassān ibn ʿAṭiyya, 'Revelation was granted to the prophet of God and Gabriel brought him the *sunna*, which explains it.' Al-Awzāʿī also said, 'The book is in greater need of the *sunna* than the *sunna* is of the book.' Abū ʿUmar [Ibn ʿAbd al-Barr] says that al-Awzāʿī meant that the *sunna* passes judgement on the book, and clarifies its intentions. ʿĪsā ibn Yūnus related to us from al-Awzāʿī, from Makḥūl, 'The Qurʾān is more in need of the *sunna* than the *sunna* of the book.' From the same source, it is transmitted from al-Awzāʿī that Yaḥyā ibn Abī Kathīr said, 'The *sunna* passes judgement on the book, but the book does not pass judgement on the *sunna*.' Al-Faḍl ibn Ziyād said that he had heard Aḥmad ibn Ḥanbal, when asked about the report which states that the *sunna* passes judgement on the book, say, 'I dare not say this –

that the *sunna* passes judgement on the book; rather it explains the book and clarifies it.' Al-Faḍl likewise said that he had heard Aḥmad say, 'The *sunna* does not abrogate any part of the Qur'ān; nothing abrogates the Qur'ān except the Qur'an.' Abū ʿUmar [Ibn ʿAbd al-Barr] says that this is the view of al-Shāfiʿī, that the Qur'ān is abrogated only by the Qur'ān, because of God's words, *If We exchange for one verse another* and so forth (Q 16/101) and *Whatever verse we abrogate* and so forth (Q 2/106). Most of the followers of Mālik agree with this, except Abū 'l-Faraj. He attributes to Mālik the opinion of the Kufans [that is, the Ḥanafīs] on this matter [i.e., that the *sunna* can abrogate the Qur'ān].

II *Chapter: On those who interpret or deal with the Qur'ān while being ignorant of the sunna*

1. Abū ʿUmar [Ibn ʿAbd al-Barr] says that the people of innovation, all of them, have turned away from the *sunna* and interpreted the book in a manner not consistent with the *sunna*. They have strayed and they have caused others to stray. We seek refuge with God from failure, and we ask for success and freedom from error through his mercy. Warnings against this are transmitted from the prophet in numerous forms; amongst them are the following.

2. ʿAbd Allāh ibn Muḥammad ibn ʿAbd al-Mu'min ibn Yaḥyā told us that al-Ḥusayn ibn ʿUthmān al-Ādamī told him that ʿAbbās al-Dūrī told him that ʿAbd Allāh ibn Yazīd al-Muqrī told him that Ibn Lahīʿa told him on the authority of Abū Qubayl who said that he heard ʿUqba ibn ʿĀmir al-Juhanī say that he heard the messenger of God say, 'The destruction of my community lies in the book and in business.' Someone asked, 'What is the book and what is business?' The prophet replied, 'They learn the Qur'ān and they interpret it in a manner not consistent with God's revelation. And they love business, and so abandon communal prayer and Friday prayer, and disperse.'

   Aḥmad ibn Qāsim told us that Aḥmad ibn Abī Dulaym informed him that Ibn Waḍḍāḥ told him that Dhuḥaym told him that Abū Ṣāliḥ told him on the authority of Layth on the authority of Abū Qubayl on the authority of ʿUqba ibn ʿĀmir that the prophet said, 'The worst that I fear for my community is the book and business. As to business, many seek it out of love for it, and they abandon communal prayer. As to the book, many interpret it, and they dispute on this basis with those who are believers.'

   I read to ʿAbd al-Raḥmān ibn Yaḥyā the report that he had said that Abū Bakr ibn Aḥmad, known as Bukayr of Mecca, told him that ʿAbd Allāh ibn Aḥmad ibn Ḥanbal told him that his father told him that Zayd ibn al-Habbāb told him that Muʿāwiya ibn Ṣāliḥ told him that Abū 'l-Samḥ told him that Abū Qubayl told him that he heard ʿUqba ibn ʿĀmir say that he heard the messenger of God say, 'The worst that I fear for my community are two things: the Qur'ān and business. As to the Qur'ān, hypocrites will learn it in order to dispute with believers. As to business, they seek a comfortable life, and, following their desires, they abandon prayer.' He also said, 'The worst I fear for my community is a hypocrite, learned in language, who disputes on the basis of the Qur'ān.'

3. Salama ibn Saʿīd told us that al-Ḥusayn ibn Rashīd told him that al-ʿAbbās ibn Muḥammad al-Baṣrī told him that Abū ʿĀṣim told him that ʿAbd Allāh ibn Bakr al-Sahmī told him that ʿAbbād ibn Kathīr told him on the authority of Abū Qallāba on the authority of [ʿAbd Allāh ibn] Masʿūd who said, 'You will find people who summon you to the book of God. But they have thrown it behind them. You must have knowledge and avoid innovation; you must avoid obstinacy and hold on to what is ancient.'

4. Saʿīd ibn Naṣr told me that Qāsim ibn al-Aṣbagh told him that Ibn Waḍḍāḥ told him that Mūsā ibn Muʿāwiya told him that Ibn Mahdī told him on the authority of Ḥammād ibn Zayd on the authority of ʿAmr ibn Dīnār that ʿUmar said, 'I fear on your behalf two things: the man who interprets the Qurʾān as it should not be interpreted and the man who competes with his brother for property.'

5. Muḥammad ibn Aḥmad informed us that Muḥammad ibn Aḥmad ibn Yaḥyā told him that Aḥmad ibn Muḥammad ibn Ziyād al-Aʿrābī told him that Muḥammad ibn ʿAbd al-Malik al-Daqīqī told him that Yazīd ibn Hārūn told him that Ibn ʿAwn told him on the authority of Rajāʾ ibn Ḥaywā from a man who said that they were sitting with Muʿāwiya who said, 'That which most tempts to error is the man who reads the Qurʾān but has no learning in it. He teaches children, slaves, women and the community and they dispute with the people of knowledge.'

6. ʿAbd al-Wārith ibn Sufyān told us that Qāsim ibn Aṣbagh told him that Aḥmad ibn Zuhayr told him that al-Walīd ibn Shajāʿ told him that Mubashshir ibn Ismāʿīl told him that Jaʿfar ibn Burqān told him on the authority of Maymūn ibn Mihrān who said, 'The Qurʾān has become threadbare in the breasts of many, and they have sought something else, namely *ḥadīth*. Of those who desire this knowledge there are some who take it as a means to seek the goods of this world. And some who learn it in order to dispute with it. And some who learn it that they may be pointed out. But the best of them are those who learn it in order thereby to obey God.'

7.2 Ibn Qudāma on the status of the *mujtahid*

Muwaffaq al-Dīn ʿAbd Allāh ibn Aḥmad ibn Qudāma al-Maqdisī was a Ḥanbalī ascetic, jurist and traditionalist theologian. He was born in 541/1146 at Jammāʿīl, near Jerusalem, studied in Baghdad, and spent most of his life in Damascus, where he died in 620/1223. While in Baghdad, he studied for a short time with the famous Ḥanbalī Ṣūfī preacher ʿAbd al-Qādir al-Jīlānī (d. 561/1166), after whom the Qādirī order is named, as well as with more mainstream Ḥanbalī teachers such as Ibn al-Jawzī (d. 597/1200). He is also said to have taken part in Saladin's campaign against the Franks in Jerusalem in 583/1187.

Ibn Qudāma's experience with al-Jīlānī, which was cut short only by the latter's death, seems to have left him with a good opinion of Sufism in general. He is better known, however, for his fierce criticism of the traditions that he disliked, especially the theology (*kalām*) of the Ashʿarites. He accused the scholastic theologians of straying from the apparent meaning of the texts of revelation and the interpretations of the pious predecessors, by placing too much emphasis on rational speculation.

Ibn Qudāma's *Rawḍat al-nāẓir* was influenced significantly by the Shāfiʿite Abū Ḥāmid al-Ghazālī's (d. 505/1111) famous work of the same genre, his *al-Mustaṣfā*. The discussion of *ijtihād* (legal reasoning) is the seventh of eight chapters in this concise and clearly organized work of *uṣūl al-fiqh* (methodology of jurisprudence). Ibn Qudāma's approach to *ijtihād* seems to be consistent with his views on rational speculation in theology. In the first part of the passage presented below, he can be seen as playing down the significance of the additional proofs besides the Qur'ān and the *sunna,* especially the contributions of one's predecessors in a particular juristic school tradition. He also expresses his frustration with the indeterminate nature of much of the jurisprudential scholarship in his day. Ibn Qudāma urges his fellow jurists to focus on the goal of finding the single and correct ruling in each situation, rather than producing increasing numbers of skilfully argued efforts, and treating them all as being of equal worth. This reveals much about the tensions between the desire to discover God's law in a more concrete and black and white form, as represented by Ibn Qudāma, and the justificatory and exploratory aspirations of the majority of classical jurists, who confronted the sources of the law through the past tradition of their respective schools (see section 7.4 for the approach of al-Nawawī which contrasts with that of Ibn Qudāma).

Further reading

Wael Hallaq, 'Ijtihād,' in John L. Esposito (ed.), *The Oxford encyclopedia of the modern Islamic world,* New York/Oxford 1995, vol. 2, pp. 78–81.

Henri Laoust, *Le Précis de droit d'Ibn Qudāma,* Beirut 1950.

George Makdisi, 'Ibn Ḳudāma al-Maḳdisī,' in *Encyclopaedia of Islam*, new edition.

—— *Ibn Qudāma's censure of speculative theology. An edition and translation of Ibn Qudāma's* Taḥrīm an-naẓar fī kutub ahl al-kalām, London 1962, introduction.

Source text

Ibn Qudāma, *Rawḍat al-nāẓir wa-jannat al-munāẓir fī uṣūl al-fiqh*, Riyadh 1993, pp. 959–64, 975–6, 982–7 and 990–6.

Chapter: On the status of the mujtahid

1. Know that *ijtihād* etymologically means expenditure of effort, and the utmost exertion of capacity in a task. It is a word only used for an activity involving effort. One says it of carrying a millstone but not of carrying a mustard seed. In the technical terminology of the *fuqahā*ʾ it signifies specifically the expenditure of effort in order to know the rules of law. Full *ijtihād* is that one should expend effort in the search [for knowledge] to the point where one feels in oneself a total incapacity to extend the search any further.

2. It is a condition for a *mujtahid* that he have complete mastery of the productive sources of juristic conclusions. These are the principles which we have set out [above], namely: *kitāb*, *sunna*, *ijmāʿ*, *istiṣḥāb al-ḥāl*, *qiyās* and its dependent arguments; also overall considerations in reaching a juristic decision, and the assessment of relevant priorities amongst these. As to the question whether justice is a condition in the *mujtahid*, [the answer is] that it is not so. . . . But it is a condition of the permissibility of relying on his opinions. If a man is not just, his *fatwā*s are not accepted.

3. With regard to knowledge of the book (*kitāb*), it is incumbent that a *mujtahid* know that part of it which is related to juristic conclusions; that is about 500 verses. It is not a condition that he should know them by heart, but he should know their whereabouts so that he can find the required verse in time of need. In respect of knowing the *sunna*, it is a condition that he know those *ḥadīth* which relate to juristic rules. These, though many, are finite in number. There is no alternative to knowing the *nāsikh* and the *mansūkh* (that is, the rules of abrogation) in regard to *kitāb* and *sunna*, but it is sufficient that a *mujtahid* know in a particular case that the relevant proof is not abrogated. The *mujtahid* needs to know in regard to a *ḥadīth* he is using in a particular case that it is 'sound' and not 'weak'. This may be known either through the *mujtahid*'s knowledge of transmitters and their probity or by taking the *ḥadīth* from the 'sound' collections, the ones whose transmitters are approved by the scholars. As to *ijmāʿ*, he needs to know the cases where it is established. But it is sufficient that he should know about the problem upon which he has to give an opinion (*fatwā*), whether it is (a) something upon which there is *ijmāʿ* , or (b) something upon which there is dispute, or (c) a new case. He should also know *istiṣḥāb al-ḥāl*, as we have set out in an earlier chapter.

4. He needs to know how to set up proofs and the conditions related to proofs. He also needs to know something of grammar and language so that he is capable of understanding the speech of the Arabs. [He needs sufficient knowledge] to distinguish the direct, the apparent and the ambivalent in speech, also the true

and the metaphorical, the general and the particular, the secure and the doubtful, the absolute and the qualified, the denotative and the connotative, the morphological and the semantic. But he does not need to know more than is directly related to *kitāb* and *sunna*, whereby he can gain mastery over the import and the precise intention of a passage.

5. As to the ramifications of *fiqh*, he has no need of these, for these were produced by *mujtahids* after acquiring the status of *ijtihād*. So how can they be a condition for a status which is itself conceptually prior to these ramifications?

6. It is not a condition of *ijtihād* in respect of a particular problem that a *mujtahid* have reached the grade of *ijtihād* in all problems. Rather, when he knows the proofs of a single question, and the modes of considering it, he is a *mujtahid* in that question, even if he is ignorant of juristic conclusions in other areas. . . . Do you not realize that the companions and the *imāms* after them used to suspend decision in some problems? Mālik ibn Anas was asked forty questions and to thirty-six of them he replied, 'I don't know.' But this suspension of decision does not exclude him from the grade of *ijtihād*. God knows best. . . .

7. Problem: Truth lies with the opinion of one *mujtahid*; the others are in error. This is true in *furūʿ al-dīn* and in *uṣūl al-dīn*. But if it relates to *furūʿ al-dīn* in an area where there is no decisive proof based on revealed text or *ijmāʿ*, then [the error] is excused, there is no sin involved and the *mujtahid* gets a reward for his *ijtihād*. So say some Ḥanafīs and some Shāfiʿīs. Some of the theologians say that every *mujtahid* is correct, and that there is not [in a problem of *ijtihād*] a [firm] proof that can be searched for. There are variant views from Abū Ḥanīfa and from al-Shāfiʿī which support this opinion.

8. Some of those who consider that every *mujtahid* is correct claim that the proof in this matter is decisive. [Proofs of this are given at some length and are refuted, pp. 976–82.]

9. The evidence that the truth lies in one single decision is to be found in *kitāb*, *sunna*, *ijmāʿ* and logic (*maʿnā*).

    9.1. As for *kitāb*, the proof lies in God's words, *David and Solomon, when they gave judgement on the field – for the people's flocks had strayed there – we were witness to their judgement. We conferred understanding on Solomon; to each we gave judgement and knowledge* (Q 21/78–9). If they had been equal in getting the right answer, there would have been no significance in specifying that Solomon had understanding. This, too, is evidence against those who claim that sin is not removed from one in error. For God praised and commended both, as is evident from His saying, *To each we gave judgement and knowledge.*

    9.1.1. Someone may ask how it is possible to attribute error to David since he was a prophet. Or how do you know that he gave judgement by *ijtihād*, granted the dispute on the possibility of that [i.e., of prophets judging by *ijtihād*]? Or, further, if he was in error, how can one in error be praised, since he merits blame for an error? And, all of this being the case, is it not possible that they were both correct at the time but that revelation was given subsequently in agreement with only one of them? We reply as follows. Error is permissible in prophets, but they cannot be confirmed in error. We have explained this earlier. If minor sins are conceivable on the part of prophets, why should error be forbidden, error of the type that involves no sin, error whose perpetrator is rewarded? If it were not so, our own prophet would not have been censured for his judgement on the slaves taken at Badr, nor for the permission he granted to hold back at the raid on Tabūk. God said, *God has forgiven you for what you permitted them* (Q 9/43). Further, the prophet said, 'You come to me with disputes, but some of you are more forceful in arguments than others. I judge only as I hear. So when I decree to one person something that belongs by right to his brother, let him not take it; for I give him only a slice of hellfire.' This proves that he could decree to one man something that belongs by right to his brother.

9.1.2. They may say, 'How do you know that he [David] gave judgement by *ijtihād* ?' We would then say, 'The Qur'ānic verse is evidence for that. For, if the judgement were based on a text [that was decisive], God would not have singled out Solomon as understanding, to the exclusion of David.'

9.1.3. They may say, 'The text was revealed subsequently in agreement with Solomon.' We would then say, 'If the judgement given by David had been correct together with that of Solomon, then change of judgement as a result of subsequent revelation would not have prevented God from "conferring understanding" on both of them at the time of the judgement; nor would it have occasioned the specification of Solomon as correct. It is the same as if the judgement had been changed by abrogation.'

9.2. As for the *sunna*, the evidence lies in the *ḥadīth* mentioned above. The prophet declared that he decreed to one person something that belonged by right to that person's brother. If there were any sin in that, the prophet would not have done it. If the decree he issued were itself the judgement of God, he would not have said, 'When I decree to one person something that belongs by right to his brother. . . .' Further, God's judgement does not vary according to the variety or similarity of the 'forcefulness' of disputants. . . .

9.2.1. Ibn ʿUmar, ʿAmr ibn al-ʿĀṣ, Abū Hurayra and others relate that the prophet said, 'If a judge (*ḥākim*) exercises *ijtihād* and hits the mark, he gains two rewards, and if he errs, he gains one.' This is the version of ʿAmr, as given by Muslim. It is a *ḥadīth* which the community has accepted. . . .

9.2.2. We do not say that the *mujtahid* is charged (*taklīf*) with getting the correct judgement. We only say that for every problem there is a specific correct answer, known to God, and the *mujtahid* is charged with searching for it. If he exercises *ijtihād* and gets the correct answer, he gets two rewards; if he errs he gets one reward for his effort, his *ijtihād*. He is in error, but the sin attendant upon error is removed from him. It is like the problem of the *qibla*. The person who is correct in establishing the right direction, when there is difference of opinion amongst the *mujtahids*, is only one. The others are certainly in error. . . .

9.3. As for *ijmāʿ*, it is well known in cases beyond number that the companions erred, when acting as *mujtahids*. For example, when Abū Bakr issued a response on *kalāla*, he said, 'I am only giving my opinion. If it is correct, it is from God. If it is an error, it is from me and from the Devil. God and his prophet are not to be blamed for it. . . .'

9.4. As for logic, there are several aspects to this.

9.4.1. The argument of those who claim that [all parties] are correct is impossible in itself, because it leads to a combining of contradictories, for example as in the case of date-wine which is both permitted (*ḥalāl*) and forbidden (*ḥarām*), that a woman's marriage without a *walī* is both valid and invalid, that the life of a Muslim who has killed a *dhimmī* is both forfeit and inviolate. . . . In these cases [it is argued] there is no specific ruling, and so the ruling of every single *mujtahid* is true and correct in spite of their contradictions of one another. A certain scholar has said that this theory begins in sophistry and ends in *zandaqa* (heresy). This is because it begins in making a thing and its opposite both true, and it ends by informing *mujtahids* in cases of conflicting evidence that they can [simply] choose the most attractive ruling among the various *madhhabs*.

9.4.2. They may say that it is not impossible that a thing be both *ḥalāl* and *ḥarām* with respect to different people. For a legal judgement is not an attribute belonging to the essence of a thing, so there is no contradiction in stating that a thing is *ḥalāl* for Zayd, and *ḥarām* for ʿAmr. It is like a married woman [they claim] who is *ḥalāl* for her husband, but *ḥarām* for all others. This is plain. Indeed the situation is not impossible for one person in different states and conditions. Prayer, for example, is obligatory (*wājib*) for someone who is actually in a state of impurity, as long as he thinks he is pure; but it is *ḥarām* if he knows of the impurity. And travel by sea is permissible (*mubāḥ*) to one whose opinion is overwhelming as to his likely safety, but *ḥarām* to one whose opinion is overwhelming as to the likelihood of shipwreck. The answer to all this is that their theory leads to the combining of contradictories in one person. For the *mujtahid* does not limit his judgement to his own self, but judges that date-wine is *ḥarām* to everyone, while another *mujtahid* judges it permissible to everyone. How can it be *ḥarām* to everyone and *mubāḥ* to everyone at the same time? How can a woman married without a *walī* be both *mubāḥ* to her husband and *ḥarām* to him at the same time? Furthermore, even if this were not impossible in itself it would lead to impossibility in some respects. For, if a *mujtahid* finds a conflict of proofs [and understands this to mean] that he must merely choose between one judgement and its opposite, then, if one *mujtahid* marries a woman with no *walī* and another marries her subsequently, deeming the first marriage invalid, how can she be *mubāḥ* to both husbands?

9.4.3. If every *mujtahid* were correct, it would be permissible for each of two *mujtahid*s, searching for the *qibla*, merely to follow his companion; because each of them would be correct and his prayer would be valid. Why should one not follow the one whose prayer is correct in itself? If this were the case, we could roll up the carpet of disputation in matters of *furūʿ*, for everyone would be correct. There would be no point in dissuading someone from his opinion or informing him of his opponent's opinion.

9.4.4. The *mujtahid* is charged with *ijtihād*; there is no dispute on this. *Ijtihād* is a search, and this requires that there be a thing searched for. If there is for a particular case no specific judgement, then what are we searching for? If one knows for sure that Zayd is neither ignorant nor learned, then is it conceivable that one could search for a [defensible] opinion as to his being [or not being] learned? If a man believes that date-wine is neither *ḥalāl* nor *ḥarām*, how should he search for a single answer?

They may say that the *mujtahid* is not actually seeking God's judgement on a matter, but is merely seeking an overwhelming opinion, and then God's judgement corresponds to the overwhelming opinion. It is, they say, like one who wishes to travel by sea. He is informed that if he has an overwhelming opinion that he will be drowned, he is forbidden to go. But if he has an overwhelming opinion that he will be safe, he is permitted to go. And, before the emergence of his opinion, God had no judgement in regard to him, except precisely his own *ijtihād*, following his opinion. So divine judgement is completely new at the time of a person's formulating an opinion and comes into existence only after it. Likewise, they claim if two witnesses testify before a judge, then God's judgement in the case is based on the judge's opinion. If he has an overwhelming impression as to the veracity of the testimony, it is *wājib* to accept it. And if he has an overwhelming opinion of the mendacity of the testimony, it is not *wājib* to accept it. We would reply that they say that what is sought is merely opinion. But opinion must be about something. If a person is convinced of the non-existence of a judgement, how is it conceivable that he can have an opinion on its existence? Opinion is only conceivable in relation to something that really exists. They say that the existent [i.e., a judgement] comes into existence following the opinion, and this leads to infinite regress. The sea-traveller [according to them] is not actually seeking the divine judgement on a matter, but is seeking a sense of safety or disaster. These are things of which he may have a sense. Likewise the judge is seeking a sense of the veracity or mendacity of the witnesses, though this is not the same as the judgement which is entailed by this knowledge. This is opposed to what we believe. The thing sought is the judgement itself, which [for them] does not exist; so how is a search for it conceivable? Further, if we know that God has no particular judgement on a matter, then why is *ijtihād* obligatory? For, in that case, we would know, by means of rational thought, prior to revelation, the non-existence of *wājib* duties, and the absence of blame attending upon action or inaction. . . .

9.4.5. They may say that proofs that lead only to opinion are not proofs as to the true nature of juristic problems; they infer this from the variant qualities attributed to one problem. We would say that this is false.

We have demonstrated for every problem a proof and we have explained the nature of its significance. If it were true that juristic problems were devoid of relevant proofs then the *mujtahid* and the ignoramus would be equal. It would then be permissible for the ignoramus to formulate judgements on the basis of his opinion; for, granted the absence of relevant proofs, he would be equal to the *mujtahid*. In fact, the difference between them lies precisely in the *mujtahid*'s knowledge of proofs and in his rational investigation into their validity or invalidity. The resistance of some natures to accepting a proof does not detract from its significance as a proof. There are many intellectually demonstrable matters on which people are at variance, but they continue to believe that intellectual arguments are decisive. It is not denied that in some juristic problems the evidence is weak, its point unclear, and opposing evidence present. The result is that such cases are obscure to the *mujtahid*, and a variety of opinions consequently emerges. But some are clear and the error of those who oppose the evidence in such cases is manifest. Both types of evidence (the clear and the unclear) constitute proofs.

9.4.6. Further, if [rationally defended] opinion does not constitute evidence, how do you know that it does not? Denial of the relevance of opinion here necessarily entails denial of the argument that opinion does not constitute evidence [i.e., to deny that a rationally defended opinion constitutes evidence is self-refuting, since that claim is itself based on the affirmation of a rationally defended opinion].

7.3 Al-Nawawī on the ranks of *muftīs*

For a biography of Yaḥyā ibn Sharaf Muḥyī 'l-Dīn al-Nawawī (631/1233–676/1277), see above, section 6.2.

Al-Nawawī's *Majmūʿ* is a commentary on the *Muhadhdhab* of Abū Isḥāq al-Shīrāzī (d. 476/1083; see section 7.6). In its introduction, al-Nawawī presents a set of eight discussions which stand as a prologue to the study of jurisprudence, the seventh of which is on the topic of issuing *fatwās*, that is reasoned responses to specific juristic questions.

In this discussion, those deemed qualified to practise *ijtihād* (legal reasoning) and give *fatwās*, and thus fulfil a communal duty (*farḍ kifāya*) and relieve others from having to do so, are divided into three categories: the independent *muftī*, the affiliated *muftī* and the deficient *muftī*. In this way, even those communities whose members may have very limited proficiency in jurisprudence can be accommodated in the scheme. Such *muftīs* would need to rely most heavily on the works of predecessors in the juristic school, a requirement of higher-ranking *muftīs* as well, albeit to a lesser degree, who remain *muqallid*, or subject to the authority of the independent *muftīs* who preceded them.

Further reading

Norman Calder, 'Al-Nawawī's typology of *muftīs* and its significance for a general theory of Islamic law,' *Islamic law and society*, 3 (1996), pp. 137–64; a detailed analysis of this source text.

—— 'Taḳlīd,' in *Encyclopaedia of Islam*, new edition.

Wael Hallaq, '*Iftā'* and *ijtihād* in Sunni legal theory: a developmental account,' in M. K. Masud, B. Messick, D. Powers (eds), *Islamic legal interpretation: muftis and their fatwas*, Cambridge MA 1996, pp. 33–43.

M. K. Masud, B. Messick, A. Dallal, '*Fatwā*,' in John L. Esposito (ed.), *The Oxford encyclopedia of the modern Islamic world*, New York/Oxford 1995, vol. 2, pp. 8–17.

Source text

Al-Nawawī, *Al-Majmūʿ sharḥ al-Muhadhdhab*, Cairo n.d., vol. 1, pp. 70–5.

1. Abū ʿAmr [Ibn al-Ṣāliḥ, d. 643/1245] said that *muftīs* are of two categories, independent and otherwise.

    1.1. Category 1. The independent *muftī*. The conditions of the independent *muftī* are as follows:

    (a) he should have acquired knowledge of the proofs of *sharʿī* rules . . . ; these have been elaborated in works of *fiqh*, and so become easy of acquisition, praise be to God;

    (b) he should know the conditions and aspects of proofs and how to derive rules from them . . . ; this can be acquired from works of *uṣūl al-fiqh*;

(c) he should be familiar with the Qur'ān, *ḥadīth*, the rules of abrogation, language and linguistics, dispute and variation amongst scholars . . . ;
(d) he should be possessed of knowledge and experience in these matters;
(e) he should know *fiqh* and be a master of its major problems and divisions.

One who acquires these qualities is an independent and absolute *muftī* through whom the communal duty is discharged.

1.2. He is independent and absolute because he freely manipulates arguments without submission to or limitation by any *madhhab*.
1.3. Abū ʿAmr said that the condition of his learning the problems of *fiqh* is not laid down in many famous books. This is because it is not a condition of the rank of *ijtihād*, for *fiqh* is the result of and posterior to *ijtihād*, and what is posterior to a thing cannot be a condition of it. But Abū Isḥāq al-Isfarāʾīnī, Abū Manṣūr [Ibn al-Sabbāgh] al-Baghdādī and others have made it a condition. That knowledge of *fiqh* is a condition in the *muftī* through whom the communal duty of *iftāʾ* [issuing of *fatwā*s] is discharged is the valid view, though it is not a condition in the independent *mujtahid*.
1.4. It is not a condition in the *muftī* that all the rules of the law should be in his head. It is sufficient that he should memorize the majority and be capable of getting at the rest quickly. . . .
1.5. Further, the condition of acquiring all the knowledge we have itemized is relevant only to the absolute *muftī*, one who covers all topics of the law. As to the *muftī* who works only in a specific area, like pilgrimage or inheritance, it is sufficient that he know that area. This is according to al-Ghazālī, his companion [Ibn] Barhān, and others. There are some who have denied it absolutely, but Ibn al-Sabbāgh permitted it in inheritance, and the more valid view is that it is permitted absolutely.

2. Category 2. There have been no independent *muftī*s for ages past. *Fatwā*s belong now to those affiliated to the *imām*s of the accepted *madhhab*s. The affiliated *muftī* is of four grades.

2.1. Grade 1. This *muftī* does not submit *(taqlīd)* to his *imām* either in *madhhab* or in proofs, because he has the quality of independence. He is linked to him only because he follows the *imām*'s method of *ijtihād*.
2.2. Abū Isḥāq [al-Shīrāzī] claimed this quality for our companions. But he said of the companions of Mālik, Aḥmad and Dāwūd, and most of the Ḥanafīs, that they belonged to the tradition of their *imām*s by virtue of submission. He then said that the correct stance is that adopted by our companions, namely that they follow the *madhhab* of al-Shāfiʿī but not in submission to him. Rather, finding his method of *ijtihād* and analogy the most sound, and granted there is no escape from *ijtihād*, they followed his path and sought knowledge of rules by the method of al-Shāfiʿī. Abū ʿAlī al-Sinjī

said much the same, namely, that we follow al-Shāfiʿī to the exclusion of others, because we find his opinions the weightiest and most just, not out of submission to him.

2.3. I [al-Nawawī] say that these opinions of Abū Isḥāq and al-Sinjī are in agreement with the command of al-Shāfiʿī which is reported by al-Muzanī in the introduction to the *Mukhtaṣar*, and by others, namely that he announced the prohibition of submission whether to him or to others.

2.4. Abū ʿAmr said that the claim that they absolutely did not practise *taqlīd* is not sound, nor consonant with their practice or the practice of most of them.

2.5. A certain master of *uṣūl* in our tradition states that there has been no independent *mujtahid* since the time of al-Shāfiʿī. This being the case, the *fatwā* of a *muftī* of this type is like the *fatwā* of the independent *muftī* in respect of acting on it, and in respect of its being assessed for *ijmāʿ* or in juristic dispute.

3.1. Grade 2. He is a *mujtahid* limited to the *madhhab* of his *imām*, but independent in the establishment of his principles by proof. However, he does not in his proofs go beyond the principles and methods of his *imām*.

3.2. It is a condition in this *muftī* that he know *fiqh*, *uṣūl* and the arguments that lead to judgements; that he understand the methodology of proofs and analogies; that he be experienced in deducing and deriving rules, and capable of relating what is not textually recorded from the *imām* to the *imām*'s principles. He is not free from the taint of *taqlīd* since he lacks some of the tools of the independent *muftī*, lacking expertise, for example, in *ḥadīth* and Arabic; these are frequently lacking in the limited *muftī* (*al-muqayyad*). Further, he takes the texts of his *imām* as a basis for deriving rules, just as the independent *muftī* does with the texts of the law; and he may well be content with the proofs of his *imām* in disregard of opposing opinions, like the independent *muftī* in respect of his texts.

3.3. This is the quality of our companions, those whose opinions are preserved; the *imām*s of our tradition are, most of them, thus. One who acts on the *fatwā* of such a one submits to his *imām*, not to the limited *muftī*.

3.4. The apparent meaning of the words of our companions is that the communal duty of *iftā'* is not discharged by a *muftī* of this type. But Abū ʿAmr said that with such a *muftī*, the discharge of the communal duty is evident in respect of *iftā'*, but not in respect of the renewal of the sciences which support the giving of *fatwā*s. This is the case because he takes the place of his independent *imām*, as deduced from a valid principle, namely the permission of submission to a dead person.

3.5. The limited *muftī* may be independent in a specific question or topic of the law, as explained above. He may issue *fatwā*s on matters on which the *imām* has left no text, based on deduction from his principles. This is the correct view which corresponds to practice; it has been the recourse of *muftī*s for ages past.

3.6. In these circumstances, if he delivers a *fatwā* based on his deduction, the questioner is *muqallid* to his *imām* and not to him. This is what the Imām al-Ḥaramayn said. . . . Abū ʿAmr said that this should be construed in the light of a dispute reported by Abū Isḥāq al-Shīrāzī and others, as to whether it is permissible to attribute to al-Shāfiʿī the deductions of our companions. The more valid of the two views is, no.

3.7. At times he will deduce from a specific text of his *imām* and at times he will not find such a text and he will deduce based on his principles. . . .

4.1. Grade 3. He does not reach the rank of the early scholars whose views are preserved but he has a trained intelligence, knows the *madhhab* of his *imām*, is familiar with his proofs and can deploy them, and is generally capable of organizing and presenting arguments towards a juristic preference. He falls short of the former types because of his deficiencies in knowing the *madhhab*, or in experience of inference, or in knowledge of interpretive argument, etc. This is the quality of many of the moderns up to the end of the fifth century, author jurists, who organized and presented the *madhhab*, and wrote the books which are the prime focus of scholarly study today. They do not match the previous types in making deductions.

4.2. As to their *fatwā*s, they produced these in a manner the same as or close to the manner of the others, using analogy for untransmitted problems, and not limiting themselves to overt analogy. Amongst them are some whose *fatwā*s have been collected but, in their integration within the *madhhab*, they do not reach the quantity of those of the scholars of the early generations.

5.1. Grade 4. He masters the learning, transmitting and understanding of the *madhhab*, in its clear and its difficult aspects, but he has some weaknesses in control of argument and organization of analogy. His transmission and his *fatwā*s based on it depend on the writings of the *madhhab* as he reports them, whether the texts of the *imām* or the elaborations of the *mujtahids* within the *madhhab*. What he does not find in transmitted form . . . he may link to transmitted material and give *fatwā*s on this basis; likewise in respect of whatever can be brought under an established principle in the *madhhab*. In cases different from this, he must abstain from giving *fatwā*s. Such cases are rare, however, for it is very unlikely, as the Imām al-Ḥaramayn said, that a problem will arise which has no textual reference in the tradition, or which cannot be linked to the meaning of a text, or brought under a principle.

5.2. The conditions of this *muftī* are that he have a trained intelligence, and that he has mastered a large quantity of *fiqh*. Abū ʿAmr said, with regard to this and the previous type of *muftī*, that it is sufficient for him to have the bulk of the rules in his head, and that he be able in time of need to get at the rest quickly. . . .

6.1. Someone may ask, what of one who has learnt one book or several within the tradition, but is deficient, lacking the qualities of those described above; if the layman can find no other in his town, may he have recourse to such a one? The answer is, if there is a *muftī* in another town such that he can get to him, he must, in so far as it is possible, approach him. Otherwise he should mention his problem to the deficient person, and if the latter finds it, quite specifically, in a reliable work, and if he is one whose reporting is acceptable, then he should transmit it to the questioner in its textual form. The layman is then *muqallid* to the founder of the *madhhab*.

6.2. Abū ʿAmr said, 'I have found this in the writings of a certain scholar and evidence supports it.' If he does not find the specific problem written out he may not use analogy on other written sources to which he has access; this is true even if he believes it to be an example of analogy with no element of distinction, for he may imagine this to be the case where it is not.

7.1. Someone may ask, may a *muqallid* give *fatwā*s in areas where he is *muqallid*? The answer is that Abū ʿAbd Allāh al-Ḥalīmī, Abū Muḥammad al-Juwaynī, Abū 'l-Maḥāsin al-Rūyānī and others have declared it definitively forbidden. But al-Qaffāl al-Marwazī has said it is permitted.

7.2. Abū ʿAmr said that those who prohibited it intended only that the *muqallid* should not transmit his ruling in his own name; he should rather attribute it to the *imām* to whom he is *muqallid*. On this basis, we acknowledge *muftī*s who are *muqallid*s. They are not real *muftī*s, but since they take the place of real *muftī*s and perform their functions, they are counted amongst them. They should only say, for example, 'The *madhhab* of al-Shāfiʿī is such and such.' Even if they fail to make this attribution, it is to be understood as a situation too familiar to require overt expression; there is no harm in that.

8.1. The author of the *Ḥāwī* [Ibn al-Qāḍī, d. after 340/951] said that if a layman knows the ruling on a particular problem, with its attendant evidence, there are three opinions [on his giving *fatwā*s in this area]. Firstly, it is permissible for him to give *fatwā*s, and it is permissible to submit to his rulings, because he has acquired knowledge in this field just as the scholar has. Secondly, it is permissible only if the evidence is in either the book or the *sunna*; otherwise it is not permissible. Thirdly, it is not permissible, absolutely; and this is the most valid view. God knows best.

7.4 The *fatwās* of al-Nawawī

For a biography of Yaḥyā ibn Sharaf Muḥyī ʾl-Dīn al-Nawawī (631/1233–676/1277), see section 6.2.

Although innumerable *fatwās* that were issued have not survived, those of the prominent jurists have often been preserved in compilations prepared by their students. Such written compilations developed into a genre of their own, expanding beyond strictly juridical issues. The selections presented below illustrate the variety that is found in the collection of al-Nawawī's *fatwās* compiled by his student ʿAlā al-Dīn ibn al-ʿAṭṭār al-Dimashqī, from short answers, to more lengthy, reasoned responses. It is stated in the introduction that Ibn al-ʿAṭṭār selected for his compilation the *fatwās* which he thought would be of benefit to as wide a readership as possible.

Further reading

M. K. Masud, B. Messick, A. Dallal, '*Fatwā*,' in John L. Esposito (ed.), *The Oxford encyclopedia of the modern Islamic world*, New York/Oxford 1995, vol. 2, pp. 8–17.
K. Masud, B. Messick, D. Powers (eds), *Islamic legal interpretation: muftis and their fatwas,* Cambridge MA 1996.

Source text

ʿAlā ʾl-Dīn ʿAlī b. Ibrāhīm b. al-ʿAṭṭār al-Dimashqī, *Fatāwā al-Imām al-Nawawī*, ed. M. al-Arnāʾūṭ, Damascus 1352/1933, pp. 52, 56, 103–5.

I *Question:*

1. Is eating and drinking while standing up disapproved?
2. What is the answer derived from the *ḥadīth*s about this?

The answer:

1. Drinking while standing up without needing to do so is disapproved, but not forbidden. Eating while standing up is permitted if there is the need to do so, but if there is no need then it is contrary to the most virtuous way, though it is not said to be 'disapproved' (*makrūh*) as such. This is established in al-Bukhārī's *al-Ṣaḥīḥ* through the transmission of the companion Ibn ʿUmar indicating that they used to do this. This has precedence over what is found in Muslim's *al-Ṣaḥīḥ* on the authority of Anas, saying that he disapproved of it.

    1.1. Returning to the issue of drinking while standing up, in Muslim's *al-Ṣaḥīḥ* it is said that the prophet proscribed it, while in al-Bukhārī's *al-Ṣaḥīḥ* and other sources there are sound *ḥadīth*s saying that the prophet did it himself.

The *ḥadīth*s about its proscription (*nahī*) indicate that it was more than just disapproved, while the *ḥadīth*s saying that he did it himself indicate that it is not forbidden (*ḥarām*).

II Question:

1. Is it permissible to give *zakāt* to an adult Muslim who does not pray out of laziness, even though he believes that prayer is compulsory for him?

The answer:

1. If he is an adult who has been continually neglectful of prayer until the time of payment of *zakāt*, it is not permissible to give it to him, because he is considered legally incompetent; it is not correct for him to take possession of it himself, but it is permissible to pay it to his guardian to safeguard it for this legally incompetent one. If he had already developed into a mature adult who prays and then suddenly afterwards he started to neglect prayer, and the judge has not declared him legally incompetent, it is permissible to pay it to him, and it is correct for him to keep it himself, just as in all his independent actions.

III Question:

1. Is marriage for the sake of the hereafter, or for carnal pleasure in this world?

The answer:

1. If one intends it to be an act of obedience, by following the example of the messenger of God, or to produce a righteous child, or to purify one's soul and keep under control one's sexual organs, eyes and heart and so forth, then it is for the sake of the hereafter and is meritorious. If one does not do it with such intentions, then it is permissible for the sake of carnal pleasure in this world, and in that case it is neither meritorious, nor sinful.

IV Question:

1. Is it permissible for a Muslim woman to unveil and reveal parts of her body in front of Jewish, Christian and other non-Muslim women?

2. Is there any difference of opinion concerning this in the Shāfiʿī tradition, and what is the proof?

The answer:

1. She is not allowed to do that unless the non-Muslim woman in question is her slave.

2. This is the correct opinion according to the Shāfiʿī tradition, and its proof lies in God's words, *Tell the believing women to lower their gaze and guard their sexual organs; that they should not display their beauty, apart from what appears [ordinarily]; that they should bring down their headscarves over their bosoms, and not display their beauty except to their husbands, their fathers, the fathers of their husbands, their sons, the sons of their husbands, their brothers, the sons of their brothers, the sons of their sisters, or their women* (Q 24/31), which means that, for Muslim women, non-Muslim women are included under the proscription mentioned at the beginning of the verse. Moreover, our chief ʿUmar ibn al-Khaṭṭāb wrote to ʿUbayda ibn al-Jarrāḥ when he was in Syria, commanding him to forbid Muslim women from doing that. God knows best.

V *Question:*

1. Is it permissible to gaze at handsome young men, or not?

2. If a man is fond of young men and spends his wealth on them, and under their spell gives one of them a large sum, while he cannot bear to give a single dirham to a poor person with dependents who is in need, is it then forbidden for him to meet with them and to spend his wealth in this way?

3. If they have sex is it sinful or not?

4. Does any honourable reputation that he may have had become void as a result of their having sex and persistence in it, or not?

5. Have any of the scholars discussed giving permission for this, or not?

The answer:

1. Mere gazing at handsome young men is forbidden, whether it is out of lust or for any other reason, except when there is a legitimate need, such as in buying and selling them, for medical treatment or educational purposes and so forth; in these legitimate cases it is only permissible to the extent that is necessary, and any more than that is forbidden.

   1.1. God said, *Tell the believing men to lower their gaze!* (Q 24/30). Moreover al-Shāfiʿī and other scholars have written about the prohibition of gazing at them without a legitimate need, using as support this glorious verse, even though it is intended to refer to women, for some of the young men are more beautiful than many women and they can cause more harm than any woman, and lead one to more dubious and wicked ways than any woman can. It is therefore more forbidden.

   1.2. The sayings of the pious predecessors in discouragement and as warnings about looking at them are too numerous to compile here; they called them filth, because they are considered legally impure, and in all that I have mentioned it makes no difference whether the person gazing is considered virtuous or not.

2. Seclusion with young men is more strictly forbidden than gazing at them, because it is more obscene and evil, no matter whether the one who is in seclusion with him is considered virtuous, or not.

3. Having sex with young men in the manner mentioned is forbidden for the one doing it as well as for the others present, and paying for it is extremely forbidden.

   3.1. Whoever has sex with them in this manner, wilfully so, has gone astray – his testimony is rejected and both his transmissions and his rank before God become null and void.
   3.2. The ruler must prevent them from doing this, reprimand them severely and stop them, and others of their kind, from such behaviour by force. Everyone capable who knows about them must censure them according to his ability, and those who are incapable of doing so must report their behaviour to the ruler if they can.

4. None of the scholars has discussed giving permission for this behaviour, according to the description of it given here. God knows best.

VI Question:

1. Is it permitted to go to astrologers and believe in what they say, or not?

2. Al-Nasāʾī related on the authority of the prophet that he said, 'The prayer of the one who goes to them and believes in them is not accepted.' Is this sound?

3. Clarify for us what is said on the authority of the prophet, and what the scholars say.

The answer:

1. Many *ḥadīth*s have proved that it is forbidden, including this one on the authority of Ṣafiya bint Abī ʿUbayd on the authority of one of the wives of the prophet that he said, 'Whoever goes to a fortune-teller to ask him about something, and believes in him, will not have his prayers accepted for forty days.' Muslim related this in his *Ṣaḥīḥ*.

2. It is on the authority of Qubayṣa ibn al-Mukhāriq who said that he heard the messenger of God say, 'Predicting by the flight of birds and such use of omens is divination.' Abū Dāwūd related this with a good chain of transmission (*bi-isnād ḥasan*).

   2.1. Abū Dāwūd said, 'Such prediction consists of tracing lines for flight paths and holding down a bird; it is that you see a good or bad omen in its flight: if it flies to the right it is a good omen, and if it flies to the left it is a bad omen.'
   2.2. Al-Jawharī said that 'divination' is a word used to refer to 'idols', 'fortune-telling', 'sorcery', 'astrology' and such things.

3. It is on the authority of Ibn ʿAbbās that the messenger of God said, 'Whoever seeks to learn information from the stars seeks to learn a branch of witchcraft.' Abū Dāwūd related this with a sound chain of transmission (*bi-isnād ṣaḥīḥ*).

4. It is related that Muʿāwiya ibn al-Ḥakam said that he said to the messenger of God, 'I am newly converted from ignorance (*jāhiliyya*) with God's bringing of Islam and there are men among us who visit fortune-tellers.' He said, 'Don't visit them!' I said, 'There are men who see evil omens.' He said, 'That's just something they find in their own hearts, so don't believe them!' Muslim related this.

5. It is on the authority of Abū Masʿūd al-Badrī that the messenger of God proscribed paying for the following: dogs, whores and fortune-tellers. Al-Bukhārī and Muslim both related this.

6. It is related that ʿĀ'isha said that people asked the messenger of God about fortune-tellers, and he said, 'They have nothing!' They then said, 'Messenger of God, they sometimes speak about something and it comes true.' The messenger of God said, 'That is a word of God that the jinn have snatched from the ears of His saint, and then mixed with a hundred lies.' Al-Bukhārī and Muslim have both related this.

7. It is on the authority of Abū Hurayra that the messenger of God said, 'Whoever visits a fortune-teller and believes in what he says or enters a woman in her buttocks has nothing to do with what has been revealed to Muḥammad.' Abū Dāwūd related this with a weak chain of transmission (*isnād ḍaʿīf*).

8. The scholars have said that involvement with these affairs is forbidden as well as going to them and believing in them. Giving money to them is also forbidden, and it is incumbent on anyone who is tempted by something like this to repent quickly.

7.5 Ibn Ḥazm on dispute and variation in law

Jurist, theologian, philosopher and poet, Abū Muḥammad ʿAlī ibn Aḥmad Ibn Ḥazm spent his whole life (384/994–456/1064) in Muslim Spain and became the most significant promulgator of the short-lived Ẓāhirī ('literalist') school of law. He came from a high-ranking family which acted as part of the administrative hierarchy surrounding the Umayyad caliphs of Spain. During his lifetime, caliphal power collapsed and the last Umayyad caliph disappeared in 1031. Subsequently, Spain was ruled by a number of independent dynasties in military and cultural competition.

Ibn Ḥazm's education in Cordoba covered all the disciplines of Islamic culture, at a time when Cordoba was a pre-eminent centre. Politically active as a youth, he abandoned politics after 1031 and devoted himself to writing and teaching. His early work relates to poetry and morals and includes the famous *Ṭawq al-ḥamāma* ('The ring of the dove'), on poetic diction and psychological truth. His theological writings are numerous, and notoriously argumentative. In jurisprudence he was opposed to the Mālikī school, which prevailed in Muslim Spain, and instead adopted the principles of a minor school derived from Dāwūd al-Ẓāhirī (d. 270/884), a pupil of Ibn Ḥanbal (d. 241/855). Following him, Ibn Ḥazm abandoned the interpretive tradition which had grown up with the older schools, and insisted on a purely literal (*ẓāhirī*) reading of revealed texts. His *Kitāb al-muḥallā* is a monument of juristic erudition and incisive criticism. In dogmatic and theological matters, he attempted a similar literalist approach to revealed texts, and produced again an idiosyncratic synthesis opposed to the Muʿtazilites and the Ashʿarites. His great work in this area is his *al-Fiṣal fīʾl-milal* ('Book of sects'), which demonstrates correct dogma by exhaustively analysing heretical deviations, including those of the Jews and Christians.

Ibn Ḥazm's *al-Iḥkām fī uṣūl al-aḥkām* is concerned with the methodology of jurisprudence (*uṣūl al-fiqh*). The extract presented below offers an explanation and justification for the emergence, after Muḥammad's death, of differences of opinion (*ikhtilāf*) on juristic issues among the prophet's immediate successors, the 'pious predecessors'. However, this is not to say that Ibn Ḥazm looks favourably on *ikhtilāf* among later generations, as is made apparent later in the extract. Instead, he expresses optimism that the compilation of authoritative *ḥadīth* into a limited number of canonical collections should restrain *ikhtilāf*, and thus lead to a narrower, more fixed definition of the law. In addition to this overall theme, Ibn Ḥazm's Ẓāhirī tendencies are also evident in his attitude towards exegetical tools and the use of supplementary sources of knowledge to interpret and evaluate the apparent meaning of the texts of revelation.

Further reading

Roger Arnaldez, *Grammaire et théologie chez Ibn Hazm de Cordoue; essai sur la structure et les conditions de la pensée musulmane*, Paris 1956.

—— 'Ibn Ḥazm,' in *Encyclopaedia of Islam*, new edition.

Ignaz Goldziher, *The Ẓāhirīs: their doctrine and their history,* trans. and ed. Wolfgang Behn, Leiden 1971.

Ibn Ḥazm, *The ring of the dove: a treatise on the art and practice of Arab love*, trans. A. J. Arberry, London 1953.

Source text

Ibn Ḥazm, *Al-Iḥkām fī uṣūl al-aḥkām*, Cairo 1978, part 2, pp. 301–7.

Chapter on the reason for dispute amongst the imāms in the early generations of this community

Question: Why did [Mālik ibn Anas] and those before him abandon many *ḥadīth*?

Answer: May God grant you success, we have already explained this matter earlier in the present work, but since what we shall be presenting in later chapters will require repetition of what we have already said, it must also be repeated here.

1. The fact is that Mālik and the others are human beings. They forget, just like other men. A man may have memorized a *ḥadīth* but be unable to bring it to mind [on a suitable occasion] with the result that he gives a *fatwā* opposed to the *ḥadīth*. This may occur too with verses from the Qurʾān. ʿUmar, for example, commanded that the bride-price of women should not exceed a figure which he mentioned; then a woman reminded him of God's words, *And you may give one of them a* qinṭār (Q 4/20). ʿUmar promptly abandoned his opinion, saying, 'Everybody is more learned than you, ʿUmar; a woman has given the right answer while the *amīr al-muʾminīn* has erred.' On another occasion he ordered the stoning of a woman who had given birth after only six months [of marriage]. ʿAlī then reminded him of God's words, *The bearing and the weaning [of a child] is thirty months* (Q 46/15) and *Mothers suckle their children for two full years* (Q 2/233). And so ʿUmar rescinded the command to stone the woman [because the two phrases in the Qurʾān reveal that a pregnancy of six months is a possibility]. ʿUmar intended to attack ʿUyayna ibn Ḥiṣn but ʿUyayna said, 'You are not giving us our due, nor judging between us with justice.' Ḥurr ibn Qays ibn Ḥuṣn ibn Hudhayfa then reminded ʿUmar of God's words, *Turn away from those who are ignorant* (Q 7/199). This, said Ḥurr, is one of the ignorant. So ʿUmar desisted. ʿUmar too, on the day the prophet died, said that the prophet of God was not dead nor would he die unless he was the last of us, or words to that effect. Then someone recited to him the Qurʾānic words [addressed to the prophet], *You are subject to death and they are subject to death* (Q 39/30). The sword fell from ʿUmar's hand and he threw himself to the ground. 'It is as if I had never read these words before,' he said.

   Now, if this is possible with respect to the Qurʾān, it is still more possible with respect to *ḥadīth*. One may forget it completely.

2. Or, one may not forget it, but, remembering it, interpret it imagining that it contains some element of specification or abrogation or some such thing. But such readings may not be adopted except on the basis of a text or *ijmāʿ*; for they

are only the opinion of some observer, and it is not permitted to follow (*taqlīd*) such a one nor to accept his opinion.

3. Everyone knows that the companions were associated with the prophet of God in Medina, as a community. They had to earn a living, being at that time extremely short of food. All of this is recorded, textually. The prophet, Abū Bakr and ʿUmar were driven from their houses by hunger. Some were busy working in the markets, others were overseeing the date palms. But there was always a group attending the prophet whenever they found any free time. All of this cannot be denied. Abū Hurayra, remembering this time, said, 'My brothers amongst the Emigrants were distracted by their bargaining in the markets, my brothers amongst the Helpers by their tending to the palm plantations. But I was poor; I attended the prophet of God on condition only that my stomach was full.' ʿUmar confirmed this when he said, 'I missed such *ḥadīth* from the prophet, being distracted by bargaining in the markets.' He said this in the *ḥadīth* concerning Abū Mūsā's *istiʾdhān*.

   So, the prophet used to be asked questions of the law and would give judgements, or issue commands, or act in a particular manner and only those present would remember. Those who were absent would know nothing about what they had missed.

4. When the prophet died and Abū Bakr came to power, the companions were scattered because of their participation in *jihād*; some to deal with Musaylima, some the apostates; some went to Syria, some to Iraq; and some remained in Medina with Abū Bakr. Abū Bakr, when faced with a problem about which he knew of no command from the prophet, would ask those companions who were around him in Medina about the problem. If they provided an answer he would have recourse to it. Otherwise he would exercise *ijtihād*, having no other option. During ʿUmar's period in power, the conquests took place and the dispersal of the companions increased. The need for juristic decisions emerged in Medina and elsewhere. Naturally, if any companion who was present had preserved a report from the prophet on that matter, it would be used. Otherwise the governor of that particular city would exercise *ijtihād*, although the prophet's ruling might be known to a companion in another city. It might be that an inhabitant of Medina had been present when an inhabitant of Egypt had not, that an Egyptian had been present when a Syrian had not, a Syrian and no Basran, a Basran and no Kufan, a Kufan and no Medinan. All of this can be found in the reports that have been preserved, as a necessary result of the facts we have presented. Some companions were absent from sessions at times when others were present; and on the following day perhaps the one who had been absent was present and so on; with the result that each one knew only what he had witnessed and was ignorant of what he had missed. All of this is plain to the intellect.

   The rule of *tayammum* [using sand for ablutions when no water is available] was known to ʿAmmār and others, but unknown to ʿUmar and Ibn Masʿūd who said that impurity can only be cleansed with sand if water has not been available for two months. The ruling on *masḥ* [wiping of the shoes in prayer rather than washing the feet] was known to ʿAlī, Ḥudhayfa and others, but unknown to ʿĀʾisha, Ibn ʿUmar and Abū Hurayra, all Medinese. The capacity of a son's daughter to inherit along with the daughter was known to Ibn Masʿūd, but unknown to Abū Mūsā. The ruling on *istiʾdhān* was known to Abū Mūsā and Abū Saʿīd, but unknown to ʿUmar. The permission for a menstruating woman to avoid the Kaʿba prior to circumambulating it was known to Ibn ʿAbbās and Umm Salīm, but not to ʿUmar and Zayd ibn Thābit. . . . [many more examples are then given]

There are very many examples of this kind of thing. The companions continued thus and were succeeded by the successors. These too were associated with a particular geographical area and learnt their juristic skills from the companions who lived in that area. They did not go beyond the *fatwā*s of the local companions. This was not because of mere *taqlīd*, but simply because they took from them and related from them, except in so far as some small quantity of information reached them from companions in other cities. The situation is exemplified in the way the people of Medina mostly followed the *fatwā*s of Ibn ʿUmar, the people of Kufa mostly the *fatwā*s of Ibn Masʿūd, and the people of Mecca the *fatwā*s of Ibn ʿAbbās.

After the successors came the *fuqahāʾ*, like Abū Ḥanīfa, Sufyān and Ibn Abī Layla in Kufa; Ibn Jurayj in Mecca; Mālik and Ibn al-Mājishūn in Medina; ʿUthmān al-Battī and Sawwār in Basra; al-Awzāʿī in Syria; and al-Layth in Egypt. They continued in the same manner, each one taking from the successors in his area whatever juristic views they had propounded, and exercising *ijtihād* in areas where they had no transmitted information – even when that could be found in other areas.

God does not charge a soul beyond its capacity (Q 2/286). All the figures we have mentioned were granted, in so far as they correctly gauged the prophet's ruling, a double reward; in so far as the ruling remained hidden from them, they were granted a single reward.

5. It might happen that two *ḥadīth*, apparently in conflict, reach one authority. He would tend towards one of them through some exercise of preference based on the principles we have described as valid or invalid in the preceding chapters of this book. A different authority might tend towards the alternative *ḥadīth* using the same principles. For example, two views are transmitted from ʿUthmān concerning marriage to two sisters, it being declared *ḥarām* in one verse, but *ḥalāl* in another verse of the Qurʾān. Also Ibn ʿUmar was inclined to declare that marriage to women of the people of the book was forbidden totally, on the basis of the verse, *Do not marry females of the idolaters until they believe* (Q 2/221). He claimed that he knew of no idolatry greater than that of a woman who could say that Jesus was her Master. Hence he let that view overcome the permission rendered available in a different verse of the Qurʾānic text. Ibn ʿAbbās made the *ʿidda* of a pregnant woman the later of the two possibilities, either parturition or fourteen months. Some companions interpreted the rulings on the domestic donkey as being related to their status in *khums*, others to their function as bearers of people, others to their eating habits and still others simply to their nature. This is just like the interpretation of what came earlier regarding the drinking of wine; as God said, *There is no sin on those who believe and do good deeds regarding what they eat* (Q 5/93).

In such manner Mālik and those before him abandoned certain *ḥadīth* and certain verses of the Qurʾān; and in such manner their peers disputed with them. Some adopted what others abandoned and vice versa.

6. There are, in fact, ten factors leading to this situation.

6.1. A particular report does not reach a particular authority and he gives a *fatwā* on the basis of a text that has reached him. . . .
6.2. An authority becomes convinced that the transmitter of a report has not remembered it correctly. . . .
6.3. He becomes convinced that a particular report has been abrogated, just as Ibn ʿUmar thought regarding the verse about marrying women from the people of the book.
6.4. He gives one text precedence over another, thinking it superior, but this is without significance if it is not confirmed by the Qurʾān or *sunna*.
6.5. He gives one text precedence over another because of the numbers who act on it or the status of those who accept it; this too is without significance. . . .
6.6. He gives precedence to a text that is not sound over a text that is sound, being ignorant of the fault in the former.
6.7. He gives to a general statement a particular reading, based only on his own opinion.
6.8. He adopts a general reading which it is not necessary to adopt, abandoning that which confirms a particular reading.
6.9. He interprets a report so as to avoid its apparent meaning (*ẓāhir*), without any proof, on the basis of some causal factor that he imagines to be present.
6.10. He abandons a sound text because of the words of a companion, imagining that he has knowledge justifying his abandonment of the text.

These are the erroneous opinions which have led to that variety of views (*ikhtilāf*) of which God had foreknowledge that it would arise. We ask God to provide confirmation of the truth through his generous kindness. Amen.

7. Subsequently, travel to distant parts became common, the people mingled and met one another. Some undertook the task of gathering, compiling and organizing the prophet's *ḥadīth*, with the result that they were transferred from distant lands to those who had never heard of them, and so constituted decisive evidence for those who now heard them for the first time. *Ḥadīth* were now collected that demonstrated the truth of one among several interpretations that had arisen around particular *ḥadīth*. Sound *ḥadīth* could be distinguished from unsound. Those exercises of *ijtihād* could be declared false which had led to something opposed to the words of the prophet, or to the abandonment of his practice. On hearing a report and recognizing that it constitutes valid evidence, an authority was now deprived of all excuse for continuing to oppose it. All else was stubbornness, ignorance, *taqlīd* and sin.

7.6 Al-Shīrāzī on the distribution of alms

Ibrāhīm ibn ʿAlī Abū Isḥāq al-Shīrāzī was born in 393/1003 in Firuzabad in Persia. He was schooled by various Shāfiʿī masters in Shiraz and Basra and he later taught in Baghdad, including at the prestigious Niẓāmiyya school, which was constructed in his honour by the vizier Niẓām al-Mulk. Towards the end of his life he travelled in Khurasan. He died in 476/1083.

Al-Shīrāzī wrote two works on practical law (*furūʿ*), the *Kitāb al-Tanbīh fīʾl-fiqh* and *al-Muhadhdhab fī fiqh al-imām al-Shāfiʿī*. These two works are counted among the five key reference texts for the Shāfiʿī school, and the *Muhadhdhab* was considered by Yaḥyā al-Nawawī (for whom, see section 6.2) to be one of the two most important works of this school ever produced. Al-Shīrāzī's particular contribution to juristic discussion includes his emphasis on the primacy and independence of the legal approach to the sources of the law from all other approaches, including that of the theological schools, and his adoption of systematic methods of interpretation and extraction of the law from the texts of revelation.

The *Muhadhdhab*, al-Shīrāzī's 'crowning achievement', was composed between 455/1063 and 469/1076. He states that its overall aim is 'to deal with the sources of law for the Shāfiʿī *madhhab* along with their proofs and the problems which arise from the sources and the causes thereof' (*Muhadhdhab,* vol. 1, pp. 2–3). In the extract presented below, al-Shīrāzī considers how the owner of 'hidden' goods, those not easily accessible to inspection, should arrange for the payment of his *zakāt.* In what reads like an abstract analysis, the three viewpoints presented in the example of *ikhtilāf* (difference of opinion; paragraphs 2.0–2.3) included here, neatly prioritize, in turn, each of the three main areas of concern: the owner's personal duty to God, the governor's communal duty and the right of the needy to receive *zakāt.* The hypothetical and exploratory character of this passage is representative of the bulk of works of *furūʿ al-fiqh*.

Further reading

Norman Calder, 'Law,' in Seyyed Hossein Nasr, Oliver Leaman (eds), *History of Islamic philosophy*, London 1996, vol. 2, pp. 979–98, with a full analysis of paragraphs 1 and 2 of this excerpt.

—— 'Friday prayer and the juristic theory of government: Sarakhsī, Shīrāzī, Māwardī,' *Bulletin of the School of Oriental and African Studies*, 49 (1986), pp. 35–47.

E. Chaumont, 'Al-Shīrāzī, al-Shaykh al-Imām Abū Isḥāḳ,' in *Encyclopaedia of Islam*, new edition.

Source text

Al-Shīrāzī, *Al-Muhadhdhab fī fiqh al-imām al-Shāfiʿī*, Beirut 1379/1959, vol. 1, p. 175.

Chapter: On the distribution of alms (ṣadaqāt).

1.1. It is permissible for the owner of wealth to distribute *zakāt* on 'hidden' goods by himself. Hidden goods are gold, silver, trade goods and precious stones. This is based on the *ḥadīth* from ʿUthmān, that he said in the month of Muḥarram, 'This is the month of your *zakāt*, so he who has a debt, let him pay his debt; then, let him pay *zakāt* on the remainder of his wealth.'

1.2. It is permissible for him to appoint an agent to distribute it on his behalf. This is because *zakāt* is a claim on wealth, and it is permissible to appoint an agent to execute it, as with debts between men.

1.3. It is permissible that he pay his *zakāt* to the governor (*imām*). This is because the *imām* is the representative of the poor. His status is like that of a guardian to an orphan.

2. On the question of which is the best mode of conduct, there are three views.

2.1. The best mode of conduct is that the owner of wealth should distribute his *zakāt* by himself. This is the plain meaning of the text [i.e., of the *ḥadīth* quoted in paragraph 1.1.]. Further, he is secure in respect of his own paying, but not secure in respect of anyone else paying.

2.2. The best mode of conduct is that he should pay the *imām*, whether the *imām* is just or unjust. This is because of what is related concerning Mughīra ibn Shaʿba. He said to a client of his, who had the stewardship of his property in al-Ṭāʾif, 'What do you do about alms (*ṣadaqa*) on my property?' The client replied, 'Some of it I distribute directly as alms, and some of it I give to the authorities.' Mughīra asked what he knew about the latter portion. The client explained that they buy land and marry women with it. Mughīra said, 'Pay it to them; for the messenger of God commanded us to pay them. Also because the *imām* is more knowledgeable about the poor and the extent of their need.'

2.3. Amongst our companions there are some who say that if the *imām* is just, payment to him is the best mode of conduct; but if he is unjust, then distribution by the owner of wealth himself is best. This is because of the prophet's words, 'He who asks for it as it should be, let him be given it; he who demands more than he should, let him not be given it.' It is also because the donor is secure in paying it to a just *imām*, but is not secure in paying it to an unjust *imām*, for the latter may spend it on his own desires.

3. As for 'manifest' goods [as opposed to 'hidden' goods], these are animals, cereals, fruit, minerals and so forth. There are two views on the distribution of *zakāt* on these goods.

3.1. Al-Shāfiʿī said in his older works that it is obligatory to pay it to the *imām*; if one distributes it oneself, one is subject to liability. This is based on the Qurʾānic verse, *Take from their wealth* ṣadaqa *that you might purify and cleanse them* (Q 9/103). This is also because this is property in which the *imām* has the right of demand, with the consequence that payment to him is obligatory, as with *kharāj* and *jizya*.

3.2. In his later writings, al-Shāfiʿī said that it is permissible for the owner to distribute the *zakāt* on manifest goods himself. This is because it is *zakāt* and the owner of wealth may distribute it himself, just as with 'hidden' goods.

7.7 Al-Sarakhsī on *zakāt*

The illustrious Ḥanafī jurist Muḥammad ibn Aḥmad ibn Abī Sahl Abū Bakr al-Sarakhsī (d. *c*. 500/1106) lived and worked in Transoxiana. References in his *Kitāb al-mabsūṭ* reveal that he dictated it from prison. Later biographies elaborate on this point with an emphasis on his unrivalled knowledge, his integrity and his commitment to his own school tradition.

The *Kitāb al-mabsūṭ* is considered to be the most important of the works of al-Sarakhsī, or *Shams al-a'imma* ('the sun of the leaders') as he is traditionally referred to, as well as one of the most important works ever produced within the school. It is a commentary on the epitome (*mukhtaṣar*) known as *al-Kāfī* by Muḥammad ibn Muḥammad al-Marwazī (d. 334/945 or 344/955), which in turn was an epitome of works by Muḥammad al-Shaybānī, who wrote the foundational works of the Ḥanafī school. Therefore al-Sarakhsī effectively reintroduced and explored the rules originally compiled by al-Shaybānī, although al-Marwazī's work dictates the overall framework of al-Sarakhsī's *Mabsūṭ* and provides the basic rules. Al-Sarakhsī expands and explores juristic material, often through discussion of differences of opinion (*ikhtilāf*), both within the Ḥanafī tradition and among the other major schools, and by providing explanations and justifications.

In the extract presented below, al-Sarakhsī's discussion revolves around his perception that there are tensions arising between God's demands and the rights and duties of the *zakāt* donors, *zakāt* recipients, tax-collectors and the governor (*imām*). In part I, he presents three situations in which the owner of camels can refuse to pay a collector, exploring and enriching, in the process, the possibilities and implications of the rules he has inherited. Part II contains a *ḥīla* (juristic contrivance), where al-Sarakhsī displays his wit and ingenuity by arguing that tyrants are themselves 'the poor', and thus rightful recipients of *zakāt*. This clearly relates to the realities of his day, and is intended to relieve the burden of the *zakāt* donor, by asserting that his religious duty to give *zakāt* to the poor is fulfilled even through payment to tyrants who will use it simply for their own benefit.

Further reading

Norman Calder, 'Exploring God's law: Muḥammad ibn Aḥmad ibn Abī Sahl al-Sarakhsī on *zakāt*,' in Christopher Toll, Jakob Skovgaard-Petersen (eds), *Law and the Islamic world, past and present*, Historisk-filosofiske Meddelelser 68, The Royal Danish Academy of Sciences and Letters, Copenhagen 1995, pp. 57–73; includes an analysis of the passage presented here.

—— 'Al-Sarakhsī,' in *Encyclopaedia of Islam*, new edition.

—— 'Friday prayer and the juristic theory of government: Sarakhsī, Shīrāzī, Māwardī,' *Bulletin of the School of Oriental and African Studies*, 49 (1986), pp. 35–47.

Source text

Al-Sarakhsī, *Kitāb al-mabsūṭ*, Beirut 1406/1986 (reprint of the Cairo 1324 edition), vol. 2, pp. 161–2 (part I), 180 (part II).

I [Three problems related to the distribution of zakāt]

1. The collector arrives. The owner [of camels] says, ‘I have not had these animals for a whole year’; or he says, ‘I owe a debt which is greater that their value’; or he says, ‘These animals are not mine.’ He then swears that this is so. He is believed in all cases. This is because he is responsible for *zakāt* duties that are obligatory on him. *Zakāt* is an act of worship purely for the sake of God, and the word of a responsible person is always acceptable in regard to acts of worship that are obligatory (solely) as being due to God. Hence if the owner denies that *zakāt* is obligatory, for any of the reasons just given, the collector must believe him. He is, however, required to swear.

    1.1. The requirement to swear is not specified in one tradition from Abū Yūsuf. He said that no oath is required because oaths are irrelevant in regard to acts of worship. It is like one who says, ‘I have fasted’, or, ‘I have prayed’; he is believed without an oath. But according to the main tradition, Abū Yūsuf said that what is required is the affirmation of a responsible person, together with an oath. In other acts of worship oaths are not relevant because there is no one who will be deemed to be calling the worshipper a liar. But here the collector is [implicitly] denying the claim he puts forward. Hence he is required to swear.

2. The owner says, ‘Another collector has already taken my *zakāt*; and he swears that this is so. If there has not been another collector in that year his word is not accepted. This is because a responsible man is believed if he affirms what is probable; but if he affirms what is improbable, he is not believed. In this case, the owner affirms what is improbable. If there has been another collector that year, his word stands. This is true whether or not the owner brings forward a certificate of payment. So it is in the *mukhtaṣar* [of al-Marwazī]. This is the tradition as derived from the *Kitāb al-jāmiʿ al-ṣaghīr* [of al-Shaybānī].

    2.1. In the *Kitāb al-zakāt*, however, al-Shaybānī says that [this is only true] if he brings forward a certificate of payment. This implies that showing a certificate of payment is a condition for believing the owner in this case. This is the tradition from Ḥasan ibn Ziyād from Abū Ḥanīfa. The reason for this is that the owner has affirmed something and brought evidence that it is true. The custom is that when a collector takes *ṣadaqa*, he gives a certificate of payment. Hence the owner’s affirmation is accepted if accompanied by this evidence. Otherwise it is rejected. It is like the case of a woman who affirms that she has given birth: if the midwife also bears witness to it, her word is accepted, otherwise not.

    2.2. The other view [that a certificate is not required] – which is the more valid view – rests on the fact that a certificate is in writing, and all writing is similar. Also the owner may inadvertently neglect to take the certificate, or may lose it subsequently. So it should not be made decisive in this matter. The rule is that the owner’s word is accepted if accompanied by an oath.

3. The owner says, 'I have paid my *zakāt* directly to the poor.' He is not believed and, according to our tradition, *zakāt* is taken from him [i.e., a second payment].

3.1. According to al-Shāfiʿī, he is believed. This is because *zakāt* is obligatory only for the sake of the poor, as proved by the Qurʾānic statement, Ṣadaqāt *are only for the poor, the miserable* and so on (Q 9/60). Furthermore God says, *On their wealth is a claim for the beggar and the deprived* (Q 51/19). Hence, if the due sum is transferred to the rightful recipient, and the rightful recipient has the capacity to receive that due sum, the duty of the donor is fulfilled. It is like the case of one who buys something from an agent, and then transfers the price directly to the one who appointed the agent. In this case, the collector receives the *zakāt* in order to pass it to the poor and the donor has relieved him of this burden by placing it directly where it belongs. So there can be no claim against him [by the collector].

3.2. The argument for our view is as follows. *Zakāt* is a financial duty implemented in full by the *imām* [governor, local political authority] by virtue of legitimate authority. The person subject to the duty does not have the capacity to deprive the *imām* of his right to implement it. It is like the case of one subject to *jizya* who decides to pay it directly to the soldiers; [this is not permitted].

This argument may be explained in two ways:

3.2.1. *Zakāt* is due solely for God's sake. So it can be implemented only by one who is appointed as deputy for the implementation of what is due to God. This is the *imām*. Accordingly, the duty of the donor is not fulfilled except by transfer of his *zakāt* to the *imām*. We conclude that even if the donor is known to be telling the truth when he affirms that he paid the *zakāt* directly to the poor, it is taken from him a second time. His duty, as between him and God, is not fulfilled by direct payment to the poor. This analysis accounts for the preferred view of one of our *shaykh*s, namely, that the *imām* has the right of choice in deciding where to distribute the *zakāt* and the donor may not deprive the *imām* of this right of choice.

3.2.2. The collector is deemed agent to the poor. What is collected is due to the poor. But the right of collection has been transferred to the collector so that the poor do not retain the right of demand on their own behalf. Accordingly it is not obligatory to pay them, if they request it. It is like the case of a debt due to a minor: if the debtor pays it to the minor and not to the minor's guardian [it is not valid]. According to this analysis, a man is, however, deemed to have fulfilled his duty as between himself and God if he pays directly to the poor.

4. The plain meaning of the phrase, 'he is not believed' [as used by al-Marwazī in the base text] is an indication of this position [i.e., it conforms to the second analysis].

But this implies that if the donor is known to be telling the truth the collector should not interfere with him. This is because the poor have the capacity to receive what is their due; though it is not obligatory to pay them on their demand. Deeming the collector to be a representative of the poor is to give him a capacity of supervision under the law. Accordingly, if the donor pays directly to the poor, when the latter make no demand on the former, the aim of the duty of *zakāt* has been achieved. It is different from the case of the minor, for he does not have the capacity to receive what is due to him, so the duty is not fulfilled by paying him directly.

II [Another problem from the Kitāb al-zakāt]

1. Outlaws conquer one of the lands of the people of justice and collect the alms (*ṣadaqa*) due on their property. Subsequently the *imām* re-conquers the land. He may not collect these dues a second time. This is because he has failed to provide protection and 'collection depends on protection'.

1.1. This ruling is different from that of the merchant who passes the customs officer of a rebel people and is taxed. If he subsequently passes the customs officer of the people of justice he may be taxed a second time. This is because the owner exposed his own property to the rebels when he took it through their land. So he is not excused. In the former situation, however, the owner of property did nothing. Rather, the *imām* failed in his duty of protection, so he may not collect a second time.

2. However, the ruling is issued that the owner of property in case of conquest by outlaws should pay, as between him and God, a second time. This is because they do not collect our wealth as *ṣadaqa*, but through mere lawlessness. They do not distribute it as *zakāt* should be distributed. Hence the owner should pay what is incumbent on him for the sake of God. Whatever they took from him was mere injustice.

   Likewise with respect to the *dhimmī* community: if the outlaws take their poll tax, the *imām* may not extract from them further taxation, because he has failed to provide protection.

3. As to the collections made by the Sultans of our time, these tyrants, whether alms, tithes, *kharāj* or *jizya*, al-Marwazī did not deal with them. Many of the religious leaders of Balkh promulgate the ruling that payment is required a second time, as between the owner of goods and God, as in the case of land conquered by rebels. This is because we know that they do not distribute the collected wealth as it should be distributed.

3.1. Abū Bakr al-Aʿmash used to say that on *ṣadaqāt* they rule that repetition is required but on *kharāj* this is not so. This is because the rightful recipients of *kharāj* are the military, and these are the military: if an enemy appeared they would defend *dār al-islām*. *Ṣadaqāt*, however, are for the poor and the needy, and they do not give it to the poor and the needy.

3.2. The more valid view is that these illegitimate collections fulfil for the owners of wealth the duty of *zakāt* – as long as they formulate at the time of payment the intention of giving alms to them [i.e., to the unjust Sultans]. This is because the wealth that they possess is the property of the Muslims, and the debts they owe to Muslims are greater than their own wealth. If they returned to the Muslims what they owe them, they would possess nothing. Accordingly they have the status of the poor [and are therefore legitimate recipients of *zakāt*!]. Muḥammad ibn Salama even said of ʿAlī ibn ʿĪsā ibn Yūnus ibn Māhān, the governor of Khurasan, that it was permissible for him to receive alms. There was a prince in Balkh who needed to perform atonement for an oath he had sworn [and failed to keep]. He asked the *fuqahā*ʾ how he should perform atonement. They issued the ruling that he should fast for three days [which is the mode of atonement due from a poor man; a rich person would normally be expected to feed a certain number of the poor or to free a certain number of slaves]. He wept and complained to his retinue, 'They say that my debts are greater than my wealth and my oath-atonement is that due from one who owns nothing.' The same considerations are valid in the case of exactions collected today, as long as the donor formulates the intention at the time of payment that this is his tithe or his *zakāt*. This is permissible along the lines we have just enunciated.

7.8 Al-Ṭūsī on the division of *khums*

Abū Ja'far Muḥammad ibn al-Ḥasan al-Ṭūsī (d. 460/1067) left his native Tus, in what is now north-eastern Iran, to study in Baghdad, where the political situation was at the time more favourable to Shī'īs. His best-known teacher was al-Shaykh al-Mufīd, a leading exponent of Twelver Shī'ism's rationalist tendency, which was becoming increasingly influential. In 436/1044, al-Ṭūsī became al-Mufīd's second successor as the leader of the Shī'ī community in Baghdad, and he was also appointed to the most prestigious chair in the religious sciences at the capital. This was in recognition of his own towering achievements in scholarship already by this time. Eventually in 448/1057, after Baghdad fell to Sunnī forces who burnt his home and library during an assault on the Shī'ī quarters of the city, al-Ṭūsī left for Najaf, thus bringing about the transfer of the centre of Shī'ism also between these two cities. He was by far the most important representative of Twelver Shī'ī jurisprudence since its emergence in the second half of the fourth/tenth century, and so it is perhaps no surprise that his authority continued to be recognized by his successors for a century and a half after his death.

Al-Ṭūsī himself refers to over forty works that he had written. He is best known for his works in the areas of *ḥadīth*, jurisprudence and theology. His two *ḥadīth* collections, entitled *al-Istibṣār* and *Tahdhīb al-aḥkām*, eventually came to constitute half of the set of four canonical Shī'ī *ḥadīth* collections. Al-Ṭūsī argued for the acceptance of *ḥadīth*s reported by just a single authority (*āḥād*), in this way helping to increase the corpus of authoritative *ḥadīth* available to be used for Shī'ī jurisprudence as proofs. As a successor to Shaykh al-Mufīd, al-Ṭūsī relied heavily on reasoned argumentation none the less, and so his contribution can be seen as a bringing together of rationalist and traditionist approaches in Shī'ism at this critical juncture in its historical development. The passage presented below is taken from the discussion of *khums* (see the *ḥadīth*s on this topic presented in section 3.4 above) in the chapter on *zakāt* in al-Ṭūsī's voluminous exploration of jurisprudence, *al-Mabsūṭ fī fiqh al-Imāmiyya.* It is concerned specifically with the issues of the division of *khums*, the *anfāl* (spoils belonging rightfully to the prophet, or the Imām as his successor, but often promised as 'bonus' shares to warriors), and what should be done with *khums* during the Occultation, when the Imām, who is meant to receive and distribute it, is no longer available. Al-Ṭūsī argues that *khums* must still be paid, and demonstrates how three of its six divisions can still be distributed. Later Shī'ī jurists would build on his presentation to argue for the use eventually of all six shares of *khums* during the Imām's absence.

Further reading

Mohammad Ali Amir-Moezzi, 'Ṭūsī, Muḥammad ibn al-Ḥasan,' in *Encyclopaedia of Islam*, new edition.

Norman Calder, 'Feqh,' in *Encyclopaedia Iranica*.

—— '*Khums* in Imāmī Shī'ī jurisprudence, from the tenth to the sixteenth century AD,' *Bulletin of the School of Oriental and African Studies,* 45 (1982), pp. 39–47.

Abdulaziz Sachedina, '*Al-Khums:* the fifth in the Imāmī Shī'ī legal system,' *Journal of Near Eastern studies,* 39 (1980), pp. 276–89.

Source text

Al-Ṭūsī, *Al-Mabsūṭ fī fiqh al-Imāmiyya*, ed. M. T. al-Kashfī, Tehran 1967, vol. 1, pp. 262–4.

I Chapter on zakāt – Section mentioning the division of khums

1. When the Imām receives *khums* he should divide it into six portions, the first three of which are God's share, the prophet's share and the prophet's relatives' share.

    1.1. These three portions belong to the Imām who is standing in the place of the prophet. He spends it as he pleases, such as on his own expenses, family expenses, whatever burdens he has to bear and providing for others.

    1.2. The remaining three portions are the shares of the orphans, the poor and the wayfarers belonging to the prophet's family. No other categories of people have any right to receive *khums.*

        1.2.1. The Imām must divide the latter three portions among the recipients according to their needs and annual expenses, which are calculated modestly, without favouring one group over another; he must give to all of them according to what has been mentioned, both taking into account their needs and treating equally recipients of either gender.

    1.3. If there is a surplus left over then it belongs exclusively to the Imām, and if there is a deficiency he must make it up from his own wealth.

    1.4. The orphans and the wayfarers are given their share regardless of whether they are in need or not, because the evident meaning of the expression that is used encompasses all of them.

II Section mentioning the anfāl and who is entitled to it

1. *Anfāl* includes all abandoned land the owners of which have died; all land on which horses and camels have not stepped [to take it by force], or which has been handed over by its owner out of obedience and not as a result of killings; mountain-tops, the depths of valleys, jungles and barren land without owners; the share of the prophet of booty, whether fixed or transportable, taken from defeated kings who had originally taken possession of the items without using force; the inheritance of those without heirs; and all booty before it is divided, such as beautiful slave-girls, fugitive horses, the finest clothing and similar property and slaves which have no match [that could enable their division amongst all recipients of booty].

2. If enemies are killed during a war without the permission of the Imām and the booty is taken, all of it belongs to the Imām exclusively, since all that was mentioned as belonging to the prophet exclusively belongs to the one who is standing in his place in any particular era from amongst the Imāms.

2.1. It is not permissible for the booty to be used except with the Imām's permission.

2.1.1. Whoever makes use of part of the booty without his permission is a sinner. Whatever increase and benefit he should acquire from it belongs exclusively to the Imām.

2.1.2. When someone uses part of this booty by the command of the Imām, or with his permission or assurance, he must bring to the Imām what he agrees upon as a condition to his use, either a half or a third of it. The remainder belongs to him. All of the above applies when the Imām is present.

3. During the Occultation Shīʿīs have been given a dispensation allowing them to make use of the following things that belong to the Imām and which they cannot avoid dealing with: captured women, dwellings on land belonging to the Imām and trade goods acquired in warfare, but nothing else besides.

4. There are different opinions amongst the Shīʿa with regard to what should be done during the Occultation with the *khums* that is collected in the stores, treasuries and other places, since there is no textual revelation specifying a solution.

4.1. Some hold the opinion that it is permissible during the time of the Imām's concealment to apply what we have been permitted with regards to captured women and trade goods seized in warfare. However, acting in accordance with this view is not permitted because it is contrary to the cautious approach and involves using the property of someone else without being certain of his permission.

4.2. Another group holds the opinion that *khums* must be preserved as long as the donor is alive; when his death approaches he should appoint a trustworthy member of the Imāmi fraternity as executor to deliver the *khums* to the Imām on his return, or if necessary in turn to appoint a successor as executor to deliver the *khums*, and so on.

4.3. Another group holds the opinion that the *khums* must be buried, because the earth will disgorge its contents at the final resurrection [once the Imām has returned].

4.4. Another group holds the opinion that the *khums* must be divided into six portions: the three portions belonging to the Imām should be buried or consigned to someone trustworthy. The remaining three portions should be distributed to the orphans, the poor and the wayfarers of the prophet's family who are entitled to their portions while they can still be identified.

4.4.1. The distribution of the *khums* must be carried out on this latter basis because those entitled to it can be identified and it is only the person responsible for receiving and distributing the *khums* who is not available; this makes the situation like that of *zakāt* in that it is permissible to distribute it.

4.4.2. The distribution of *khums* is permissible like the case of *zakāt*; although the person responsible for receiving it is not available he does not oppose it, and there is already a precedent in seeking out *zakāt* even though the one to whom it should be taken is not available.

5. If an agent carries out one of the previously mentioned alternative opinions, namely burial or the appointment of an executor to deliver the *khums*, he remains blameless. However, it is not permissible to act according to the first opinion mentioned above, under any circumstance.

7.9 Al-Muḥaqqiq al-Ḥillī on the distribution of *zakāt*

Najm al-Dīn Abū 'l-Qāsim Ja'far ibn Ḥasan al-Ḥillī, known as al-Muḥaqqiq al-Ḥillī, was a leading jurist of the Twelver Shī'ī school in the seventh/thirteenth century. He was born in about 602/1205–6 in the town of Hilla, which is situated between Baghdad and Kufa, and spent most of his life there. His family could already boast many jurists among them, including his father who was one of al-Muḥaqqiq's own teachers. When Naṣīr al-Dīn al-Ṭūsī visited Hilla on a mission from the Ilkhan Hulegu, he is reported to have addressed al-Muḥaqqiq as the leading representative of the scholars of the town, and to have even attended one of his study sessions. The best-known of al-Muḥaqqiq's numerous students in Hilla was his own nephew, Ibn Muṭahhar al-Ḥillī. Al-Muḥaqqiq died in 676/1277. While some report that his body was carried to Najaf for burial next to the shrine of 'Alī ibn Abī Ṭālib, the first Shī'ī Imām, others say that he was buried in Hilla, where his tomb has itself become a place of pilgrimage.

The *Sharā'i' al-islām,* which is al-Muḥaqqiq's best-known work, is one of the most influential works of Twelver Shī'ī jurisprudence ever to have been written, attracting numerous commentaries over the centuries. Al-Muḥaqqiq's other works include an abridgement of the *Sharā'i'* which also attracted many commentaries, as well as a commentary on the *Nihāya* of Shaykh al-Ṭā'ifa Muḥammad ibn Ḥasan al-Ṭūsī. He also produced a number of theological writings as well as works on jurisprudential methodology (*uṣūl al-fiqh*), logic, philology, and even a few volumes of poetry.

It is important to appreciate that the similarities between works of Shī'ī and Sunnī jurisprudence far outweigh the differences. In form, Twelver Shī'ī works such as al-Muḥaqqiq's *Sharā'i'* belong to the same genre as Sunnī codifications of the law. Twelver Shī'ī jurists also adopt the same norms and juristic techniques as the Sunnī jurists. The most obvious difference lies in the central importance of the 'Imām of the age', to whom, for instance, Shī'īs should ideally give their *zakāt* for distribution. Unlike Sunnīs, they did not come to the opinion that temporal rulers have the right to collect *zakāt*. According to al-Muḥaqqiq in the *Sharā'i'*, in the Imām's absence the donor should pay *zakāt* to 'the trustworthy jurist of the Imāmī Shī'īs' because he knows best 'the places' where it should be distributed (paragraph 3). Eventually the explanation given by Shī'ī scholars for why it should be given to the jurist would be that he actually represents the Imām in his absence.

Further reading

Norman Calder, 'Feqh,' in *Encyclopaedia Iranica*.

—— 'Zakāt in Imāmī Shī'ī jurisprudence, from the tenth to the sixteenth century AD,' *Bulletin of the School of Oriental and African Studies,* 44 (1981), pp. 468–80.

Etan Kohlberg, 'Al-Ḥelli, Najm-al-Din,' in *Encyclopaedia Iranica*.

Moojan Momen, *An introduction to Shī'ī Islam*, New Haven 1985, pp. 184–207.

Source text

Al-Muḥaqqiq al-Ḥillī, *Sharāʾiʿ al-Islām,* ed. ʿAbd al-Ḥusayn Muḥammad ʿAlī Baqqāl, Qum 1994, vol. 1, pp. 194–7.

I *Chapter on zakāt – section 3: Regarding those with the authority to distribute the charity*

1. There are three who are eligible: the donor, the Imām and the assistant of the Imām.

   1.1. The owner of wealth has the right to take responsibility for distributing the charity incumbent on him, either by himself or through someone whom he appoints for the purpose.

   1.2. It is better to take it to the Imām, especially in the case of manifest wealth, such as crops and livestock.

      1.2.1. If the Imām should ask for it then it is obligatory to give it to him. If the owner of wealth has already distributed it, this is the situation: some have said that it does not suffice, while others have said that it suffices even though he has transgressed. The former opinion is closer to the correct procedure.

   1.3. The guardian of a child, just like the owner of wealth, also has the right to give out the charity himself.

2. It is incumbent on the Imām to appoint someone to collect the charity. It must be paid to him upon request.

   2.1. If the owner of wealth says, I've distributed it already, his word is accepted – neither evidence nor oath is required.

   2.2. The collector is not permitted to distribute it unless he has the permission of the Imām. If he is granted the permission he may take his share before distributing the remainder.

3. In the absence of an Imām it is paid to the trustworthy jurist of the Imāmī Shīʿa, for he can discern better where it should be distributed.

   3.1. It is best to share it among each of the categories of recipients, and to identify a specific group in each category, although it is permissible to pay it all to members of one category, and even to a single individual within one of the categories.

   3.2. It is not permissible to give a share to categories that are not represented, nor to those who live outside, even if they have the right to be in the region.

   3.3. Moreover it is not permitted to postpone payment when one has the power to pay it promptly; such actions would constitute error for which one is answerable.

3.3.1. The same applies to one who keeps hold of wealth that belongs to someone else, refusing to give it upon request; or the one who does not pay up in accordance with the instructions he has received, or gives what he has been entrusted with to someone other than the specified recipient.

3.4. If he cannot find someone who has the right to receive the charity, then it is permissible to take it to another region. There is no accountability should it be lost, unless this is due to his negligence.

4. If the wealth of the donor lies outside of the region where he lives the best course is to pay the charity in that region. It is permissible though for him to pay it in his home region instead. If he transports the required amount to his own region then he is responsible for any loss.

II Section 4: appendix

The following issues have been raised:

1. If the Imām or the tax-collector has taken possession of the charity its donor is no longer responsible, even if it should get lost.

2. If the donor should not manage to find someone who has the right to receive the charity it is best for him to set it aside. If he should die before having distributed it, he must transfer it in his will.

3. If a slave who is bought with charity dies without any heir, the original donor of charity who bought him receives the inheritance. The alternative opinion has been expressed that the Imām should receive the inheritance instead. The former view is more manifestly correct.

4. If the charity needs to be measured or weighed, the owner of the wealth is liable for the additional expenses involved. The alternative opinion has been expressed that the expenses should be calculated as part of the total amount of his obligatory charity (*zakāt*). The former view is more manifestly correct.

5. If there is more than one reason on account of which a poor man has the right to receive charity (e.g., poverty and participation in *jihād*), it is permissible for him to receive a separate share for each of the reasons.

6. The least amount that is given to a poor man is that which is incumbent on the minimum amount of taxable wealth, ten carats of gold or five dirhams. The opinion has been expressed that it should be the additional amount that is incumbent for the next wealth-bracket, two carats of gold or one dirham. The first opinion has more support. There is no maximum limit for a single payment. However, if it takes the form of successive payments and reaches a sufficient amount for a year's provisions, it is forbidden for him to take any more.

7. If the Imām takes possession of *zakāt* he must offer a prayer for the benefit of the donor; the alternative opinion has been expressed that it is merely recommended, which is more prevalent.

8. It is reprehensible for someone to take possession of one's own accord of what has been given out as charity, whether that charity was of the obligatory type, or merely the recommended type. However, there is nothing wrong with the charity returning to someone as inheritance or the equivalent.

9. It is recommended that livestock given as charity should be branded in their most protruding and conspicuous parts [e.g., the base of the ears of sheep, or the hinds of camels and cattle]. It should be branded with the name of the tax for which it has been taken, whether *zakāt*, *ṣadaqa* or *jizya*.

7.10 Nāṣir-i Khusraw on *zakāt*

The most reliable source of information about the life of Abu Muʿīn Nāṣir ibn Khusraw ibn Hārith Qobādhiyānī Balkhī is his much celebrated travelogue, the *Safarnāma.* He had worked as a civil administrator and embraced the school of Ismāʿīlī thought, before, in 437/1045, embarking on a seven-year journey westwards from his home in the Balkh province of Khurasan. He reached Mecca via north-western Persia, Mesopotamia, Syria and Palestine, before heading towards Egypt, where the longest portion of his absence from home was spent. This was a logical choice, for Egypt had been ruled by Ismāʿīlīs since the Fāṭimid conquest in 358/969, so Nāṣir-i Khusraw was able to receive training to be an Ismāʿīlī missionary during his period of residence there.

On his return to Persia, Nāṣir-i Khusraw eventually settled in the village of Yumgan in the Hindu Kush mountains of Badakhshan, probably to avoid persecution at the hands of the Sunnī Seljuqs. He stayed here for most of the remainder of his life, during which time he composed most of his works, all of which were written in Persian. In addition to the aforementioned *Safarnāma* and Ismāʿīlī writings, such as the *Wajh-i dīn*, he composed a highly esteemed collection of poetry, his *Dīvān*. These works have established him as one of the foremost thinkers in the history of Ismāʿīlism, as well as one of the most accomplished literary figures of his generation who wrote in Persian.

The *Wajh-i dīn* consists of fifty-one chapters, or 'discourses', about half of which coincide with chapters that can be found in legal manuals, including those on prayer, almsgiving, the *ḥajj* and fasting. However, rather than being concerned with the outward requirements of the *sharīʿa* for their own sake in the manner of a jurist, Nāṣir-i Khusraw offers his own inner interpretation, or *ta'wīl*, of selected details relating to the 'wisdom', or *ḥikma*, which lies behind all outward expressions. It was because of such inner interpretations of religion that the Ismāʿīlīs were referred to as the Bāṭiniyya, or 'esoterics'. Nāṣir-i Khusraw's method of *ta'wīl* enables him to demonstrate that Islamic law and revelation have an inner meaning which is of benefit to one's soul, in addition to the outward meaning that concerns one's body. As illustrated in the passages presented here, his inner interpretations tend to focus in particular on the Ismāʿīlī epistemological doctrine of *taʿlīm*, namely the belief that the key to knowledge and true certainty lies in the charismatic Imām of each age and his representatives. Allusions in this text to the members of the hierarchical structure of authority in Ismāʿīlism, such as the enunciating prophet (*nāṭiq*), the founding Imām (*asās*) and the missionary (*dāʿī*), indicate the influence of Neoplatonic cosmology, which exerted a significant influence on virtually all of the Islamic intellectual traditions during this period.

Further reading

Henry Corbin, 'Nāṣir-i Khusraw and Iranian Ismāʿīlism,' in R. N. Frye (ed.), *The Cambridge history of Iran*, Cambridge 1975, vol. 4, pp. 520–42.

Farhad Daftary, *The Ismāʿīlīs: their history and their doctrines*, Cambridge 1990.

A. C. Hunsberger, *Nasir Khusraw, the ruby of Badakhshan*, London/New York 2000.

W. M. Thackston (trans.), *Safarnāma: Nāṣer-e Khosraw's Book of travels*, Albany NY 1986.

Source text

Nāṣir-i Khusraw, *Wajh-i dīn*, ed. G.-R. Aavani, Tehran 1977, pp. 206–8 (part I), 220–1 (part II), 222–3 (part III) and 226–7 (part IV).

I *The twenty-eighth discourse: concerning the proof for zakāt and the inner interpretation of what this term means*

1. With God's guidance, we say that giving *zakāt* purifies the believer while also benefiting his soul, since the purification of his soul depends on the purification of his body, the purification of the body depends on the purification of food, and the purification of food depends on making one's wealth *ḥalāl*, which depends on setting aside God's rightful share.

2. The one who is worthy of taking God's share from the servants is his messenger, since he who follows His command can also represent him, as God Himself has said to the prophet, *Take the poor-tax from their wealth, thereby purifying and cleansing them, and bless them, since your blessing brings them peace* (Q 9/103). No believer questions obedience to the command of the messenger of God, Muṣṭafā, nor does he fail to realize that whoever gives *zakāt* to him receives a blessing from the messenger and whoever receives a blessing is at peace, while those who fail to give *zakāt* do not receive any blessing and therefore are not at peace. Similarly the believer recognizes that whoever gives charity becomes purified and finds benefit, while whoever fails to give it does not become purified nor find benefit.

3. In addition to the command which God gave to the messenger to take *zakāt* from the believers, the payment of *zakāt* is mentioned frequently in the Qur'ān, such as, *Establish the ritual prayer and pay the* zakāt*!*' (Q 22/78 etc.). It has also been reported that the messenger said: 'The one who withholds the payment of *zakāt* lies in hellfire!'

4. While ritual prayer is incumbent on everyone, rich or poor, *zakāt* is incumbent on the rich, but not the poor. God made it obligatory just like ritual prayer as a test for mankind, promising paradise for those who give it, as well as the listing of their names amongst the righteous, while those wretched ones who withhold it are filled with the dread of punishment and are listed amongst the wicked. God said, *I warn you of a blazing fire for which only the wretched one who lies and turns his back is destined; the righteous one who spends his wealth for purification* [*yu'tī mālahu yatazakkā*; translated into Persian by Nāṣir-i Khusraw as 'the one who gives the *zakāt* due on his own wealth'] *will avoid it* (Q 92/14–18).

5. The messenger of God provided the details of the *zakāt* that is mentioned in the Qur'ān, instructing about which type of wealth is subject to *zakāt* and which is not, just like he provided the details of ritual prayer. The intention of all these instructions is to convey the wisdom which is veiled beneath them, so that people are led by the signifier to the signified, and, by means of such guidance from

God, escape from hellfire: whoever puts into practice the outward requirement, seeks the meaning contained therein and clearly recognizes it as an expression of gnosis of God, will be delivered. In this way, people with knowledge will cling to God's allies and flee from the devotees of Satan of their day. If it were not the case that God, by making *zakāt* obligatory apart from on certain types of wealth, intends that mankind should know the inner meaning of His guidance and to cling to those individuals who possess the treasury of His certain knowledge, then why should *zakāt* not be incumbent on every single camel and on all types of wealth?

II *The thirtieth discourse: concerning the zakāt on camels and its interpretation*

1. With God's guidance, I say that *zakāt* is obligatory on three types of animals, namely the camel, the cow and the sheep, and these three represent the three lofty ranks in the hierarchy of religion, namely the enunciating prophet (*nāṭiq*), the founding Imām (*asās*) and the Imām, all of whom came to life through mankind and during that life received their portion from the holy spirit and will never cease to live. I will now explain these three types of charity.

2. With regard to the charity on the camel, I say that the camel signifies the enunciating prophet, for the camel bears heavy loads on long journeys and there is no journey longer than that between the corporeal and spiritual worlds; moreover the heaviest load is the speech of God, which the enunciating prophet bears, as God stated, *We will send down to you weighty words!* (Q 73/5).

3. A camel is first of all killed by splitting the top of its heart; then it is sacrificed by saying, 'In the name of God.'

   3.1. The slaughter represents making the initial pledge to attain to knowledge of the truth.
   3.2. When the name of God is uttered over it the camel is decapitated. This represents when the believer makes the inner pledge to the religious leaders that he will separate from what is futile, since such things are represented outwardly by the head of the camel.
   3.3. Slaughtering the camel represents when people, while within the limits of the corporeal world, make the pledge to attain to the spiritual world and rise higher.
   3.4. Blood pours out of the heart when it is killed, signifying that in the spiritual world, when the second pledge is made, doubt and uncertainty leave the heart of the novice (*mustajīb*), thus purifying him.
   3.5. As I said, at first the breast of the camel is split, and only after that is its head cut off: this signifies that from the start the enunciating prophet is connected to the spiritual realm and uncertainty leaves his heart, before he becomes detached from all of mankind, corresponding with the interpretation of the utterance of the name of God over the camel when it is killed.

3.5.1. In the slaughter of a cow or a sheep first of all the head is cut off, and only after that is the knife stabbed into its heart in order to empty it of blood: the meaning of this is that the founding Imām must first of all take a pledge to separate from the world of opposites and join with the enunciating prophet, in order to reach the second rank and thereby be permitted to take on the mission. This is because it is only after recognizing the spiritual realm that his heart becomes pure.

III *The amount of zakāt payable on camels*

1. Whoever owns fewer than five camels is not required to pay *zakāt* on them. The number five represents the two spiritual roots and the three spiritual branches which the owner has not attained to with regards to the prophetic message.

2. When there are five camels then it is obligatory to pay charity to the amount of one sheep on them.

3. With every additional five camels an additional sheep is required, until there are twenty-five camels, at which point a yearling female calf is required. The Arabs call that baby camel 'daughter of the womb'.

   3.1. The interpretation of the four sheep required for twenty camels is that they represent the four [lower] ranks in the hierarchy, namely the proof (*ḥujja*), the missionary (*dāʿī*), the ordained (*maʾdhūn*) and the novice (*mustajīb*). This means that when the enunciating prophet fulfils his rank of prophethood, thereby attaining to the five higher ranks which are appropriate for him, he brings out each of the aforementioned four members of the mission.

4. When there are twenty-five camels, a yearling calf must be given, the so-called 'daughter of the womb': the womb represents the internal mission, and the yearling calf represents the Imām when he has not yet reached his full status. Once he is fully developed, then he will receive the mission in the world.

5. When there are ten further camels, reaching the total of thirty-five, then a two-year-old female calf, the so-called 'suckling daughter', must be given. That represents the Imām who is receiving benefit from the founding Imām, his spiritual mother from whom he receives the milk of inner interpretation.

IV *The interpretation of the charity on cattle – the sacrifice of the cow*

1. We say that every intelligent person knows that there is much benefit that can be derived from cattle in this world, and that the prosperity of people lies in the amount of their cattle. This is because all ploughing and cultivation is carried out by means of cattle, and this is an important task through which one prospers. The first things that grow on the earth are plants, while our mothers and

fathers also grow on this earth due to these plants, so that if the number of plants, which are the first to exist, decreases, then people also decrease as their numbers are generated by the plants.

2. Every intelligent person also knows that the life of man is based on two things: the body and the soul. Since it is the cow that supports and produces nourishment for the body, it is used as the analogy for the nourisher of the soul which provides it with food – thus the cow is the analogy for the founding Imām.

3. The Arabic for cow is *baqar*. In Arabic, to express the meaning 'he opened its stomach' they say *baqara baṭnahu*. Thus the founding Imām is the one who opens the stomach of the outward expression of the book of the *sharī'a*, and brings out its wisdom and inner interpretation from within. It is for this reason also that Muḥammad-Bāqir was called 'Bāqir', since he brought out the correct interpretation after the world had appeared dark like the night.

4. When we say that in the sacrifice of cattle seven cows suffice, while it is not permissible to sacrifice more than one camel, there is a sign in this. This is because the enunciating prophet established one member of the hierarchy and that was the founding Imām, while the founding Imām established seven of them, namely the seven Imāms to whom God entrusted the interpretation of things and their mission.

Chapter 8

Ṣūfism

8.1 Al-Ghazālī on the path of the Ṣūfīs

On al-Ghazālī (d. 505/1111) and the book from which this passage is taken, *al-Munqidh min al-ḍalāl* ('Deliverance from error'), see above, section 6.4. As was suggested above, the entire treatise is probably better understood as a work of epistemology. The aim is to show that right knowledge will deliver one from error. Here, he speaks autobiographically about the knowledge of the Ṣūfīs, the last group whom he describes on his quest for knowledge. It is therefore with the Ṣūfīs that al-Ghazālī finds his thirst for certain knowledge of the truth satisfied. He describes the practical steps necessary for purifying one's heart, and the importance of direct experience, or ' taste', for mystical knowledge. Al-Ghazālī discovers that the path of the Ṣūfī saints can bestow on the seeker direct experiences that are comparable with the experiences of prophets, in this way providing irrefutable proof of the truths of religion. Following the discussion provided here, he is able to argue for the reality of prophecy in general, through a faculty of perception grounded in the soul, which can be verified by non-prophets through 'taste' (i.e., direct experience) on the path of the Ṣūfīs.

Further reading

Farid Jabre, *La notion de la* ma'rifa *chez Ghazali*, second edition, Beirut 1986.

Eric L. Ormsby, 'The taste of truth: the structure of experience in al-Ghazālī's *al-Munqidh min al-ḍalāl*,' in Wael B. Hallaq, Donald P. Little (eds), *Islamic studies presented to Charles J. Adams*, Leiden 1991, pp. 133–52.

Source text

Farid Jabre, *Al-Munqid min aḍalāl (Erreur de délivrance)*, Beirut 1959, excerpts from pp. 35–40 of the Arabic text.

Section: The path of the Ṣūfīs

1. When I had done with these sciences, I turned my efforts to the Ṣūfī way. I came to know that their way became complete only through both knowledge and practice. The sum of their sciences is the removal of the soul's deficiencies, and cleansing it of its reprehensible and vicious qualities, so as to achieve a heart empty of all save God and adorned with the constant remembrance of God.

2. Knowledge was easier for me than practice. So I began by acquiring their knowledge from their books, such as the *Qūt al-qulūb* of Abū Ṭālib al-Makkī [d. 386/998], the works of al-Ḥārith al-Muḥāsibī, and the disparate fragments deriving from al-Junayd, al-Shiblī, Abū Yazīd al-Basṭāmī and others. In the end I understood their aims in so far as these were a matter of knowledge, and appreciated their way as far as was possible through learning and listening. And I realized that their most singular characteristic was such as could be appreciated not through learning but only through 'taste', 'state' (*ḥāl*) and change of qualities. How different it is to know the definitions of health and of fullness, together with their causes and conditions, and to be healthy and full; to know the definition of drunkenness . . . and to be drunk. In fact the drunkard, while drunk, does not know the definition or the science of drunkenness – he knows nothing about it – while the sober man may know the definition and the principles of drunkenness, and be quite free of the state itself. The doctor, while sick, may know the definition and the causes of health, and its medicines, and yet lack health. Similar to this is the difference between knowing the truth of asceticism together with its conditions and causes, and being in a 'state' comprising asceticism and abstention from things of this world.

3. I knew then for sure that they were masters of 'states' and not purveyors of words. All that could be achieved through knowledge, I had achieved. What remained could not be learned through study and listening but required 'taste' and practice.

4. Now, I had acquired through the sciences I had studied and the paths I had followed in investigating the two types of science, revealed and rational, a firm and certain faith in God, in prophecy and in the last day. These three principles of faith had become firmly rooted in my soul, not through specific discursive proof, but through causes, connections and experiences, the details of which could not be enumerated. It was also evident to me that I had no expectation of the happiness of the other world except through piety, and through control of the desires of the self. The foundation of all this lay in cutting the link between the heart and worldly things, through turning away from the abode of illusion and towards the abode of eternity, and advancing with the utmost resolution

towards God. It could not be achieved except through abandonment of rank and wealth, and flight from distraction and entanglement. . . .

[Al-Ghazālī here describes the difficulties he had in achieving a determination to abandon position, fame, comfort and so forth. Ultimately, however, his plans change.]

5. I left Baghdad. I distributed such wealth as I had, preserving only a bare sufficiency, and maintenance for the children. (I found excuse for this in the thought that the wealth of Iraq is earmarked for the welfare of society, it being a *waqf* on behalf of all Muslims. I could see no wealth in the whole world that a scholar might more fittingly draw on for his children.) I went into Damascus, and stayed there for about two years, with no distractions save retirement and seclusion, spiritual exercises and moral striving. I was concerned to cleanse the soul, to train the morals, and to purify the heart for memory of God, in accord with what I had learnt from the books of the Ṣūfīs. I practised seclusion for a while in the mosque at Damascus, climbing the minaret during the day and locking its door behind me. Then I travelled to Jerusalem, entering there the Dome of the Rock every day and locking its door behind me. Then I was moved to carry out the duty of Pilgrimage, to seek help from the blessings of Mecca and Medina, to visit the tomb of the prophet of God, after visiting the tomb of Abraham. So I went to the Hijaz. Then various cares and the summons of my children drew me back to my homeland, and I returned there, after having been the furthest of all creation from such an act. There, too, I preferred retirement, out of desire for seclusion and the purification of the heart. But the vicissitudes of time, the demands of my family and the necessities of making a living all conspired to change in me the nature of my desire and to sully the purity of my seclusion. Only at scattered moments did my situation achieve purity. My desire for this end was, however, not affected and though obstacles pushed me away, I would return. So it was for ten years. During these periods of seclusion various things were revealed to me that can be neither computed nor adequately analysed.

6. As much as I shall say – that it might be beneficial – is this, that I came to know for sure that the Ṣūfīs were following the path of God, the Ṣūfīs in particular, and that their conduct was the best of conduct, their path the surest of paths, their morals the purest of morals. Even more, if the wisdom and intellect of the wise were united, together with the knowledge of those *ʿulamāʾ* who understand the secrets of the law, in order to change one aspect of their conduct and morals and to replace it with something better, they would be unable to do so. For all their movements and their ways of being still, in their manifest and in their hidden aspects, are derived from the light of the lamp of prophecy; and there is not, on the face of the earth, beyond the lamp of prophecy any higher source of light.

7. What can one say about a path for which the purification – the first of its conditions – is complete purification of the heart from all save God; to which the key – corresponding to the act of reciting the opening of the daily prayers – is complete drowning of the heart in memory of God; and of which the end is

complete annihilation in God? This indeed is its end only in relation to its beginnings, those which belong to the realm of choice and acquisition. These in truth represent the first part of the way; what precedes this is but, as it were, the entrance hall.

8. Early in the way visions begin, such that Ṣūfīs in waking hours perceive angels and the spirits of prophets, and hear from them voices, and derive from them benefits. Their state then proceeds from the witnessing of forms and likenesses to levels of perception which transcend the boundaries of speech. None who tries to give expression to these can do so without his words containing manifest error which it is impossible to guard against. But, overall, the matter culminates in a closeness which one group have imagined to be 'incarnation' (*ḥulūl*), another group 'union' (*ittiḥād*) and another 'connection' (*wuṣūl*). All of this is error. The nature of the error we have explained in our book *al-Maqṣad al-asnā* ('The noblest aim'). Indeed one to whom such a state is given should say no more than the poet:

> What happened, happened; I'll not remember it.
> Don't ask about it; just think well of it.

In sum, he who is not granted anything through 'taste', will be able to perceive of the truth of prophecy only the name. The miracles of the saints are in truth [the equivalent of] the first steps of the prophets. Such was the first state of the prophet of God when he came to Mount Ḥirā' to practise there seclusion with his Lord and worship, so that the bedouin said, 'Muḥammad is in love with his Lord!'

9. This is a state which can be realized through 'taste' by those who follow the path of the Ṣūfīs. Those who are not granted 'taste' may become certain of its existence through experience and intimacy, if they increase their companionship with the Ṣūfīs until they achieve a sure and certain understanding based on circumstantial evidence. Those who share their company will derive from them this faith, for they are a people whose companions are not left in distress. Finally, for those who are not granted the possibility of the companionship of Ṣūfīs, let them acquire sure knowledge of the possibility of that state through rational demonstration, as we have explained in our book, *ʿAjāʾib al-qalb*, 'The wonders of the heart', contained in the *Iḥyāʾ ʿulūm al-dīn* [Book 21]. To comprehend this state through rational demonstration is 'knowledge'. To participate in that state is 'taste'. To accept it as a result of experience and intimacy, with good will, is 'faith' (*īmān*). These are the three degrees referred to in, *God raises those of you who believe and those of you who are given knowledge in degrees* (Q 58/11).

10. Beyond these degrees are an ignorant people. They deny the basis of all this, they express astonishment at such claims, they listen and they scoff. They say, 'Amazing!' How they rave! But concerning them God has said, *Amongst them are some who listen to you, but when they leave you they say to those who have been given knowledge, What did he say so haughtily? They are the ones upon*

whose hearts God has set a seal. They follow their whims (Q 47/16). *God has made them deaf and blind* (Q 47/23).

11. What became clear to me through my experience of their path is the truth and the essence of prophecy.

8.2 Al-Sarrāj on the *sunna* and musical audition

Abū Naṣr ʿAbd Allāh ibn ʿAlī al-Sarrāj (d. 378/988) was a Ṣūfī scholar from Tus, in present-day north-eastern Iran. Very little information is available about his life. The main source of information is his sole-surviving work, the *Kitāb al-lumaʿ fī ʾl-taṣawwuf*, which indicates that he travelled widely in the Near and Middle East to meet a large number of teachers and transmitters.

The *Kitāb al-lumaʿ* details the states and stages of the mystical itinerary, describes the distinctive practices and customs of the Ṣūfīs, and defines a large set of their technical terms. It is particularly remarkable for its breadth of coverage and its accommodating approach: it includes chapters on conventional Muslim issues, such as the chapter presented below on the veneration of the prophet, as well as chapters which deal with issues specific to Ṣūfism that may be considered controversial, such as the lengthy section on musical audition (*samāʿ*), a chapter of which is presented below, and the several chapters on the 'overflowing utterances' (*shaṭaḥāt*) attributed to Abū Yazīd al-Basṭāmī and others.

The *Kitāb al-lumaʿ* consists of a collection of chapters, each forming a discrete and autonomous treatise in itself. They also take diverse forms, the range of which is indicated by the chapters presented below. The chapter on the importance of the *sunna* for Ṣūfīs consists entirely of citations, a selection from among the large stock that circulated about the Ṣūfī attitude towards the ultimate sources of authority in Islam. In contrast, the chapter on the audition of poetry relies almost exclusively on reasoned arguments as proof for the validity of this distinctive practice of the Ṣūfīs.

As the oldest systematic presentation of Ṣūfism, al-Sarrāj's *Kitāb al-lumaʿ* is considered the first and most authoritative work of the Ṣūfī manual genre. It has served as the main source for the later, more accessible works of al-Qushayrī (section 8.4) and Hujwīrī (section 8.5), through which it has become familiar throughout the Muslim world.

Further reading

Richard Gramlich (ed. and trans.), *Schlaglichter über das Sufitum: Abū Naṣr as-Sarrājs Kitāb al-Lumaʿ*, Stuttgart 1990; a fully annotated German translation.

P. Lory, 'Al-Sarrādj, Abū Naṣr,' in *Encyclopaedia of Islam*, new edition.

R. A. Nicholson (ed.), *The Kitāb al-lumaʿ fi ʾl-taṣawwuf of Abū Naṣr ʿAbdallāh ibn ʿAlī al-Sarrāj al-Ṭūsī*, Gibb Memorial Series, Leiden/London 1914, introduction and summary.

Source text

R. A. Nicholson (ed.), *The Kitāb al-lumaʿ fi ʾl-taṣawwuf of Abū Naṣr ʿAbdallāh ibn ʿAlī al-Sarrāj al-Ṭūsī*, Leiden/London 1914, Arabic text pp. 103–4 (part I) and 283–5 (part II).

I *Chapter dealing with what has been mentioned about the Ṣūfī shaykhs with regard to their following the messenger of God*

1. The shaykh said that he heard ʿAbd al-Wāḥid ibn ʿUlwān say that he heard al-Junayd say, 'This knowledge of ours is interwoven with the *ḥadīth* of the Messenger of God.'

2. I heard Abū ʿAmr Ismāʿīl ibn Nujayd say that he heard Abū ʿUthmān Saʿīd ibn ʿUthmān al-Ḥīrī say, 'He who makes the *sunna* the ruler of his soul in speech and action expresses wisdom, while he who makes lust the ruler of his soul in speech and action expresses innovation.' God said, *If you obey him you will be rightly guided* (Q 24/54).

3. I heard Ṭayfūr al-Basṭāmī say that he heard Mūsā ibn ʿĪsā, the one known as ʿAmmī, say that he heard his father say that Abū Yazīd said to him, 'Let us go to see this man who has made himself famous for sainthood.' He was a sought-after man, famous in his locality for asceticism and piety. Ṭayfūr had identified his name and family for us. ʿAmmī's father said, 'We went and when he came out of his house and entered the mosque he spat towards the *qibla*, and so Abū Yazīd said, "Let's go back," and he turned away without greeting him, and said, "This is unfaithful to one of the customs of the messenger of God, so how can he be faithful about what he is claiming with regard to the stations of the saints and God's elite!"'

4. I heard Ṭayfūr say that he heard Mūsā ibn ʿĪsā say that he heard his father say that he heard Abū Yazīd say, 'I intended to ask God to spare me from the need for the provision of food and women, then I thought to myself, "How can it be permitted for me to ask God for this when the apostle of God did not ask him for it?" So I did not ask him. Then God spared me from the need for the provision of women, such that I do not care whether a woman meets me or a wall!'

5. I heard Abū 'l-Ṭayyib Aḥmad ibn Muqātil al-ʿAkkī al-Baghdādī say, 'I was with Jaʿfar al-Khuldī on the day of al-Shiblī's death, when Bundār al-Dīnawarī, who was a student of al-Shiblī, approached us. He had been present at his death, so Jaʿfar asked him, "What did you see him do at the time of his death?" He answered, "When he could no longer speak and his forehead was dripping with sweat he indicated that I should do his ablutions for him in preparation for prayer, so I did that. However, I forgot to run my fingers through his beard, so he grabbed my hand and ran my fingers through his beard himself."' Abū 'l-Ṭayyib said, 'Jaʿfar wept, saying, "What can you say about a man who wouldn't leave out cleaning his beard during ablutions even when he was about to die, when he couldn't speak and his forehead was dripping with sweat!"'

6. I heard Aḥmad ibn ʿAlī al-Wajīhī say that he heard Abū ʿAlī Rūdhbārī say, 'My teacher in Ṣūfism was Junayd, my teacher in jurisprudence was Abū 'l-ʿAbbās ibn al-Surayj, my teacher in grammar was Thaʿlab and my teacher in the *ḥadīth* of the messenger of God was Ibrāhīm al-Ḥarbī.'

7. Dhū'l-Nūn was asked, 'Through what did you attain knowledge of God?' He answered, 'I attained knowledge of God through God, and I gained knowledge of what is other than God through the messenger of God.'

8. Sahl ibn ʿAbd Allāh said, 'Sometimes the truth would keep trying to penetrate my heart for forty days, but I wouldn't allow it to enter except with two witnesses in the form of the book and the *sunna*!'

9. This is what I have with me at the moment concerning what the Ṣūfīs believe about following the messenger of God. I dislike verbosity, so I've been brief for the sake of conciseness. Through God alone can one find success.

II Chapter mentioning those who have chosen the audition of poetry

1. The shaykh said: The proof for the opinion of the group who have chosen musical audition of poetry takes the form of that saying of the prophet, 'In poetry there is wisdom,' and his utterance, 'Wisdom is the goal of the believer.' This group have maintained that the Qur'ān is God's speech and His speech is one of His attributes, so it is a divine truth which a human being cannot endure when it is manifested; this is because it is uncreated and so created attributes cannot endure it. Moreover, it is not possible for one part of it to be better than another part, nor can it be embellished by means of created music, but rather created things are made beautiful by it: it is the most beautiful of things, and created things of beauty are not considered beautiful when compared with it. God said, *We have made the Qur'ān easy to remember, but do any remember it?* (Q 54/17). And He also said, *If we had sent down this Qur'ān to a mountain, you would have seen it humbled, split apart by the fear of God* (Q 59/21). Therefore, if God were to send it down to men's hearts with its divine truths, and open up to their hearts an atom of veneration and awe for it during recitation, they would be torn apart, startled, confounded and perplexed.

2. It is common for somebody to recite the Qur'ān in public, but without anyone experiencing any tenderness in their heart during the recitation. If a beautiful voice were used for the recitation, or pleasant, moving melodies, tenderness and delight would then be experienced in listening, and if that beautiful voice and that pleasant melody were used for something other than the Qur'ān, that same tenderness, delight and pleasure would be experienced then as well. Though they may think that the tenderness, purity, enjoyment and the ecstasy were from the Qur'ān, if that were really the case then they would always experience this without any interruption whenever the Qur'ān is recited.

3. Pleasant melodies have affinities with men's inner dispositions; this relationship is based on pleasure, and is not divine. The Qur'ān is God's speech, and its relationship is a divine one, not one based on pleasure. Verses of poetry also have such a relationship based on pleasure, not a divine one. Although those who engage in musical audition differ in rank and specific characteristics, there is in

each case an affinity with one's inner dispositions, pleasure for the soul and enjoyment for the spirit, because they are in harmony with those subtleties in a beautiful voice and pleasant melodies. The same can be said for poems, for they contain lofty meanings, tenderness, eloquence, subtlety and allusions; if these voices and melodies were to be combined with this poetry, they would be in harmony with each other because of their mutual affinity and similarity, and this would be more pleasurable, less difficult to endure and less dangerous for listening hearts because created things resemble each other.

4. Those who have chosen audition of poems over audition of the Qur'ān have done so out of reverence for the Qur'ān and respect for the danger in it, because it is a divine truth and men's souls shrink from it, die due to its effects and become annihilated by its delights and pleasantness whenever the rays of its truths shine their radiance on them and make manifest to them their divine meanings.

5. This group have said, 'As long as our human nature remains, we still have our attributes and enjoy pleasures, and our spirits delight in moving melodies and pleasant voices, our taking delight in poetry, through which we witness the continuance of such pleasure, is better than our taking delight thus in God's speech, which is His attribute, that is His speech which was made manifest and will return to Him.'

6. A group of religious scholars have disapproved of trilling the Qur'ān, and combining melodies with the Qur'ān is not allowed according to them. God said, *Recite the Qur'ān in a measured rhythm!* (Q 73/4). Those who do this do it only because human dispositions make men shrink from the audition of the Qur'ān and its recitation, since it is a divine truth. They therefore recite it with a beautiful voice in order thus to attract the dispositions of ordinary men so that they will want to listen. If hearts were fully engaged, each present moment fulfilled, innermost spirits pure, souls disciplined and human dispositions withdrawn, there would be no need for this. Through God alone can one find success.

8.3 Abū Nuʿaym's biography of al-Basṭāmī

Abū Nuʿaym Aḥmad ibn ʿAbdallāh al-Iṣfahānī (d. 430/1038), the assumed author of the *Ḥilyat al-awliyāʾ*, which is recognized as one of the most important sources for the early development of Ṣūfism, is none the less remembered in later sources more for his importance as a Shāfiʿī *ḥadīth*-transmitter than as a Ṣūfī. While the other major works ascribed to him, namely the *Dhikr akhbār Iṣbahān* and the *Dalāʾil al-nubuwwa*, confirm his interest in the collection of historical material and the biography of the prophet, it is remarkable that his *magnum opus* should have been the ten-volume *Ḥilyat al-awliyāʾ wa-ṭabaqāt al-aṣfiyāʾ*, which belongs to a tradition in which he is not remembered as a prominent representative. His maternal grandfather, Ibn Maʿdān al-Bannāʾ, was most probably the source of Abū Nuʿaym's interest in Ṣūfism; Ibn Maʿdān's importance as a Ṣūfī is reflected in the fact that he is commonly identified as the teacher of ʿAlī ibn Sahl al-Iṣfahānī (d. 307/920), who was the most celebrated Ṣūfī from Isfahan up to this point in time. The introduction of the *Ḥilyat al-awliyāʾ* confirms that he was Abū Nuʿaym's forerunner in Ṣūfī scholarship, and the inclusion of members of his school at the end of the work suggests that Abū Nuʿaym was himself also a follower of the living tradition of Ṣūfism in Isfahan which he had established.

The *Ḥilyat al-awliyāʾ* consists of approximately 650 biographies (amounting to approximately 4,000 pages in the printed edition). An overall chronological principle is evident in the order of presentation of biographies in this work of the Ṣūfī *ṭabaqāt* genre, since they begin with the four 'rightly-guided' caliphs and culminate with Abū Nuʿaym's own contemporaries. The time-span is covered predominantly by individuals who are not usually identified as Ṣūfīs, including the generations of the pious predecessors, the first six Imāms of Shīʿism, the founders of the main law schools (apart from Abū Ḥanīfa, for polemical reasons) and other jurists, theologians and pietists. These religious authorities are attributed with some Ṣūfī utterances (amongst other material) in their respective biographies, even though they may not usually be remembered in this way. Despite the wide net that has been cast, the controversial al-Ḥusayn ibn Manṣūr al-Ḥallāj (d. 309/922) has been excluded for polemical reasons.

Most of the biographies of individuals who are recognized primarily as having been mystics are found in the tenth volume. This includes the biography of Abū Yazīd, which is typical in format of the biographies in the *Ḥilya* in general. It begins with an introduction in rhyming prose (*sajʿ*), which is immediately followed by a long sequence of discrete segments of biographical information, less than half of which are introduced by a complete chain of authorities (*isnād*). This sequence of biographical segments is followed by concluding remarks, presented as the opinions of Abū Nuʿaym, and, finally, a *ḥadīth* transmission by Abū Yazīd.

The translation presented here is representative of a number of distinctive features of the structure of the text of the *Ḥilya*, including the signs of growth, interpolation and interference with the text, the recurrence of variants and the competing influence of key-word, thematic and *isnād* associations on the juxtaposition of individual segments. All of these characteristics suggest that the text may have undergone a number of redactions. Since this passage is taken from the very start of the biography, it includes the introduction and the biographical segments which follow immediately after it. The latter consist mostly of short anecdotes and pithy utterances, including some of the bold, uncompromising utterances about his own spiritual experiences and rank with which Abū Yazīd is traditionally associated. Consistent with the remainder of this work and other contemporary works is the use of the term *ʿārif* (gnostic) to refer to the Ṣūfī, as distinct from, for example, the *zāhid* (ascetic) and the *ʿābid* (pietist).

Further reading

G. Böwering, 'Besṭāmī (Basṭāmī), Bāyazīd,' *Encyclopaedia Iranica.*
R. G. Khoury, 'Importance et authenticité de textes de *Ḥilyat al-awliyāʾ*,' *Studia Islamica*, 46 (1977), pp. 73–113.
W. Madelung, 'Abū Noʿaym al-Eṣfahānī,' *Encyclopaedia Iranica.*
Jawid A. Mojaddedi, *The biographical tradition in Sufism: the ṭabaqāt genre from al-Sulamī to Jāmī*, Richmond 2001, chapter 2.

Source text

Abū Nuʿaym al-Iṣfahānī, *Ḥilyat al-awliyāʾ*, Cairo 1932–8, vol. 10, pp. 33–7.

Abū Yazīd al-Basṭāmī

1. The shaykh and *ḥāfiẓ*, Abū Nuʿaym, said, 'Among them is the lone roamer, the solitary wanderer Abū Yazīd al-Basṭāmī. He roamed and withdrew, he wandered and then returned. He withdrew beyond the limits to the originator of perceptible and knowable things. He separated himself from creation and stayed consistent with the truth. He was helped by secret retreats, and strengthened by his mastery of piety. His allusions are plain but their meaning is hidden; to those who understand them they give security, but to those who reject them they are a source of temptation.'

2. ʿUmar ibn Aḥmad ibn ʿUthmān related to us that ʿAbd Allāh ibn Aḥmad ibn Mūsā al-Ṣirfī related to him that Aḥmad ibn Muḥammad ibn Ḥasan related to him that ʿUmar al-Basṭāmī related to him on the authority of Abū Mūsā that Abū Yazīd said, 'My love for you is no surprise, since I'm a poor slave; your love for me is the surprise, since you are a powerful king!'

3. ʿAbd al-Wāḥid ibn Bakr related to us saying that al-Ḥasan ibn Ibrāḥīm al-Damaghānī said that Mūsā ibn ʿĪsā related to him, saying that he heard his father say that he heard Abū Yazīd say, 'O God, you created mankind without their knowledge and you invested upon them a trust without their choosing it, so if you don't help them who will?'

4. Muḥammad ibn al-Ḥusayn (al-Sulamī) related to us saying that he heard Manṣur ibn ʿAbd Allāh say that he heard Yaʿqūb ibn Isḥāq say that he heard Ibrāhīm al-

Harawī say that he heard Abū Yazīd al-Basṭāmī say, 'When I started I was mistaken about four things: I imagined that it's me who remembers him, that it's me who knows him, that it's me who loves him and that it's me who seeks him. When I finished I realized that his remembrance came before mine, his knowledge preceded mine, his love was prior to mine and that he sought me first until I started to seek him.'

5. ʿUmar ibn ʿUthmān related to us that ʿAbd Allāh ibn Aḥmad ibn Mūsā related to him that Aḥmad ibn Muḥammad ibn Jābān related to him that ʿUmar al-Basṭāmī related to him on the authority of Abū Mūsā that Abū Yazīd said, 'God has an elite among his servants, who, if he were to veil them in heaven from vision of himself, would appeal for help to get out of heaven just like the inhabitants of hell appeal for help to get out of hell!'

6. I heard al-Faḍl ibn Jaʿfar say that he heard Muḥammad ibn Manṣūr say that ʿUbayd ibn ʿAbd al-Qāhir said, 'A group of people sat around Abū Yazīd, while he hung his head down for a while, and then he raised it to them to say, "While you have been sitting down before me, here I have been, roaming my thoughts, looking for a rotten grain which you can bear, to extract it for you, but I did not find anything." '

7. He said that Abū Yazīd said, 'I was absent from God for thirty years. My absence from him was as a result of my mentioning him, for when I refrained from it I found him in every state.'

8. A man said to me, 'Why do you not travel?' Abū Yazīd said, 'Because my companion does not travel and I am staying with him.' The questioner opposed him by means of an analogy, saying, 'Ablution with still water is disliked!' Abū Yazīd responded, 'They did not see any fault with sea water; its water is clean and its dead things are lawful!' Then Abū Yazīd said, 'You may see the rivers flowing with droning and murmuring until they approach the sea; when they mix with it their murmuring and turbulence subsides, and the sea water does not notice them: neither an increase appears in it, nor would a decrease appear in it if they were to leave it.'

9. ʿUmar ibn Aḥmad related to me that ʿAbd Allāh ibn Aḥmad related to him that Aḥmad ibn Muḥammad related to him that ʿUthmān related to him on the authority of Abū Mūsā, saying that Abū Yazīd said, 'For thirty years whenever I wished to mention God I always rinsed and washed my tongue, deeming Him too high to mention Him.'

10. ʿUthmān ibn Muḥammad al-ʿUthmānī related to me that Abū 'l-Ḥasan al-Rāzī said that he heard Yūsuf ibn al-Ḥusayn say that he heard Yaḥyā ibn Muʿādh say that he heard Abū Yazīd al-Basṭāmī say, 'I did not cease to wander in the field of unity until I entered the enclosure of unicity. Then I did not cease to wander inside the enclosure of unicity until I departed to everlastingness, and I drank from his cup such a drink that, thanks to its memory, I will certainly not thirst ever again.'

10.1 Yūsuf said 'I used to hear this speech in different words from Dhū 'l-Nūn, there being an addition to it; Dhū 'l-Nūn would not utter it except when excited and overwhelmed by his ecstasy. He used to say that, and follow it with, "Yours is the glory and beauty, Yours is the perfection. Glory be to you, glory be to you. May the tongues of praise and the mouths of glorification venerate you. You, you, eternal, eternal. His love for me is eternal."'

11. Abū 'l-Faḍl Aḥmad ibn Abī ʿImrān related to me that Mūsā related to him that Manṣūr ibn ʿAbd Allāh related to him, saying that he heard Abū ʿImrān Mūsā ibn ʿĪsā say that he heard his father say that Abū Yazīd said, 'I was absent from God for thirty years. My absence from Him was a result of my mentioning Him, for when I refrained from it I found Him in every state, until it was as if He was me!'

12. Aḥmad ibn Abī ʿImrān related to me that Mūsā related to him that Manṣūr related to him that a man came to Abū Yazīd and said, 'Give me some advice.' He told him, 'Look at the sky!' and his companion looked at the sky. Then Abū Yazīd asked him, 'Do you know who created this?' He answered, 'God.' Abū Yazīd said, 'The one who created it is watching over you wherever you are, so beware!'

13. Aḥmad related to me that Manṣūr told him that Mūsā related to him the following: a man came up to Abū Yazīd and said, 'I've heard that you fly in the air.' He responded, 'And what's so surprising about that? Carrion can fly, and surely a believer is nobler than such a bird!'

14. Aḥmad ibn Ḥarb sent him a rug with a note in which he had written, 'Pray on it at night!' Abū Yazīd wrote back to him, 'I have gathered together the acts of worship of the people of heaven and the seven climes, put them into my pillow and placed that under my cheek [for when I sleep]!'

15. I heard al-Faḍl ibn Jaʿfar say that he heard Muḥammad ibn Manṣūr say that he heard ʿUbayd say that he heard Abū Yazīd say, 'I divorced the world three times, absolutely and irrevocably. Then I turned to my lord by myself and called out to Him for help: "My God, I pray to you with a prayer which is divest of all but You!" When He knew the sincerity of my heart's prayer and my despair over my carnal soul, the first thing that came to me by way of a reply to this prayer was that He caused me to forget myself completely; and He set up created beings in front of me despite my shunning them.'

16. ʿUmar ibn Aḥmad ibn ʿUthmān related to me that ʿUbayd Allāh ibn Aḥmad related to him that Aḥmad ibn Muḥammad ibn Jābān related to him that ʿUmar al-Basṭāmī related to him on the authority of Abū Mūsā that Abū Yazīd said, 'There are so many faults in acts of obedience that you don't need to look for sins!'

17. ʿUmar related to me that ʿUbayd informed him that Aḥmad told him that ʿUmar informed him on the authority of Abū Mūsā that Abū Yazīd said, 'As long as

the worshipper reckons that there is someone more evil than himself in creation he is still proud.'

18. Muḥammad ibn al-Ḥusayn (al-Sulamī) informed me that he heard Manṣūr ibn ʿAbd Allāh say that he heard Abū ʿImrān Mūsā ibn ʿĪsā say that he heard his father say that Abū Yazīd said, 'For thirty years I struggled against my carnal soul, but I did not find anything harder than scholastic knowledge and putting it into practice. If it were not for the differences of opinion of the scholars I would have grown weary; the differences of opinion of the scholars are a blessing, except with regard to stripping bare divine unity.'

19. Abū Yazīd said, 'Whoever lets his lusts stay with him does not understand his carnal soul.'

20. Abū Yazīd said, 'Heaven is of no consequence for the lovers of God,' and 'Those who love God are veiled by their love.'

21. ʿUmar ibn Aḥmad related to me that ʿUbayd Allāh ibn Aḥmad related to him that Aḥmad ibn Muḥammad related to him that ʿUmar told him on the authority of Abū Mūsā who said that Abū Yazīd said, 'Those who are most veiled from God belong to three categories, each veiled by different things: the first is the ascetic, by his asceticism, the second is the pietist, by his piety, and the third is the scholar, by his knowledge.' Then he continued, 'The poor ascetic has worn his uniform of asceticism and gone to the centre of the ascetics. Now if that poor fellow knows that God called the entire world "little", how much does he possess of it, and how much of that has he renounced?' Then he continued, 'The real ascetic is the one who looks at God with a gaze which stays fixed and never reverts to anything else, not even to himself. The pietist is the one who sees the gifts God has in store for his piety, rather than the acts of piety themselves, such that he only understands piety as a means of acquiring God's gifts. As for the scholar, if he were to know that all that God has revealed is just a single line from the Preserved Tablet, then how much of that line has he understood, and how much of his knowledge has he put into practice?'

22. Muḥammad ibn al-Ḥusayn (al-Sulamī) informed us, saying that he heard Aḥmad ibn ʿAlī say that he heard Yaʿqūb say that he heard al-Ḥusayn ibn ʿAlī say that Abū Yazīd said, 'Gnosis concerning the essence of God is ignorance, knowledge about the essence of gnosis is perplexity, and making allusions by a teacher is associationism (*shirk*)!'

23. And he said, 'While the gnostic is preoccupied with what he hopes for, the ascetic is preoccupied with what he eats!'

24. And he said, 'Blessed is the one who has only one preoccupation, whose heart is not distracted by what his eyes see, nor by what his ears hear.'

25. And: 'The one who has gnosis of God renounces everything that might distract him from God.'

26. Aḥmad ibn Abī ʿImrān related to us that Manṣūr ibn ʿAbd Allāh said that he heard Abū ʿImrān Mūsā ibn ʿĪsā say that he heard his father say that Abū Yazīd said when asked about the sign of the gnostic, '*When the kings enter a village they destroy it* (Q 27/34).'

27. And he said, 'I am amazed how someone who has gnosis of God can worship him!'

28. And someone said to him, 'You are one of the seven supreme saints (*abdāl*) who are the supports of the earth.' He responded, 'I am all seven!'

29. And someone asked him, 'When does someone attain to the level of the top men in this affair?' He answered, 'If he realizes the faults of his carnal soul then he attains to the level of the top men.'

30. And he said, 'God has some servants who, if he were to veil them from him for the blink of an eye and give them all of the heavens, would not feel any need for them – so how could they rely on the world and its adornment?'

8.4 Al-Qushayrī on the term Ṣūfī, Ṣūfī states and satisfaction

Abū 'l-Qāsim ʿAbd al-Karīm al-Qushayrī (d. 465/1072) was born into a privileged Arab family from among those who had settled near Nishapur, the city where he spent most of his adult life. It was apparently on the instruction of his teacher in Ṣūfism, Abū ʿAlī al-Daqqāq (d. 406/1016 or 412/1021), that he studied Ashʿarite theology and Shāfiʿite jurisprudence under the leading authorities in Nishapur as a young man. Some Ashʿarite theological writings are included among his approximately twenty extant works, indicating the continued importance of this theological school for him. Indeed, he is said to have become their leading representative in Nishapur. However, his most important work by far is the *Risāla*, which is possibly the most popular prose work on Ṣūfism ever to have been written. Although the earlier works of al-Sarrāj and al-Sulamī which overlap in scope with al-Qushayrī's *Risāla* are considered the most authoritative in the Ṣūfī tradition, they have in fact become familiar to most readers through the latter work, for al-Qushayrī bases his biographies on those of al-Sulamī and his thematic discussions on the corresponding discussions of al-Sarrāj. Like these two illustrious predecessors, al-Qushayrī is remembered in the later Ṣūfī tradition primarily for his scholarship. His *Risāla* has been translated into numerous languages and has attracted many commentaries.

Al-Qushayrī's *Risāla* consists of four main sections, followed by an appendix. The first section, which is by far the shortest, is theological in content, confirming al-Qushayrī's Ashʿarite allegiance; the second section is made up of biographies in an overall chronological pattern, thus representing the *ṭabaqāt* genre; the third section offers definitions of technical Ṣūfī terminology; and the fourth section consists of thematic chapters on the theory and practice of Ṣūfism. The appendix deals with various issues, under the rubric 'Advice to disciples'.

The passages presented here in translation are taken from the second, third and fourth sections of the *Risāla.* The first passage translated here is the introduction of the biographical section. It links the subjects of the first biographies back to the time of the prophet of Islam, while also accounting for the relatively late emergence of the term *ṣūfī.* The definition of *ḥāl* displays al-Qushayrī's tendency in the third section to define terminology himself using, for illustration, citations of the sayings of past Ṣūfī authorities, as well as occasionally from the texts of Muslim revelation. This specific term is perhaps the most frequently used of all, since it is the generic term for an inner experience bestowed by God on the mystical itinerary. The discussion of *riḍā* is consistent with al-Qushayrī's systematic method in the fourth section of beginning each chapter with citations from revelation, even if they should be only loosely related. He follows this form of introduction with his own comments and the opinions of past Ṣūfīs on the issue concerned.

Further reading

A. J. Arberry, *Sufism: an account of the mystics of Islam,* London 1950, pp. 74–83.

R. Gramlich (ed. and trans.), *Das Sendschreiben al-Qusayrīs über das Sufitum*, Stuttgart 1987; a fully annotated German translation.

Jawid A. Mojaddedi, *The biographical tradition in Sufism: the ṭabaqāt genre from al-Sulamī to Jāmī,* Richmond 2001, chapter 4.
Barbara R. Von Schlegell (trans.), *Principles of Sufism,* Berkeley 1990; an English translation of most of the fourth section, including the entirety of the chapter on *riḍā.*
Michael Sells, *Early Islamic mysticism,* Mahwah NJ 1996; a source book for early Ṣūfism, which includes (pp. 99–149) a translation of the third section of the *Risāla.*

Source text

Al-Qushayrī, *Risāla*, Cairo 1972, pp. 34 (part I), 54–5 (part II) and 150–2 (part III).

I Chapter mentioning the shaykhs of this path and those aspects of their sayings and behaviour which indicate veneration for the sharīʿa

You should know that the best of the Muslims after the apostle of God were not called, in their own time, by a title of distinction other than companionship of the apostle of God (*ṣuḥba*), since there was no virtue higher than that. Thus they were called the *ṣaḥāba* and when those of the second period took over from them, those who had associated with the *ṣaḥāba* were called the *tābiʿūn*, this being considered the most noble title. Then those who came after them were called the *atbāʿ al-tābiʿīn*. Subsequently the people were at variance and different ranks became discernible. The elite of the people amongst those who were preoccupied with religion were called the *zuhhād* ('ascetics') and *ʿubbād* ('pietists'). Then innovations emerged and challenges were made between the groups, each of them claiming that the *zuhhād* were amongst their number. The elite of the traditionalists who maintained their souls with God and safeguarded their hearts from the paths of heedlessness alone possessed the name *taṣawwuf* (Ṣūfism). This name became well known for these great individuals by the year 200. In this section, we will now mention the names of a group of the shaykhs of this sect from the first generation until the time of the later ones amongst them, and briefly mention their behaviour and sayings which contain an indication of their principles and their customs, God willing.

II Chapter explaining the technical terms (alfāẓ) which are current amongst this group and explaining their difficult aspects

On the *ḥāl*.

1. A *ḥāl*, according to the Ṣūfīs, is something which affects the heart, without intention on the part of those affected, without attraction, and without acquisition. It may take the form of delight or sadness, expansion or contraction, yearning, confusion, awe or need. *Ḥāls* are gifts, in contrast to *maqāms*, which are acquisitions. From the uncreated world *ḥāls* come, from hard work and effort, *maqāms*. The person with a *maqām* is fixed in his *maqām*; the person with a *ḥāl* is in a transitory phase.

Dhū'l-Nūn al-Miṣrī was asked what the meaning of the gnostic (*al-ʿārif*) is. He replied that he was here, but now he is gone. Some shaykhs said that a *ḥāl* is like a lightning flash. If the condition lasts, it is the soul's learning. Some also say that a *ḥāl* is like its name; it alights in the heart (*taḥillu*) and disappears in an instant. They recite the following:

It's not a *ḥāl* if it did not alight
And what alights must pass and fade from sight:
Like when a shadow reached its full length, then
It starts to shrink and disappear again.

2. Some authorities have suggested that the *ḥāl* lasts and can endure. They say that if it does not survive, or come in constant succession, then it is not a *ḥāl* but an impulse or an insight; and one who experiences these has not yet arrived at the level of *ḥāls*. Only when the quality survives is it called a *ḥāl*. This is like Abū ʿUthmān al-Ḥīrī, who said, 'For forty years now God has not put me in a *ḥāl* that I have disliked.' He was talking about being maintained in a state of satisfaction (*riḍā*), for *riḍā* is one of the *ḥāl*s.

3. The necessary resolution of this dispute is to admit that the proponents of remaining at length in a *ḥāl* are correct. For that condition may become, as it were, a pasture, in which one may be given training. However, to one who has achieved such a *ḥāl*, there will be further *ḥāl*s and these will be transitory, not lasting, at a higher level than those which have become for him a pasture. If, in turn, these transitory phenomena become lasting, as the *ḥāl*s before them did, then the person affected will move on to a higher state, to *ḥāl*s beyond these, and more subtle. Eternally he will move in this process of advancement.

I have heard the teacher Abū ʿAlī al-Daqqāq comment on the prophet's words, 'My heart is in darkness, and I call seventy times a day for God's mercy.' He said that the prophet was eternally advancing in his *ḥāl*s. When he advanced from one *ḥāl* to a *ḥāl* that was higher, he gained a vantage point on the *ḥāl* he had left behind, and, in relation to his new position, his former one was darkness. His *ḥāl*s were eternally advancing.

3.1. Infinite are the possibilities in God of subtle and more subtle experience. If the truth of the truth which is God most high is glory, and if to arrive at Him in truth is impossible, then God's slave is eternally advancing in his *ḥāl*s. There is no point which he can reach for which there is not within God's compass a higher possibility which God can bring him to. According to this insight is the Ṣūfī saying interpreted: 'The virtues of the pious are the sins of the advanced.' Junayd was asked about this and recited the following verse:

Transient lights, they gleam when they appear,
They tell of union, mysteries they make clear.

III On satisfaction (riḍā)

1. God says, *God is satisfied with them and they with Him* (Q 5/119).

2. ʿAlī ibn Aḥmad al-Ahwāzī informed us, saying that Aḥmad ibn ʿUbayd al Baṣrī related to him from al-Karīmī, who said that Yaʿqūb ibn Ismāʿīl al-Sallāl related to him from Abū ʿĀṣim al-ʿAbādānī, who had it from al-Faḍl ibn ʿĪsā al-Raqqāshī, from Muḥammad ibn al-Munkadir, from Jābir, that the prophet of God said the following.

   While the people of paradise were engaged in a discussion, there appeared to them at the gate of paradise a light. They raised their heads, and beheld the Lord looking down on them. 'People of paradise,' He said, 'ask of me anything.' 'We ask of you satisfaction with us.' 'My satisfaction has already settled you in my house, and given you my bounty. This is the time of its fulfilment, so ask again.' 'We ask you for more of the same.' They were brought stallions of red ruby with trappings of green emerald and red ruby. They rode on the stallions, who moved their hooves with the utmost grace. And God commanded trees laden with fruit. And maidens came, brown-eyed maidens, saying, 'We are soft, free of harshness; we are eternal, undying, partners to a people who are believers and noble.' And God commanded heaps of white musk, sweetly smelling, and it evoked in them a perfume which was called evocation. Finally the horses brought them to the Garden of Eden, which is the citadel of paradise. And the angels said, 'Lord, the people have arrived.' 'Welcome, righteous ones,' said the Lord, 'welcome, obedient ones.' And the veil for them was drawn aside and they looked upon God and enjoyed the light of the Merciful, so each saw not the other. Then He said, 'Escort them to their palaces, with gifts.' So they returned, and each saw the other. That, said the prophet, is the meaning of God's word, *Hospitality from a merciful, a generous [host]* (Q 41/32).

3. The Iraqis and the Khurasanis are in dispute on the question of *riḍā*, as to whether it is a *ḥāl* or a *maqām*. The people of Khurasan say that *riḍā* is one of the *maqām*s and that it comes at the end of *tawakkul* (reliance). The meaning of this is that it is to be interpreted as something accessible to God's slave through his own act of acquisition. As to the Iraqis, they say that *riḍā* is one of the *ḥāl*s. It is not an acquisition by the worshipper; rather it is a gift that alights in the heart, like all the *ḥāl*s.

   The two views may be reconciled by asserting that the beginning of *riḍā* is an acquisition by the worshipper, and it is, at that stage, a *maqām*. But its end is a *ḥāl* and is not an acquisition.

4. The mystics have spoken much on *riḍā*, each one expressing his own situation and experience. They are varied in the manner of their expression, as they are diverse in their experience and share of *riḍā*. But the basic condition of knowledge, that which cannot be done without, is this, that he alone has *riḍā* who does not oppose God's decree.

   I have heard the master Abū ʿAlī al-Daqqāq say that it is not *riḍā* merely that you should not feel that there is vicissitude, rather that you should not oppose God's predestinary decree. What is required of God's slave is that he should feel *riḍā* in the divine decree in so far as he has been commanded so to feel. Not all that is by God's decree is required or permitted to evoke *riḍā* in God's slave: he should not feel *riḍā* at the sins of humans or the trials visited on the Muslims.

5. The sages have said that *riḍā* is God's high gateway, meaning that one who is honoured with *riḍā* has found the most generous welcome, has been honoured with the highest status.

   I heard Muḥammad ibn al-Ḥusayn (al-Sulamī) say that Abū Jaʿfar al-Rāzī related to him that al-ʿAbbās ibn Ḥamza related to him, that Ibn Abī ʾl-Ḥawārī related to him that ʿAbd al-Wāḥid ibn Zayd said that *riḍā* is God's high gateway and the paradise of this world.

6. Know that the slave can scarcely feel *riḍā* with God except after God feels *riḍā* with him, for God has said, *God is satisfied with them and they with Him* (Q 5/119).

   I heard from the master Abū ʿAlī al-Daqqāq that a pupil said to his master, 'Can the slave know that God has *riḍā* with him?' 'No,' he replied. 'How can one know that, since his *riḍā* is of the invisible world?' 'But the saint knows,' said the pupil. 'How so?' 'If I find that my heart has *riḍā* with God, I know that He has *riḍā* with me.' 'You have spoken well, O my servant,' said the teacher.

7. The tale is told that Moses said, 'O my God, guide me to deeds that, when accomplished, will evoke in You *riḍā* with me.' 'You cannot bear that,' said the Lord. Moses fell prostrate before the Lord, beseeching him. So God spoke directly to him, 'O son of ʿImrān, My satisfaction (*riḍā*) lies in your satisfaction with My decree.'

   The shaykh Abū ʿAbd al-Raḥmān al-Sulamī told us that Abū Jaʿfar al-Rāzī said that al-ʿAbbās ibn Ḥamza related that Ibn Abī ʾl-Ḥawārī related that he heard Abū Sulaymān al-Dārānī say the following. When the slave forgets his own desires, he has acquired *riḍā*. I heard him say that he had heard al-Naṣrābādhī say, 'He who desires to attain the quality of *riḍā*, let him cling to that wherein God has placed His *riḍā*.'

8.5 Hujwīrī on drunkenness and sobriety

Abū ʾl-Ḥasan ʿAlī ibn ʿUthmān al-Jullābī al-Hujwīrī was born in Ghazna and settled eventually in Lahore, where he wrote the *Kashf al-maḥjūb*. As his sole-surviving work, this is the main source of information about his life. The contents of the *Kashf al-maḥjūb* suggest that he was first and foremost a Ṣūfī, one who had also received a traditional scholastic education in theology. Hujwīrī's teacher in Ṣūfism was probably the relatively little-known Abū ʾl-Faḍl al-Khuttalī, whom he describes as his role model on the Ṣūfī path. The *Kashf al-maḥjūb* also alludes to meetings with other Ṣūfī teachers, during travels in an area extending from Syria (where Khuttalī was based) to the Punjab. Hujwīrī died in Lahore where his shrine is today the most celebrated pilgrimage destination. The dates given traditionally for his death are 456/1063–4 and 464/1071.

The *Kashf al-maḥjūb* is the oldest surviving work of its kind written in Persian. Similar to Qushayrī's *Risāla,* it is a dual-generic work, covering both the *ṭabaqāt* (biography collection) and manual genres. While sections one and three are made up of thematic chapters, section two consists mostly of biographies. The biographies are grouped into chapters in an overall chronological pattern, from the companions of the prophet until Hujwīrī's own contemporaries, including Khuttalī. They are followed by an innovative chapter on contemporary Ṣūfīs. This divides his contemporary Ṣūfīs into twelve particular groups, by presenting what are mostly contentious issues related to Ṣūfism as their distinctive doctrines. It seems to be largely of Hujwīrī's own construction.

In this context, the *Ṭayfūriyya* (named after Abū Yazīd Ṭayfūr al-Basṭāmī, d. 261/865) and the *Junaydiyya* (named after Abū ʾl-Qāsim al-Junayd, d. 297/910) are said to follow the doctrines of drunkenness (*sukr*) and sobriety (*ṣaḥw*) respectively. The relative merits of such approaches are presented in the specially devoted section, translated below, which is sandwiched between the brief accounts of each of these two groups. This lengthy discussion of an issue of debate is typical of Hujwīrī's method of presenting contentious topics, in that, despite making categorical statements in favour of one and in opposition to the other group, he none the less strives to accommodate both viewpoints. He achieves this ultimately by distinguishing between positive and negative types of both drunkenness and sobriety. This passage illustrates Hujwīrī's distinctive preference to present reasoned arguments, however inconsistent they may sometimes be, rather than to rely primarily on citing past authorities. It also reveals his overriding interest in the Ṣūfī theory of annihilation and subsistence in God, through his association of drunkenness and sobriety with those experiences. This passage also represents a key stage in the development of the belief that Abū Yazīd and Junayd represented opposite poles of Ṣūfism, for it is the first time that they are associated with doctrines of 'drunkenness' and 'sobriety', an association which would become firmly established in the later Ṣūfī tradition.

Further reading

G. Böwering, 'Hojviri, Abu 'l-Ḥasan 'Ali ibn 'Oṯmān,' *Encyclopaedia Iranica*.
Jawid A. Mojaddedi, *The biographical tradition in Sufism: the ṭabaqāt genre from al-Sulamī to Jāmī*, Richmond 2001, chapter 5.
—— 'Getting drunk with Abū Yazīd or staying sober with Junayd: the creation of a popular typology of Sufism,' *Bulletin of the School of Oriental and African Studies*, 66 (2003).
R. A. Nicholson (trans.), *The Kashf al-mahjub: the oldest Persian treatise on Sufiism*, Leiden/London 1911 (second edn 1936), republished as *The revelation of the mystery*, intro. Carl W. Ernst, Westport CT 1999. This translation is based on a single manuscript which appears to be deficient in significant parts of the work; this can be witnessed by comparing the translation presented here with its corresponding translation (pp. 184–8 of the 1936 second edition).
Annemarie Schimmel, *Islam in the Indian subcontinent*, Leiden 1980.

Source text

'Alī Hujwīrī, *Kashf al-maḥjūb*, ed. V. Zhukovski, reprint Tehran 1993 (first published St Petersburg 1899), pp. 230–4.

Discussion of drunkenness and sobriety

1. You should know that 'drunkenness' (*sukr*) and 'rapture' (*ghalaba*) are expressions that those with knowledge of spiritual truths have used for the rapture experienced through love of God, while 'sobriety' (*ṣaḥw*) is an expression for attainment of the goal. They have discussed these issues extensively; one group reckons that sobriety is better than drunkenness, while another group disagrees, holding the view that drunkenness is better than sobriety.

2. Abū Yazīd (Basṭāmī) belongs to the second group. His followers say that sobriety causes the reinforcement and balance of human attributes which is the greatest of veils before God. Drunkenness causes the reduction of blemishes and human attributes, the loss of one's will and freedom to choose, as well as the annihilation of one's self-control for the sake of subsistence in a higher potentiality, one that exists inside one and in opposition to one's own human nature, and which is more perfect, advanced and complete than that.

2.1. David was in the state of sobriety when God attributed His own action to His prophet, *David killed Goliath* (Q 2/252); Muṣṭafā (Muḥammad) was in the state of drunkenness when God attributed to Himself one of His prophet's actions, *You did not throw when you threw, but God threw* (Q 8/17). What a difference between the two slaves: the one who subsists in himself and is affirmed by his own attributes when it is said, 'You did it yourself as a miracle,' and the one who subsists in God, his own attributes having been annihilated, to whom it is said, 'We did what we did.' Thus the attribution of the servant's own action to God is better than the attribution of God's action to the servant, for if God's action is attributed to the servant then he subsists in himself, while if the servant's action is attributed to God he subsists in God. When the servant subsists in himself it is like when David glanced at Ūriyā''s wife when he shouldn't have and saw what he saw, while when the servant subsists in God it is like when Muṣṭafā glanced once at a woman like that, which was forbidden for men. This is because the former was in sobriety, while the latter was in drunkenness.

3. Those who prefer sobriety to drunkenness include Junayd. His followers say that drunkenness is a blemish since it causes a disturbance of one's state, the loss of soundness and reduction of self-control. The basis of all spiritual affairs is seeking, either by means of one's annihilation or one's subsistence, by one's effacement or one's affirmation, and if one's state lacks soundness there is no point to it because the hearts of the seekers of God must be stripped of all impressions. By blinding oneself one can never find release from the grip of worldly things, or escape their baneful effects. The reason why people remain preoccupied with things other than God is that they fail to see them for what they are: if they saw them properly they would escape.

3.1. There are two types of correct vision: one is to see a thing with an eye to its subsistence and the other with an eye to its annihilation. If you behold with an eye to its subsistence you see that all things must be deficient in their subsistence for they do not subsist in themselves in their state of subsistence. If you behold with an eye to its annihilation you see that all existent things must be annihilated in God's subsistence. Both of these characteristics will turn you away from existent things, and that's why the prophet asked in his supplication, 'O God, show me things as they are' – whoever sees finds peace. This is also the meaning of God's words, *Consider well, those of you with discerning vision* (Q 59/2) – so long as one does not see, one does not become free. None of this can be achieved except in the state of sobriety, and the proponents of drunkenness do not have an inkling about it. For instance, Moses in drunkenness could not bear the revelation of one theophany and consequently lost his wits, while the messenger of God in a state of sobriety travelled from Mecca as far as 'two bows' length away' in the heart of a theophany, and each moment he became more aware and conscious:

> Glass after glass I drank wine till I burst,
> It neither made me drunk nor quenched my thirst!

4. My own shaykh, who was of the Junaydian school, used to say that drunkenness is the playground of children while sobriety is the place of the annihilation of men. I, ʿAlī ibn ʿUthmān al-Jullābī, say in agreement with my shaykh that the perfection of the state of the possessor of drunkenness is sobriety, and the least degree of sobriety provides vision of the deficiency of mankind. Therefore, a sobriety which highlights inadequacies is better than a drunkenness which is itself an inadequacy.

4.1. It is related that Abū ʿUthmān Maghribī in the beginning withdrew into the desert for twenty years, not hearing any human voice until his body had wasted away and his eyes had become as small as the eye of a needle, such that he no longer resembled a human. After the twenty years he was instructed to associate with people. He thought to himself that he should begin by associating with the devotees of God and those who live next to his house as this would be more blest. He headed for Mecca, where the shaykhs were made aware in their hearts that he would be arriving, and came out to welcome him. They found that he had transformed in appearance, hardly resembling a living creature anymore. They asked, 'Bū ʿUthmān, for twenty years you've lived in such a manner that Adam and his progeny are at a loss to understand your condition. Tell us why you went, what you saw, what you found and why you returned.' He answered, 'I went in drunkenness, I saw the harm caused by drunkenness, I found despair and I came back helpless.' The shaykhs all said, 'Bū ʿUthmān after you it is forbidden for anyone to talk about sobriety and drunkenness, for you have done the subject justice by showing the harm caused by drunkenness.'

4.2. Therefore drunkenness is simply to imagine that you have been annihilated while your attributes remain, thus representing a veil. However, sobriety is seeing your subsistence in God while your attributes are annihilated, which is the ultimate unveiling. In short, if someone asserts that drunkenness is closer to annihilation than sobriety this is absurd, because drunkenness is an attribute over and above sobriety; so long as the servant's attributes increase he remains clueless, but when they decrease the seekers can nurse hope for annihilation. This is the climax of their experience in drunkenness and sobriety.

5. The following story has been passed down about Abū Yazīd, which has been interpreted the wrong way around: Yaḥyā ibn Muʿādh wrote a letter to him, asking, 'What do you say regarding someone who becomes drunk with one drop of the sea of love?' Bāyazīd wrote in response, 'What do you say regarding someone who, if all the oceans of the world were to become the wine of love, would drink them all and still scream out about being thirsty?'

5.1. People assume that Yaḥyā has alluded to drunkenness and Bāyazīd to sobriety. The opposite is the case for the sober one is the one who cannot bear a drop, while the drunk is the one who, in drunkenness, drinks everything and still needs more, since drinking is the means of prolonging drunkenness. It is more fitting for like to pair with like. Sobriety is opposed to drunkenness; it is not compatible with drink.

6. Drunkenness is of two types, the first by the wine of affection and the second by the cup of love. The drunkenness of affection has a secondary cause for it is produced by vision of personal benefit. The drunkenness of love is without such a cause for it is produced by vision of God, the benefactor Himself. Therefore whoever sees the benefit, sees by means of Himself and therefore sees himself, while whoever sees the benefactor, sees through him and so does not see himself. Although the latter is in drunkenness, his drunkenness is [actually] sobriety.

7. Sobriety is also of two types: one is sobriety through heedlessness, and the other is the sobriety of love. A sobriety which is related to heedlessness is the greatest of veils, and a sobriety which is related to love is the clearest of unveilings. Therefore the one which is associated with heedlessness, although it is sobriety, it is actually drunkenness, while the one which is linked with love, although it is drunkenness it is actually a sobriety. When the foundation is firm then sobriety is like drunkenness and drunkenness like sobriety. When that foundation is missing they are both worthless.

8. In short, sobriety and drunkenness are in the path of men, caused by diversity. When the Sultan of Truth shows his beauty sobriety and drunkenness both appear to be intruders, since they are interconnected, the end of one representing the beginning of the other. Beginnings and ends exist only where there is separation, and those things which belong to separation are all judged equal. Union is the elimination of separations, regarding which the poet says,

   When morning breaks above the star of potent wine
   Sober and drunk shall stand as equals at that time.

9. In Sarakhs there were two Ṣūfī masters, Luqmān and Abū 'l-Faḍl Ḥasan. One day Luqmān approached Abū 'l-Faḍl and found him with a notebook in his hand, so he said, 'O Abū 'l-Faḍl, what are you seeking with a notebook?' He replied, 'The same thing you are seeking by abandoning notebooks!' Luqmān asked, 'So why are we at odds?' Abū 'l-Faḍl answered, 'You're the one who sees a dispute between us because you asked me what I was seeking! Sober up from this drunkenness and release yourself from sobriety, so that the dispute will disappear and you will come to know what it is that we are both seeking!'

8.6 Rūmī and the *Mathnawī*

Jalāl al-Dīn Muḥammad Rūmī was born in 604/1207 in Balkh, in what is now northern Afghanistan. His father, Bahā' Walad, was a popular preacher and teacher of the religious sciences as well as a Ṣūfī, and Jalāl al-Dīn followed in his footsteps in each of these areas. Around 610/1213, the approach of the Mongols prompted Bahā' Walad to flee Balkh with his family. They eventually settled in Konya, in present-day Turkey, which is why Jalāl al-Dīn, who spent most of the remainder of his life there, became known as Rūmī ('of the West'). In 642/1244, a wandering mystic from Tabriz called Shams al-Dīn arrived in Konya and started a much celebrated teacher–student relationship with Rūmī which changed the course of his life. From dry scholarship and pious exhortations, Rūmī was inspired by Shams al-Dīn to write volumes of mystical poetry. Rūmī's intense relationship with Shams aroused jealousy and suspicion among his own students, and consequently, within a couple of years of arriving in Konya, Shams finally left without a trace.

Although he wrote a number of important prose works as well, Rūmī is best known for his poetry: the collection of thousands of ghazals, quatrains and other short pieces, which he entitled the *Dīwān-i Shams-i Tabrīz*, and his six-volume didactic work, the *Mathnawī*, which contains over 25,000 couplets in total. (Rūmī dedicated his own *Dīwān* of poetry to Shams-i Tabrīz as a gesture of his own annihilation in the love of his inspiring mentor.)

The *Mathnawī* was written during the 660s/1260s at the request of Rūmī's disciple Ḥosām al-Dīn Chalabī. The title of this work is the generic name for its verse form, the *mathnawī*, or couplets following the rhyme pattern *aabbccdd* and so on. Before Rūmī, the Persian poets Sanā'ī and 'Aṭṭār had established the *mathnawī* as an effective form in which to write didactic Ṣūfī poetry, but Rūmī's work is considered the supreme example.

Like other mystical *mathnawī*s, it consists mostly of stories that serve to illustrate the specific teachings of Ṣūfism. Not having a frame-narrative, they appear to be held together relatively loosely without any obvious principle of order. The characters of Rūmī's stories, which are mostly based on those recounted in earlier written sources, range from prophets and kings to shepherds and slaves, and often animals also feature. Rūmī is renowned for his ability to expound and illustrate mystical doctrines through the description of everyday situations. His *Mathnawī* is also distinctive for the frequency with which he breaks off from narratives in order to comment on, or expand, a specific point – often at great length and through further, shorter narratives – suggesting that for him the importance of the message far outweighed stylistic concerns.

While it has been described as 'the Qur'ān in Persian' by the fifteenth-century Ṣūfī poet 'Abd al-Raḥmān Jāmī, the *Mathnawī* has also been influential on Turkish literature and culture, since most of Rūmī's successors in the Mevlevī Ṣūfī order came from the region where he settled rather than his homeland. Rūmī died in 1272 in Konya, where his shrine today is one of the most popular pilgrimage sites in the whole Islamic world. His successors named their order 'Mevlevi' after him, for they referred to him as Mevlana, 'Our master', but they are better known in the West today as the 'whirling dervishes' because of the unique form of dance which they perform for worship.

The translations offered here include the famous first eighteen couplets, which Rūmī is said to have composed before being asked to write a *mathnawī* work, two narratives, describing the early Ṣūfī Bāyazīd (Abū Yazīd) Basṭāmī encountering a poor old Ṣūfī shaykh and Moses encountering a simple shepherd, respectively. Also included is a passage on the necessity of following a guide on the Ṣūfī path, which refers to the archetypal teacher–student relationships between Muḥammad and 'Alī, and between Khiḍr and Moses, to which the relationship between Shams-i Tabrīz and Rūmī would be added in the later Ṣūfī tradition.

Further reading

Franklin Lewis, *Rumi: past and present, east and west*, Oxford 2000.

R. A. Nicholson, *The Mathnawi of Jalal'uddin Rumi*, London 1925.

Rumi, *The Masnavi: Book 1*, trans. Jawid Mojaddedi, Oxford World's Classics Series, Oxford forthcoming.

Annemarie Schimmel, *The triumphal sun: a study of the works of Jalāloddin Rumi*, second edition, Albany NY 1993.

Source text

Jalāl al-Dīn Muḥammad Rūmī, *The Mathnawi of Jalal'uddin Rumi,* ed. R. A. Nicholson, London 1925, Persian text vol. 1, vv. 1–18 (part I); vol. 1, vv. 2943–80 (part II); vol. 2, vv. 1720–96 (part III); and vol. 2, vv. 2218–51 (part IV). This is still the most readily accessible edition and offers the advantage of a line-by-line literal prose translation to refer to, not to mention extensive commentary for books 1 to 4. The translations offered here employ rhyme and metre in order to convey the musicality and pithy, aphoristic form of the Persian original, through an equivalent English verse form, heroic couplets. Earlier versions have appeared in a different format in the journal *Sufi* (2000–2).

I The song of the reed

Now listen to this reed-flute's sad lament
About the heartache being apart has meant:
'Since from the reed-bed they uprooted me
My song's expressed each human's agony,
A breast which separation split in two
Provides the breath to share this pain with you:
Those kept apart from their own origin
All long to go back to rejoin their kin;
Amongst the crowd to mourn alone's my fate,
With good and bad I've learnt to integrate,
That we were friends each one was satisfied,
But none sought out my secrets from inside:
My deepest secret's in this song I wail,

But eyes and ears can't penetrate the veil:
Body and soul are joined to form one whole,
But no one is allowed to see the soul.'
It's fire not air the reed-flute's mournful cry,
If you don't have this fire then you should die!
The fire of love is what makes reed-flutes pine,
Love's fervour thus gives potency to wine;
The reed consoles those forced to be apart,
Its melodies will open up your heart,
Where's antidote or poison like its song
Or confidant, or one who's pined so long?
This reed relates a tortuous path ahead,
Recounts the love with which Majnūn's heart bled:
The few who hear the truths the reed has sung
Have lost their wits so they can speak this tongue;
The day is wasted if it's spent in grief,
Consumed by burning aches without relief,
Good times have long passed, but we couldn't care
If you're with us our friend beyond compare!
While ordinary men on drops can thrive
A fish needs oceans daily to survive:
The way the ripe must feel the raw can't tell,
My speech must be concise, and so farewell!

II *The Ṣūfī guide*

Follow the journey's guide, don't go alone,
The path is filled with trials that chill the bone!
Even on routes which numerous times you've used
Without a guide you're hopelessly confused,
Beware now of this path you've not yet tried!
Don't go alone, keep focused on your guide!
If you're not safe in his protective shade
The ghoul's deep wails will leave you stunned, afraid,
Diverting you straight into further harm,
Much shrewder men than you could not keep calm;
Heed the Qur'ān on those who went astray
And how the wicked Satan made them pay:
He lured them all a thousand miles from here,
Reducing them to nakedness and fear.
Look at their bones and hair, and now take heed,
Don't be an ass, don't let your passions lead!
Grab hold of its thick neck and pull it back
Away from lust towards the guide's own track,
If left alone this donkey's bound to stray
Towards the field with golden mounds of hay,
Don't you forget to hold with force its leash,

Or it will bolt for miles to find hashish!
A donkey stoned – what greater enemy!
That donkey's ruined countless, can't you see?
If you're unsure of what's correct, just do
The opposite of what it wants to do,
'Consult them, then do just the opposite!
Or else you'll always be regretting it.'
Don't ever tolerate your carnal lust,
They'll lead you off the path, betray your trust, (Q 38/26)
While nothing conquers passion better than
The company of fellow travellers can:
The prophet summoned ʿAlī to his side,
'Hey, lion of God, brave hero of my pride,
Don't count on courage on its own to cope,
Take refuge also in the tree of hope:
Enter the realm of that pure intellect
Whom no opponent can from truth deflect.
Just like Mount Qāf, he reaches to the sky
His spirit like the Simorgh soars so high,
We could continue with this man's applause
Until the end of time without a pause,
He is the sun, though human to our sight,
Please understand that "God knows best what's right."
ʿAlī, in preference to all pious deeds
Follow the one whom God's direction leads,
Others persist with acts of piety,
Hoping to flee their egos' tyranny,
Take refuge here instead with this true guide,
Just leave the hidden enemy aside!
Of all the acts of worship it's the best,
It makes you far superior to the rest.'
If he accepts, surrender to the guide
Like Moses, who with Khidr once had tried,
Stay calm, don't question what he should commit,
So he won't say, *Enough, Now we must split!* (Q 18/8)
If he destroys their boat, don't you go wild,
Don't tear your hair out if he kills a child!
Since God has said this man's hand's like his own,
And, *Up above their hands rests God's alone*, (Q 48/15)
With God's own hand he slays the helpless boy,
To bring him back with new, eternal joy;
The few who tried this journey on their own
The guide still helped, they didn't walk alone:
His helping hand's for all across the land,
It has to be then naught but God's own hand,
If he can stretch his help out far and wide
There's even more for those stood by his side,
If absent ones receive such gifts for naught

Imagine what those present shall be brought,
You can't compare his faithful followers
With those who choose to be mere onlookers;
Don't be too delicate when he's around,
As weak as water, crumbly like the ground,
If each blow leaves you bitter don't expect
Without pain like a mirror to reflect.

III Moses and the shepherd

Once Moses overheard a shepherd pray:
'O you whose every whim we all obey,
Where do you live that I might meet you there
To mend your battered shoes and comb your hair,
To wash your clothes and kill the lice and fleas,
To serve you milk to sip from when you please,
To kiss your little hand, to rub your feet,
To sweep your bedroom clean and keep it neat?
I'd sacrifice my herd of goats for you,
This loud commotion proves my love is true.'
He carried on in this deluded way,
So Moses asked, 'What's that I hear you say?'
'I speak to my creator there on high,
The one who also made the earth and sky.'
Moses replied, 'You've truly lost your way,
You've given up the faith and gone astray,
It's gibberish and babble stupid twit,
You'd better learn to put a cork in it!
Your blasphemy pollutes the atmosphere
And tears to shreds that silk of faith so sheer,
While socks and shoes might be superb for you
How can they fit the sun, have you a clue?
If you don't shut your mouth immediately
A fire will burn up all humanity.
You don't believe? Then please explain this smoke,
And why your soul turned black when you just spoke!
If you're aware that He is God, our Lord,
Why act familiar when that is abhorred?
Friendship like this is worse than enmity,
The Lord's above such acts of piety,
For family friends reserve your generous deeds,
God has no body, nor material needs:
Milk is for babies, who must drink to grow,
And shoes for those with feet, as you must know;
Even when you address his chosen slave
Select your words with care, don't misbehave,
Since God has said, "I'm him and he is Me.

'When I was ill you never came to see':
He wasn't left alone with his disease
That servant who 'through Me both hears and sees'."
Don't talk to saints without the reverence due
It blocks your heart, and blots your record too;
If you address a man by Fāṭima's name
Though man and woman are inside the same
He'll still seek vengeance for it, if he can,
Even if he's a calm and patient man,
That glorious name which women all revere
Can wound a man more deeply than a spear;
While feet and hands are great for you and me
They'd just contaminate God's purity,
He was not born, nor does the Lord beget, (Q 112/3)
But reproducing beings are in his debt:
Those with a body once were born – that's sense,
Creation must stay this side of the fence,
That's all because we wither and decay,
Unlike our source we're bound to fade away.'
The shepherd said, 'Your words have struck me dumb,
Regret now burns my soul, and I feel numb.'
He breathed a heavy sigh and rent his cloak,
Then in the desert disappeared like smoke.
A revelation came down instantly:
'Why did you turn a slave away from Me?
Your mission's to unite all far and wide,
Is it instead your preference to divide?
As far as possible don't separate,
"Above all else divorce is what I hate",
I've given each one his own special ways
And his unique expressions when he prays:
One person's virtue is another's sin,
His meat might seem like poison, listening in;
I stand immune to all impurity,
Men's pride and cunning never bother Me,
I don't command for My own benefit,
But so My slaves themselves can gain from it;
For Indians their own dialect seems best,
But folk from Sindh think Sindhi's much more blest,
I'm not made any purer by their praise,
Their own impurities these prayers erase,
And I pay no attention to their speech
But their intention and the heights they reach:
Pure, humble hearts within are what I seek
Regardless of the haughty way they speak.'
The heart's the essence, words are mere effects,
The heart's what counts, the cackle he neglects!
I'm tired of fancy terms and metaphors,

I want a soul which burns so much it roars!
It's time to light one's heart with pure desire,
Burn thought and contemplation with this fire!
How far apart the meek and well-behaved
From ardent lovers who may seem depraved!
Each moment lovers burn themselves away:
A ruined village has no tithes to pay,
Don't pick at faults and call him a disgrace,
Don't wash the blood upon love's martyr's face!
His blood exceeds your water's cleanliness:
This martyr's blemish beats all righteousness;
Those at the Kaʿba scrap the *qibla* rule:
What use are boots to divers in the pool?
You don't seek guidance from those drunken men,
So why insist they mend their rags again?
The lovers stand beyond religion's hold,
From God himself truth's creed and laws they're told:
If rubies have no seal stamped there's no harm,
Midst seas of grief love stays serene and calm.
Then in the depths of Moses God concealed
Such secrets that can never be revealed,
Into his heart poured words, pure and refined,
Transparent just like speech and sight combined,
He lost his wits and then found them anew,
From pre- to post-eternity he flew,
I'd just waste time by trying to explain,
It's far beyond the ordinary brain:
This mystery would blow your brain to bits,
While writing it the firmest pencil splits;
Moses, on hearing God's reproach, just ran
Towards the desert searching for that man:
He followed footprints that the shepherd laid,
Scattering dust throughout the track he'd made,
Footprints of drunkards are a special kind
Distinct from those the sober leave behind:
He starts just like a rook, steps straight ahead,
Then bishop-like diagonally instead,
Sometimes just like a wave's crest rising high
And then as if a fish has slithered by,
Occasionally he'd write his thoughts in sand
Like fortune-tellers reading what is planned,
At last when Moses found the shepherd there
He gave the message, 'God's decree is fair,
Don't bother with mere custom anymore
But let your heart express what's in its core!
True faith salutes your infidelity,
Through you the world has found security,
Absolved by God *whose will must be fulfilled* (Q 14/27)

Scream out, without the fear that you'll be killed!'
The shepherd said, 'I've gone beyond that stage,
My heart's blood cannot still this thirst assuage,
I've even passed that tree at heaven's end
A thousand spheres beyond – I still ascend:
You cracked the whip and made my stallion vault
Above the heavens with a somersault!
For spurring me towards divinity
God bless that hand which cracked the whip for me!
Right now my state's beyond what tongues can say,
What I've described gives just a glimpse away.'
The image in the mirror that you see
Is yours, and not the mirror's property,
The breath inside the reed its player has blown
Is just a tiny portion of his own,
Whenever you give praise to God, beware
It's worth no more than this poor shepherd's prayer!
You might suppose your own immaculate,
But still for God they're all inadequate,
So when the veil is lifted don't protest:
'What's now revealed we never could have guessed!'

IV The pilgrimage of Bāyazīd

For Mecca Bāyazīd one day set out
To make the pilgrimage, to be devout,
At every town he passed along the way
He'd seek what local sages had to say:
He'd wander asking, 'Who here has the light?
Who only leans on truth's supporting might?'
God said, 'When on your travels always seek
The few who take from Me each word they speak!'
Seek treasure, shun the world of gain and loss,
This world is second-best, no more than dross!
In hope of wheat whoever sows his seeds
Soon finds his field has also sprouted weeds,
But if it's weeds you sow no wheat will rise,
Seek masters of the heart, the meek and wise!
Head for the Kaʿba when it's time to go
And you'll see Mecca too, as all must know:
God was, on his *miʿrāj*, the prophet's aim,
He saw the throne and angels all the same.
A new disciple built a house one day,
The master passed and saw it on his way,
He questioned the disciple as a test,
Knowing that his intentions were the best:
'Why did you put a window over here?'

'To let the light come in to make things clear.'
'That's secondary, it's not like breathing air,
Your primary need's to hear the call to prayer!'
While travelling Bāyazīd searched far and wide
To find his epoch's Khidr, the perfect guide,
He found him like a crescent hunched and pale,
Majestic, speaking just like those we hail,
His heart like sunshine though his eyes were blind
Like elephants seeing India in their mind:
Countless delights are seen with eyes shut tight,
But when they're opened none are seen in light!
While you're asleep the mysteries are shown
Your heart's a window viewing the unknown,
The mystic even dreams when wide awake,
Prostrate and feel the ground beneath him shake!
So Bāyazīd then asked him, 'How are you?'
The man was poor and had a family too,
'O Bāyazīd, why did you take this road?
Where is it that you're carrying that load?'
'To *ḥajj*, since day-break I've been travelling.'
'For your expenses how much did you bring?'
'Two hundred silver coins is all I've got,
I've tied them to this garment with a knot.'
'Just walk around me seven times right here,
That's better than the *ḥajj* for you, fakir!
Then hand your coins to me, you generous man,
Complete your *ḥajj*, fulfil your mission's plan!
You've run to Ṣafā, entered purity,
You've done the *ʿumra*, live eternally!
He judges me much loftier, I swear,
Than that mere house of bricks they flock to there:
That Kaʿba is the home of piety,
But I possess his deepest mystery,
Inside the Kaʿba no one's ever stepped
And none but God will my pure heart accept,
When you've seen me, you've seen the lord as well,
Truth's Kaʿba you've just circled, can't you tell?
To serve me is obeying God's decree
So don't suppose he's separate from me:
Open your inner eye, see if you can
Perceive the light of God inside a man!'
This wisdom pierced right into Bāyazīd,
Just like an earring, making him take heed,
For he had heard such wisdom from this friend
Enabling him to reach the journey's end.

8.7 Shāh Niʿmat Allāh Walī on the path to union

Sayyid Nūr al-Dīn b. ʿAbd Allāh Shāh Niʿmat Allāh Walī (730/1330–834/1430) was born in Aleppo, but spent most of his life in Persia, where he founded the Ṣūfī order named after him, the Niʿmat Allāhiyya. Shāh Niʿmat Allāh's teacher in Ṣūfism was the Yemenite shaykh ʿAbd Allāh Yāfiʿī (d. 768/1367). After succeeding Yāfiʿī and travelling widely, Shāh Niʿmat Allāh first settled in Transoxiana, where he quickly attracted a large following. However, the fame that he acquired resulted in his expulsion by Tamerlane, most likely on the advice of the Ṣūfīs in his entourage who belonged to the rival Naqshbandī order. After further travels, Shāh Niʿmat Allāh finally settled in the area of Kerman, in south-eastern Persia. His magnificent tomb in Mahan, just outside the city of Kerman, was built on the orders of the Bahmanid sultan Aḥmad Shāh, who had invited him to the Deccan. Shāh Niʿmat Allāh's son and successor, Shāh Khalīl Allāh, took up this invitation, and thus his successors all came to be based in the Deccan for some 250 years, until the order returned to its native Persia.

Shāh Niʿmat Allāh was himself a Sunnī, although, like the majority of Ṣūfīs, he also expressed a deep reverence for the family of the prophet, attributed to the twelve Imāms a special role in the path to sainthood (*wilāya*) and considered affiliation with regards to the law (*sharīʿa*) as secondary to affiliation in the Ṣūfī path (*ṭarīqa*). The Niʿmat Allāhī order has thus functioned in the context of both Sunnism and Shīʿism in Persia (before and after the Safavid dynasty). More recently, they have experienced an unprecedented revival in the secular Iran of the mid to late twentieth century, followed by a rapid spread to North America and Europe.

Shāh Niʿmat Allāh was a prolific writer of both prose and poetry. His surviving works reveal that he was heavily influenced by the Ṣūfī belief in the unity of being (*waḥdat al-wujūd*) as propounded by the followers of Ibn al-ʿArabī (d. 638/1240), on whose *Fuṣūṣ al-ḥikam* Shāh Niʿmat Allāh wrote his own commentary. His poetry strikes the reader as focusing on a combination of the theme of divine love prevalent in the poetry of Rūmī and the theme of the unity of being associated with Ibn al-ʿArabī.

The following three passages are taken from the 'treatises' (*rasāʾil*) of Shāh Niʿmat Allāh. Ranging from brief comments to lengthy discussions, these writings mostly consist of balanced rhyming clauses of poetic prose, frequently supported by verse. These three passages describe the Ṣūfī path to union through detachment, divine love and poverty, all of which are central themes in the Persian Ṣūfī writings of this period. It is clear that Shāh Niʿmat Allāh's treatment of them is based on the principle that God is Absolute Being, while everything else is His manifestation. Shāh Niʿmat Allāh's clear and succinct expositions shed light on a number of subtle paradoxes, such as the status of a Ṣūfī who utters statements like 'I am the Truth.'

Further reading

Hamid Algar, 'Niʿmat-Allāhiyya 1. The founder and the development of his order,' *Encyclopaedia of Islam*, new edition.

Jean Aubin, *Matériaux pour la biographie de Shah Niʿmatullāh Wali Kirmani*, Tehran and Paris 1983.
Terry Graham, 'Shāh Niʿmatullāh Walī: founder of the Niʿmatullāhī Ṣūfī order,' in L. Lewisohn (ed.), *The legacy of medieval Persian Sufism*, London and New York 1992, pp. 173–90.

Source text

Shāh Niʿmat Allāh Walī, *Rasāʾilhā*, ed. J. Nūrbakhsh, Tehran 1976, vol. 1, pp. 134–7 (part I), 167–70 (part II) and 208–15 (part III).

I Guidance for seekers

1. You must know that when the attachments and obstacles of created things are present the Sultan behind the curtain of the royal tent will not reveal the truths of His essence, behind the fine veil of His attributes and the subtle highlands of His acts, for the beggars in the lowlands of His effects, and that love of the futile is incompatible with love of God. Turn away from every changing thing until you find Him in all manifestations.

2. So turn away from everything and find thus what you seek.
Once you've abandoned everything He'll then reveal a cheek.

Necessarily, the seeker of God must turn away from futile essences, accidents and desires, and resolve to follow the path of love towards the Lord, not letting the dust of enjoyment of perceptibles, nor the dust of attachment, enter through the window of his senses, and not letting the dust of the oratory of his own existence rise up either, for the nurturing of blameworthy qualities and the strengthening of the commanding self is caused by all of that. The commands of the commanding self to commit hypocrisy seek authority without being entitled to it.

The mystical wayfarer must follow *Say, If you love God follow me so God may love you* (Q 3/31), and turn the commanding self from something that gives commands to something that follows them, and fulfil the order to *All of you turn to God* (Q 24/31) from the barren plains of egotistic ignorance and the deserts of bestial delusion – *They are like cattle, only worse* (Q 7/179) – and return in peace to the nearness to God possessed by mankind – *We have honoured the sons of Adam* (Q 17/70).

3. At this stage he's a regular renunciant.
He's an ascetic who still suffers greed and want.

The essence of asceticism is to renounce voluntarily both this world and the hereafter. As it has been said, 'Asceticism for those other than the mystic is a mere transaction: they buy the goods of the hereafter with the goods of this world. For the mystic it is to transcend what preoccupies his inner being from God and to rise above everything that is other than God.' So it is necessary to advance and not to stay fixed in the station of asceticism more than this, for the devil's whispering to one's soul is not cut off by sensual deprivation and the removal of greed.

> This is the rank of the beginners, friend,
> But those who don't know think that it's the end.

4. The others are like that, but the purest are like this:

   By day and by night, hidden and in the open, they strive to acquire noble characteristics, and, through the love of the drunkenness from witnessing the truth, they drink the wine of religious devotions from the goblet of spiritual exertion; they are preoccupied with cleansing and purifying their heart and soul, and, to the soothing melody of 'Love is what lasts, and any love which fades is not real love' in the tune of 'My sickness, and my cure!' they sing this song:

> Pain you inflict's the cure of those in agony
> And those who feel need and direct to you their plea.

4.1. These men of vision, who are the title-page of the scroll of detachment and the sermon in the exordium of the book of unicity, are drawn by the attraction of 'One of God's attractions to which the actions of men and jinn correspond.' They are the supreme truths in the world and the fulfilment of the essence of man, embellished outwardly with their fine conduct and adorned inwardly through their efforts on the mystical path. They have broken off from the futile to join with God, and like me they have flung off their shoulders the cloak of hypocrisy of humanity, to plunge like a drop into the sea of effacement in God; they have become annihilated from human characteristics and, by the decree of 'You were created with God's characteristics,' they have attained subsistence in divine attributes.

> Subsistent in God after self-annihilation
> He is the glass, the wine, the server and companion.

4.2. So understand this, and avoid making a mistaken assumption, like a bat that flies away from the nest of certainty and confirmation to the realm of doubt and rejection, by claiming that he is saying that he is God. He is the slave of God; he is separate from creation and for God his name is ʿAbd Allāh ('slave of God'), as God has said concerning the reality of his messenger, *Yet when the slave of God stands up* . . . (Q 72/19),

> Niʿmat Allāh's rank is precisely this,
> By God, it is a station of sheer bliss!

II On poverty

1. The messenger of God said, 'The *sharīʿa* is my words, the mystic path is my actions, the truth is my state, gnosis is my capital, intellect is my faith, love is my foundation, yearning is my vehicle, fear is my comrade, knowledge is my weapon, clemency is my companion, trust is my garment, contentment is my treasure, sincerity is my rank, certainty is my refuge, and poverty is my pride; I pride myself in it above all other achievements.' He also said, 'Poverty is to be black-faced in both worlds,' and 'Poverty almost reaches the point of being infidelity.'

2. Scholars have commented about each one of these sayings. Those who assert Divine unity (*muwaḥḥidān*) have also made allusions to them. The summary of all this is that real poverty is the non-existence of ownership; therefore, whenever a poor man reaches the point where he has absolutely no possessions left whatsoever, he has attained to true poverty and to the point of excelling other existents in this, for when the messenger of God said that poverty is pride he did not mean merely superficial poverty. In Mecca there were many people who were poor according to their appearance, but were not completely lacking possessions.

    2.1. The meaning of 'non-existence of ownership' is that the poor man has nothing that can be attributed to himself as a possession, to the extent that he becomes annihilated from himself, such that, 'The poor man does not need anything and nothing needs him.' This is the station of pure unity and absolute oneness, notwithstanding the fact that unity becomes confirmed each time an excess is shed, for 'Unity is the shedding of excesses.' This is the reason why it has been said, 'When poverty is perfected there is only God left.'

3. If we examine the saying, 'Poverty is to be black-faced in both worlds,' in this context what is meant by 'black' is the annihilation of the mystic wayfarer in both worlds, this world and the hereafter. This is because black is darkness, and wherever it is used it has the meaning of non-existence and annihilation, since God has said, *God is the patron of those who believe; He takes them out of darkness into light. The patrons of those who disbelieve are false deities; they take them out of light into darkness* (Q 2/257).

    3.1. Therefore, the meaning of true poverty is this, for true poverty cannot be established except through the annihilation of the mystic wayfarer in both worlds; this is the non-existence of ownership and the shedding of excesses, and all that has been attributed to him is shed from his own being and its dependencies, so that he has no possessions left at all. There is no doubt now that he is poor, and so he has attained to the rank of poverty, becoming 'white-faced' in this world and the hereafter. God has said, *Illustrious in this world and the hereafter and one of those who are brought near* (Q 3/45). Whoever has not attained these aforementioned characteristics and claims to have poverty is black-faced in this world and the hereafter. God said, *'Those of you whose faces have been blackened – did you disbelieve after having believed? Then taste the punishment for having disbelieved!'* (Q 3/106).

4. The saying, 'Poverty almost reaches the point of being infidelity,' means in essence that this kind of poverty gets close to infidelity. That is, since the end of true poverty is the non-existence of ownership and the shedding of excesses which have been attached to oneself, then nothing remains apart from the pure being of the one essence, for that is God's being. This compels the individual to say, 'Glory be to me! How glorious my station is!' and 'There is nothing inside my robe apart from God,' and 'I am the Truth.'

   4.1 It is clear that in the *sharīʿa*, on the basis of its outward form, it is infidelity, although in the *ṭarīqa* (mystic path) and the *ḥaqīqa* (truth-reality) it is true. We refer to their report, 'If something exceeds its limit, then its opposite is reflected.' Up to this point my speech has been a secret.

   The strong expression travels rapidly
   I fear the reins will slip away from me

   For the wise man the allusion suffices.

5. Since the end of poverty is the beginning of divinity and lordship, it is not the cause of infidelity. However, if the mystic wayfarer has attained perfection he knows that removing from view the existence of others and eliminating superficial possessions will not cause the attainment of divinity and the permanence of lordship and wealth, but rather it will cause his needlessness and withdrawal to last, and he will abide in the station of pure unity and absolute oneness. This is what is meant by poverty by the people of God. God knows what is correct, and it is to him that we return.

III Treatise on love

1. God said, *Say, If you love God follow me so God may love you* (Q 3/31). In the Torah it states, 'Sons of Adam, I truly am your lover, so you owe it to me to be my lover.' The messenger of God said, 'God is beautiful and He loves beauty.'

   Love is a station with divinity
   Love is much better than mere royalty.

2. This glorious station has four names:

   The first is *ḥubb*, so listen as you should
   From the beloved to what sounds so good.

   2.1 The sign of *ḥubb* is that the heart of the lover is free of the impurity of contingents and desires, and the lover must seek the beloved from the beloved and not look for anything else.

I speak these sweet words from the one I love,
Share secrets like companions in the cave;
If you seek the beloved from himself
You'll know the one whose perfect form I crave.

2.2 The next name is *wadd*, which is the demonstration of love: a thing of beauty is called the demonstration of love (*wadūd*) because it has been established on earth.

In love *wadūd* is very necessary
For the beloved gave such a decree.

God said, *The Merciful will give them* wadd (Q 9/96), meaning steadfastness in love to the hearts of his servants. This is the meaning of *wadd.*

2.3. The third is *ʿishq*, which is overflowing love. God said, *Those who believe love God intensely* (Q 2/165).

Love came and then the brain packed up and left.
It broke that vow that it had made and left.
When he saw that the king had entered drunk,
His poor old servant jumped straight up and left.

2.3.1. With the appearance of the light of the sun of jealousy of what is other than the burning of *ʿishq*, the lamp of the intellect loses its own light. When the power of the sultan of love seizes the throne of the royal court of the existence of the lover, with the sword of jealousy it annihilates everything else.

The fire of His fierce jealousy lights up
And with one breath burns other things all up.
'For others in this realm there is no space' –
He taught this Arabic through His pure grace.

2.3.2. *ʿIshq* is a pain which you can't know about unless you feel it, and if you read this *Treatise on Love* of mine with your intellect alone, you cannot understand. The term *ʿishq* is derived from the noun *ʿashaqa* [a vine which kills the tree it grows around], so whenever it grows around the tree of the existence of the lover,

It seizes him from his feet to his head.
That tree collapses when it's finally dead.

2.3.3. Since overflowing and excessiveness cannot be part of God's eternal attributes and *ʿishq* is excessive love according to experience, if you have experienced it that is, the terms *ʿishq* and *ʿāshiq* do not apply to God.

2.3.4. When the water of life of love flows in all the rivers of the spiritual forces and the streams of the bodily parts of the lover, and the fountainhead of being leads him to the crashings of the torrent of *ḥubb* in the seas of love,

> To us he is one of the lovers now,
> Immersed within the vast and boundless sea.
> With love of the beloved in his heart,
> Like soul in body flowing endlessly.

Any sound he hears, he hears from the beloved; any words he utters, he takes from the beloved; and in everything that he looks at he sees the beloved, and he seeks the beloved from the beloved.

> Bravo! This love is so superb and sweet.
> If you have it, come here so we can meet!

2.3.5. When the blood flowing in the veins of Zulaykha boiled and her heart screamed, in order to hold back depravity she began to bleed; each drop of blood which dripped on the tablet of the ground at that moment joined together to form the name of Joseph on that spot.

> When you have smeared your own blood by his door
> It's 'Joseph' that your heart writes on the floor.

2.4.
> The fourth term used for love's *hawā*, my friend,
> Something that's sweeter who can comprehend!

Hawā leads to the effacement of the will of the lover in the beloved, and the relationship with the beloved overwhelms at first whatever is in his heart.

> Whoever should possess such a *hawā*
> Has in his heart our very own *hawā*.

3. The cause of love is either beauty or beneficence. If it is beauty: 'God is beautiful and loves beauty.' If beneficence: 'Beneficence is not perfected except by God, and there is no beneficent one but God.'

> The path of love is one that leads this way,
> For love of Him you'll love the world today

4. On the evidence of 'The slave does not cease to approach me with supererogatory acts until I love him . . .', supererogatory acts are a cause of love, and supererogatory acts are an excess. The forms in the world are an excess in relation to being: supererogatory acts are loved by the beloved of God, just as the forms of the world are loved by God, the eternal beloved. The jealousy of the eternal beloved necessitates that he not love anything other than Himself, so consequently the reward is 'And when I love him I am the hearing with which he hears and the sight with which he sees.' My sight and hearing he bestows.

Glossary-Index

ʿAbbāsids	dynasty of caliphs ruling from 750, through the era of the flowering of Islam, and coming to a final end in 1258, although it had lost any meaningful power several centuries earlier with the rise of the Buwayhids. 19, 83
ʿAbd al-Jabbār	Muʿtazilī jurist, theologian, d. 415/1025. 152–4
Abū Bakr	first caliph after Muḥammad, d. 13/634. 26, 47–8, 74, 81, 84, 137, 149, 161
Abū Dāwūd	compiler of authoritative work of Sunnī *ḥadīth*, d. 275/889. 47–9
Abū Nuʿaym	Shāfiʿī school *ḥadīth* transmitter, Ṣūfī, d. 430/1038. 237–42
Abū ʿUbayd	theologian, *ḥadīth* and Qurʾān scholar, d. 224/838. 134–42
Abū Yazīd al-Basṭāmī	early Khurasanian Ṣūfī mystic, d. 261/874. 229, 233–4, 237–42, 248–51, 254, 260–1
ahl al-sunna waʾl-jamāʿa	'the people of the *sunna* and the community'; Sunnī Muslims. 134–5
akhbār	traditions; singular *khabar*. 151
ʿAlī ibn abī Ṭālib	Muḥammad's cousin and son-in-law, first Imām of the Shīʿa, fourth caliph after Muḥammad and foremost among his disciples according to the Ṣūfīs, assassinated 40/661. 20, 34, 55, 74, 85–7, 104, 111–3, 140–1, 161, 256
al-ʿAllāma al-Hillī	Shīʿī theologian, d. 726/1325. 166–9
asbāb al-nuzūl	'occasions of revelation' of the Qurʾān. 27, 73–9
aṣḥāb	'companions'; group members. 147–9
Ashʿarī	school of theology derived form al-Asdhʿarī, a theologian from Basra and Baghdad, d. 324/935–6. 121, 155, 159, 243
ʿaṣr	one of the daily five prayers, held in the mid-afternoon. 125
āya	verse of the Qurʾān; also used with the general meaning of 'sign' from God. 98
Barāhima	traditionally identified as the Brahmins of India; a theological group who held that prophecy was unnecessary and therefore impossible. 166–7, 169

basmala the statement 'In the name of God, the All-merciful, the All-compassionate'. 3, 82, 98

al-Bukhārī compiler of most important Sunnī collection of *ḥadīth*, d. 256/870. 39–47, 80–1, 102, 197

Burāq the winged creature which carried Muḥammad on his 'night journey' (*isrā'*) from Mecca to Jerusalem. 19–25

dār al-islām the 'house of Islam', the geographical area under the control of Muslim caliphs. 213

dhimmī a member of a protected community, especially referring to the Jews and Christians who live under Muslim rule. The right to practise their own religion was guaranteed by their payment of a special poll tax, the *jizya*. 50, 52, 90–3, 189, 213

Dhū 'l-Nūn Miṣrī early Ṣūfī from Egypt, considered the most authoritative of his generation, d. 248/862. 235, 240, 245

al-Fārābī philosopher based in Baghdad, d. 339/950. 166, 170–7

al-Farrā' grammarian, lexicographer, exegete from Kufa, d. 207/822. 108–10

Fāṭimids dynasty of Ismā'īlī caliphs who ruled over North Africa during the period 297–567/909–1171, establishing their capital in Cairo in 358/969. 83, 223

fatwā a reasoned legal response rendered by a *muftī* to a specific juristic question. 45, 186, 192–201, 203, 205–6

fiqh jurisprudence, the science of religious law, as described by the jurists known as the *fuqahā'*. 187, 192–3, 195

Fūrat al-Kūfī Shī'ī exegete from Kufa, d. ca 310/922. 111–13, 149, 186, 205, 214

furqān literally 'separator' or 'criterion', understood to be a name of the Qur'ān. 10

furū' the elements of religion (thus *furū' al-dīn*) within law and ritual which must be learned through study or followed according to the example of a learned person. 148, 187, 190, 207

Gehenna *jahannam*, one of the names of hell used in the Qur'ān. 7, 113, 117, 125–6, 132

al-Ghazālī theologian, philosopher, jurist, mystic, d. 505/1111. 150–1, 228–32

ḥadīth a tradition or written report, being the source material for the *sunna* of Muḥammad. 32–3, 36–58, 80, 97, 128, 137–41, 141, 143–5, 147–8, 166, 178, 180–2, 184, 186, 193–4, 197–8, 200, 202–3, 205–6, 208, 215, 234, 237

ḥāfiẓ one who has memorized the Qur'ān. 129–30, 238

ḥajj pilgrimage to Mecca performed in the month of Dhū'l-ḥijja, one of the 'five pillars' of Islam; a requirement for all Muslims, if they are able, once in a lifetime. 139, 181, 223, 261

ḥāl a temporary 'state' of spiritual experience bestowed by God in Ṣūfism. 243–47

ḥalāl that which is 'lawful' within Islamic law. 180–1, 189–90, 205, 224

hamza a letter in the Arabic alphabet (glottal stop). 110

ḥanīf the attribute, especially ascribed to Abraham in the Qur'ān, of being a sincere believer in God; derived from this word is the idea itself of early monotheism, *ḥanīfiyya* (and *ḥanafī* as an adjective). 129, 132

ḥarām that which is 'forbidden' within Islamic law. 180–1, 189–90, 198, 205

hijra	Muḥammad's migration from Mecca to Medina in the year 622 CE, understood as the date for the beginning of the Muslim *hijrī* calendar. 19, 136
Hujwīrī	mystic from Ghazna who settled in Lahore, d. between 456/1063–4 and 464/1071. 248–52
Ibn ʿAbbās	early authority in *ḥadīth* and exegesis, d.68/687. 19–26, 31, 34, 54, 75–8, 99–101, 116, 138
Ibn ʿAbd al-Barr	jurist of the Mālikī school in Spain, d. 463/1070. 178–84
Ibn ʿAṭiyya	Spanish traditionist and exegete, d. 541/1147. 80–2, 98–9, 101–2
Ibn Bābawayh	Shīʿī collector of *ḥadīth*, theologian, d. 381/991. 50–3
Ibn Ḥajar	*ḥadīth* scholar, teacher, judge, d. 852/1449. 42–6
Ibn Ḥazm	jurist, theologian, philosopher and poet from Spain, d. 456/1064. 202–6
Ibn al-Jawzī	jurist, theologian, historian from Baghdad, d. 597/1200. 159–62
Ibn Kathīr	preacher, scholar of law, *ḥadīth*, and Qur'ān of Damascus, d. 774/1373. 128–33
Ibn Qudāma	Ḥanbalī ascetic, jurist and theologian of Damascus, d. 620/1223. 185–91
Ibn Qutayba	Qur'ān and *ḥadīth* scholar from Kufa and Baghdad, d. 276/828. 147–9
Ibn Saʿd	traditionist, compiler of an early biographical dictionary, d. 230/845. 30–5, 84
ʿidda	the 'waiting period' required of a woman after divorce or death of a husband before remarriage. 58, 205
iʿjāz	doctrine which states that the Qur'ān cannot be imitated; the 'inimitability' of the Qur'ān. 98
ijmāʿ	'consensus', one of the four main sources of law in Sunnī Islam, the others being Qur'ān, *sunna*, and *qiyās*. 80, 149, 156–7, 186, 189, 203
ijtihād	the use of one's 'personal effort' in order to make a decision on a point of law not explicitly covered by the Qur'ān or the *sunna*; the person with the authority to do this is called a *mujtahid*. 185–196, 204–6
ikhtilāf	'difference of opinion' especially in legal matters. 202, 206–7, 210.
imām	literally the 'model', here generally referring to the prayer leader in the *ṣalāt* who stands in front of the rows of worshipers, keeping their actions in unison during the prayer. The word is also used in other contexts. It is a title of the revered early leaders of the Shīʿa who are the source of authority in that community; these Imāms are ʿAlī ibn abī Ṭālib and certain of his descendants who were designated as holding the position. The word is also commonly used as a title of the founders of the Sunnī schools of law - Abū Ḥanīfa, Mālik ibn Anas, al-Shāfiʿī and Ibn Ḥanbal - and similarly for other significant religious figures. 38, 50, 53, 101, 103–4, 111, 132, 158, 163–5, 187, 193–5, 208, 210, 212–13, 215, 216–27
Imāmī	generic name given to the largest group of the Shīʿa, the Ithnā ʿAshariyya ('Twelvers'). 163–5, 215–20
īmān	faith; one who has faith is a *mu'min*. 134–42, 144, 231
iʿrāb	the endings of words in Arabic which serve to make the syntactical function of those words apparent in a sentence. 97
Ismāʿīlī	branch of the Shīʿa with a distinct gnostic metaphysics; the name derives from their beliefs about the lineage of the Imāms which they

	see as passing through Ismāʿīl, the son of the sixth Imām Jaʿfar, who predeceased his father; also known as the Bāṭiniyya. 164, 223–7
isnād	the chain of authorities through whom a *ḥadīth* report has passed; the list of these people forms the first part of the *ḥadīth* report, the text which comes after it being called the *matn*. 30, 32, 47, 60, 97, 105, 164, 200–1, 237
isrāʾ	Muḥammad's 'night journey' to Jerusalem, connected to the heavenly ascension, *miʿrāj*. 19–26
istiʾdhān	asking permission to leave. 204–5
istiṣḥāb al-ḥāl	the principle by which a previously existing judicial situation was held to still exist unless it could be proven that it had ceased to exist or had been modified. 186
istiʿādha	the formulaic statement seeking protection from Satan said before reciting the Qurʾān. 98
jāhiliyya	the 'age of ignorance', historically seen to be before Muḥammad but in a general religious sense referring to ignoring, or ignorance of, Islam; especially used with moral overtones. 130, 136, 140, 200–1
jihād	'striving for the faith' or 'holy war', sometimes seen as a 'sixth pillar' of Islam. 38, 48, 137, 204, 221
jizya	a poll tax levied on non-Muslim males who were counted among the 'people of the book', usually Jews and Christians; see also *kharāj*. 90, 92, 209, 212–3, 222
al-Junayd, Abū 'l-Qāsim	Ṣūfī based in Baghdad, considered the most authoritative of his era, d. 297/910. 229, 234, 245, 248, 250
kalām	literally, 'speech', often the speech of God; also refers to a mode of theological discussion framed in terms of an argument, and thence to speculative theology as a whole. 147–51, 156–8, 185
kalima	a word. 98
kharāj	a land tax levied on non-Muslims; see also *jizya*. 209, 213
khums	literally 'one-fifth'; the portion of the booty from military raids to which Muḥammad was entitled and which, within Shīʿism, became a tithe payable to the Imām and his representatives for booty and other categories of possessions. 50–3, 205, 215–8
kitāb	literally 'book'; in legal discussions it is usually 'the book', meaning the Qurʾān. 186–7
al-Kulaynī	Shīʿī *ḥadīth* scholar, d. ca 329/940. 54–8
lutf	divine grace, favour and help. 154, 167
madhhab	a school of law formed around one of the early figures significant in juristic discussions (e.g., Abū Ḥanīfa, Mālik ibn Anas, al-Shāfiʿī, Ibn Ḥanbal); plural: *madhāhib*. 36, 193–6, 207
madrasa	religious school, or seminary. 143, 146, 150, 166
mahdī	the 'guided one' who is expected to appear prior to the judgement day in order to restore righteousness in the world. 164
Mālik ibn Anas	eponymous patron of the Mālikī law school, d. 179/795. 36–8, 44, 149, 178, 183, 187, 193, 202–3, 205–6
maqām	a lasting 'station' on the mystical itinerary of Ṣūfism acquired by the mystic. 244, 246

miʿrāj	the 'heavenly ascension' of Muḥammad, reported to have taken place around the year 6 of the *hijra*, in which he met with the prophets of the past, was shown visions of heaven and hell, gazed upon God and was given the command of five prayers a day for all Muslims. 19–26, 260
mubāḥ	'permissible' in Islamic law. 189
muftī	a jurist who is authorized to give a *fatwā* or legal decision on a religious matter. 192–6
al-Muḥaqqiq al-Ḥillī	Shīʿī jurist, d. 676/1277. 219–22
mujaddid	a renewer or the faith, stated in a *ḥadīth* report to appear in the Muslim community every one hundred years, in order to revive the spirit of Islam through the process of *tajdīd*, 'renewal'. 54
mujtahid	a jurist who is qualified to exercise *ijtihād* or personal effort in making legal decisions on matters where there is no explicit text of the Qurʾān or the *sunna* to be followed. 185–96.
mukallaf	a person who is obliged (accepting of *taklīf*) to fulfil religious duties. 152–3, 167, 169
muʾmin	someone who has *īmān*, 'faith'. 134–42, 144
al-Muqaddasī	traveller, geographer of the near east, d. 375/985. 88–9
muqallid	the one who acts within the bounds of *taqlīd*, the legal authority of the past. 192, 196
Muqātil ibn Sulaymān	traditionist and Qurʾān commentator, d. 150/767. 64, 71–2, 77, 105–7
mutʿa	literally 'enjoyment'; temporary marriage in Shīʿism. 54–8
mutakallimūn	the theologians; those who use *kalām*. 150–1
Muʿtazila	a theological school of thought which blossomed in the eighth and ninth centuries; it stressed human free will and the unity and justice of God, and embraced Greek rationalist modes of argumentation. 50, 119, 121, 147, 152, 156–9, 163, 202
al-Nasafī	Ḥanafī jurist, theologian, d. 537/1142. 155–8
Nāṣir-i Khusraw	Ismāʿīlī jurist and thinker, d. ca. 465/1072 – 470/1077. 223–7
al-Nawawī	teacher, jurist, commentator on *ḥadīth* in Damascus, d. 676/1277. 143–6, 192–201
al-Nawbakhtī	Shīʿī scholar and theologian, d. between 300/912 and 310/922. 163–6
Qadariyya	a theological grouping of early Islam which held the doctrine of freewill. 145
al-Qāʾim	'the one who rises,' an epithet for the Twelfth Imam, Imam Mahdī. 165
qibla	the direction in which Muslims face in prayer (towards the Kaʿba in Mecca), marked by the *miḥrāb* in a mosque. 21, 136–7, 189–90, 234, 259
qiyās	'analogy', one of the four main sources of law in Sunnī Islam, the others being Qurʾān, *sunna*, and *ijmāʿ*. 147, 186
al-Qummī	Shīʿī legal scholar, exegete, d. early 4th/10th century, after 307/919. 103–4
al-Qurṭubī	jurist, exegete from Spain, d. 671/1272. 97–102
al-Qushayrī	Ashʿarite theologian, mystic of Nishapur, d. 465/1072. 243–7
rakʿa	cycle of postures through which a person moves in performing the *ṣalāt:* standing, bowing, prostrating, kneeling. 22–4, 180, 182
Ramaḍān	the ninth month of the Muslim calendar, the month of fasting. 23, 139

ijtihād, 'personal effort', and frequently has a negative sense in the modern context. 151, 193, 204

al-Ṭarafī — Spanish religious scholar, collector of stories of the prophets, d. 454/1062. 59–63

ṭarīqa — the Ṣūfī 'path'; a Ṣūfī order or brotherhood. 262, 266

taṣawwuf — Ṣūfism, the mystical way in Islam. 244

taslīm — the saying of *al-salām ʿalaykum*, 'Peace be upon you'. 139

tawātur — transmission that is 'broadly authenticated', as in the case of the Qurʾān, the text of which is fully reliable because it has been transmitted through so many *isnāds*, and similarly for some *ḥadīth* reports which are uncontested in their authenticity. 156–8

tawḥīd — doctrine holding to the proclamation of the unity of God. 152–3

taʾwīl — interpretation, often with an allegorical or symbolic sense, and thus often seen as speculative. 147–8, 223–7

al-Thaʿlabī — exegete, collector of stories of the prophets, d. 427/1035. 59, 64–73

al-Ṭūsī, Muḥammad — Shīʿī theologian and jurist, d. 460/1067. 54, 215–9

al-Ṭūsī, Naṣīr al-Dīn — philosopher, Shīʿī theologian, d. 672/1274. 166–9

ʿulamāʾ — the learned class, especially those learned in religious matters (singular: *ʿālim*) 132, 149, 230

ʿUmar ibn al-Khaṭṭāb — second caliph after Muḥammad, assassinated 23/644. 37–8, 47–8, 54–5, 74, 80–1, 84, 130, 140, 149, 161

ʿUmar ibn ʿAbd al-ʿAzīz (ʿUmar II) — Umayyad caliph, ruled 99/717–101/720. 38, 90–3

Umayyads — the first dynasty of caliphs, ruling from 661 until the takeover of the Abbasids in 750. 83

umma — the community; the transnational body of Muslims. 132

ʿumra — the 'visitation' of holy places in Mecca, the lesser pilgrimage; it can be performed at any time of the year but is also joined to the *ḥajj*. 261

uṣūl — the 'roots' or fundamentals of religion and law (thus *uṣūl al-dīn* or *uṣūl al-fiqh*) which form the basis of theology and jurisprudence. 185, 187, 192, 194, 202, 219

ʿUthmān — third caliph after Muḥammad, assassinated 35/656. 33, 81, 83–7, 161

wādī — a river bed which is only filled with water at certain times of year. 26

al-Wāḥidī — philologist and Qurʾān scholar, d. 468/1076. 27, 73–9, 122

waḥy — prophetic revelation. 178

wājib — necessary; something which is obligatory in Islamic law. 169, 190

walī — a guardian for marriage purposes; a 'friend' of God in mysticism, a saint. 189

waqf — religious, charitable endowment. 230

al-Wāqidī — traditionist, biographer of Muḥammad, d. 207/822. 27–9

al-Yaʿqūbī — historian from Khurasan, d. 284/897. 88–9

zakāt — alms tax, one of the 'five pillars' required of all Muslims. 36–49, 51–2, 133, 136–9, 144, 181–2, 198, 207–27

al-Zamakhsharī — philologist, theologian, Qurʾān commentator, d. 538/1144. 119–20, 122, 128